HALIFAX

WARDEN OF THE NORTH

THOMAS H. RADDALL

Updated edition with three new chapters
by Stephen Kimber

Nimbus Publishing Limited
PO Box 9166
Halifax, NS B3K 5M8
(902) 455-4286 www.nimbus.ns

Printed and bound in Canada

Front cover: Dusan Kadlec, "Towing Out - Halifax Harbor C.1898"
Image Size - 24" X 36" Visit www.dusankadlec.com to view more of Dusan Kadlec's limited edition prints

Interior and Cover design: John van der Woude

Library and Archives Canada Cataloguing in Publication

Raddall, Thomas H., 1903-1994
Halifax, warden of the North / Thomas H. Raddall.

ISBN 978-1-55109-715-2

1. Halifax (N.S.)—History. I. Title.
FC2346.4.R34 2010   971.6'225   C2009-907290-4

First published in 1948 by McClelland and Stewart Limited; revised edition, 1971; reprinted in 1993 by Nimbus Publishing; updated 2010.

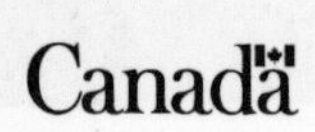

We acknowledge the financial support of the Government of Canada through the Book Publishing Industry Development Program (BPIDP) and the Canada Council, and of the Province of Nova Scotia through the Department of Tourism, Culture and Heritage for our publishing activities.

To my wife
—T. H. R.

Contents

A Note on the Edition

HALIFAX: WARDEN OF THE NORTH WAS FIRST published by McClelland & Stewart in 1948. In 1965, Doubleday Canada issued a revised edition of the book, updated to 1964 by Thomas H. Raddall and including a new preface. In 1971, McClelland & Stewart published a third edition of the book with further revisions and amendments from Raddall. This edition of the book includes Raddall's latest revised and updated text, as well as three new chapters written by Stephen Kimber, which extend the history from 1964 to present day. Both the bibliography and the index in this edition have been updated to include references for the new chapters.

Preface

I FIRST SAW HALIFAX FROM THE DECK OF THE OLD ALLAN liner *Carthaginian* when she ended a voyage from England one bright morning in May 1913. I was not an immigrant in the usual sense of the term, for my father was one of a small band of instructors from the famous British Army School of Musketry at Hythe, Kent, sent out to join the Canadian permanent force at the request of the Dominion Government. He took his family with him and we made our home at Halifax. Officially the British Army's connection with Canada had ceased in 1906, and it surprised me in after years to realize that we were in all probability the last of a long procession of imperial soldiers and their families who had settled in Halifax all the way back to 1749.

A typical child of the service, I was born in the married quarters of an army establishment and made my first tottering steps in a barrack square, so that when we came to Halifax and my father took me to see the Armouries, the Citadel, Wellington Barracks, the harbor forts, the ranges at Bedford and the militia camp on McNab's Island, it seemed a natural step from the old life across the sea. Gradually I came to know that the city had another and larger side, which had nothing whatever to do with the army and a great deal to do with commerce and the sea. The latter part of this discovery was fascinating, perhaps because my blood was half Cornish, a very salty fluid. When my father was killed in France a few years later I dropped my schoolbooks in the old Halifax Academy and went off to sea, like many a Bluenose boy before me.

This opened a new and remarkable world, and the first (and not the least) of its revelations was the harborside of Halifax, the purlieus of Water Street, and the queerly assorted folk who cater to the needs of ships and crews. It was a viewpoint hitherto unknown to me; indeed even now I am astonished to find how few Haligonians living west of Citadel Hill know more than a hint of the life along the waterfront, despite the fact that their own life depends so largely on the harbor and the ships that pass in and out. Yet I found the sailor's viewpoint equally restricted, for he rarely ventured over the hill. I suppose that is why one dour old salt told me, as we watched the city drop away on my first outward voyage, "Ay, take a good look! It's the best view of Halifax—from the stern, outward bound."

Thus as the years went by I found myself in the rare condition of knowing the city from three sides, having seen it with the curious eyes of youth from each angle, and having heard with youth's avid ears the separate tales and traditions of soldier, townsman, and sailor. This was important, for I came to Halifax at a time when the old memories were preserved with care, when the long stroll was still the proper way to spend a Sunday afternoon, and when almost any man or woman could point out the sites of things past and tell their tale. All this was hearsay, of course, but the fascination deepened later on when I began to inspect the sources of the city's story.

Some of these were revealed to me by the late Harry Piers, curator of the Provincial Museum, an enthusiastic antiquarian whose mind and shelves were stored with information about the city in which he had spent his life. At that time I was posted in the (now defunct) Marconi wireless station at Camperdown near the harbor mouth, where I was able to carry out some minor researches for him. Thereafter I went to see him whenever I had the chance, and by good fortune I often found with him George Mullane, himself an antiquarian of note and one of the last surviving contemporaries of Joseph Howe. I spent many an hour in their company and we must have made an odd group—the two elderly gentlemen and the young sailor "brass-bound fit to play music"—for I had only recently left ship duty and wore my uniform (the only decent clothes I had) when in town.

Years later when I became a novelist my researches took me to the Public Archives of Nova Scotia, where I made the acquaintance of Dr. Daniel Cobb Harvey, and of his assistants Dr. James Martell and Miss Margaret Ells, each thoroughly familiar with the material I sought and all interested in my problems. Very soon I found that the great difficulty in writing an historical novel about Nova Scotia was the very richness of the material. It was a struggle to keep the history in the background where it belonged, for it had an insistent way of intruding upon the story, a habit I had to watch and repulse.

The insistence of history was doubly hard to resist because the temptation came from without as well as within. For example, Colonel Theodore Roosevelt, having read certain of my historical tales, urged me to write a history of the eighteenth century in Nova Scotia "using the Macaulay or Parkman approach." I demurred, pointing out that I was a novelist and that the enormous significance of Nova Scotia's role in the American Revolution had been made clear by the researches of modern historians, notably J.B. Brebner and W.B. Kerr. Later James Martell urged me to write a history of Halifax, because in the process of familiarizing myself with the background of two of my novels I had gathered a great amount of the necessary fact. Again I refused, pleading that it was out of my field. Then my publishers made the same suggestion and I yielded. Their request came in 1944 when Halifax was in the midst of a great war, and I stipulated that I should not attempt the work until two or three years after the war's close so that the full story might be told.

That is how and why this account of Halifax during its first two centuries came to be written. It is not a history, for properly a history must record every incident, every date, and copious statistics, all documented with care. It would take several volumes, whereas my object was to write a single readable book based on selective research. In the first writing I made laborious footnotes, documenting every pertinent fact; but as the work went on I realized that they would only bore the average reader and I therefore cut them out. For those whose interest is in the sources I have included an appendix showing books and documents I consulted. But even there I have not attempted to list the various newspapers or the great number of letters, pamphlets, diaries, and other documents from which I gleaned information. (Examples: the reports of the Provincial Museum, the White Collection of manuscripts, the memoirs of the Chevalier de Johnstone, the diary of Edward Binney, the poetical squibs of Dr. Croke, Margaret Ells' paper entitled "Governor Wentworth's Patronage," the diary of William Dyott, correspondence of the Reverend Mather Byles, a paper entitled "Social Conditions in Nova Scotia, 1749-1783" by Katherine Relief Williams, the journal of Jeffrey Amherst, the journal of Captain Knox, reports of the Canadian Historical Association, files of the *Gentleman's*

Magazine, the notes of Titus Smith, the collections of the United Services Institute, Halifax.)

Fortunately for all of us the Nova Scotia Historical Society for many years has been gathering and in many cases printing the informative papers originally read before its members. The best known of these (and still the most valuable for the student of Halifax history, despite its imperfections) is the *History of the Settlement of Halifax* by Thomas Beamish Akins, first read as a paper before the Halifax Mechanics' Institute in 1839 and in later years enlarged. It was published by the Nova Scotia Historical Society in 1895, four years after Akins' death. He had been thirty-four years a Commissioner of Public Records for Nova Scotia, and he left behind amongst other valuable things the Akins Collection of books, pamphlets, and manuscripts which now is housed in the Nova Scotia Archives.

I acknowledge with the utmost gratitude the generous help of Dr. D.C. Harvey, whose own writings in the *Canadian Historical Review*, the *Dalhousie Review*, and other journals and books must be read by anyone wishing to get an authentic and comprehensive picture, especially in that postcolonial period which Harvey aptly terms "The Spacious Days of Nova Scotia." I am equally indebted to Dr. James Martell, author of *Halifax during and after the War of 1812*, *Military Settlements in Nova Scotia after the War of 1812*, and other important studies which have been published under the aegis of the Public Archives; and to Miss Margaret Ells, formerly of the Archives staff, whose manuscript history of Nova Scotia in the period 1782-1812 was of great value.

I owe a debt also to Dr. C. Lindsay Bennet and the librarians of Dalhousie University; to Miss Anne Donahoe, librarian of the Nova Scotia Legislature; to Dr. C. Bruce Fergusson of the Archives staff; to Mr. John P. Martin of St. Patrick's School; to Squadron Leader Maynard Colp, OBE, RCAF; and to Mr. J.A.C. Moore, Captain John P. Dwyer, Mr. Ralph Letts, Mr. J.F. McManus and the many others who in various ways have contributed their help and knowledge. To all I offer here my thanks and my hope that this book will be deemed worthy of their trouble.

Thomas H. Raddall
Liverpool, Nova Scotia
January 30, 1964

1.
The Indians

Chebooktook. *The legend of Glooscap. First explorers and missionaries. The French plan a fortress.*

THE FIRST INHABITANTS WERE A SAVAGE FOLK WHO called themselves *Meeg-a-maage,* a name which the English twisted first into Mickamuck and finally into Micmac. The Micmacs spent their winters inland, where the caribou and beaver hunting were best and there was shelter from the bleak Atlantic winds; but as soon as spring melted the ice on lakes and rivers and brought the migratory birds and sea fish back to the coast they embarked in their canoes for the harbors on the Atlantic face of the Nova Scotia peninsula. Here, with fish and wild fowl to be had for little labor, where at worst the squaw could dig up a meal from the nearest clam flat, they spent the summers at ease.

The site of Halifax port and anchorage they knew simply as *Che-book-took* ("at the biggest harbor"), a name which the white men rendered Chebucto. The northwest arm of the harbor they called *Waeg-wol-tich-k* ("it runs down to an end") because it had the look of a great river flowing out of the hinterland and was nothing of the sort. The narrows leading from the harbor proper into what now is called Bedford Basin they called *Kebek,* a name commonly given to a strait at the head of a tidal estuary—whence Quebec on the St. Lawrence. The steep wooded hillside where white men later built the town of Halifax was merely *Goo-ow-ak-a-de* ("place of many pines"). All Micmac place names were descriptive, and so the suffix *ak-a-de* ("place of") occurred frequently. This deceived the early French explorers, who considered it the name of the country and marked it "Acadie" on their maps.

The aboriginal Haligonians appear to have wintered on the Fundy side of the Nova Scotia peninsula. Each spring they paddled up the

Shubenacadie River, crossed over a handy portage to the Dartmouth lakes, or over another to the Sackville River, and so came to Chebucto. The return of warm weather, of birds and fish and the pleasant life by the sea, was celebrated with a feast on the shore of the harbor, a custom continued long after the white men came. Their camping places naturally lay at the mouths of the streams flowing into Chebucto; for here in May, just when the wild pear was in snowy bloom, the brooks swarmed with alewives on the way upstream to spawn, followed in June and July by throngs of salmon.

There is a tradition amongst the Micmacs that their ancestors caught trout in the now vanished stream which once flowed down Citadel Hill on the site of George Street, hunted moose in the swamp which is now the Common, and killed wild duck in its boggy pools, of which only the Egg Pond and the small lake in the Public Gardens survive. As late as 1928 a small Indian tomahawk head, made of stone, was found on the Citadel slope at the head of Buckingham Street, the site of another ancient stream flowing down to the harbor.

The Micmacs were a stocky people with brown skins, black eyes and coarse black hair, hunters and fishermen all, and their arts were few and primitive. The women made a crude and brittle pottery by scraping clay out of the stream banks, molding it by hand, decorating it with a pointed stick and a simple rocking stamp, and baking it in the camp fires. They were skilled in basketry and in leatherwork, which they embellished with dyed porcupine quills. The men hunted and made war with stone-headed tomahawks, spears and arrows, and knives of flint and sometimes of split beaver teeth.

The finest thing they made with their crude tools was the birch bark canoe, a craft admirably designed for the kind of life they led. In it they made their seasonal migrations up and down the rivers and along the coast. As the canoe could be carried easily over the portages from one river to another it gave their war parties a tremendous range; they covered the whole of the Maritime Provinces, made frequent journeys to the St. Lawrence, and attacked their enemies in New England. They were bold seafarers, venturing to the Magdalen Islands and Newfoundland, and harpooning seals, porpoises and other creatures of the deep.

The Micmacs were nature worshipers, but they had a queer whimsical mythology drawn about a giant man-spirit named Glooscap who had made the world, created the first Micmac from an ash tree, and frequently changed men back to trees or stones or animals according to his mood. It was a tongue-in-cheek mythology (the very name Glooscap means "fibber") and in general it served as a means of entertainment, a collection of fables told about the winter fires. Yet one of their whimsies was remarkable in the light of later events. There was a belief amongst them that Glooscap, weary of the eternal wars amongst his chosen people, had departed towards the sunset in his magic canoe, and that some day a race of pale-faced strangers would come out of the sunrise to rule them and the lands which had been theirs.

How long they lived this gypsy life and cherished these notions is anybody's guess. Possibly the idea of pale strangers from the east sprang from actual visits by the Norsemen, whose sagas describe a coast very like that of Nova Scotia and a savage people very like the Micmacs. All that is certain is that soon after John Cabot's voyage in 1497 European fishermen made their way to the Grand Banks and pushed on to dry their catch on the shores of the new land. For at least a century before permanent European settlement the coasts of Newfoundland and Nova Scotia were frequented by these venturesome cod fishers. Eventually they struck up a barter for furs with the savages and this led to the establishment of summer trading posts, always in some modest harbor with a narrow entrance easily defended with muskets or small cannon. The very size of Chebucto made it impractical for these purposes, and so for a century and a half "the biggest harbor" remained merely a port of call.

When the first French chronicler, Samuel de Champlain, arrived on the coast of "Acadie" in 1604 with De Monts, seeking a place for permanent settlement, he passed Chebucto by, noting it later as *"une baie fort saine"*—a good safe bay. They sailed on around the western end of the Nova Scotia peninsula and eventually founded a settlement at Annapolis, which they called Port Royal. There, slowly, the new French colony put its roots down in the rich soil of the Annapolis Valley and Minas Basin, while the Atlantic face of the peninsula remained a wilderness dotted with small fishing and trading posts. Yet the deep shelter and central position of Chebucto made it useful to seafarers, and the congregation of savages there for the spring feast soon caught the attention of traders and missionaries.

By 1698 there was a French fishing station at Chebucto, placed on McNab's Island, where there was a good beach for drying the cod, and close to the harbor entrance. At this time Father Louis Peter Thury was busy among the savages there. He is the first recorded missionary at Chebucto and possibly it was he who conceived the idea of using the spring feast, which corresponded roughly to the Christian feast of Easter, as a means of promoting his mission work. At any rate the old Micmac festival, always celebrated seven days after the first new moon in May—the alewife month—became a Christian holiday, dignified in later years with the name of St. Aspinquid of Agamenticus.

The life of the early French missionaries was hard, for they lived with their savage charges even on the warpath, and nearly perished of cold and starvation in the winters. Father Thury himself died and was buried by the Indians on the shore of Chebucto about the year 1699, when the French abandoned their fishing post at the harbor mouth. When the French botanist Diereville, sent out to obtain plants for the royal gardens, visited Chebucto in October 1699 in the ship *La Royale Paix*, three Micmac chiefs came off in a bark canoe, professed themselves Christians, and took him to see Thury's grave, which they had marked with pebbles from the beach.

The abandoned fishing station in the wild beauty of Chebucto moved Diereville to poetry. In free translation, it begins:

This harbor is of great extent:
Nature a basin there has lent
Around which grow the fir trees green,
Producing a most pleasing scene.
Upon its bank a structure odd
Erected for the drying cod...

By this time the wandering and unpoetic English had discovered Chebucto for themselves. In 1698 the Governor of Acadie reported to France that an English ship had been trading with the savages at Cap Sambre (Sambro, at the mouth of Chebucto), and that his officers had found an English vessel fishing there and had ordered it off the coast. The rivalry for possession of Acadie had begun. Yet the importance of Chebucto was still only dimly realized, and the first glimmer came when a new French governor, Brouillan, put in to the harbor on his way to Port Royal in the summer of 1701. He wrote: "This port is one of the finest that Nature could form.

It is true that to make it secure would cost rather dear because its entrance is wide and very easy of access. I found there two or three hundred savages, who represented to me the grief they felt in having received the knowledge of true religion without the means of cultivating it."

Brouillan's ship was wind-bound at Chebucto, so to save time he went with several Indians overland to Minas Basin and thence to Port Royal. He does not say, but the Indians must have taken him by the easy canoe route via the Waverley Lakes and down the Shubenacadie River, their favorite highway between the Bay of Fundy and *Uk-che-gum*, the ocean; and this must have shown him the strategic value of a garrison at Chebucto, which could control the traffic with the interior. Apart from this lay the obvious advantage to French warships in a large and safe port on the Atlantic side of the peninsula; for Port Royal could be reached only on a favorable wind and at the whim of the Fundy fogs and tides.

The notion of a settlement at Chebucto certainly developed soon after Brouillan's visit. In 1705 his officer Bonaventure was writing, "I do not think the inhabitants of St. Malo or of other places would engage to settle a place like Chibouctou until they see that His Majesty has laid the foundations of a fort." That was the rub—the fort. And His Majesty delayed until the march of events put Chebucto out of his reach forever. In the meantime, it remained a convenient shelter and watering place for French ships coming on the coast from Europe, and for wandering New England fishermen and traders. The savages continued to gather there for the summer season, and in the spring of 1705 we find Father Felix Pain, almoner of the Port Royal garrison, journeying across the peninsula to be present at the Chebucto feast and see that the Micmacs made their Easter devotions.

At this time Governor Brouillan had gone to France to defend himself against charges made by his personal enemies and to press the needs of the infant colony in Acadie. He returned in September 1705 a dying man. An old wound in the face had developed into a cancerous sore, and just as his ship *Le Profond* arrived off Chebucto he expired, uttering a wish that his heart be buried at Port Royal. His body was committed to the sea at the entrance to Chebucto, and Father Pain, having spent the summer with the Micmacs there, went as a passenger in *Le Profond* to Port Royal. There, with ceremony, the late governor's heart was buried in a small casket outside the fort.

Alas, poor Jacques François de Brouillan! There was no rest for his heart even at his beloved Port Royal, for during the siege of 1707 the British sappers dug up the casket, broke it open, and scattered the contents abroad. But his bones have lain on the sea floor outside Halifax for more than two centuries and a half, under the great fleets passing in and out of "this port... the finest that Nature could form."

The fall of Port Royal was a nasty blow to King Louis and his ministers, for the growing French empire along the river and gulf of St. Lawrence was left without a sentry box at its mouth. All the long delays and procrastinations now recoiled upon their powdered wigs. However, the peace negotiations were not concluded, and they had some hope of retaining the Atlantic side of the peninsula. In 1711 they sent De Labat, the engineer officer of their former garrison at Port Royal, to examine Chebucto and make a plan for a fortress there. De Labat's map still exists, an interesting document.

Cape Sambro he calls properly Cap St. Sambre. Devil's Island is "Ile Verte." McNab's Island is "Ile de Chibouquetou." George's Island is "Ile Ronde ou Raquette"—Round or Snowshoe Island. All around the harbor and Bedford Basin he marked *"coste boisée"*—wooded shore. The Northwest Arm he did not explore, although he shows the mouth of it; but he took careful soundings along the Eastern and Western Passages and straight up the harbor into Bedford Basin. He must have consulted the savages on some points, for he shows the mouth of Sackville River and remarks "Fifty paces to the first portage"—the beginning of a canoe route to the Bay of Fundy. The alternate route via Dartmouth Cove and Banook Lake he does not show at all. Perhaps the Indians wished to keep it secret. Certainly they made good use of it later on, when the British settled at Chebucto and built a fort to guard the Sackville portage.

But the most interesting part of De Labat's map is his plan for the French fortress. The present site of Halifax he ignored, marking it simply "wooded shore" like all the rest. The French town was to be built on McNab's Island near the abandoned fishing station described by Diereville in 1699. The main harbor fort was to stand on the steep bluff opposite Mauger's Beach, exactly where the British afterwards built their powerful York Redoubt. In addition De Labat planned a battery where the Mauger's Beach lighthouse now stands, another inside McNab's Cove to guard the fishermen's beach, a third on Lawlor's Island to watch the

Eastern Passage, and a fourth at Point Pleasant immediately facing the town and guarding movement in or out of the Northwest Arm. Whatever his failures at Port Royal, De Labat had a sound military eye at Chebucto, and the British in later years built their outer forts exactly where he had decided the French should build theirs.

Nothing came of De Labat's efforts, of course. His masters had awakened to the importance of Chebucto much too late. In 1713 the Treaty of Utrecht conveyed the whole Nova Scotia mainland to British possession, and the French had to be content with the island of Cape Breton as their future guard post to the St. Lawrence. There, in a small bleak harbor on the northeast coast, they began to build the fortress originally intended for Chebucto. They called it Louisburg.

2.
The French: 1710–1746

Captain Coram. The conflict of interests. Nova Scotia and Bonnie Prince Charlie. The tragic story of D'Anville and his great armada.

IF THE FRENCH HAD BEEN BLIND TO THE VALUE OF Chebucto, the British were no less so. Having taken Port Royal and changed its name to Annapolis they proceeded to forget the whole province, even the wretched British garrison of Fort Anne, which was left more or less to its own resources for forty years, like the children of Moses in the wilderness. From time to time a little manna fell from New England, but that was all. The New Englanders were keenly conscious of Nova Scotia, whose very shape was that of a cannon pointed at their Boston heart, and were determined not to see it fall into French hands again. Indeed as time went on they saw it as a weapon for the conquest of Quebec and the end of French dominion in America. Also they had a commercial interest.

Nova Scotia lay close to the cod banks which were the life of New England's trade, and it made a convenient place for fishermen to get firewood and water and to dry their catch. In theory, now that the Nova Scotia peninsula belonged to the British Crown, they had full use of the coast and could even settle if they wished. Actually the British authority did not extend past the crumbling ramparts of Fort Anne. The rest was a wilderness of rock and forest inhabited by roving bands of Micmacs, fiercely hostile to whites who spoke the English tongue. For forty years after the conquest of Nova Scotia each fishing season brought its sorry tale of New Englanders murdered in lonely harbors up and down the coast. The Indian hostility was clearly French-inspired; in fact the Micmacs had a constant market for English scalps in Louisburg and other French posts to the north. And so there arose a conviction that

Britain must establish a fortress on the seaward face of the peninsula. Every finger pointed to Chebucto.

In England itself there was a sudden stir of interest. In 1718 Captain Thomas Coram, that energetic sailor-philanthropist who established the Royal Foundling Hospital (and whose portrait Hogarth painted with a globe at his feet and a fleet of ships in the offing) proposed a settlement at Chebucto. He applied for a grant of land and for a bounty on pine pitch, which he planned to manufacture and ship to England for naval stores. At the same time a more elaborate proposal was put forth by Sir Alexander Cairnes, James Douglas, and Joshua Gee, the political economist. They proposed to settle at least two hundred people at Chebucto within three years, to cultivate the lands about the harbor for the raising of hemp, and to produce pitch and turpentine from the surrounding forest for His Majesty's Navy. They also wished to regulate the fishery.

This drew the immediate opposition of the New Englanders, jealous of their fishing rights upon the Nova Scotia coast. Their London agent, Dummer, pressed these objections and as a result both English plans fell through. Then another voice was heard. Writing from the miserable fort at Annapolis in 1720, Governor Philipps declared: "This country will never be of any consequence in trade until the seat of government be removed to the eastern coast." He suggested that two hundred soldiers be sent from England to establish a settlement on the seaward face of the peninsula, naming Chebucto amongst the possible sites, and adding that three ships of war should be stationed at the chosen port. In the following year his deputy, Paul Mascarene, made similar suggestions. Both were pigeonholed in London and forgotten, and Chebucto continued to hold nothing but camps of savages surrounded by somber woods.

By 1725, however, there was a path through the forest from the French villages at Minas Basin, for in that year Acadian drovers were bringing cattle and sheep overland to Chebucto for shipment to Louisburg by the vessel of an enterprising Yankee trader. And the traffic grew, so that in 1731 Governor Philipps issued a proclamation forbidding it; but he lacked troops and ships to enforce his words and the smuggling went on.

In 1734 and again in 1738 the impotent governor at Annapolis urged the home government to establish a garrison on the east coast, adding that this might "invite a new set of people that are Protestants to venture their lives and fortunes." Always London was deaf and blind. And all this time the French went on building the great fortress and naval base at Louisburg, calling it proudly "the Dunkirk of the West," maintaining close relations with the Acadians and Indians in Nova Scotia, and preparing for a day when they would seize the pitiful fort at Annapolis and bring Acadie under the lily banner once again.

In 1744 an opportunity came with the outbreak of war between England and France, news of which arrived at Louisburg before it reached Boston. A naval force from Louisburg seized and destroyed the New England fishing post at Canso, and a force of French rangers and Indians struck at Annapolis itself. Fortunately, Paul Mascarene, the English governor at Fort Anne, was a man of resolution; and the attack was beaten off. But New England was thoroughly alarmed and roused. As a result there was a counterstroke, the great expedition of Yankee farmers, hunters, and townsmen which captured Louisburg by a combination of luck and daring in the summer of 1745. France was thunderstruck. Indeed it was a feat that astonished the world. But England had something else to think about.

The news of Louisburg's fall had barely reached London when there was news of quite another kind. Bonnie Prince Charlie had landed in Scotland. Within a few weeks the Highlands were aflame, and by December the Jacobite army had penetrated England as far south as Derby. The subsequent fate of Prince Charlie's romantic enterprise is well known. Less known is the profound effect it had on English and French fortunes in Nova Scotia.

The all-but-successful invasion of England by an army of wild Highlanders had given King George and his ministers a shock—just as the capture of "the Dunkirk of the West" by an army of wild New Englanders had shocked King Louis and his court. There was a way of reconciling these twin annoyances, of cancelling one against the other; but this was not discovered until peace was signed in 1748. In the meantime things were happening across the sea.

The French officers at Quebec were busy with schemes for the recapture of Louisburg. They proposed that a fleet of warships and 2500 regular troops come out from France, retake Louisburg, and for good measure seize Annapolis. If Annapolis proved too strong the expedition would establish itself at Chebucto or Lahave and so place Nova Scotia firmly in French hands again. As it happened, such a force was available in the spring of 1746. Originally gathered for an invasion of England or Scotland in support of Prince Charles, it lay at Brest when the Scots' cause came to grief at Culloden. The fleet consisted of 37 warships and 34 transports and fireships, manned by 6790 officers and seamen. The transports had on board two battalions of the Regiment de Ponthieu and single battalions of the Saumur, Fontenay le Comte, and Royal de la Marine regiments, numbering 3150 in all, and commanded by General Pommeril.

The gathering of this force was well known to Prince Charlie's followers in the Highlands and upon it they based high hopes of raising the Stuart banner once more. When they learned that the French fleet had left Brest in command of the Duc d'Anville in May 1746 they were jubilant; but the last hope of the Stuart cause was dashed to the heather when the Highlanders learned, weeks later, that France thought more of New Scotland than of the Old and that D'Anville had sailed for Chebucto instead.

The story of this great armada is one of the most tragic in the history of America. The officers and men of D'Anville's fleet sailed believing that their destination lay in Britain. D'Anville alone knew the truth, and when he revealed it to his crews at sea they were almost mutinous. The fleet was to cross the Atlantic to the lonely harbor of Chebucto and there join forces with a French squadron from the West Indies under Admiral Conflans. The combined fleet and army would then recover Louisburg, seize Annapolis as a matter of course, and go on to destroy Boston. To assist in these operations Quebec was sending a strong force of rangers and Indians to Nova Scotia in advance. On paper the scheme was magnificent. The force to be concentrated at Chebucto would be the greatest ever seen in America. But D'Anville's seamen had a wholesome dread of the long ocean passage and the wild American coast; and all their fears were realized.

Battered by storms and delayed by calms, the great fleet was all summer on the sea. Scurvy broke out, and lack of sanitation in the crowded troopships brought on a contagion of typhus which raged throughout the fleet. With crews depleted by death and enfeebled by disease the armada arrived off Sable Island in September, just in time for the terrific equinoctial storms which make the Nova Scotia coast one long lee shore at that season of the year. Such a storm smote the fleet off Sable Island. Some of the ships went down with all on board. Others, with broken spars and tattered canvas, sheered away from the ill-omened coast and made their way to the West Indies or back to France. About half the fleet held on slowly for Chebucto.

Meanwhile the advance guard of the fleet, the frigates *L'Aurore* and *Castor*, which sailed from Brest in April, had reached Chebucto early in the summer. The senior officer, Du Vignan, busied himself in raiding English shipping, using Chebucto as a base. In this he was highly successful, taking an English warship of ten guns and at least eight vessels laden with cattle, fish, and dry provisions, all of which were brought into the harbor as prizes and later anchored in Bedford Basin. The Indians had gathered at Chebucto for the summer and the notorious French priest Le Loutre, who had come out in *L'Aurore*, took charge of them. To purchase their assistance part of the captured cattle and stores were turned over to the savages, who doubtless held high feast upon the Basin shore.

As the summer weeks went by Du Vignan became worried, for his provisions were getting low and he had 168 English prisoners cooped aboard the ships. Eventually he turned over the prisoners to one Repentigny, who with 150 Indians was to march them to Quebec. On August 12 Du Vignan sailed for France, convinced that D'Anville's expedition had been given up. The fate of the miserable captives in the hands of Repentigny's savages may be imagined. If any survived the journey of five hundred miles through the forest there is no record of it.

Early in September, Admiral Conflans arrived from the West Indies with four ships of the line. Doubtless the Indians told him of Du Vignan's departure, for, after waiting and cruising some days off Chebucto, Conflans came to the same decision and sailed for France. Thus when D'Anville arrived at Chebucto on September 10 in his battered flagship he found the great anchorage empty except for the canoes of the Micmacs and a solitary transport of his own fleet. He had been three months beating his way across the sea, his crews were starving, the troops were perishing of disease, and he had seen the fleet smashed and scattered on the very threshold of Acadie. To cap his misfortunes he now realized that the ships sent to Chebucto in advance had gone home to France, despairing of his coming.

Within a week of his arrival three of the transports came in, laden with sick and with doleful tales of the dead. It was too much for poor D'Anville. He died very suddenly of what his officers termed apoplexy and his crew declared to be poison. Which was right no one ever knew, but when the admiral's bones were exhumed at Louisburg nearly two centuries afterwards it was found that the French surgeons had trepanned the skull in an effort to satisfy their curiosity.

Vice-Admiral d'Estournel turned up with the surviving ships of the fleet at sunset on September 27, the day of D'Anville's death, and was amazed to find himself the leader of this ruined enterprise. On the following day D'Anville's corpse was buried without ceremony on George's Island, and D'Estournel called a conference of the senior army and naval officers, advancing his own view that the remains of the expedition should return to France at once. There was a hot debate, led chiefly by a stocky irascible old man, Jacques Pierre de Taffanell, Marquis de la Jonquière, who afterwards became Governor of Canada. For all his fine name and title Jonquière was ill educated; he had been on sea service in various parts of the world since the age of twelve, and no doubt the iron of such a life had found its way to his tongue.

The remarks of Jonquière and others so stung D'Estournel that the sensitive and bewildered man rushed to his cabin, bolted the door, and threw himself on his sword. When the door was broken down he lay dying, and muttered: "Gentlemen, I beg pardon of God and the King for what I have done, and I protest to the King that my only object was to prevent my enemies from saying that I had not executed his orders." And with a macabre touch of irony he named Jonquière to succeed him in the command.

Jonquière was no weakling and he took charge with a will. Before the expedition could attempt any fighting its health must be restored, and to this end he sent a demand to the Acadian settlements for fresh provisions, moved the whole fleet into Bedford Basin, and put the troops and the sick ashore. Probably he used De Labat's chart, for the chosen spot for his encampment lay about Birch Cove, towards which the French engineer had taken his chief soundings. Here for two weeks, in rude shelters of canvas and brushwood scattered in small clearings along the shore, the feeble soldiers and sailors lay and died like rotten sheep. The scurvy could be relieved by fresh meat and vegetables brought over the trail from Minas Basin, but there was no cure for the typhus.

After leaving France, something like 2400 men of this luckless expedition perished by storm and disease. Of these at least 1135 died at Chebucto. Some were buried ashore; but graves were hard to dig amongst the tree roots, and the bones of many were found a few years later scattered about the woods beside the water. Most of this grim company probably were flung into the Basin depths, sea fashion, with a shot or two at their feet to carry them down. And death was not confined to the French. Their savage allies stole the clothing of those who perished ashore, caught the pestilence themselves, and fled into the forest carrying the disease to other camps of the tribe. It is said that three quarters of the Micmacs in western Nova Scotia perished of this plague.

By now the tough Jonquière realized that his force was too feeble to attempt the storm of Louisburg, but he still had hopes of Annapolis, where the small fort was in ruins and the English garrison were starved and mutinous. It was now October, the hardwood trees about the Basin shore had begun to shed their gaudy leaves, the northern lights marched in the sky at night like the frost giants of the Micmac tales, and in the mornings the stones were white with their very breath. It was now or never. Ramesay and his *Canadiens* and savages had marched to Annapolis and lay encamped before the place, but they could not remain long at this season of the year.

At Chebucto the French troops embarked. The sick were taken aboard five vessels prepared as hospital ships. The *Parfait*, a warship of fifty guns no longer seaworthy, was set afire with other vessels, including captured English ships from the West Indies and Carolina and several New England fishing craft. They made a fine blaze on the sheltered water of Bedford Basin, a spectacle for the wondering savages, and for nearly a century afterwards the charred hulks could be glimpsed beneath the surface. On the morning of October 13, 1746, the fleet sailed, still powerful in appearance—forty-two ships of all kinds—but in reality one vast floating charnel-house. An English prisoner in one of them saw dead men cast overboard all the way out of the harbor and along the western coast of Nova Scotia.

Jonquière had no better luck than D'Anville. Off Cape Sable another storm scattered the fleet into the Atlantic, where some ships sank and most of the others crawled painfully away to France. Two ships managed to round the cape and enter Annapolis Basin; but there they found a pair of English men-o'-war anchored before the fort and departed in haste. So ended the great expedition.

In Boston, where the news of its coming created as great a stir as the Spanish Armada did in Elizabethan England, its defeat caused a frenzy of pious thanksgiving. The greatest threat ever made against the English colonies in America had been destroyed without the firing of a shot. No wonder the New Englanders looked upon God as their personal property. The great harbor of Chebucto was left with its shores and bottom littered with French bones—and poor Jacques de Brouillan had company at last.

3.
The English: 1748

Merry England under George II. The peace of Aix-la-Chapelle. An English fortress and colony for Nova Scotia.

We turn now to England, the England of George the Second, that strutting, greedy, noisy little man whose head lies easiest in the lap of a mistress and whose heart is forever in Hanover; the England of Horace Walpole, Pitt, Fox, and Carteret; of Richardson, Fielding, Smollett, Hogarth, and Sterne; of Whitefield and the Wesleys; of Handel, Lady Mary Montagu, Eugene Aram, Butcher Cumberland, and "the King over the Water."

It is an England ruled not by king or people but by nobles and gentry of the Whig party, powerful, patriotic in their fashion, but corrupt in every practice from the election booth to the last least commissary contract. It is an England still rural, awaiting the Industrial Revolution; a green land worked by the many to enrich the few, with only the most miserable of roads, with no large city outside London. It sings (to Dr. Arne's tune) of ruling the waves, yet it is powerless against the swarm of armed smugglers on its own coasts; and though maintaining armies abroad it is unable to put down the footpads and highwaymen who infest its roads to the very gates of London.

It is the England of a wealthy, brilliant, idle, rakish upper class, a pious and steady-going middle class rising but impotent still, and a vast wretched impoverished populace whose only pleasure is cheap gin. And this England, through a series of miracles performed by daring wanderers, has an empire stretching from the Ohio forest to the Bay of Bengal!

England has just fought a war with France and come off the field second best; Butcher Cumberland had found it easier to slaughter poor

Scotsmen in the Highlands than to conquer the well-furnished armies of Marshal Saxe. Yet England is shaken still by that eruption in the Highlands. It could happen again, for Prince Charlie remains the darling of the French court, Paris is full of Scots eager to set the heather afire once more, and England itself is alive with Jacobites toasting the king across the water. The ruling Whigs are contemptuous of King George, but he is their figurehead and they must bolster his throne by every means at their command. And so they come to the peace table at Aix-la-Chapelle. The French are arrogant, for they have won victories in Europe and India and written off D'Anville's expedition as bad luck. The English are anxious to please, and their only trump at the table is a miracle across the sea, the capture of Louisburg by a rabble of American townsmen and plowboys.

The talk is long and devious. Slowly the English unfold their great desire—French recognition of the House of Hanover as the lawful sovereigns of England. They want France to renounce the House of Stuart and expel the Young Pretender from her soil. The French demur, of course. They care not a rap for Prince Charlie, but he has a nuisance value. The English play their trump—the return of Louisburg. The Frenchmen catch their breath. Is it possible? Louisburg, built at a cost of millions, the key to Quebec, to Canada! They take it, quickly. They even offer a trading post in India. And so the thing is done. France signs. England signs. It is the eighteenth of April, 1748. The English envoys hurry home. Good news for His Majesty—the end of the Pretender! Good news for the merchants—a trading post in India! Good news for the people—"peace in our time." Nobody thinks of America.

But America is outraged. The colonies are proud of their maiden effort in the field of arms. They have spent great sums, the swamps about Louisburg are rich with their dead. They suffer under the bloody raids and growing menace of a French empire spreading from Canada down the Ohio and Mississippi to the Gulf of Mexico, cutting them off from the vast West. With Louisburg in their hands they were ready to strike at Quebec, the very throat of French dominion in America, and put an end to that menace forever. This has been their dream for years. And now England, without consulting them at all, without so much as a by-your-leave, has promised Louisburg to France. Worse! An English garrison has taken over the fortress from the colonials, repaired every breach, restored every gun, replaced every plank and nail. The Dunkirk of the West is to be handed back to France intact, as if the siege had never been!

The colonies howl with rage, and the howl is echoed in England itself. London newspapers attack the peace with venom. The *Evening Post* comes out with catchy doggerel like this:

> *A New Ballad on the Glorious Times* (to the tune of *Derrydown*)
> *"Cape Bretons expensive, as well hath been proved,*
> *And therefore the burthen is wisely removed;*
> *Which burthen French shoulders we'll settle again on,*
> *And add our own stores, our provisions and cannon."*

Hastily the Whig government seeks to make amends. The cost of the Louisburg expedition is refunded to the New England colonies—just in time, for they are bankrupt. And the cost in blood? The New Englanders want something more for their effort. They demand a transatlantic security against further attack from Louisburg, against another armada like that of D'Anville. William Shirley, Governor of Massachusetts, makes no bones about it. He wants an English fortress on the harbor of Chebucto, no less, and in its protecting shadow a settlement of English or German Protestants to offset the dour Acadians of Nova Scotia—precisely what the English officers in Nova Scotia have been advocating for a generation. At last the point sinks home.

His Majesty's Government decides to build this armed town at Chebucto. Money is voted; a plan is commanded. The matter of a garrison is simple enough. In the early summer of 1749 the English troops at Louisburg are to hand the fortress back to the French under the terms of the peace treaty. They can then move down the coast and establish themselves at Chebucto. And what about the settlers, Shirley's "English or German Protestants"? The English towns, especially London, are full of Protestants just now—discharged soldiers and sailors, and workmen trade-fallen with the war's end, all protesting very loudly against the sudden hard times and the infamous peace.

4.
1749

The plan of Trade and Plantations. Cockney colonists. Governor Cornwallis. The great expedition. Choosing a site at Chebucto.

THE PLAN FOR THE NEW SETTLEMENT WAS DRAWN UP by the Board of Trade and Plantations, whose president, Lord Halifax, submitted it to the government in the autumn of 1748. In the following spring an advertisement appeared in the London *Gazette*, dated at Whitehall, March 7, 1749. It began: "A proposal having been presented unto His Majesty for the establishing of a civil government in the Province of Nova Scotia in North America, as also for the better peopling and settling of the said province, and extending and improving the fishery thereof by granting lands within the same, and giving other encouragement to such of the officers and private men lately dismissed from His Majesty's land and sea service as are willing to accept of grants of land and to settle with or without families in Nova Scotia..."

It was a long-winded document, promising fifty acres of land to every qualified settler plus ten acres for every member of his family, together with arms, ammunition, and "a proper quantity of materials and utensils for husbandry, clearing and cultivating the lands, erecting habitations, carrying on the fishery, and such other purposes as shall be deemed necessary for their support." Every officer under the rank of ensign was to have eighty acres, ensigns were to have two hundred acres, lieutenants three hundred acres, captains four hundred acres. Every officer above the rank of captain was to have six hundred acres, with an additional thirty acres for each member of his family. All were promised rations for one year after their arrival in Nova Scotia. All were promised "a civil government... whereby they will enjoy all the liberties, privileges and immunities enjoyed by His Majesty's subjects in any other of the Colonies and Plantations in America under His Majesty's Government." All were promised "proper measures for their security and protection."

Apparently the Lords of Trade and Plantations had some doubt about the qualification of soldiers and sailors for pioneering in the wilderness, and so they added a paragraph offering the same grants and advantages to "carpenters, shipwrights, smiths, masons, joiners, brickmakers, bricklayers and all other artificers necessary in building or husbandry." The prospective settlers were to apply by letter or in person to the Plantations office in Whitehall or to the commissioners of the Navy at Portsmouth and Plymouth, and the books would be closed on April 7. The transports would be ready to receive the emigrants on board on April 10, and the expedition would sail on the twentieth.

This was very short notice at a time of year when the English highways were at their miserable worst. Few of the common people were scholars enough to read the advertisement, much less to write a letter of application to the Lords of Trade. No doubt the advertisement passed by word of mouth, but even this was slow in the England of 1749, where public conveyances were few. London itself was linked with the north by a covered wagon in which the passengers sat on straw, and as Parkman tells us, "spent the better part of a fortnight in creeping from York to London."

Few applicants came from rural England. Nor were His Majesty's discharged soldiers and sailors eager to join the exodus; they knew too much about life in His Majesty's garrisons abroad. The people who swarmed into Whitehall to register themselves with their wives and children were largely the poor of London, a rabble of cockneys wholly unfit for a life in the American wilderness, attracted simply by the promise of free victuals. Among them were fifty or sixty former officers of the army and navy, unable to resist the generous offers of land, and a few gentlemen volunteers in search of adventure.

The Lords of Trade received much good advice from Shirley, and the Chebucto expedition was marvelously well organized in view of the inefficiency and corruption of that age. The ships were loaded with everything from fire engines to fishing gear, bricks, seeds, blankets, woolens, and shoes, not to mention stores of salt beef, pork, and ship biscuit. There were French Bibles for the enlightenment of the Acadians and hatchets and gewgaws for the good will of the Indians. There was a hospital complete with instruments, drugs, surgeons and surgeon's mates, apothecaries, and a midwife. There were field guns, swivel guns, muskets, powder and shot. There were surveyors' instruments. There was stationery. There was a sum of nearly £4000 in gold and silver for the governor's use. There was everything but a printing press.

The rush of cockneys eager to receive His Majesty's bounty in Nova Scotia outran all expectations. More passengers had to be crammed into the chartered vessels, more ships engaged, more stores provided. As a result the fleet lay in the Thames for more than a month beyond the scheduled sailing time. In view of the crowded state of the transports the Board took unusual sanitary precautions and installed ventilators with pumps to ensure a circulation of air below decks, a decided novelty in ships of that time.

The command of this venture into the wilds was given to Colonel Edward Cornwallis, a handsome military bachelor of thirty-six who had fought at Fontenoy, commanded a regiment in the Highlands against Prince Charlie, and now was anxious to distinguish himself in Nova Scotia. He had turned over his regiment in the Highlands to a Major James Wolfe, who would distinguish himself in Nova Scotia later on. Horace Walpole speaks of Cornwallis as "a brave sensible young man of great temper and good nature"—a perfect picture of the man—and Wolfe afterwards mentioned Cornwallis' "approved courage and fidelity."

More than this, Cornwallis was incorruptible—a very rare quality in colonial governors of his time. He was slender, somewhat over middle height, an aristocrat to his fingertips, conscious of his dignity and inclined to be cool and ceremonious except when the "great temper" took charge. We are told he had a pleasant voice, fine eyes, and a winning expression. Later on his voice acquired a rasp, and so did his pen, as troubles mounted and the harsh winters of the new colony destroyed his health.

His aide and right-hand man was a young army bachelor like himself, Richard Bulkeley, tall, handsome, Irish, wealthy, a former king's messenger and captain of dragoons whose equipment for the wilderness included a valet, a groom, a butler, three blood horses and a vast amount of baggage. Another aide was Captain Horatio Gates, son of the Duke of Leeds on the wrong side of the blanket, a capable young officer who in later years was to make his name famous on the wrong side of the field in the American Revolution.

On May 14, 1749, Cornwallis and his staff sailed from England in the sloop of war *Sphinx*. The transports left some days later, slowly making their way down the Channel, calling at Portsmouth, and finally setting forth on the long voyage to a land almost as unknown as the moon. They carried 2576 passengers for Chebucto, distributed as follows:

	TONS	PASSENGERS
Charlton	395	213
Cannon	342	190
Winchelsea	559	303
Wilmington	631	340
Merry Jacks	378	230
Alexander	320	172
Beaufort	541	287
Rockhampton	232	77
Everly	351	186
London	550	315
Brotherhood		27
Baltimore	411	226
Fair Lady		10
		2576

In addition to these there were the *Sphinx* with Cornwallis and his suite, the transport *Sarah*, which sailed later from Liverpool with the hospital stores and staff, the small vessel *Union*, and other store ships. All in all, the first fleet probably carried three thousand people to Chebucto.

The *Sphinx* steered for Cape Race, that famous landmark on the way to the New World, and met head winds. The transports took a more southerly course and had better weather, so that despite their tubbish hulls they arrived on the coast only a few days behind the captain-general. The *Sphinx* sighted the coast of Nova Scotia on June 14; but as nobody on board had ever seen it before, and there was no chart worthy of the name, she stood offshore until she met by good fortune a Yankee sloop carrying two pilots to the British garrison at Louisburg. With these she headed for the land, touched at Merliguish (the site of Lunenburg), and entered Chebucto on June 21—a day celebrated by the Haligonians ever since.

It was that time of year in Nova Scotia when after the bleak east winds of April and May the sun breaks forth with almost tropical heat, when trees, shrubs, and grasses have a lush green only to be matched in Ireland, when the open spaces by the water are speckled white with wild strawberry blossoms, when huckleberry, blueberry and lambkill bushes are in bloom; when the forest floor is bright with lady's-slipper, bluet, sarsaparilla, starflower and false Solomon's-seal, when violets bloom along the brook sides and the swamps are a blue fire of iris, when small fruit has begun to form on the Indian pear branches and the leaves of young poplars make a silver flutter against the somber background of the pines. More important to the settlers, it was a time when the cod had moved inshore from the Banks, when haddock and pollack were schooling in every sea creek and salmon were swarming up the streams.

It seemed to be a land of plenty if not quite one of milk and honey, and Cornwallis dashed off an enthusiastic dispatch to the First Lord of the Admiralty (the Duke of Bedford) saying: "...the coasts are as rich as ever they have been represented. We caught fish every day since we came within fifty leagues of the coast, the harbour itself is full of fish of all kinds; all the officers agree the harbour is the finest they have ever seen... the country is one continual wood, no clear spot to be seen or heard of...I have been ashore in several places...D'Anville's fleet only cut wood for present use but cleared no ground...they encamped their men upon the beach...I have seen but few brooks nor have as yet found the navigable river that has been talked of."

The illusion about a "navigable river" persisted until every nook of the great fiord had been explored. For a time the Northwest Arm was thought to be such a stream and it was given the name of Sandwich River, but nothing flowed into the Arm except a few springs and a brook tumbling down the slope from the Chain Lakes. A similar torrent fell down the ridge into Dartmouth Cove on the east side of the harbor. The only river worthy of the name at all was a shallow stream pouring into the head of Bedford Basin, and even here the savages had to portage their canoes.

The rest of the fleet appeared outside Chebucto five days after Cornwallis arrived, but as the wind was unfavorable it was several days before the transports got into the anchorage. They were unharmed by the long voyage and the only casualty in a six weeks' passage was the fatal illness of one child. It was a triumph of navigation and of the new-fangled ventilators, which the Admiralty later installed in all its ships on foreign service.

Meanwhile Cornwallis had sent to Annapolis for the acting governor, Paul Mascarene, who arrived with his staff in Chebucto on July 12. On the following day Cornwallis opened his commission as Governor and Captain-General of Nova Scotia, and in their presence took the oaths of office. On July 14 he organized a civil government, with Mascarene, Captain Edward How, Captain John Gorham, and the civilians Benjamin Green, John Salisbury, and Hugh Davidson sworn in as councilors. They held their first meeting in the great cabin of the *Beaufort* transport, sitting about an oaken table which is still to be seen in the Province House, Halifax, and "the formation of the Board was announced to the people by a general salute from the ships in the harbour and the day was devoted to festivity and amusement."

Mascarene, then nearing the end of his long career in Nova Scotia, had been stationed at Fort Anne nearly forty years. How was an army officer with a useful knowledge of the French and Indians in the province. Gorham commanded a corps of rangers largely composed of New England Indians, half-breeds, and white adventurers, with whom he had been posted at Fort Anne. Green was a New Englander, a graduate of Harvard who had come to Nova Scotia with the army that conquered Louisburg and remained there as a government official. Davidson was an Englishman who sailed out with Cornwallis and become the first Provincial Secretary. Salisbury was a dissipated and quarrelsome Englishman, a protégé of Lord Halifax whom Cornwallis could not ignore—the first of a long procession of black sheep sent out to the colony with offices of various kinds in the hope that they would make a fortune or perish in the wilderness. Thus the first council contained something of everything and was no doubt as representative a government as could have been found in Nova Scotia at the moment.

The first and most urgent requirement was a site for the town. A British naval captain on the Nova Scotia station, Thomas Durell, had looked into Chebucto some time previously and sketched a plan for the settlement. The sailor's eye was taken by the broad shelter of the Basin—now dubbed Bedford Basin in honor of the First Lord of the Admiralty—so easily defended by a battery at the Narrows. The New Englanders objected to a site eight miles from the harbor mouth as inconvenient for the fishery. Cornwallis himself liked Point Pleasant, his soldier's eye seeing how easily a town there could be defended from the land side. But here the sailors stepped in, pointing out that the water off Point Pleasant was shoal and rocky, and exposed to southeast gales. So the governor compromised, picking a site two miles farther up the harbor on the west side, just inside George's Island.

Here the water was deep, and the land sloped to the crest of a sugarloaf hill, all covered with forest, which someday might be made into a citadel comparable with that of Quebec. Thus the new town would be screened from the northwest winds of winter—a point the French had overlooked in building Louisburg—with the result that the inhabitants of Chebucto and their descendants were fated to cling to a slope as sparrows cling to the easterly pitch of a roof. All in all the choice was not only good, it was miraculous, for Cornwallis was thinking in terms of a patch of dwellings and barracks on the harbor slope; he could not foresee a time when the town would spread entirely over the Chebucto peninsula, with the advantage of sea water on three sides.

The landing place was a small marshy cove in the western shore, where a brook trickled into the harbor from a spring on the side of the big hill. In after years the cove and the strip of marsh along the shore were filled with earth and rubbish, and all that remains of the inlet today is the dock called Market Slip. It is quaint to think that at one time the tide reached almost to the site of the present Custom House. The brook was the town's first source of drinking water, and when it dried up the bed was filled and became part of George Street, which followed it up the slope.

Overshadowing the landing place at the head of the cove stood a great hardwood tree whose branches, according to tradition, were the town's first gallows. Tradition says also that the first settlers found skeletons in tattered French uniforms, some with rusty muskets clutched in their bony fingers, lying in the moss or propped against rocks and trees. These relics of D'Anville's expedition must have made the cockneys ponder. There were other grisly souvenirs on the Basin shore, and on McNab's Island, for a chart of Chebucto made at this time shows Mauger's Beach as "Dead Man's Beach."

The earliest English map, apparently made by Thomas Durell, shows the Northwest Arm as "Sandwich or Hawk's River." Thrum Cap is "Red

Island." McNab's is "Cornwallis Island," so named for the governor but granted to his nephews, one of whom became Archbishop of Canterbury. The point now occupied by part of the Dockyard is shown as Gorham's Point, named for the commander of the rangers, whose house is shown there, well outside the town. Another small spit near the foot of what is now Cornwallis Street is termed "Bing's Beach," and as the Basin is shown as "Bedford formerly called Torrington Bay" we may assume that they were named for John Byng, son of Lord Torrington and possibly a captain on the Nova Scotia station at this time. If so it was a bad omen for Cornwallis, who in later years was to be associated with Byng in the disgraceful retreat from Minorca.

The captain-general ordered the settlers to work at once, and soon discovered what sort of subject had answered His Majesty's advertisement in the *Gazette*. The ragtag and bobtail of London had stepped straight out of Hogarth's prints into the wilds of Chebucto, where they interpreted the "liberties, privileges and immunities" promised in the *Gazette* to mean liberty to do what they liked, the privilege of subsistence on His Majesty, and immunity from anything resembling hard work.

After three weeks' sad experience of their qualities the exasperated governor wrote to the Board of Trade: "I beg leave to observe to your Lordships that amongst them the number of industrious active men proper to undertake and carry on a new settlement is very small. Of soldiers there are only 100, of tradesmen, sailors and others able and willing to work, not above 200." The rest were a shiftless lot, full of complaints, many in rags, others sick or feigning sickness to avoid the labor of clearing the townsite. A large number of sailors, out of a berth with the peace, had taken advantage of a free passage to Nova Scotia and now were skipping off to New England in the Yankee trading and fishing craft which swarmed in and out of the harbor. Most of the others had come for a year's free subsistence, which they proposed to enjoy at leisure. The sun was hot; black flies and mosquitoes swarmed and bit; the work of clearing the tall pines and undergrowth from the stony hillside looked interminable. It was much more pleasant to sit in the breeze by the shore and grumble about the arrangements.

For they had something to grumble about. It was obvious now that each settler would have to be satisfied with space to build a hut inside the town defenses; for the rest of his promised land he would have to accept five acres in the wilderness beyond, a forbidding green gloom full of flies and, probably, Indians. The accounts of a deep and fertile soil in Nova Scotia had deceived them all, from the First Lord of Trade to the last cockney in the ships. These reports had come from the Fundy side of the province where the French had settled long ago and where there was very good soil indeed. The seaward face of the country was another matter. Only in a few narrow river valleys was arable soil to be found. The rest of this rugged landscape consisted of thin sour clays and forest humus liberally studded with boulders. The Chebucto peninsula especially was hopeless: a hill, a swamp, and a plateau of slate rock thinly covered with soil. The modern traveler entering Halifax by rail is well aware of this, for after passing Bedford Basin his train carries him through a cutting, miles long, in which he sees little but sheer slate walls until the track emerges on the harbor. The settler of 1749 had to learn all this by grubbing in the thin topsoil.

Meanwhile the expedition's engineer John Bruce and the surveyor Charles Morris laid out the new town on the harbor slope of Citadel Hill. The plan conceived in London was ambitious. The *Gentleman's Magazine* declared: "That city is at first to consist of 2,000 houses, disposed into fifty streets of different magnitudes. In the middle of the town is to be a spacious square with an equestrian statue of His Majesty." On the spot, Bruce and Morris laid out a town much more modest, in blocks 320 by 120 feet, and with less than a dozen streets. Each block contained sixteen house lots 60 feet deep with a 40-foot front. The streets were 55 feet wide.

The "spacious square" was in fact a rectangle of rough ground on the steep face of the hill. It was proposed to build a church at the north end of it, and at the south end a combined jail and courthouse. Eventually the church (St. Paul's) was built at the south end; but the first courthouse occupied a site on Buckingham Street to the north, and the first jail was established in a stone house built by Colonel Horsman near the site of St. Mary's Basilica far to the south. The "equestrian statue of His Majesty" never materialized, and Halifax was spared the sight of George II mounted on anything so uncongenial as a horse. For many years the "square," dignified with the title of Grand Parade, was used as a place of assembly by the militia and garrison. An old print shows a company of redcoats drawn up facing the slope, with the noses of the rear platoon on a level with the knees of the foremost. Until the Parade was leveled in the closing years of the century it must have made a fine toboggan slide for the youngsters of early Halifax.

The streets quite evidently were named in honor of the patrons of the expedition and leading British statesmen of the day. Thus Holles (now spelled Hollis) Street was a delicate compliment to the Prime Minister, Henry Pelham, whose mother was Lady Grace Holles. Bedford Row was named for the Duke of Bedford, Granville Street for the Right Honorable George Granville, Barrington Street for Viscount Barrington of Ardglass, Argyle Street for the Duke of Argyle, Grafton Street for the Duke of Grafton, Albemarle Street for the British ambassador to Paris, Sackville Street for Sackville, Duke of Dorset, who was president of the council, George Street for the lewd and irascible little man who held the throne, and Prince and Duke streets just in case anyone important had been overlooked.

And the town itself? What else but the title of the chief Lord of Trade and Plantations? Halifax, of course! For various points in the province, as well as for certain Halifax streets, the pioneers chose the family names of English noblemen. Haligonians should be thankful that for the name of their city the title was chosen instead. The name of the Earl of Halifax was George Dunk.

5.
1749

Gorham's Rangers. A treaty with the savages. Scalps and skirmishes. The first winter brings disease and death.

THE ENGLISH GARRISON OF LOUISBURG HANDED OVER the fortress to the French in accordance with the treaty of peace, and Cornwallis sent his empty transports to bring them down the coast. Hence the settlers' promised security and protection arrived in the form of Hopson's and Warburton's regiments. The raw new town suddenly swarmed with red coats, white breeches and black gaiters, the beginning of a long military procession that was to extend through a century and a half. These were the typical Tommies of the eighteenth century, a swearing, drinking lot who had been in garrison at Gibraltar and then at Louisburg. They had been accustomed to solid ramparts and weatherproof quarters: here they found neither, and we can hear their opinion of Halifax echoing across the years.

For warfare in the forest, the only sure protection against Indian raids, such troops were worthless. Better stuff were the shabby men of Philipps' Regiment from Annapolis, where they had spent long years in the decrepit log-and-earth fort with the savage war whoop in their ears. But in truth the only troops at Halifax worth His Majesty's pay were the men of Gorham's Rangers, a company of sixty swarthy adventurers, many of them full or half-blood Mohawks, and all familiar with the Nova Scotian warpaths. These wild men in buckskins, and their canny drawling commander, offended the governor's sight. He was glad of an excuse to send them out of the town.

It was a good excuse, of course. Cornwallis knew that the savages who gathered at Chebucto in time past had come by canoe from the interior, probably by way of the Sackville River. So he sent Gorham's rangers to the head of Bedford Basin with orders to build a barrack and fort from which they could guard the Sackville portage. That the savages had an alternative route by way of the Dartmouth Lakes apparently did not occur to him. Probably he did not know of its existence. Indeed the most striking fact about the whole expedition, this brain child of the Lords of Trade, was that nobody troubled to explore the forest about the harbor before it came or for many painful months after it arrived.

Cornwallis was counting heavily on peace with the savages. To this end he had sent the adroit and forest-wise Captain How among the tribes as soon as possible, to call the chiefs together for a treaty. Three chiefs came, together with nine warriors acting as deputies for the others. They represented the Micmacs about Fundy Bay, the Malecites on the St. John River, and their kinsmen of Passamaquoddy. The remnants of the Micmac tribe who had lingered about Chebucto after the typhus epidemic of 1746 vanished soon after the Halifax fleet arrived, and Cornwallis seems to have made little effort to gather them into his treaty-making. These savage visitors from the hinterland were a different sort, dressed in rags of French homespun ornamented with beads and bits of bright cloth, with ribbons and sometimes a clay pipe drawn through holes pierced in their ears, and each face was a mask of daubed vermilion streaked with black stripes across nose and forehead.

The captain-general received them aboard the *Beaufort*, probably at that same table which is now preserved in Province House, and the *Sphinx* fired a salute of seventeen guns as they arrived. They came aboard in full war paint and noisy with rum, ominous signs to anyone but the innocent Cornwallis; but How seems to have held his tongue and doubtless Gorham (who knew them best) was at his post at the far end of the Basin. Another thing was ominous. The interpreter was an Acadian named André, one of a people strongly suspected of complicity in Indian raids.

The Indians were shown a treaty made in Boston far back in 1725 which some of the older ones recognized, having signed it with their own totems. Said Cornwallis: "I have instructions from His Majesty to maintain amity and friendship with the Indians and to grant to those in these provinces all manner of protection." This sounded very well in English but it must have puzzled the Indians. From whom were they to be protected—their long-time friends, the French? And who was to protect them—the redcoats, whom they held in the greatest contempt? Whatever their thoughts they answered the captain-general dutifully, or so the interpreter declared, and when they were asked to renew the treaty on another sheet of written parchment they did so in good cheer, drawing their totems—a fox, a porcupine, and so on—with remarkable skill at the foot of the paper. Cornwallis then bestowed gifts brought all the way from England, and the savages paddled over to the *Sphinx*, on whose deck "they solaced themselves with singing and dancing...one continued bellowing and noise." And away they went, while their amused hosts fired another seventeen-gun salute in parting.

Gorham, How, or anyone acquainted with Indian customs could have told Cornwallis that all this was wrong, that there should have been a ceremony in the savage fashion with a ceremonial washing away of the war paint and the solemn burial of a hatchet, with frequent references to "the bright chain of friendship" and other terms important in savage oratory. As it was, the exultant warriors returned to their tribes with the war paint still on their faces, able to boast that they had worn it in the presence of the English chief and performed a war dance on the very deck of the thunder ship. The totems on the parchment did not mean a thing. Within a few months certain of the settlers, including Cornwallis' own gardener, found this out at the cost of their scalps and lives, and the bloody tale was to go on for nearly eleven years.

The chief trouble was that Cornwallis had too many things on his mind. Apart from the savages, he was fetching delegations of stubborn Acadians from the Fundy shore, though they would only refuse the proffered oath of allegiance; he was trying to induce his mob of cockneys to fell trees as an abatis about the town for their own protection; he was overseeing the efforts of the unskilled soldiers in making small log-and-earth forts at chosen points about the slope. He was trying to empty the transports and get them off charter, trying to get his stores under cover, to get building material from Boston, to erect a sawmill on the Dartmouth stream, to get a fishery started, to get a proper road cut through the forest from Minas Basin. He was trying to decide upon a system of laws and at the same time trying to maintain some sort of order among his unruly colonists.

The latter proved the most trying of his problems. He managed to get them to work by dividing them into companies under leaders of their own choosing, and eventually he had to pay them at a rate far exceeding that of the redcoats who sweated beside them. But he could not keep them sober. When the garrison moved down from Louisburg they brought in their train a swarm of sutlers and camp followers, mostly from New England, whose chief stock in trade was rum, strong to match the thirst of all and cheap to match their resources. A straggle of drinking dens and shanties appeared along the beach, and so began the long and lively career of Water Street.

The times were violent. Before long the law had its first murder case. One Peter Carteel ran amuck with a knife aboard the *Beaufort* (the floating seat of Nova Scotia's Government), killing the boatswain's mate and wounding two others. He was convicted and hanged. At the same time Cornwallis was busy instilling discipline into Philipps' Regiment (still quartered mostly in the Annapolis Valley) by ruthless shootings and hangings which must have astonished the Acadians and Indians. In the midst of all this there was a curious little episode when the new French governor at Louisburg sent the warship *Le Grand Saint Esprit* to Halifax for the remains of the Duc d'Anville. Cornwallis gave polite assistance, and the sweating mob on the harbor slope was treated to the spectacle of a uniformed party on George's Island digging up the bones of the ill-fated admiral and carrying them solemnly aboard for reburial in the Louisburg garrison chapel. Such an example of respect for the dead should have impressed the cynical cockneys; but, sad to relate, it did not.

Towards the summer's end an Indian war party came down the Dartmouth Lakes and attacked the crew of the governor's sawmill just above Dartmouth Cove. Four men were killed, indeed butchered in such a fashion that the settlers' rum-heated blood was chilled for weeks. So much for the treaty, and early in October the council met with Cornwallis aboard the *Beaufort* to discuss the next move. They decided not to declare war on the Micmacs, "as that would be to own them a free people, whereas they ought to be looked upon as rebels to HM Government or as banditti ruffians." Instead they called upon all His Majesty's officers, civil and military, and all His Majesty's subjects, to take and destroy the Micmacs wherever they might be found. And they offered ten guineas for each Indian, living or dead, "or his scalp as is the custom of America."

The price went higher later on and for years there was a merry trade, the French buying scalps at Louisburg, the English buying scalps at

Halifax, and no one certain, as the money chinked on the table, whether these scraps of withered skin and clotted hair belonged to man, woman, or child, or whether they were English, French, or Indian. In this grisly fashion began the rivalry between the two fortresses which could end only in the destruction of one or the other. For the present and for some years yet the English would tread softly; the disparity between the armed camps was too great. Louisburg was really a fortress, with walls and ramparts bristling with cannon. Halifax was little better than a transatlantic almshouse for the London poor, and its defenses were a joke.

By mid-September Cornwallis could report to the Lords of Trade that he had victualed 1574 *settlers* in the past week—roughly half his people. The rest were still aboard their transports waiting to be settled. A month later he wrote that about 300 houses had been "covered in," and that he had completed a barricade of felled trees about the town and built two forts on the perimeter. These forts were little more than log blockhouses. The houses were mostly cabins of logs and saplings stood on end and in some cases sheathed with boards. (The typical "colonial" cabin of logs laid horizontally was introduced into America by the Finnish and Swedish settlers of Delaware; it had yet to appear in the north.)

The residence of Cornwallis himself was a modest frame house in the government plot just above the landing cove, where the South African War memorial now stands. There were some more pretentious homes. Colonel Horsman built himself a stone mansion, the stone imported probably from England. For most of the people ashore there were the wooden huts, and tents of ship canvas and brushwood in which they huddled against the increasing cold. Many had to winter aboard the ships, whose decks were roofed over against the snow but whose heating facilities were poor, to say the least.

In this fashion the Haligonians began their first winter, half ashore and half afloat, and it would be hard to say which had the worst of it. Unclean, undisciplined, clutched together for warmth, existing on rations of salt meat and hard tack, the cockneys soon developed typhus, which in those days passed under various names—"ship fever," "gaol fever," "hospital fever"—but killed as thoroughly under one name as another. Just as D'Anville's men had perished of it in this very scene, so the English colonists perished in the winter of 1749-50. We are told that more than a thousand died—one in every three. It was like the great plague of London, tales of which must have lingered in the cockney mind. Their callousness was such that, two days after Christmas, "all housekeepers were ordered to notify deaths within twenty-four hours to one of the clergymen, under pain of fine and imprisonment. Persons refusing to attend and carry a corpse to the grave when ordered by a justice of the peace were to be struck off the ration list and sent to prison. Vernon, the carpenter, was ordered to mark the initial letters of the deceased upon each coffin."

The burial ground lay just outside the defenses to the south, a spot since known as St. Paul's Cemetery. Here the dead were thrust away into the frozen earth with little ceremony, and little or nothing to mark the graves. Like any London cemetery of the period it was held inexhaustible, one generation burying itself upon another, so that none of the inscribed stones now to be seen there hark back to the beginning. We may picture the rum-primed gravediggers, the shivering guard of redcoats watching the forest, the perfunctory parsons, the unwilling mourners, the pine coffins with their carved initials, and the air of gloom over all.

It seems brutal to suggest that all this was for the best. It is the truth. Typhus, no respecter of persons, lays a particular hold on the unclean, the drunken, the shiftless, the physical dregs of a populace. In a single winter Halifax was purged of its worst human element, and the loss was neatly offset by an influx of New Englanders, tough, resourceful scions of the Pilgrims and Puritans, accustomed to making a living in a stony land. Thus quickly changed the human face of Halifax.

Cornwallis, not to frighten the Lords of Trade, said little or nothing of the epidemic in his dispatches; indeed he reported cheerfully at the winter's end that there never had been more than twenty-five sick in the hospital ship at a time, leaving the noble lords to infer that all was well. The arithmetic of the ration lists agreed with their inference, for the shrewd Yankees quickly installed themselves on the mess books and so the sum came right.

6.
1750–1755

The first street lighting. The building of Mather's and St. Paul's. Arrival of the Huguenots and Germans. The artful Mauger. Michael Francklin. The influx of Americans. The first newspaper. The rigors of justice. A slum is born.

THE LORDS OF TRADE WERE NOT SO EASILY DECEIVED about the cost of the expedition, already more than double their estimate and rising steeply all the time. They quibbled over the captain-general's expenditures and his new demands, and hot-tempered Cornwallis wrote back: "Not a pound shall be expended by me unnecessarily, but without money you could have had no town, no settlement and indeed no settlers. 'Tis very certain that the public money cleared the ground, built the town, secured it, kept both soldiers and settlers from starving with cold, and has brought down 1,000 settlers from the other colonies. Lots in Halifax are now worth 50 guineas. If there was no public money circulating lots would be given for a gallon of rum. The money is laid out in building forts, barracks, storehouses, hospitals, churches, wharves, etc., public works all that seem necessary."

A good deal of the unforeseen cost arose from the obtaining of supplies at Boston, where the chief royal purveyors, the firm of Apthorpe & Hancock, charged all that the Crown would bear. Among other expenses, Cornwallis had sent Bulkeley there to obtain timber for St. Paul's, and (to provide light of a more earthly kind) to buy four hundred lanterns for the landing places and the rough streets and lanes of Halifax. These lanterns were hung on posts about eight feet high, a mode of street lighting followed spasmodically and with small success for many years. The lanterns were too easily stolen or smashed by roistering seamen, who habitually carried cudgels three or four feet long, as we may see in Short's prints of the town. Haligonians of the colonial period were glad to stay indoors o' nights.

In 1750 St. Paul's was opened for worship, although there were no pews. Cornwallis was pleased with it, writing that it was modeled after "Marybone" in London, although it looks more like St. Peter's in Vere Street. It stood with its back to the Parade, facing south towards Prince Street as if in disdain of the redcoats trying to march and wheel on the rough slope, although in truth it was the garrison church as much as anything else. Many years later the Prince Street entrance was removed and the present entrance made facing the Parade. The whole structure was of pine and oak brought by ship from Boston and Portsmouth, New Hampshire, like most of the frame buildings erected in Halifax at this time.

Thus came into existence the mother temple of the Church of England in Canada. Its principles were broad from the first. Dissenters were permitted to hold prayer meetings in St. Paul's on Sunday afternoons, and at various later times congregations of Micmac Indians and of Hessian soldiers gathered within its doors to hear services in their own tongues. Eventually the dissenters had their own meeting house, for the Yankee influx had filled the town with nonconformists. This edifice, called Mather's Church (probably in memory of Cotton Mather, the eminent New England preacher) was built on the other side of Prince Street and much farther down, opposite the present Legislature. Later on, in some way still mysterious, the name became St. Matthew's. Like St. Paul's, it was financed largely by the Crown, an enormous concession for those bigoted times. Roman Catholics, still under the frown of English law since Elizabethan days, were not permitted a church at all, not even a priest. Catholics in Halifax in the early days were chiefly soldiers of the garrison and their wives and children; they were the beginning of an Irish colony which grew steadily as time went by.

The years following 1749 were busy ones. Cornwallis, after the sad experience of the cockneys, requested the Lords of Trade to send out more suitable settlers, preferably German farmers. And so they came in hundreds each summer for the next three years, poor people from the Rhineland, most of them, but with a strong proportion of "Swiss." There were some Swiss in fact, but the early chroniclers were hazy about European divisions and many of the immigrants they wrote down as "Swiss" actually were French Protestants from Montbéliard in the Belfort Gap, near the foothills of the Alps. These are said to have comprised about one third of the continental immigrants. But they came with the folk who called themselves *Deutsche* and the English settlers knew them all as "Dutch"—hence Dutchtown, the north suburb of Halifax in colonial times, and Dutch Village on the isthmus.

The "Dutch" folk were settled on a pair of rough lanes running north from the Citadel slope which they called Brunswick and Gottingen. Later immigrants were granted land on the peninsula as far out as the isthmus. To protect them Cornwallis built three blockhouses at intervals from Bedford Basin to the head of the Northwest Arm, connected by a narrow military road which was patroled by redcoats and rangers of the garrison. The south blockhouse stood in what is now the angle of Chebucto Road and Armdale Road, nearly opposite the entrance to Simpson's department store. The central blockhouse stood in what is now the north angle of Bayers Road and Connaught Avenue. The north blockhouse was near the present entrance of Fairview Cemetery on Windsor Street, and the central driveway of the cemetery is all that remains of the old military road.

Thus within a short time the colony abandoned the original crude circle of felled trees and pushed its defenses to the Dutch Village valley. On the plateau behind the blockhouse line the frugal Germans cleared the forest and tilled the soil, but their produce was small and Halifax had to rely on food supplies from New England and across the sea. Cornwallis continued to hope for co-operation from the Acadian farmers on the Bay of Fundy, but these hopes dimmed as the influence of the fanatical Le Loutre made itself felt. The Acadian produce made its way to French posts at Baie Verte and on the St. John River, but chiefly to Louisburg; and the conviction grew that Halifax and its garrison and fleet never could be fed at home until the Acadians had been plucked from British soil and replaced by farmers from New England.

Americans were flocking to Halifax, but they were not farmers. They were fishermen and traders looking for a harvest from the sea and from the town. There were other settlers of all sorts. One half-pay naval captain named Bloss built himself a mansion and maintained a staff of sixteen Negro slaves. Another settler well supplied with Negro labor was Joshua Mauger, a diligent and artful schemer who had laid the foundation of a fortune in the West Indian slave trade and still manned his ships with faithful blacks. He had come to Louisburg to share in the plunder after the conquest of 1745 and later removed with the garrison to Halifax.

This man soon put a finger into every Halifax pie. He had a fishery station on McNab's Island at the place still called Mauger's Beach (pronounced "Major" by the Haligonians), a rum distillery near the site of the Dockyard, a large warehouse and shop in the town, a chain of trading posts in the Indian country, a contract as victualer to His Majesty's fleet, and a busy and lucrative smuggling business with the French at Louisburg. His smuggling soon brought him into violent contact with Cornwallis; but Mauger's money and influence in Britain talked louder than the governor's furious dispatches, and, the man remained like an evil spider with a web reaching into every part of the province, to the West Indies, and to Britain.

Another adventurer (but of a very different stamp) was Michael Francklin, a young English gentleman who landed at Halifax in 1752 with £500 in his pockets and a firm ambition to make it grow into a fortune. He began with a rum shop in George Street, went on to fine wines and breadstuffs and the dried fish trade to Spain and Italy, engaged in army and navy supply contracts, married a Boston girl of the influential Faneuil family, became a member of the Nova Scotia Legislature and eventually lieutenant governor of the province. His whole life was a romance. While still new to Halifax he was carried off by Indians and spent months in captivity in the forest. There he learned the Micmac language and customs and obtained an influence with the savages that he put to good use later on.

One party of English immigrants arrived after a long delay at the Azores. With them was an odd character, a Sicilian soldier of fortune, Peter, Marquis of Contes and Gravina, who soon tired of the town life and joined the rough-and-ready men of Gorham's Rangers. Not all the Americans attracted to Halifax came from New England. In 1751 the New York *Weekly Post-Bag* remarked: "We have advice from Halifax in Nova Scotia that there is such a number of New Yorkers got to that place since the first settlement of it as will nearly fill one of the largest streets in the town; and that they are about to form themselves into a Society or Company by the name of the Free New York Fishery Company at Nova Scotia; and that all that come there from New York, provided they come there as one of King David's soldiers (see 1 Samuel, chap. 22, verse 2), shall be permitted to join them and draw shares according to the stock they bring."

No doubt it was for the benefit of these soldiers of King David as much as the cockney settlers of King George that the council in 1750 forbade the collection of debts contracted in England and elsewhere. Certainly Halifax, like every new settlement in the wilds, attracted "every one that was in distress, and every one that was in debt, and every one that was discontented." Those who can find no pleasure in the past must look with a single eye to the future, and in the end they are the conquerors.

In the first three years most of the original cockney settlers vanished by death or desertion, and their places were taken by the shrewd Americans and to some extent by the patient "Dutch." But there persisted for nearly one hundred and fifty years a steady influx from Britain, chiefly English, Scots, and Irish servicemen and their families, stationed in the port for years and finally settling there upon discharge. These left their mark on Halifax, which long retained a distinct Old-Londonish atmosphere with traces of Cork and Aberdeen, all in the midst of a bustling Canadian city.

The numerous "Dutch" were soon reduced, for Cornwallis was anxious to make another strong settlement on the coast, and in 1753 he removed most of the Germans and Huguenots to what now is called Lunenburg. But for this, Halifax might have remained a city with a certain Old-German atmosphere as well. As it is, many Haligonians bear the old "Dutch" names, somewhat Anglicized, and retain the steadfast characteristics of their forbears although in appearance, manner, and speech they are indistinguishable from the rest.

The bitter experience of the cockneys at Halifax left a dismal impression on the folk at home, whose opinion of colonial enterprises in America at this time was very low. The impression is well portrayed in a series of lampoons printed on the backs of playing cards in England about this period. The eight of diamonds is devoted to a gibe at Halifax, inaccurately drawn—Citadel Hill is shown near the head of the Northwest Arm—but sadly accurate in its suggestion. A trio of would-be farmers are being attacked by huge wild beasts on the shore of the Arm. Inland, a mob of savages brandishes spears and bows, while two settlers at Point Pleasant are engaged in the lugubrious task of sorting a number of severed arms and legs. On the site of Halifax itself three indolent fellows play at dice. The doggerel beneath declares:

He that is rich and wants to fool away
A *sporting sum in North Americay,*
Let him subscribe himself a headlong sharer,
And asses' ears shall honour him or bearer.

The sporting sums voted by a parliament committed to build and maintain the new fortress town in Americay made Halifax a sort of boom town for the neighboring New Englanders. They continued to come and set up shops and taverns and every other device to catch the trade of the army and inhabitants. In 1751 Bartholemew Green arrived from Boston with the first printing press and set it up in a building on the lower side of Grafton Street, and on this press in March of the following year his partner, John Bushell, printed the maiden issue of the *Halifax Gazette*, the first newspaper in Canada. It was a modest thing about the size of a half sheet of foolscap, with a woodcut at each side of the title, one showing a ship in full sail, the other a fowler hunting game. The news was clipped from English newspapers, months old, but we learn a good deal of early Halifax from the advertisements.

Two gentlemen advise the public that they will teach spelling, reading, writing in all its different hands, arithmetic in all its parts…at the Sign of the Hand & Pen at the south end of Granville Street." Elizbeth Render advises that she keeps a reading school on Barrington Street, and that she also cleans gold and silver lace and stiffens silks and mournings. There is an "Academy" on Grafton Street where young gentlemen are speedily instructed in the true arts of spelling, reading, writing, arithmetic, French, Latin, and dancing—and the dancing lessons may be attended by young ladies as well.

Richard Bulkeley warns against cutting wood on Cornwallis' Island. Henry O'Brien takes boarders at the Heart & Crown "on the Beach"—that is to say, on Water Street. John Sharpe does business "at the sign of the Recruiting Sergeant, near the Parade." Samuel Sellon deals in real estate at the sign of the Spread Eagle, an inn long known in Halifax as the "Split Crow." Captain Piggott conducts his affairs "at the Duke of Cumberland's Head." Jews are already established in the firm of Nathan & Levy, which later became Nathan & Hart. Hart was probably connected with the well-known Jewish family of Hart in Quebec and Montreal, and there is reason to believe that the grandfather of Bret Harte, the American novelist, spent some time with his Halifax relations on first coming to America.

Although many of the settlers continued to draw His Majesty's rations for five years after the town was founded, the shops were full of goods for those with money or credit—"good pork, beef, wheat and rye flour, Indian meal, butter, cheese, mould and dipped candles, rum, tobacco, milk, bread, sugar, braziers' ware, choice Hampshire bacon, house frames, glazed window sashes, perukes, and iron backs for chimneys," all are advertised in the *Gazette*. A conveyancer did a thriving business in bills of lading, bonds, charter parties, deeds, leases, mortgages, writs, and wills "at the corner of Sackville Street by the Beach."

There were blacksmiths, cabinetmakers, joiners, attorneys, bakers, tallow chandlers, soapmakers, linen drapers. There was a brewery, and Mr. Mauger's distillery. There was also a busy slave trade conducted by the avaricious Mauger, who regularly sold Negro men, women, and children at Major Lockman's store and elsewhere. Major Lockman was a German, a retired army surgeon, and the north extension of Barrington Street for many years bore his name.

Thus Halifax, nourished by parliamentary grants, took root in the stony soil of Chebucto. The Indians, often accompanied by Acadian adventurers, continued to raid Dartmouth and the skirts of Halifax itself, carrying off prisoners and scalps to the French posts at Louisburg, Beausejour, and elsewhere. The price of Indian scalps at Halifax went up to £30, and the English officer Bartelo and the New England officer Gilman each raised a troop of rangers to engage in this exciting and sometimes lucrative business.

It was a harsh and cruel time, even in the town itself. Men were hanged for petty burglary. A woman who stole "2 saucepans, 1 copper pott, a quart & pint pewter pott, 2 brass candlesticks, all of a value of five shillings" was able to escape the death sentence only by benefit of clergy. (She was branded in the hand with the letter T for Thief and thrown in the common jail for two months.) When a simple carpenter hanged himself the governor commanded that he be buried without Christian rites at the nearest crossroads, and the coroner was ordered "to cause a stake to be driven through the said body and such other marks of infamy to be set up *in terrorem* as heretofore has been used and accustomed in like cases."

The streets were still rough with stones and old tree stumps. In spring and autumn they were deep in mud, in summer deep in dust, and grass grew wild along the waysides. For water the inhabitants relied upon the town pumps, the chief of which stood at the side of George Street not far from the governor's door; and as they flung their slops and garbage into the gutters their ills were many and severe. The first log huts had been sheathed with boards and fitted with steep shingled roofs to shed the winter snow, and with a plentiful supply of lumber at last the streets began to present rows of frame houses built on low foundations of dry stone wrenched from the hillside. Shops were small and crude, most of them simply a front room in a dwelling, with goods exposed on a broad shutter let down on hinges in the day and closed up at night.

A custom brought to Halifax by the New Englanders was the noisy celebration of Guy Fawkes or Gunpowder Plot Day on the fifth of November. It was a familiar holiday to the old-country English; but in New England, especially in Boston, it had become the excuse for annual riot and commotion. Effigies of Guy Fawkes, the Pope, and anyone politically unpopular at the moment were mounted on wagons and drawn about the streets by a yelling mob of men and boys, usually accompanied by a figure representing the Devil, pitchfork in hand and covered with tar and feathers. There were rival mobs with similar effigies and wagons, and when they met in the streets there was a battle royal for each other's images. Halifax had a smaller population than Boston and doubtless the annual affair was on a smaller scale, but it was so noisy and destructive that in 1752 the governor and council forbade all persons from "assembling and carrying about effigies on the anniversary of the holyday commonly called Gunpowder Treason."

Every townsman between the ages of sixteen and sixty was subject to militia duty and from time to time they mustered for drill on the Parade, each in his everyday clothes and armed with musket and cartridge pouch. The regulars were housed in wooden barracks, one at the south side of Citadel Hill at what became known as Royal Artillery Park, the other on the north side at the corner of Brunswick and Cogswell streets. A lane between the two cantonments, running along the harbor slope of the hill, was known as "Barrack Street" for a century and a half, despite its official name of Brunswick Street. Here gathered an evil slum of grog sellers, pimps, and prostitutes who battened on the dissolute soldiery.

On the waterfront the seamen resorted to dens along "the Beach," and when for a bit of spice the tars went roistering up the hill to Barrack Street, or the redcoats ("lobster-backs") came down to sample the delights of Water Street, there were scuffles and sometimes riots, with the seamen swinging their cudgels (a favorite challenge was "D'ye want a rub-down with my oaken towel?") and the soldiers drawing bayonets, and all the queer denizens of those parts diving to cover. Thus in its earliest days the heart's core of Halifax became sandwiched between two slums, a situation which long remained a reproach and a problem to its citizens.

7.
1755–1758

The feud with Louisburg. Governor Lawrence. Ten thousand scalping knives. The soldiers of New and Old England. The merry game of privateering. Lord Loudon's great fiasco. Death of the war chief Cope. Boscawen, Wolfe, and Amherst. The life of a soldier.

HALIFAX REMAINED AN OUTPOST IN THE WILDS, A sop to the pride and anger of the New Englanders, until war with France broke out again in 1755. The war brought a change which grew very swiftly with the influence of William Pitt, who saw that the proper way to strike at France was not in Europe but on the sea and in her colonies abroad. Foremost in Pitt's mind was the conquest of Canada. He proposed to accomplish this largely with sea-borne armies, a plan which brought Halifax into its true role at last, as a base for far reaching enterprises on land and sea. But Pitt was not yet in power and the British were to muddle as usual until sheer desperation showed them their one true course.

Cornwallis had gone home in 1752, broken in health. His young aide, Horatio Gates, had married a Nova Scotia girl and gone off to his destiny in New York. Only Bulkeley stayed, enchanted somehow with this wild country and the raw new town. Colonel Hopson reigned as governor for a year and then went home to England. The acting governor now was the tough soldier Lawrence, a veteran of fighting in Europe and America, who still bore a scar from Fontenoy. He stood six feet two inches, a big west-country Englishman with a bluff affability but a will as ruthless as a sword.

Events moved swiftly in 1755. Both nations had prepared to make Acadie a battlefield. In May, Lawrence received warning that a French fleet and four thousand regular troops were on their way to Louisburg intending an invasion of Nova Scotia. This was startling; Lawrence estimated his available force at three thousand, and the defenses of Halifax were very poor. The crest of Citadel Hill, from which a hostile force could shoot down the very chimneys of the town, remained unfortified. The log forts on the lower slope were in a tumbledown state. On the waterfront two or three batteries existed, George's Island had been partly cleared of trees and armed with cannon, and what was called the Eastern Battery had been erected to watch the eastern passage of the harbor at a point near the site of Imperoyal. None of these could prevent the French from entering the main harbor channel and landing troops.

Fortunately a British fleet under Boscawen came up with the French on the Banks of Newfoundland, captured two of their best ships, and scattered the rest. The prizes, *Alcide* and *Lys*, were brought into Halifax harbor in triumph and their twelve hundred seamen and soldiers confined as prisoners on George's Island. On board the captured ships the British had found the Governor of Louisburg and the French war chest—specie to the value of £30,000. But among the stores on board was an item of even greater interest: twenty leather bags, each containing five hundred scalping knives for distribution to the Acadians and Indians in Nova Scotia. The discovery of these ten thousand knives sent a chill of horror through the Haligonians, whose minds were filled with memories of the bloody raids against them all through the years since 1749.

A French officer of the Régiment de la Marine admitted that he was to have taken charge of the knives and freely gave a list of the Acadians and Indian chiefs who were to receive them. One was Cope, chief of the Micmacs at Shubenacadie, foremost in his hatred of the English and the author of many an outrage against the Halifax harbor settlements. Another was Broussard, nicknamed Beau Soleil, the Acadian who had led the raid on Dartmouth in 1750 and who at this moment was in charge of the Acadian rangers fighting the British forces about Beausejour.

Fort Beausejour fell to the British in June, and Halifax was elated. But on July 23 the brig *Lily* arrived from New York with the news of Braddock's defeat and there was consternation, for if a rabble of French and Indians could cut up a disciplined British force on the Monongahela they could do it anywhere. This news reached the Acadians at a time when Lawrence had resolved to settle the Acadian problem once and for all. He summoned thirty Acadian deputies to Halifax and made a final demand that they take the oath of allegiance to the British King. They refused. Six days after the *Lily* brought her ominous message, Lawrence came to the decision long urged upon him by the New England governors, the decision which has been so deplored in sentimental prose and poetry ever since, that he must expel the Acadians from the country. To Lawrence, in the midst of dangers, there was no room for sentiment. No doubt he had seen those scalping knives. The Acadians were expelled.

The men who chiefly carried out the expulsion, Winslow's grim New England soldiers and rangers, afterwards marched to Halifax over the road from Minas and were quartered at Fort Sackville, at Dartmouth (where their chaplain preached to them in Clapham's windmill), and in the blockhouses across the Halifax peninsula. These tough men in blue coats and buckskins, accustomed to war in the forest, were regarded askance by the redcoats of the garrison. Captured French stores were at auction in Halifax at the time, and the Americans bought what one of them described as "rigemental briches." In these strangely assorted uniforms of blue and white, with their rough shoes and moccasins, their sealskin haversacks and carved powderhorns, their variety of hats and caps, their slouching gait and careless air, they were the antithesis of soldiers in the disciplined British eye. The English officers despised them, Colonel Monckton had gone out of his way to insult them, but in twenty years the British regular was to learn that such men on their own ground were invincible.

The year 1755 also brought a ghost to Halifax, the sixty-four-gun warship *Mars* of D'Anville's old fleet, captured on that doleful voyage home and for nine years a part of the British Navy. She was part of Boscawen's fleet now, but the old jinx of Chebucto was as potent as ever and the great three-decker struck and foundered on the reef known ever since as Mars Rock. Fate had brought her back to the bones of her shipmates.

For the first time Halifax experienced the clang, the jostle and prosperity of large-scale war, very different from the petty business of Indian warfare with its long silences; its sudden whoops and shots, and the draggled wisps of skin and hair that were its only loot. Now the streets were thronged with Boscawen's merry seamen in their short petticoat trousers, their red or checkered flannel shirts, their Barcelona handkerchiefs and tight little thrice-cocked hats. Lawrence's redcoats woke the dust of the narrow streets as they marched from barracks to forts, to Church Parade at St. Paul's, and to Grand Parade for inspections or the changing of the guard. The air was pierced with their drums and fifes and shaken by the boom of signal guns.

Gaunt pig-tailed rangers, padding soft-footed in their moccasins about the town, set the taverns ringing with their songs and whoops.

And now began the lively and often lucrative business of privateering against His Majesty's enemies at sea. The sharp man Mauger was quick to fit out a schooner, the *Musquito*, which brought the first prize into Halifax, a fat Dutch merchantman caught laden with French goods. The methods of Mauger's crew were worthy of the owner. Suspecting money hidden aboard, they put thumbscrews on six of the Dutchmen and a passenger to make them tell. As one of these unfortunates was dancing under the torture, Mauger's second mate took hold of the man and skipped merrily up and down the deck with him, while a privateersman played a hornpipe on the fiddle. All this was brought out by a Court of Vice-Admiralty sitting solemnly in Halifax to consider whether or not the Dutchman's cargo was fair prize.

Fourteen other privateers were fitted out by such respectable people as Malachi Salter and Michael Francklin, though whether or not their crews were as unscrupulous as Mauger's is not recorded. What with the captures of the privateers and those of the fleet, Halifax soon was loud with auctioneers selling off prize goods. Every man had plenty to drink and every lass had ribbons to wear. The goods were various and sometimes odd. One item was a church organ captured on the way to Spanish America. It found its way to St. Paul's and for many years boomed forth the tunes of Protestant hymns. At this time the population of Halifax was 1755, overwhelmed by the presence of 3000 soldiers and rangers and by Boscawen's thousands whenever the fleet was in. Under this impact the morals of the town went gutter-low, and the war had barely begun.

In 1757 the town experienced a huge new male incursion when Lord Loudon brought his army and Lord Holborne his fleet to prepare for the second conquest of Louisburg. There were eleven battalions of British redcoats, two battalions of the Royal American Regiment, and a corps of rangers under the celebrated Captain Robert Rogers, the man who later sought the Northwest Passage by way of the Great Lakes. All of these were encamped on the shoulders of Citadel Hill and on the rough knoll to the west of it, known ever since as Camp Hill. Loudon's army numbered something like twelve thousand officers and men.

In the early autumn of 1757 Halifax saw another kind of troops, a battalion of Montgomery's Highlanders, some of whom were quartered in Dartmouth. These were the first fruits of a new British policy, to utilize the fighting qualities of the Highland clans in the empire's wars abroad, and Montgomery's was the first of a long train of Scottish regiments in garrison at Halifax.

Loudon was a pompous incompetent who had been given this post for his services against Prince Charlie in 1745. He kept his troops at Halifax the summer long, complaining that the local rum made them ill, and planting acres of cabbages against the scurvy. The fleet under Holborne consisted of eleven warships and fifty transports, manned by at least four thousand seamen. The effect of this swarm added to the soldiers in the huddled wooden town may be imagined.

Through the hot summer days Loudon exercised his soldiers on the marshy surface of the Common. The American soldiers did not love him and perhaps it was no accident that twice at their musket practice a ball narrowly missed the commander in chief. Despite this military horde the Indians continued to skulk about the outskirts of the town until, one day in July, a group of strolling seamen was attacked in the pinewoods nowadays known as Point Pleasant Park. Two were carried off alive, two were killed and scalped. (No doubt a scalp with a tarred pigtail attached was a special prize to the Micmacs.)

An officer's guard was ordered to patrol the woods near the spot, but whether or not these men encountered the Indians we are not told. The notorious Micmac chief, Cope, disappeared at this time, never to be seen again, and his people have a tradition that he was killed in a fight and buried secretly in the pinewoods of Point Pleasant. Any of the family parties of Haligonians who picnic at Point Pleasant, any of the smart riders in jodhpurs who jog their horses along the bridle paths among the pines, any of the sweethearts who wander in the friendly gloom, may be treading over the bones of that famous and ferocious savage who for a decade filled their ancestors' days and nights with horror.

As one might expect with such a commander, the Loudon expedition came to a sorry end. In early August, just after the troops had been embarked for the attack on Louisburg, the man-o'-war *Gosport* took a French prize, *La Parole*, bound out of that port, and brought her into Halifax. Hidden in a barrel of fish was a packet of letters addressed to the French Government, stating among other things that a fleet of twenty-two ships of the line (not to mention frigates and smaller craft) had arrived at Louisburg and that some eight thousand French troops were in the fortress or "entrenched up to their necks" above the landing beaches. It was obvious to every Halifax shopboy that *La Parole* had been sent out to be "captured" and that the letters were intended for Loudon to read. But they frightened that pompous man out of his wits and he canceled the whole expedition.

The troops, the fleet, and the Haligonians were amazed and then filled with scorn. At Sunday service the clerk of St. Paul's announced that certain verses of the Forty-fourth Psalm were to be sung:

> *We have heard with our ears, o God, our fathers have told us what work thou didst in their days, in the times of old.*
> *How thou didst drive out the heathen with thy hand, and plantedst them; how thou didst afflict the people, and cast them out…*
> *But thou hast cast off, and put us to shame; and goest not forth with our armies.*
> *Thou makest us to turn back from the enemy: and they which hate us spoil for themselves.*
> *Thou hast given us like sheep appointed for meat; and hast scattered us among the heathen.…*
> *Thou makest us a reproach to our neighbours, a scorn and a derision to them that are round about us.…*
> *Arise for our help, and redeem us for thy mercy's sake.*

Nobody missed the significance of this, but Loudon had not spirit enough to give the clerk a wigging. When his officers arrested two Halifax merchants for declaring that the French had no more than five ships of the line at Louisburg he ordered their release before night. And away he sailed, leaving the smallpox brought by his troops, which killed seven hundred of the townsfolk in the bitter cold winter of 1757-58. Admiral Holborne, having more spirit, sailed for Louisburg to tackle the French fleet; but the season was too late. He was caught in an equinoctial gale, his fleet was badly damaged, and two of his finest ships were wrecked on the wild coast of Cape Breton.

So ended England's most ambitious effort up to that time against the French in America—one more failure, in a war of disasters. But now a new hand took the helm, the hand of William Pitt; and there was Pitt's calm voice saying: "I know that I can save this country and that no one else can." His dream was clear, to cripple the French by striking at their empire across the sea, and he knew how to make it real and what men to pick for the job. He chose Jeffrey Amherst, veteran of Dettingen and Fontenoy, a man who had seen the disgraceful surrender at Kloster Zeven, a tall, thin, beak-nosed soldier with a gift for organization. And under steady Amherst he placed a perfect counterpart, James Wolfe, the fiery and reckless young soldier who had seen Dettingen, Falkirk, Culloden, who carried a scar from the field of Laffeldt, who had seen the badly bungled landing at Rochefort and was snorting still with rage. And for the fleet there was Boscawen of course, "Old Dreadnaught" of the large clear eyes, the bold arched eyebrows and the pleasant mouth, the small man who carried his head a bit awry but saw things straight enough. Boscawen knew the North American station far better than he knew his beloved wife Fannie—he had spent so much more time there.

These men came to Halifax in the spring of 1758 with 41 warships, 120 transports, and 12,000 British troops. The shabby wooden streets were brilliant with uniforms, the shop counters jingled with guineas and silver, the taverns roared, the bawdyhouses bustled, the commissaries scrambled to obtain provisions for this enormous visitation. Amherst was late in arriving, and Lawrence was in nominal command until he came; but Wolfe was the heart and soul of things. He kept the troops busy rehearsing the landing on the Dartmouth shore and making fascines, storming ladders, and other apparatus for the assault. Boscawen himself designed a cart with enormous wheels for hauling cannon through the Louisburg swamps. Nothing was neglected, not even the health of the troops.

To ward off scurvy every soldier was obliged to drink (and pay for) a daily ration of spruce beer, a decoction invented by the New Englanders at the first siege of Louisburg. Spruce beer continued to be a compulsory tipple in Nova Scotia garrisons for many years and the recipe is worth recording here:

> *Take seven pounds of good spruce and boil it well till the bark peels off. Then take the spruce out and put in three gallons of molasses and boil the liquor again, scum it well as it boils, then take it out of the kettle and put it into a cooler. When milk-warm in the cooler put a pint of yeast into it and mix well. Then put it in the barrel and let*

it work for two or three days, and keep filling it up as it works out. When done working, bung it up with a tent-peg in the barrel to give it vent now and then. It may be used in two or three days.

Besides this powerful beverage each soldier received the usual grog allowance—one gill of rum in three gills of water—not to mention the fiery cordials of the taverns, which consumed most of his pay. As a result his sins were many and his punishments were harsh to match the stuff he consumed. Men guilty of serious military crimes were hanged on the Common or shot behind Citadel Hill, where the garrison football ground is now, and their bodies flung into the earth on the side of Camp Hill at what is now the corner of Jubilee Road and Robie Street.

Flogging was the common punishment, with the offender stripped and strung up to the triangles—three sergeants' pikes tied together at the top—and lashed with cat-o'-nine-tails in the hands of tall drummers of the regiment. A hundred lashes was considered light; for serious misdeeds a man might suffer as many as a thousand. A frequent penalty was "riding the wooden horse," with the culprit sitting naked astride a sharp wooden rail for hours, sometimes with weights attached to his feet, and sometimes carried along the street from barrack to barrack, jolting painfully whenever his bearers stumbled on the stony way.

In special cases the punishment was varied, especially if the culprit was an officer, when of course physical pain was out of the question. One lieutenant of the rangers (none other than the Sicilian adventurer, Peter, Marquis of Contes and Gravina) was convicted of "rape on a child under the age of ten years" and sentenced to walk up and down the Grand Parade for an hour on a cold December day, with a paper on his breast setting forth the crime.

In the fleet, offenders were flogged at the gangway; and for serious offenses they were flogged aboard each man-o'-war in the anchorage, going by boat from ship to ship. Mutineers and seamen convicted of piracy were hanged at the yardarm in the harbor, and their bodies later dangled in chains at Black Rock on the Point Pleasant road, or on the grim gibbets at Mauger's Beach where the swinging bones remained as warning to everyone passing in or out of the port. The good old days!

8.
1758–1759

A little dinner at the Pontac. The fall of Louisburg. Creating a dockyard. Beginning the "Great West Road." German settlers in Gottingen and Brunswick streets. Freshwater River and the Kissing Bridge. The loot of Louisburg. The first post office. Convening a General Assembly. Life in '59.

THE CHIEF HOTEL AT THIS TIME WAS THE GREAT Pontac, named after Pontack's Club in London. It was a large wooden building of three stories surrounded by verandahs, standing at the foot of Duke Street where a small cove gave easy access to the harbor. When the admiral or some well-to-do captain gave a dinner at the Pontac he had special dishes prepared on board by his own cook to supplement the Pontac's fare. These dishes were hurried ashore by picked boat crews to the Duke Street cove and thence rushed up to the dining room by a hurrying file of stewards.

Here the officers of the garrison and fleet and the merchant aristocracy of Halifax entertained each other with dinners, routs, and balls. The hotel was kept first by a Jersey man named Decarteret, and later by the more noted John Willis, who made it for years the social center of the town.

A "small" dinner given here by Wolfe on the eve of his departure for Louisburg cost that gallant young officer nearly £100. Here is the bill:

47 plates @ 20/-	£47	0	0
70 bottles Madeira @ 5/-	17	10	0
50 bottles Claret @ 5/-	12	10	0
25 bottles Brandy @ 7/6-	9	7	6
10 musicians @ 10/-	5	0	0
Supplies for musicians	2	15	0
15 special attendants @ 4/-	3	0	0
Table-master and his supper	1	10	0
	£98	12	6

To Genl. Wolfe,
Halifax,
24th May, 1758

John Willis.
GREAT PONTAC

A convivial affair it must have been, and a brilliant gathering; we can guess the names of some of Wolfe's guests. Amherst was still on the sea, groping towards Halifax in the *Dublin,* but Lawrence undoubtedly sat before one of those forty-seven plates. The stout old soldier had turned over his duties as governor to Colonel Robert Monckton and now was commanding a brigade in the expedition. Jeffrey Amherst's brothers must have been there, William a captain in the army and John a captain in the navy. With them, doubtless, were Brigadier Whitmore ("that poor old man" of Wolfe's letters); Colonel James Murray, son of Lord Elibank; Major Alexander Murray, soon to gain fame with his grenadiers at Louisburg; Colonel John Henry Bastide, chief engineer to the forces; Colonel Richard Gridley, veteran of the New Englanders' conquest of Louisburg, now called in for his knowledge, and one day to fight against some of these very redcoats in the American Revolution; Colonel the Honourable William Howe, an old comrade in arms of Wolfe, and one day to command British armies against the Americans; the Earl of Dundonald, a young captain of grenadiers, soon to die at Louisburg; Lord Rollo, colonel of infantry; Captain Hugh Debbeig, Wolfe's assistant quartermaster general; Colonel the Honourable Roger Townsend, adjutant general of the expedition; Colonel Ralph Burton, still bearing his scar from the scene of Braddock's defeat; and Brigade Major Isaac Barre, whose voice on the side of the Americans was to be heard loud and long in Parliament in the years to come.

The naval guests must have included Boscawen himself; Commodore Durell, who made the first British chart of Halifax harbor; Vice-Admiral Sir Charles Hardy, who had led a squadron into the ice off Louisburg as early as March; and Captain John Rous, the able New Englander—once a privateersman and now commanding a ship of the line—in whose cabin Wolfe was fated to write his last order at Quebec. A fine show of blue and scarlet they must have made about the Pontac's tables. They would sit down at the fashionable hour of four in the afternoon and hold on far into the night. And we can guess what sort of tunes those ten musicians played; for Wolfe, though no drunkard, was fond of a ditty called "How

Stands the Glass Around?" and another which inquired: "Soldier, Why Be Melancholy?"

No doubt there were other convivial gatherings in the town and its camps and barracks. And then one day the red-coated regiments marched down to embark. The four companies of rangers went along in their queer half-Indian dress, armed with light muskets, tomahawks, and scalping knives. The Highlanders strode down the narrow streets with kilts swaying to the music of the pipes. It must have been a fine show for the townsmen and their women and children, and a sad sight for the grog sellers and the trollops of Barrack Street.

On May 28 the fleet and transports sailed out of the harbor, filling the eastern horizon with their sails. Just outside they met Amherst in HMS *Dublin* with its soon-to-be-famous Captain George Bridges Rodney, and off they went to Louisburg. The outcome of that expedition all the world knows. The impetuous Wolfe had expected to take the fortress in ten days or so. But the siege took weeks, and when Louisburg fell at last it was too late in the season to go on to Quebec. Several of the regiments and warships returned to Halifax and wintered there.

Halifax was feeling the impact of these great events. For one thing His Majesty's Navy had determined to build a first-class dockyard. There had been a royal dock at Halifax for some time past "with all conveniences for the largest first-rate ship to heave down and careen"; but now the government purchased more land about the dock and planned a navy yard on a scale hitherto unseen in America. This and other war expenditures had produced a boom in Nova Scotia. The road from Halifax to Windsor was still just a muddy track through the forest; but now the inducements offered by Governor Lawrence, the fall of Louisburg, the rich lands awaiting settlement—especially those from which the Acadians had been removed—and the presence of a hungry market in the town and garrison of Halifax all combined to bring a rush of eager New Englanders to the western parts of the province.

Thus the old Windsor road became "the Great West Road," running all the way from Halifax to Annapolis. Along the Annapolis Valley it was little better than a horse path. From Minas Basin to Bedford Basin it followed more or less the track cut out by the Acadians in the dim years before 1749. Thence it skirted the Basin shore, climbed the Halifax plateau past what is now Fairview Cemetery and ran through the fields and pastures and wood lots of the frugal Germans (this part is still called Windsor Street) to the edge of the Common at Camp Hill. Here it swung across the swamp past the Egg Pond, skirted the southerly slope of Citadel Hill, turned down what now is Queen Street, and entered the town at the old south gate by Spring Garden Road. Until 1758 this was the only highway out of the town. But about that year Chebucto Road came into existence, leading from the north suburbs to the blockhouse and bridge at the head of the Northwest Arm and linking there with a track lately cut through the forest from Lunenburg.

In the north end of the town the German folk of Gottingen and Brunswick streets now had a house of worship, familiar still to Haligonians as "the little Dutch church." It was built on Brunswick Street, which now was linked with the notorious "Barrack Street" in a continuous if somewhat irregular line along the upper harbor slope, making a very queer contrast—the turbulent soldiers and their groggeries and bawdyhouses at one end of the road, and the pious industrious Germans at the other.

At the south end of the town the chief object of interest was the governor's garden, approached by the track called Spring Garden Road by the nostalgic Londoners. It lay on the site of the present county courthouse. Just across the road was the poorhouse, on the grounds of the present Public Library. Here were confined not only the poor but the insane. One of its most used fittings was a whipping post, for these were the days when lunatics were flogged as if some sort of devil lived within their flesh. There must have been many an edifying spectacle for the gentlefolk sniffing the flowers across the way. The poorhouse dead were buried hastily in shallow graves in the yard, and for many years there were complaints about the smell which hung over this part of Spring Garden Road.

The south end of Barrington Street then and for generations was known as Pleasant Street, for it ran towards Point Pleasant and made a favorite walk for the pioneer townsfolk on fine Sunday afternoons. Owing to the Indian raids the governor provided a guard of redcoats for these excursions, and for a long time each sunny Sabbath saw a procession of Haligonians dressed in their best, marching solemnly towards the pine point between files of bayonets and paced by fife and drum.

The usual walk took the strollers as far as the brook called Freshwater River, which flowed out of the marshy Common, passed through what now are the Wanderers' Grounds and the Public Gardens, crossed Spring

Garden Road near the present statue of Bobby Burns, passed through a bushy ravine just south of Fort Massey, and finally splashed across "Pleasant Street" into the harbor. The bridge over the stream at Pleasant Street was known for generations as the Kissing Bridge, a favorite haunt of lovers and the scene of much flirtation in the summer evenings. This brook was the chief source of fresh water for the fleet and merchant shipping, and from the Kissing Bridge loiterers could watch the sailors filling and trundling their casks down to their boats at what now is the dock between Pier A and Ocean Terminal. Time and building schemes have dried the Freshwater River and filled its ancient course, and all that remains of it today is the Egg Pond in the Common, the duck pond in the Public Gardens, and a sewer at the foot of Inglis Street. The site of the Kissing Bridge, alas, is a humdrum railway embankment where the trains clack in and out of Union Station.

The most notable change in Halifax in 1758 was the completion of a new Government House close beside the original cottage built for Cornwallis in the early days. It stood on a grassy terrace (the site of Province House), a two-storey rectangular wooden box with huge chimneys and a steep hipped roof. Before the main porch on Hollis Street stood a pair of sentry boxes constantly tenanted by tall-capped grenadiers. The grounds held several small buildings for the offices of government, all surrounded by a palisade of tall pointed pickets. The new mansion was completed in August, and Lawrence gave a great housewarming ball in honor of the victors of Louisburg. Amherst, Wolfe, and the others were there—the guests numbered more than four hundred—and the entertainment cost the jovial governor over £500.

Now that the rivalry of Halifax and Louisburg—the Rome and Carthage of the new world—had ended in final victory for the British, the decree went forth that Louisburg was to be demolished stone by stone, as Carthage was. It had been built with a good deal of cut stone brought across the sea from Caen in Normandy, and the spoilers carried it off to Halifax in shiploads with the other booty. Fine residences of these conquered stones were built in Halifax by well-to-do merchants and officials, amongst them Richard Bulkeley, who had just married young Amy Rous. The solid house he built still stands in Argyle Street, as part of the premises of the Carleton Hotel. Even the little Dutch church had a share in the loot; the bell which had rung vespers from the Louisburg garrison chapel now called the pious Germans of Halifax to prayer.

Other spoils of war were the cannon of the demolished fortress, which Lawrence carried to Halifax and placed in triumph about the streets, sunk down to their trunnions in the earth with muzzles pointing mutely skyward. There they remained nearly a century, stumbling blocks for night-faring roisterers and the delight of every dog.

There was now a "post office" at Halifax, really a depot where mail was held awaiting the attention of the addressees. In these days postage usually was paid at the receiving end, and in 1758 an officer posted upcountry complained that "upwards of 40 letters for officers and soldiers of the 43rd Regiment lately lay at the Post Office at Halifax, and the Postmaster transmitted them back to New York, not knowing how he should be repaid the postage." The delivery of mail to outside points depended on the friendly interest of travelers and coasting skippers, and this state of affairs persisted for another fifty years. There were no envelopes; the letter paper was folded into an oblong packet and sealed with a daub of red or black wax, with the address written on the outer fold. A typical letter from England addressed to a loyalist soldier discharged in Nova Scotia after the Revolution bore this superscription:

> *For Mr. Willm. Cooke belonging to the Prince of Wales American Voluntea̶res, Now in Novicotia near Port Rosieway in the Province of Halifax, North America.*
>
> *If you are a Seaman or a Sodiers Friend*
> *Pray lett this Letter goe to its Journeys End.*

In October 1758 there was a portentous gathering in Halifax, the first General Assembly of Nova Scotia. In the original instructions to Cornwallis there was a paragraph saying: "And we do hereby give and grant unto you power...to summon and call General Assemblys of the Freeholders and Planters within your Government according to the usage of the rest of our colonies and plantations in America." Cornwallis and his immediate successors had done nothing about this. Soldiers all, they regarded with a profound distrust any civilian pretensions towards government.

By 1758 Lawrence could no longer delay. The town was full of New Englanders alive with that instinct for self-government which was to set North America aflame in less than twenty years; and more were coming to settle in the province, on the governor's own invitation and on his promise that they should enjoy political privileges. So he called the first assembly, remarking glumly in one of his dispatches: "I observe that too many of the members chosen are such as have not been the most remarkable for promoting unity or obedience to HM Government here."

Still, he could comfort himself with the reflection that the powers of the assembly were very limited. The scepter lay in the hands of the governor and his self-appointed council, and surely they could keep it there. The assembly had other views. There were heard the first faint creak and grumblings of a struggle for true self-government which was to continue nearly a century. In Archibald MacMechan's words, "it meant the planting of free political institutions in what is now the Dominion of Canada...the primacy of Nova Scotia in the field of politics."

In November Jeffrey Amherst turned up again, this time to inspect the Halifax defenses. It did not take him long, for there was little to inspect. He walked to Point Pleasant, went by boat to Dartmouth, to Fort Sackville at the end of Bedford Basin, to McNab's Island, to George's Island, and he traversed the blockhouse line at the isthmus and examined the three small batteries along the Halifax waterfront. George's Island he said was "spoiled almost by cutting it down," and what he said of the Eastern Battery (Imperoyal) was true of the whole—"it is good enough against Indians." Off he went to New York to plan the invasion of Canada.

The assault on Quebec was scheduled for the next year, but in the meantime the destruction of the barracks at Louisburg had made the place untenable for most of the British army and so the troops were scattered through the American colonies for the winter. Two English regiments and two battalions of the Royal Americans came to Halifax, where in truth the accommodation was poor. Most of them spent the hard weather miserably in tents and shacks erected in open spaces about the town, drinking themselves insensible against the cold, and perishing of "camp fever." To supplement the meager army pay the soldiers were allowed to work in the town at wages laid down by authority—one shilling sixpence per day for "artificers" and sixpence a day for common labor. One of these artificers was Anthony Henry, a fifer of the Royal Americans, who knew the printing trade. He went to work at Bushell's printing press, secured his discharge from the army and within two years was sole manager of the *Halifax Gazette*, which had grown to double its former size.

In the spring of 1759 the troops went off to their supreme adventure at Quebec under the lanky red-haired Wolfe, and again the Halifax merchants (notably Michael Francklin) reaped fortunes in supplies. At this time, too, the Halifax Dockyard began to take its new important shape. The huge new mast house and other structures were built of schistose slate from a quarry across the Northwest Arm. For more than a hundred years this "ironstone" was a favorite building material in Halifax wherever a massive structure was required and permanence was the thing. It was a hard and rather ugly stone, a dark gray stuff that looked black in rainy weather, gleaming dully in every facet of its broken edges, and when the buildings became obsolete the wreckers found them very hard to pull down. Behind its granite façade St. Mary's Basilica remains an example of the ironstone buildings which once were such a feature of the town, and All Saints Cathedral, erected (1910) completely of this material, represents the last of its era.

Other building in 1759 included two large blocks of wooden barracks on the northeast slope of Citadel Hill near the corner of Brunswick and Cogswell streets, later known as the Red Barracks. They had a parade ground between them, and the cantonment lay just across the road and slightly downhill from the ruins of one of Cornwallis' log-and-earth forts, on a site since occupied by Trinity Church.

And now at last, after several fits and starts (including a scheme to finance it by a public lottery) a lighthouse was built at Sambro near the harbor entrance. Since the Louisburg lighthouse was demolished this was the only guide to mariners on the long ill-charted coast, and it is strange to record that its maintenance for years was in the hands of contractors, who furnished or failed to furnish oil for the lamps according to their whim.

Business was good in Halifax and life was pleasant. One of its busy merchants sent his wife on a visit to her relatives in Boston, and wrote a letter which gave her and posterity a glimpse of town life in his time:

Halifax, Sep. 2nd, 1759.

My Dear Sukey,

Since you have been gone the Governor has more than once enquired whether I have heard from you, and drank your safe arrival in a bumper. We are all very well, Ben goes to school regularly; Abbie's delicate skin is a little sunburnt, it is impossible to keep her always in the house. Mac is as hearty as a brick. I enclose you a journal of our dinners, company, etc., for I know you to be a very woman for curiosity. Hagar behaves better than ever. I have only to tell her what I want and it is got at the minute I order it and in the nicest manner. Jack is Jack still, but rather worse; I am obliged to exercise the cat or stick almost every day, I believe Halifax don't afford such another idle deceitful villain; pray purchase a negro boy if possible. As to your coming home I would not have you exceed the 1st of October as after that time you may expect bad weather.

I would have you bring half a barrel of neat's tongues, some butter, some nuts, also get half a barrel of good corned beef and some green pepper; but why need I mention these things to you. I find that it is not good for man to be alone, I am weary of life without you and should urge your coming home immediately were it not that I think you are happy in the company of your friends in Boston. I have purchased some geese which I shall fatten until you arrive; I know you are fond of ducklings. I have laid in most of my wood, have got the chief of my fence done; am now enclosing the fine green pasture at the back of our garden. Our Governor comes regularly every morning to see how I go on, he has this day given me a very good lot in the north suburbs.

Your very affectionate husband,
Malachy Salter.

9.
1759–1765

The savages bury the hatchet. Proclaiming a new king. The Collins murder case. "Tomahawk" the hangman. The loot of Havana.

THE WAR ROLLED ON. THE FLEET AND ARMY GATHERED at Halifax again, and Mr. Richard Short, purser of HMS *Prince of Orange*, improved his time by making some excellent drawings of the town which later he published in London. In May 1759 Wolfe had sailed for Quebec, and the prevailing toast was "British colours on every French fort, port and garrison in America!" Quebec fell on September 18. Eleven days later the news sent Halifax into a celebration that lasted several days and nights. Each night there was an "illumination" which involved fireworks and bonfires but chiefly meant that every townsman placed lighted candles in the street-facing windows of his house. In the inky darkness of the eighteenth-century streets it was very effective, and Halifax continued to celebrate the empire's victories in this manner until gas lighting robbed it of its glamor.

In 1759 Halifax had much to celebrate. The fall of French dominion in North America meant security at last, not so much from the soldiers of King Louis as from the Indians in his pay. The tribes, bewildered by the swift turn of events, called in their war parties. The evil genius of the Micmacs, the half-mad priest Le Loutre, had gone long since, disowned by his bishop at Quebec and captured by the British on his way to France. The fiery war chief Cope had vanished. And now old Father Maillard, for twenty-five years a missionary in the Acadian forests, led the savages along the path to Halifax and peace. It is strange that while so much has been written about the evils of Le Loutre so little has been said of Father Maillard, the saint who wrought this miracle in Nova Scotia history. Under his persuasion the chiefs came to Halifax one by one to make their peace. The last was Argimault, chief of the Monguash tribe, a Micmac clan; and the occasion was made one of great pomp and ceremony, attended not only by the military officers but by the members of His Majesty's Council, the assembly, the magistrates, and other officials.

Father Maillard acted as interpreter. The president of the council signed the treaty and Argimault drew his own totem with the quill. When this was done the whole gathering marched in solemn procession to the governor's garden beside Spring Garden Road and there, under a hot July sun, in a multitude of officials and staring soldiers, sailors, and townsfolk, the savage chief declared that "he now buried the hatchet in behalf of himself and his whole tribe, in token of their submission and of their having made peace, which should never be broken." So saying he laid the tomahawk in a small grave dug amongst the flowers, where it was buried forever: The promise made through Father Maillard was never broken. Fittingly, the stone County Courthouse now stands beside the spot, a symbol of peace and the rule of law.

Thus after years of blood and terror the last echo of the war whoop died away. The tide of immigration from New England now became a flood. New settlements appeared everywhere about the coasts and up the rivers. To be sure, the war with France continued until 1763; but now its dangers were remote. The fall of Louisburg alone had cut marine insurance rates on transatlantic traffic by more than half (from 25 per cent to 12 per cent). The conquest of Canada promised a trade to the north where before there had been nothing but menace. It was a rosy prospect for the Haligonians; but there was one small cloud, no bigger than King George's hand. His Majesty's Government across the sea in London consistently refused to see Halifax as anything but a weapon of war.

In 1759 the citizens sought to incorporate their town; but those imperial watchdogs Governor Lawrence, Secretary Bulkeley, and the members of the council looked sourly on the measure and refused it, despite the eloquence of Michael Francklin. Like many of his military predecessors and successors, Lawrence looked upon the civil population as so many unnecessary mouths to feed in case of siege. Besides, civilians were a nuisance, always wanting this or that, pushing their shops and houses close about the forts, cluttering the waterfront and anchorage with their fishing boats and trading ships. The original notion of a population of "planters" to supply the troops and fleet had perished in the thin stony soil of the Halifax peninsula. The other notion, a colony of ex-soldiers on the Roman model, had gone with the winds of circumstance. Lawrence himself reported in 1760 that "every soldier that has come into the province since the establishment of Halifax has either quitted it or become a dramseller."

In 1762 there was an alarm of French invasion, the last flicker of the war. Engineer Bastide hastily dug trenches on the crest of Citadel Hill, threw up a battery at Point Pleasant, and erected a signal station on Thrum Cap. Admiral Colville placed a chained boom across the Northwest Arm with a few cannon (long known as the Chain Battery) to defend it. All the scurry died away when peace came in the following year. Halifax was prosperous and growing beyond the rickety old palisades like a lusty wench bursting out of an old tight bodice. The town was spreading up the slope. Argyle and Grafton streets had become the fashionable residential section, with Hollis, Granville, and Barrington streets given over more and more to commerce. On the outskirts the simple frame cottages and log shanties of the common folk were creeping north towards the Dockyard and westward over the slopes of Citadel Hill. Lawrence was dead and buried under St. Paul's. (He had caught a chill after dancing at another grand ball in the new residency, and perished of pneumonia.) Michael Francklin, that good-looking, wealthy, and accomplished young merchant-bachelor, the catch of the town, had made a powerful connection by marrying Susannah Boutineau of Boston, granddaughter of Peter Faneuil. He had built a house on Buckingham Street "with two reception rooms decorated in great taste by artists from New York."

The spider-man Mauger was still going strong, clashing with officialdom whenever it got in the way of his schemes. But very soon now he would sell out his vast enterprises in Nova Scotia and the West Indies, retire to England, and live the life of a lord on a fortune of more than half a million pounds.

Negro slaves were still in demand, and in 1760 the *Gazette* could advertise such items as: "To be sold at public auction on Monday at the house of Mr. John Rider, two slaves, a boy and a girl about eleven years old; likewise a puncheon of choice cherry brandy with sundry other articles." And indeed there were plenty of white slaves to be had along the docks where passengers landed from Great Britain. The system of indentures by which poor English, Irish, and Scots, male and female, bound themselves out for years to pay for their passage across the sea was slavery pure and simple. So was the binding out of orphans, who frequently ran away from their masters and for whose capture rewards were advertised, exactly as though they had been blacks from Africa.

Halifax was still in great part a New England town, with undertones of Old English, "Dutch," and Irish. The Scots, a small but shrewd and capable group in Halifax from very early days, were numerous enough by 1761 to form the Scottish Guild of Merchants, out of which grew on one hand a town board of trade and on the other the North British Society, both of which flourish to this day.

Old George II was dead at last, and the accession of George III was proclaimed in Halifax with all due pomp on a keen February day in 1761. A long procession tramped through the snowy streets—a company of red-coated, miter-capped grenadiers, some constables of the town, the magistrates, the government officials, more constables, the provost marshal with two deputies on horseback, a "band of musick," still more constables, Acting Governor Jonath Belcher, Admiral Lord Colville, Colonel Foster, the garrison commander, the members of His Majesty's Council, the speaker and members of the assembly, and finally the principal merchants and inhabitants.

They marched all about the town to hear the provost marshal read the proclamation in full (it was the usual windy document of those times) at the door of the wooden courthouse at the corner of Argyle and Buckingham streets, at the north gate, at the south gate, at Government House, and finally at Grand Parade, where the shivering redcoats were drawn up and the artillery on Argyle Street just above their heads fired a salute into the wintry air. Colville's fleet in the harbor fired royal salutes in turn, beginning with the flagship *Northumberland*, a towering three-decker. A royal salute called for twenty-one guns, and what with the batteries ashore and the men-o'-war at anchor in the roadstead the frosty harbor hills echoed and re-echoed far into the afternoon.

At three o'clock the officials waited on Belcher at the Governor Lawrence's Head tavern, "where a very elegant entertainment was provided for them, and after dinner His Majesty's health was drunk under a royal salute from the batteries, and thereafter those of the princess-dowager of Wales and all the royal family, and many other loyal toasts; and the evening concluded with great rejoicings and beautiful illuminations, bonfires and fireworks played off by the Royal Artillery, the best designed and best executed of anything of the kind that has hitherto been seen in North America." It was a show such as Halifax loved, and continued to love for a century and a half.

Behind this gilt and glitter and behind the industry of the merchants and townsfolk flourished the other side of Halifax; the brothels, the drinking dens, the underworld which nourished itself on the vices of the troops and fleet. Already the town was reputed the most wicked in North America. A Yankee settler, writing home to the Reverend Dr. Styles about this Sodom of the frontier, made a famous quip: "There are 1,000 houses in the town. We have upwards of 100 licensed (drinking) houses and perhaps as many without license, so the business of one half the town is to sell rum and the other half to drink it." His arithmetic was not quite equal to his wit, and his famous generality ignored the fact that the land and sea forces, who kept most of these taverns going, outnumbered the townsfolk by five or six to one.

The sailors and soldiers were scarcely to be blamed, for their officers set the pace and the example with their gambling, their drinking bouts, their quarrels and duels, their kept mistresses and their amorous diversions in Barrack Street, Water Street, and the lanes and alleys thereabouts. In 1759 Halifax was regaled with a murder; not one of the common affairs of the back streets or the waterfront, but the slaying of one of His Majesty's officers and gentlemen, Lieutenant Collins of the Navy. His companions, Captain Sweeney, Dr. Johns, and others, testified indignantly that they had been tippling at the house of one John Field and had then gone in search of women, that they had knocked at a door and "inquired for Polly," that Polly had been refused them, indeed admission had been refused (they were beating on the wrong door), and that when they waxed strong over this flouting of their legitimate desires and diversions the householder, one Lathum, discharged a musket and killed Lieutenant Collins. Captain Sweeney promptly called the town guard and the spirited Lathum, a baker, was tried and hanged. Thus it was made clear that the Haligonian's home ceased to be his castle when the whims of His Majesty's officers were concerned.

The public hangman at this time was a character known as "Tomahawk" who lived in a lonely hut at the north end of the old blockhouse line, by the Windsor road—a few steps from the present entrance of Fairview Cemetery. His trade was a busy one in times when a man could be hanged for stealing a sheep or anything else of a few shillings' value, and executions at the foot of George Street were a common public spectacle. Between jobs he soused himself with rum, perhaps to drown his memories, and eventually he drank himself to death. The corpse was discovered by a party of larking young men, who placed a noose about the neck and dragged it across the road to the ruin of the north blockhouse. They pitched poor Tomahawk into the old latrine, where his bones could be seen by curious townsmen for the next seventy years.

The old blockhouse had a grim repute, for in the early days one garrison of careless redcoats had been surprised and slain by a Micmac war party, and their bones too were lying in shallow graves near the blockhouse wall. Lonely "Dutch" fanners on the Windsor road held the place haunted after this, and for two generations hurried past the spot when darkness overtook them on the way from town.

As if the debauchery of the garrison and the station squadron were not enough, in 1762 there was a wild visitation from the south. The British fleet and army which had captured Havana, with its enormous loot, came into Halifax. There followed a saturnalia as this rabble of gaunt sunburned adventurers (Gorham's Rangers were among them) flung their pistareens, pieces of eight, and doubloons over the tavern bars and into the laps of the prostitutes. Most of the ships remained moored in the harbor for the winter, and according to one account, the dissipation "was something beyond belief. The prize money distributed amongst so many soldiers and sailors was worth over £400,000 sterling, which they almost threw away. The birds of prey drawn here from all quarters by the hope of plunder made Halifax more like a pirates' rendezvous than a modest British settlement."

This torrent of Spanish coin was nothing strange in itself. The piece-of-eight silver dollar had long been the standard of currency in Nova Scotia as in New England; hence the expression "two bits" for a quarter dollar, which is still a common term. Indeed all sorts of coins were in circulation. "The assortment of odd coins coming into Halifax at this time was beyond belief. The Spaniards brought from the Mediterranean and Levant to their colonies coins that had been in circulation for centuries. These would be carried to Halifax in payment for fish and supplies; and the authorities, in exchange for bills drawn on the Treasury at London, would take tons of this old silver for payment of the army and navy. A merchant's till at the close of a busy day or a large collection at St. Paul's would make the fortune of a collector in the numismatic line today."

10.
1763–1775

Death of Abbé Maillard. A "Yankee" town. Rumblings of rebellion. The British troops withdraw to Boston. The importance of Michael Francklin. The feast of St. Aspinquid. Father Bailly sings the mass in secret. The quarrelsome Governor Legge.

POOR ABBÉ MAILLARD DID NOT LONG SURVIVE THE triumph of his labors amongst the savages. He had remained in Halifax after that strange ceremony amongst the flowers, and the authorities so valued his friendship and advice that they procured a government pension for him—an astonishing concession in that age when a Roman Catholic was forbidden by law to hold a public post, and a French priest, especially, was regarded as a limb of Satan. But the most astonishing thing occurred when the old man died in August 1762. He was mourned as much by the English as by the French and Indians, and since there was no other consecrated ground in which to bury him the lieutenant governor commanded a grave in St. Paul's Cemetery. There was a long and solemn procession to the graveyard. "His pall was supported by the President of the Council, the Speaker of the House of Assembly and four other gentlemen, and Mr. Wood performed the office of burial according to our form" (the Anglican) "in the presence of almost all the gentlemen of Halifax and a very numerous assembly of French and Indians."

Father Maillard had translated the Roman Catholic liturgy into the Micmac language, and to the pleasure of the Indians Mr. Wood completed the burial service by reciting appropriate parts of that liturgy in their own tongue. As an example of Christian fellowship it was unparalleled in the North America of that time, and was an omen of the good sense and tolerance which has obtained between the Roman Catholic and Protestant communities in Halifax to this day, when the religious groups are much more evenly divided and the old evil restrictions are only a memory of the past.

The end of the war with France brought a profound change to British North America. With Canada conquered and that longstanding menace on the north blown away in a gust of British gunpowder, the colonists could look upon their future in a new light. Their own part in the wars, notably their conquest of Louisburg in 1745, had given them a pleasant sense of their own power. This was realized with some misgivings by the home authorities, who had seen to it that the final invasion of Canada was carried out almost wholly by British regulars. But this in turn had meant swarms of redcoats encamped from time to time since 1755 in American towns and villages, the tipsy, blasphemous British soldiery of Hogarth's day, contemptuous of civilians, especially of colonial civilians, and arrogant in all their dealings with them.

Such a visitation had never been seen before in America except at Halifax, and the effect upon the grim psalm-singing New Englanders in particular was very great. They were shocked, resentful, and finally hostile. There were other, deeper causes for rebellion, to be sure, and these have been noted in the history books; but the personnel of the fleet and army (too often the sweepings of English jails and slums, and their officers too often the turbulent bullies so well described by Smollett) were the outward and visible signs of the imperial power, and upon them the blame for the final provocations of rebellion must be laid.

This was apparent in Halifax as elsewhere in America; but here the civil population was so outnumbered by the fleet and garrison that it had to swallow its resentment and wait with much less cheer than Micawber for something to turn up. At this time Halifax was a town with little or no middle class. The crust of its society was the governor and a coterie of timeserving officials appointed by himself or from London, together with a fawning group of merchants grown rich from army and navy contracts. There was a handful of lesser merchants and professional people, most of them New Englanders and adherents of the dissenters' church. The rest were poor fishermen, carpenters, mechanics, and laborers, with a sprinkling of truck gardeners, loggers, and trappers in the outskirts.

The census of 1767 shows a little over 3000 people, of whom 302 were English, 52 Scots, 853 Irish, 264 "Germans and other foreigners," 200 Acadians—and no less than 1351 "Americans," most of whom were from New England. In eighteen years Halifax had become literally, as well as figuratively, an outpost of New England, looking to Boston rather than to London for most of its supplies and its political sentiments. Few of the townsfolk had any reason to love or even to respect their local government, for the assembly had little real power and in any case it was usually filled with merchants of the upper class. There were civil laws, certainly, but the real rule was a kind of perpetual martial law imposed by the succession of military governors and their obedient councils. This worked in various ways, always to the disadvantage of the civil population. For example, in 1764, when the Collins–Lathum affair was rankling still, every officer commanding a man-o'-war in the harbor became ex-officio a justice of the peace, thus presenting the town with a whole bench of Captain Sweeneys.

The first rumblings of trouble came with the notorious Stamp Act in 1765. The disturbances in Boston and elsewhere had a prompt echo in Halifax, where the *Gazette* declared the disgust of the town and province at this attempt at taxation from abroad. The nominal editor of the *Gazette* was Richard Bulkeley, the Provincial secretary, an imperialist of the deepest dye. He called upon Henry, the printer, for an explanation of this effrontery; and Henry chose to blame the insertion of the offending matter upon his apprentice Isaiah Thomas, a young New Englander.

Henry was let off with an apology. But soon there was another rebellious paragraph in the *Gazette*. Soon after this a ship came to Halifax with a copy of the Pennsylvania *Journal*, printed in "full mourning," the pages framed in thick black lines, the title crowned with skull and crossbones, and the foot of the last sheet exhibiting a coffin, the birthdate of the newspaper, and a lugubrious account of its death "from a disorder called the Stamp Act." The ex-soldier Henry itched to set up the Halifax *Gazette* in the same way, but caution stayed his hand until young Thomas had a brilliant idea.

The *Gazette* came forth with the emblems of death and the rest of that seditious display, and with an ingenuous explanation: "We are desired by a number of our readers to give a description of the extraordinary appearance of the Pennsylvania *Journal* of the 30th of October last. We can in no better way comply with the request than the exemplification we have given of that journal in today's Gazette." This, in the official newspaper of the colony, created a sensation. Finally young Thomas mutilated the *Gazette's* whole supply of the obnoxious stamped paper by cutting out the stamps, and Henry perforce printed several issues on unstamped paper, in direct defiance of the law. For this he lost the *Gazette* printing contract and young Thomas was banished from Halifax.

Bulkeley imported a printer from London, Robert Fletcher, on whose utter loyalty he could rely. But Henry had only given expression to the sentiment of many Haligonians at this time; and they went on to expressions of their own, burning an effigy of the local stamp master on the rear slope of Citadel Hill, and dangling an old boot from a gallows in derision of Lord Bute, the unpopular favorite of King George. Indeed opinion in Halifax was so strong that the authorities felt obliged to put a captain's guard over the stamp master's house to ward off any attempted violence to his person.

The governor was Lord William Campbell, a young and sporting aristocrat with a wealthy Carolinian wife, both typical of a caste whose time was growing short in America. The rumble of discontent did not disturb him much, for he took his duties lightly and left the worry to the lieutenant governor, Michael Francklin, a very different sort of man. If Campbell and his lady were symbolic of the blind royalist caste in America, Francklin represented the more numerous group of loyalists who saw the trouble coming, recognized the grievances, and sought in a baffled way to bring about a compromise between revolution and the continued folly of His Majesty's Government.

Meanwhile Lord William and his handsome wife set a new pace in the gay naval and military society of Halifax. The governor loved fast horses and so did Bulkeley, and before long they had a racecourse on the North Common. With other people of wealth and sporting instincts they imported blood horses from Ireland, and from New York and Baltimore, and the spring and autumn race meets at Halifax became famous in the colonies. Michael Francklin liked horses, too, but here again he showed the difference of his quality, for he believed that the great meadows beside the Fundy tide could support a valuable horse-breeding industry; and to this end he established an experimental stud farm at his summer home in Windsor and built a manor in the meadows of Minudie, where he raised the feed for his stables.

The fashionable promenade along Barrington and Pleasant streets had become known as The Mall, and in 1766 the walk was planked from Grand Parade to the Kissing Bridge. Here on sunny afternoons paraded the belles and beaux of Halifax, beside a stream of carriages, sulkies, and smart curricles bearing Mr. Well-to-do and his wife, scarlet-coated officers with their wives or mistresses, and all the others whose means enabled them to keep a carriage-and-two or a carriage-and-four, those hallmarks of position in the times. It was a great show and it lasted fifty years.

The assembly held its sessions in the wooden courthouse at the corner of Argyle and Buckingham streets for lack of a house of its own, and continued to sit there until 1789. St. Paul's remained the chief house of worship. As the seat of the established church it could not be ignored even by dissenting merchants, many of whom rented pews there as well as in their own. But Mather's Meeting House continued to flourish, for the majority of the townsfolk were dissenters. The Scots and Ulstermen had joined with the New Englanders who met within its walls, and their influence was to change it from a purely Congregational to a Presbyterian church as the years rolled by. A succession of preachers, most of them from New England, harangued this flock; and some of them, notably the Reverend John Seccombe, were outspoken in their opinion of garrison morals, of garrison rule, and in fact of His Majesty's rule itself. Thus the governor and council came to regard the dissenters' church as a hotbed of sedition and the congregation as a gang of potential revolutionists.

Meanwhile in New England the pot of revolution was simmering already. The egregious Stamp Act had been repealed and replaced with the no less disturbing tax on tea. By 1768 General Gage in Boston was so alarmed at the unrest that he called in all the troops he could muster. Most of the soldiers came from Nova Scotia, where the outlying forts and posts had to be abandoned and Halifax itself was left with little more than a corporal's guard.

The troops, consisting of the 14th and 29th regiments and part of the 59th, with a detachment of Royal Artillery, marched down to the Halifax waterfront on a day in late September. In the roadstead lay His Majesty's ships *Beaver, Senegal, Martin, Glasgow, Mermaid, Romney, Launceston,* and *Bonetta,* waiting to take the force to Boston. The troops made a fine show as they passed through the crowds of staring Haligonians, none of whom suspected that he was witnessing the birth of a tremendous event. In the stiffly marching ranks of the 29th were the men who would start the powder of revolution flaring in a Boston ropewalk, and one was the man whose musket and bayonet were to be foremost in the so-called "Boston Massacre." He was a rough unprincipled fellow, not above assaulting a woman and stealing half her clothes, and no doubt the ladies of Barrack Street knew him to their cost. His name was Kilroy; and when the first blood of the American Revolution was shed on the Boston cobbles, Kilroy was there.

But all of this was hidden in September 1768 and Kilroy and the rest of the troops went swinging blithely through the dusty Halifax streets behind the shrill of their fifes and the *tow-row-row* of the drums, Destiny riding on their faded scarlet shoulders, and not a soul knowing or caring a whit. The departure of the troops left a strange void in the town. For the first time since 1749 the throng of redcoats was missing from the streets, and their pay from the tavern tills. For the first time since its foundation Halifax was entirely upon its own resources in the way of trade.

A natural trade had been growing, with the end of Indian terrorism and the settlement of Nova Scotia. Colonel Spry, the energetic garrison engineer, had carved a farm estate for himself out of the woods beyond the Northwest Arm—"Spryfield," now a suburb of the sprawling city. Others followed his example in the wilderness beyond the blockhouse line. The outlying roads had a new importance, and the government raised £1000 by a lottery for their repair.

Lord Campbell journeyed even farther afield. His races on the Common had produced a gambling fever in the sporting Haligonians, rich and poor, which so offended his sense of propriety that he removed his sport to Windsor, already the summer resort of Halifax fashionables. More, there was talk of a college; and Campbell and Bulkeley decided that such an institution should be built, if built at all, in the vicinity of Windsor where the students would be far removed from the wickedness of Halifax. Thus was conceived King's College, not to be born for many years to come.

Campbell, absorbed in his pleasures, remained a figurehead. The burden fell upon the able shoulders of Francklin, who strove to assure the loyalty of his town and province in the coming struggle in America. It was a difficult task, for he had to deal with a deaf and blind government in London, a grimly reactionary council at home, and a population bound by ties of blood and of trade with the people of New England. Yet he was well fitted; indeed he was the one man in Nova Scotia who was fitted for the struggle. His good looks and personal charm, his wealth, his wide mercantile contacts and interests, were no small assets in dealing with Lord Campbell, the council, and the government across the sea. His Boston wife and his intimate knowledge of the country districts and their problems gave him a powerful influence with the Yankee settlers in the province. And his knowledge of the Malecite and Micmac tongues and customs had enabled him to form a close attachment with the Indians.

This interest he carefully maintained, encouraging the Indians to hold their old-time feast in the name of St. Aspinquid on the shores of the Northwest Arm, seeing that the chiefs were received with honors befitting their rank, taking a part himself in the fireside oratory, and sending them away well pleased with gifts from the Great White Father in England. These feasts, in which many convivial townsmen joined, were held sometimes at the fishing station of Nathan Nathans, a prominent Jewish merchant, at what afterwards became known as Horseshoe Island, and sometimes at the fishing station of Captain Jordan below what is now called Franklin Street. At other times in the year Francklin received deputations of savages at his house in town, and we can see him there, patient, grave, courteous, hearing the slow interminable talk of the children of the forest, while poor Mrs. Francklin thought of the lice they were shedding on her beautiful carpets.

Another friend of the Indians was Colonel Joseph Gorham of the Rangers, who had earned their respect with his own savage warfare in days gone by and now encouraged them to call in peace at his house in Halifax. Other attention was paid them. The sedate walls of St. Paul's rang sometimes with hymns and sermons in the Micmac tongue while a brown throng sat uncomfortably in the hard wooden pews. Still the Micmacs clung to the faith of their first missionaries, mourning the departure of Father Maillard to the Good Hunting Place and begging Francklin for another priest.

Finally the wise Francklin saw to it that another priest came—Father Bailly, who arrived in 1768—and paid attention not only to the Indians but to the whites. There were many Catholic Irish in the town, apart from the many Ulstermen brought over by the tireless promoter of Nova Scotia settlements, Colonel McNutt; the south part of Halifax beyond Spring Garden Road was known as "Irishtown." Father Bailly secretly held baptisms and marriages, and sang mass in a lonely grove at Birch Cove on Bedford Basin—even in the town itself, in a barn on South Street—while Francklin and other Protestants of sense and good will looked the other way.

Had Francklin remained in actual power behind the figurehead of Lord Campbell there is no doubt that his sanity and loyalty would have stilled the whispers of rebellion in Nova Scotia despite the flood of pamphlets from Boston; for the Nova Scotians were sufficiently removed from that furious metropolis to take a cooler view of things. They could even smile, because Boston now was feeling the grip of military rule under the very troops who previously had laid it upon Halifax. But in 1773 Campbell succeeded in getting himself transferred to the governorship of South Carolina, the home of his wife, and away they went. In his place came an irascible heavy-jowled tyrant named Francis Legge, a major in the army, whose powerful connections in England had got him the post at Halifax. "It was considered better to give him a position with £1000 a year at the public expense in the wilds of America than have him bothering and squabbling with his unfortunate friends, who took this chance of getting rid of him."

This man at once conceived a violent jealousy of Francklin, and quarreled impartially with the council and with the populace, charging the public officers with corruption and the people with disloyalty. When some unknown thief burgled his desk he put it down to espionage and thereafter guarded himself and Government House as if the town and province were one vast hostile camp. The look, the speech, the very customs of the Haligonians were those of New England, even to a proclaimed day of fasting and prayer every spring and another of thanksgiving every fall and Legge firmly believed that every extravagance of the Boston mob struck a chord in the hearts of the Nova Scotians.

11.
1775–1776

The lone fourteenth colony. Legge's recall and his farewell. Howe's army comes to Halifax. Loyalists and camp followers. The sanitation of the times. King Rum.

FEW CANADIANS (AND FEWER AMERICANS) REALIZE even today how nearly the American Revolution succeeded in placing the whole continent under the Stars and Stripes. The seizure of Montreal and the attack on Quebec by a handful of Yankee adventurers have achieved some note in the history books, but the most significant thing has been overlooked. Nova Scotia, the fourteenth colony, then comprised the whole of the Maritime Provinces. The Province of Quebec was almost utterly French, conquered only sixteen years before and held in submission by the British garrison in Quebec citadel. There was nothing west of Montreal but a wilderness inhabited by Indians and a scatter of trappers and traders. Thus Nova Scotia was the key to all Canada; its ports commanded the approach to the St. Lawrence all the way from Cape Breton to Gaspé *and it was the only English-speaking part at the whole country*. Had the Nova Scotians thrown in their lot with their fellow Americans in 1776 the war must have ended with the complete disappearance of the British Flag from North America.

Indeed there were strong voices in the British Parliament urging this very thing, for the cost of maintaining the Halifax fortress and its out-settlements ran to a very doleful sum by that time, and with thirteen colonies gone there seemed little point in keeping the fourteenth. In 1780, as the war drew towards its disastrous climax, Edmund Burke rose in his place and made his famous attack on the Board of Trade and Plantations. "The province of Nova Scotia," he cried, "was the youngest and favourite child of the Board. Good God! What sums has the nursing of that ill-thriven, hard-visaged and ill-favoured brat cost this wittol nation! Sir, this colony has stood us in a sum of not less than seven hundred thousand pounds. To this day it has made no repayment. It does not even support those offices of expense which are miscalled its government; the whole of that job still lies upon the patient callous shoulders of the people of England!"

How the settlers of Nova Scotia were to repay a sum which had been expended largely in making Halifax a base for His Majesty's fleet and a springboard for the conquest of Canada the fiery orator did not say, and fortunately for the Dominion of Canada the British Parliament did not choose to write off its investment about the stony shores of Chebucto. Still more fortunately the Americans failed to grasp their opportunity in 1776, when two thirds of the people of Nova Scotia were of Yankee birth or parentage and all but the governor and the wealthy Halifax army and navy contractors were chafing under the stupidities of London rule. Rebel sentiment was not wanting; indeed there was open rebellion at the head of the Bay of Fundy, where a force of Nova Scotians besieged Fort Cumberland—the only garrisoned British post outside Halifax—and failed in their attempt only because they lacked cannon and adequate ammunition.

Early in the war the Congress sent agents into the province to see the state of the defenses and to sound the people on their attitude towards the King. They found His Majesty's forces gone to Boston and a strong sentiment against His Majesty's rule; but they also found the Nova Scotians desperately short of arms and ammunition and inclined to take a realistic view. Of all the American colonies theirs lay closest to Britain, and it had been so long under the thumb of His Majesty's forces that the Bluenoses were chary of open revolt without assistance from the south.

Delegates from Nova Scotia gathered at the town of Machias, on the vague border between Nova Scotia and Maine, where the people were anxious to see the rebel Flag hoisted over Halifax. The Congress eagerly promised troops and arms to assist a revolt; but their army chief, busy besieging the Nova Scotia garrison in Boston, turned a firm thumb down. This is what he wrote:

Camp at Cambridge, Aug. 11, 1775.

Gentlemen,

I have considered the papers you left with me yesterday. As to the expedition proposed against Nova Scotia by the inhabitants of

Machias, I cannot but applaud their spirit and zeal, but I apprehend such an enterprise to be inconsistent with the principle on which the Colonies have proceeded. That province has not acceded, it is true, to the measures of the Congress, but it has not commenced hostilities against them nor are any to be apprehended. To attack it therefore is a measure of conquest rather than defence, and may be attended with very dangerous consequences. It might be easy with the force proposed to make an incursion into the province and over-awe those of the inhabitants who are inimical to our cause, but to produce any lasting effect the same force must continue. And our situation as to ammunition absolutely forbids our sending a single ounce of it out of the camp at present.

I am, Gentlemen, &c.,
George Washington.

The real point of Washington's letter was in the tail; and so for lack of an eighteenth-century form of lend-lease the hopes of the more ardent Nova Scotia Whigs were dashed and the American opportunity passed. In the meantime Francklin and other Nova Scotians of loyalty and common sense were trying desperately to obtain Governor Legge's recall before he goaded the people willy-nilly into revolt. In January 1776 a delegation sailed from Halifax to press the matter, and the home government, suddenly alarmed, gave in at last. Legge was recalled to England, where he continued to draw his salary as governor for years, paying a meager £200 a year to his deputy in Nova Scotia.

Legge's departure from Halifax was a memorable event. The whole town flocked to the waterside to see him go. As the boat pulled away from the dock the crowd burst into yells of execration, and that flabby violent man stood up in the stem, shouting curses and shaking a fist at all Halifax, a spectacle for the frigate's crew as well as the delighted populace. To mollify Legge and his powerful kinsman the Earl of Dartmouth, Francklin was deprived of his post as lieutenant governor at the same time, and in his place came Mariot Arbuthnot, a naval officer, an easygoing fellow of Campbell's sort. But Francklin continued to exert his influence on the side of loyalty throughout the war, and to him must go the chief credit for the fact that the fourteenth colony remained under the British flag.

In the spring of 1776 the war in America took an astonishing turn. General Howe withdrew to Halifax with his army and fleet, abandoning Boston and apparently the whole royal cause in the rebellious thirteen colonies. The appearance was deceptive; the British Government was sending strong reinforcements and planning a descent upon New York and Philadelphia, the seat of the Congress. But for several months Halifax was the sole camp of the British forces in America, and the refuge of a huge migration of loyalists and their families who had left Boston in the fleet with Howe.

The little town was overrun with this invasion. The troops filled the barracks, encamped on the Citadel slopes, and covered Camp Hill with their tents. The muddy streets rang with their martial music and the stolid tramp of their army shoes. These were the veterans of Lexington and Bunker Hill, still smarting with defeat at the hands of the Yankees. Finding themselves again in what was to all appearance another Yankee settlement, they behaved in their Boston manner. There were various incidents. One occurred when the troops were improving the road across the marsh to Camp Hill. The handiest source of "fill" was the rough stone walls around the outlying pastures, and when a "Dutch" farmer named Chris Schlegal objected he was murdered for his stubbornness. Once more the King's men could do no wrong. Three soldiers were "tried" for the crime and went scot-free.

There were rumors that Washington might follow up his Boston success and descend upon Halifax overland, and so the redcoats were employed in building blockhouses on the hill since called Fort Needham and elsewhere about the Dockyard, at Three Mile House on the Windsor Road, and on the crest of Citadel Hill overlooking the town. But for the most part the troops followed the example of General Howe (who had brought his wine cellar and his handsome mistress Mrs. Loring to while away the time at Halifax) and occupied themselves with the rumshops and the bagnios of Barrack Street.

The influx of army officers and "loyalists" (that strange new word) created a tremendous demand for necessities in the town. Rents soared to the heights. So did the price of provisions. The merchants, the landlords, the brewers, the madames of the bawdyhouses reaped a harvest; but the ordinary townsfolk, as so often in the story of Halifax, found themselves in open competition with a horde of strangers for a roof above their heads and the very food upon their plates. They were regarded with suspicion by the newcomers, for there had been plain evidence of rebel sentiment in Halifax.

A great stack of hay, gathered at the port for shipment to Gage's cavalry in Boston last year, had been fired and destroyed. A shipment of taxed tea, spurned by Massachusetts and landed at Halifax, had aroused a strong agitation for a boycott if not another Boston tea party, so that the council had to take strong measures. The prominent Halifax merchants William Smith, Alexander Brymer, John Fillis, and Malachi Salter were suspected of complicity in these and similar matters. The fact that three of them had been members of the Nova Scotia Assembly made the suspicion blacker still; but there was no proof, and they escaped prosecution.

Most of the refugee loyalists had no intention of staying here; the poverty and the climate of Halifax were too violent a contrast to the well-being of life in Massachusetts. They called the country "Nova Scarcity" and hoped for a day when they could remove once more to the homes they had left. Indeed when Howe and his forces departed for New York in the early summer of 1776 the wealthier refugees went along, and formed on Manhattan the nucleus of a group of exiles which became, as the war went on, one vast unhappy multitude.

But many stayed in Halifax, amongst them a Widow Draper with her late husband's printing press and his partner John Howe, whose name was to live in the annals of Nova Scotia. Another, more typical of the poorer refugees, was the Reverend Jacob Bailey, who came in rags and patches with his wife and niece "lagging behind at a little distance, the former arrayed in a ragged baize nightgown, tied around her middle with a woolen string instead of a sash. The latter carried on her back the tattered remnants of a hemlock-coloured linsey-woolsey, and both their heads were adorned with bonnets composed of black moth-eaten stuff almost devoured by the teeth of time." There were many such, and most of them remained in "Nova Scarcity" because they had nowhere else to go.

The picture of the loyalists who came to Canada has been falsified by generations of imaginative artists depicting elegant ladies in powdered hair and fine silk gowns, and fine-looking gentlemen in silk stockings, broadcloth breeches, and velvet coats with silver buttons. All this is nonsense. There were fine ladies and gentlemen among the loyalists but the exiles were a whole political party, the Tory party of the thirteen colonies, and they included many solid folk of the middle class and a great number of poor; just as the victorious Whigs included with the avowed levelers of the Boston mob a great number of up-and-coming manufacturers like

Paul Revere, capitalists like John Hancock, and great landowners like Washington. It was not so much a revolution as a civil war, and the result was precisely as if the Liberal party in Canada today were to engage in open war with the Conservatives for several bloody and destructive years and then expel them with their women and children to the wilderness of Hudson Bay. Imagine the little port of Churchill suddenly the refuge of a homeless swarm of Conservatives, rich and not-so-rich, poor and very poor, and you have a picture to compare with Halifax in the period of the American Revolution, when to the average exile from the older colonies Nova Scotia was simply Ultima Thule and Halifax an outpost somewhere near the Pole.

Amongst the more prominent loyalists who came and then departed with Howe was the former royal Governor of New Hampshire, John Wentworth, an energetic young man with an ambitious wife. Halifax was to see much of them later on. Another was the Boston doctor John Jeffries, who had the melancholy task of identifying the body of his friend Dr. Joseph Warren, the famous rebel, on the battlefield of Bunker Hill. At Halifax, Jeffries received the appointment of surgeon general to the forces, and as the inrush of troops and refugees had brought the usual outbreak of smallpox he ordered and supervised the first mass inoculation ever seen in the town—fifteen hundred soldiers of the garrison. Not one of them died; and this was a miracle in days when the accepted practice was to transfer the disease direct by scab from an infected person, and the subsequent treatment by most doctors was to administer large quantities of mercurial pills and to swath the patient in blankets and quilts to "keep down the eruption." Some doctors would not permit the linen of a smallpox patient to be changed during the whole course of the disease, notwithstanding the filth which might accumulate.

By modern standards it was an unsanitary period in any case. The populace of Halifax (and of all other towns in Europe and America) disposed of its excreta in privies whence from time to time it was trundled through the streets in wheelbarrows or handcarts and dumped in the harbor. Most maids and housewives emptied their slop pails and chamber pots, into the nearest alley or gutter, and the spring and autumn rains carried all this filth down the slope towards the town pumps. Soap was mostly homemade and harsh. Bathing the whole body was considered dangerous. A prominent merchant and member of the Nova Scotia Assembly for a country constituency made the following observation in his diary: "This evening I begin to cure myself and family of the Lothsome Distemper, the Itch. We anoint with brimstone melted in fresh butter. I roast by the fire one hour and go to bed with the ointment upon me."

Beds hopped with fleas. Lice were everywhere, even in the tall white-powdered coiffures of fashionable women; and at church services and other assemblies it was common to see a lady draw from her muff or purse a thin bone skewer and delicately prod the more troublesome insects under her elegant thatch. To relieve the awkward spot between the shoulder blades there were special scratchers mounted on long handles, and some exquisites had theirs made of ivory in the shape of a small human hand with sharp curved fingers. Men and women of the more practical class simply rubbed their shoulders back and forth against the nearest doorpost, murmuring "God bless the Duke of Argyle" in tribute to that nobleman who, far away in Britain, had installed special knobs on his doorposts for the convenience of his footmen.

Fresh provisions were to be had only in the short summer season, and most of the year rich and poor lived on salted meat and fish, potatoes and breadstuffs. The well to do could add such things as wines and pastries, but in general the diet was very bad and many of the poorer folk suffered each winter from a malady which a modern physician would diagnose as beriberi or incipient scurvy. Vitamins were unknown in the eighteenth century: but human instinct is infallible. As soon as spring brought a touch of green to the landscape there could be seen a multitude of towns-folk, servants, and soldiers of the garrison busy digging up dandelions in the fields and along the byways for the dinner pot.

The diet gave bad complexions to all but the healthiest men and women. Still, complexions were none too good in any case, for the recurring epidemic of smallpox left its mark on every second or third face—a few pits here, a hideous mask there—and ladies of fashion were happy to paste small black patches over their worst pimples or scars and call them "beauty spots." And the diet affected the teeth of all classes. It is sad but true that even at the governor's fashionable "routs" most of those elegant officers and gentlemen, those gorgeous women in hoops and silks, had decayed teeth or uncompromising gaps in their smiles, suffered from pimples and rashes that the rouge pot could not disguise, and *smelled* in the heat of the dance despite liberal dashes of scent.

The night air even in summer was held to be bad for the health, and except when the heat was oppressive the windows were closed against it. During the cold months every house was practically sealed. The round stoves developed in French Canada were coming into use in Nova Scotia, as elsewhere in the English-speaking colonies, and of course that ingenious rebel Benjamin Franklin had invented the half stove, half fireplace which once graced every parlor and still bears his name; but most Halifax households depended on the huge old-fashioned hearth, where the blaze of dried hardwood or the glow of Cape Breton coals looked magnificent—and sent most of its heat up the chimney. From October to May rich and poor lived close to the fires. When winter came there were bitter drafts along the floors and in the halls, and the panes were crusted by frost; and by the privacy of her parlor stove the general's lady, like Sally in the kitchen, was glad to hoist her gown, hoops, and petticoats from time to time for the better warming of her posterior.

It was fashionable for young ladies to be pallid; and so they were, poor things, what with a studied avoidance of sunshine, no exercise, stuffy rooms, tight stays, monotonous diet, and a constant huddling over fires and stoves. And they suffered a fashionable disease in consequence—consumption—which carried them off right and left. Wives rich and poor were visited by another killer not so fashionable, puerperal fever—the "childbed fever" of the old chronicles. That is why the crowded earth of old St. Paul's Cemetery contains the bones of so many women under thirty.

Men, rugged creatures, suffered not so much from what they ate as from what they drank, chiefly because they drank too much. The West Indies trade had flooded the town with cheap rum, much of it made from molasses imported by two Halifax distilleries. These turned out ninety thousand gallons a year and we are told that "the liquor though inferior is preferred by labourers and Indians." Rum was to be had in every store as well as in the numerous taverns and dives. The household keg in the cellar with its spigot and mug were as common a sight as the potato bin or the barrel of salt herring. At one time the cellar under St. Matthew's Church was rented to a vintner and used for the storage of ardent liquors, and some wag composed a wicked little rhyme about "spirits above and spirits below" that went the rounds of the town. One of the refinements brought north by the loyalists was a taste for wines; but, even so, rum was king in Halifax for another half century, and drunkenness remained the vice of the age.

12.
1776–1783

Unrest and revolt in Nova Scotia. Scotch and Hessian troops. Press gangs and privateers. The trade in Negro slaves.

THE DEPARTURE OF HOWE FOR NEW YORK LEFT Halifax almost defenseless. The Royal Nova Scotia Regiment, a creation of Legge's, numbered no more than one hundred men of doubtful quality. The recruiting officers dispatched through the province had returned baffled, reporting most of the Nova Scotians hostile or at best indifferent to the royal cause. The governor had sent them off to Newfoundland to try recruiting there. The only corps in Halifax worth His Majesty's pay was Colonel Small's Royal Highland Emigrants, raised among the Scots recently settled in Nova Scotia and Prince Edward Island. These were good fighting men but few in number, still without uniforms and very poorly equipped. Outside of Halifax the only organized force in the whole province was Gorham's Royal Fencible American Regiment, stationed at Fort Cumberland on the Nova Scotia isthmus.

Again the American rebels had a wonderful opportunity and failed to realize it. When the Cumberlanders broke into open revolt against the King in the autumn of 1776 the promised support from Massachusetts failed to appear. Nevertheless the Cumberlanders besieged Gorham and his regiment and almost succeeded in storming the fort before General Massey, at Halifax, sent the Highland Emigrants and a hastily assembled force of marines to the relief. By this bold stroke (which left Halifax undefended) the Cumberland rebellion was crushed and several of the ringleaders were captured and brought to Halifax for trial. The Tory party in town was eager to see them hanged as an example, but wiser counsels prevailed and the prisoners were permitted to "escape." One of them was the young Irishman Richard John Uniacke, afterwards a notable figure at the bar and in the government of Nova Scotia.

All of this created great excitement in Halifax. The Tories had the provost marshal dismissed for his laxity at the Hollis Street jail, and the known Whigs were subjected to a furious witch hunt. At various times leading Whig merchants were brought before the council to answer charges of sedition. The Reverend Mr. Seccombe, that fiery preacher of the rights of man, was seized in the countryside and jailed for his sentiments. So it went.

There was other gossip, for these were lively times indeed. The horde of Boston refugees (many of whom lived wretchedly in tents and ships' deckhouses set up in vacant lots along the Halifax streets) included a large number who had left their old haunts for reasons that had nothing to do with loyalty. Halifax had thrust upon it, with the genuine loyalists, a collection of smooth and experienced sharpers, trollops, and cutpurses from the Boston streets, besides a curious medley of embezzlers, defaulters, and elopers, drawn from Massachusetts as though from Hamelin by the shrill fifes of Howe's departing redcoats.

One scandal was provided by that gay deceiver John Ramage, the miniature-portrait artist. In Boston, where his work had achieved some note, the dashing Irishman married a wife. She turned out to be penniless, and nine days after the ceremony in Boston's Trinity Church her husband deserted her and joined the loyalist migration to Halifax, where he cut a great dash posing as a bachelor. Before long he was taking the marriage vows again, this time before good Dr. Breynton of St. Paul's; the new love was a Mrs. Taylor. Unfortunately the real Mrs. Ramage followed him to Halifax, where there was a scene and finally a town-wide indignation. Even the governor exerted himself in her behalf. But the ill wind of war blew fair for Ramage as for many another of his stamp. When Howe went off with his troops to New York the gay deceiver and Mrs. Taylor skipped away blithely in their wake, leaving poor Mrs. Ramage to the charity of strangers.

As the British Government realized the gravity of the war in America there was a stream of transports crossing the Atlantic, most of them touching at Halifax for orders and supplies and to give their troops a march ashore after the long confinement of the voyage. From 1778 to 1781 a whole brigade of Scottish troops was stationed at Halifax, using the port as a base for descents upon the coast of New England. One of their junior officers had his quarters in Hollis Street. His name was John Moore, in later years familiar to every schoolboy as the hero of that favorite classroom recitation which began: "Not a drum was heard, not a funeral note…" By the odd chances of His Majesty's Service there subsequently lived and died in Halifax not only a naval surgeon who was present at Corunna but one of the very soldiers who "buried him darkly at dead of night, the sods with our bayonets turning."

Among the many regiments quartered at Halifax during the Revolution was a corps of Hessians, horse and foot, who were billeted a whole winter in the taverns and barns of the north suburbs, amongst the German-speaking folk of Brunswick, Gottingen, and Jacob streets. A sight long remembered in Halifax was the Sunday parade of these stiff blue-coated soldiers, each with his long pigtail wrapped neatly in an eelskin, marching to St. Paul's to receive communion and hear a sermon in their own tongue. Their officers were handsome and popular (several married Halifax girls and carried them off to Germany at the war's end) and they included such notables as Count von Muenchausen, Colonel Hatzfeld, the Baron de Seitz with his coach-and-four, his magnificent hussar uniforms, and his glittering diamond ring, and the Baron Knyphausen striding along with his tall malacca sword cane, ready to fight a duel at any moment.

At frequent intervals the fleet came in, and the Dockyard rang with the labors of shipwrights, calkers, blacksmiths, coppersmiths, riggers, and breamers. These were the days of the press gang, a common feature of Halifax life for half a century. A man-o'-war captain short of seamen was expected by his superiors to pick up his own recruits, and the easiest way was to send his men about the streets of the port seizing every unfortunate youth who fell in their path. These press gangs were armed with cudgels and cutlasses; resistance meant a broken head and later on a taste of the cat-o'-nine-tails to cure the recruit of his stubbornness.

To preserve the form of law it was customary for the admiral to obtain a press warrant from the council, who granted it under pressure from the governor on the ground that the press would rid the town of idle vagabonds. But the vagabonds knew well how to vanish at the first warning cry of "Press!" in the streets, and it was the countryman up to town for the market, the fisherman, the 'prentice boy, the young townsman out for an evening's lark, who fell into the toils. Those with influential friends or employers could count on release later on, but they were few. For two generations of almost incessant war young Haligonians vanished into the lower decks of His Majesty's ships, to die in distant battles, or of the scurvy, the typhus, or the yellow fever which in those days scourged the British service.

It was usual to grant the press gangs twenty-four hours in which to do their "recruiting," but all depended on the admiral's need. On occasion the warrant covered several days, during which all Halifax lay at the mercy of these roving armed parties. No building was sanctuary; no man was safe. Often young men were pursued into the very shops and warehouses of the ruling merchants, and as all seamen and many townsmen carried stout cudgels there were frequent scuffles and occasional riots. The system afforded a fine chance to satisfy personal grudges where a healthy young man was involved. A cuckolded husband, a disappointed suitor could betray the whereabouts of such a prospect to the gang and be certain that his rival would be removed for the duration of the war and probably forever. It was also an opportunity to empty the town jail. At the close of each assize a naval officer and his gang were sure to be at the courthouse door, waiting to take their pick of the convicted felons.

And now the old game of privateering began again, and grew in vigor as the war went on. After 1776 a host of rebel craft from New England harried the Nova Scotia coast. Most of them were without letters of marque from the rebel authorities and were, in fact, little better than pirates. At first they attacked British merchantmen only, but as naval escorts sometimes made this dangerous a good many of them turned their attention to the small ships and possessions of their Bluenose cousins. These American freebooters became so numerous and so bold that frequently they made armed expeditions ashore. The chief outports—Lunenburg, Liverpool, Annapolis, and Charlottetown—were all raided, and two of them were completely sacked.

Washington and other rebel leaders of good sense tried to curb the Yankee privateers, seeing where this sort of thing must lead. Their efforts were vain, and so vanished the last hopes of those Nova Scotian Whigs who wished to see their province become the fourteenth star in the new American flag. The hard-headed Yankee settlers of Nova Scotia were not the kind to turn the other cheek, and as the war went on a fleet of Bluenose privateers put out from Halifax and other ports to seek vengeance (and profit) on the coast of New England. So the die was cast.

The prospect of fighting and prize money attracted the adventurous, the entry of France into the war enlarged the field, and, as the crews signed under His Majesty's letter of marque were in theory exempt from His Majesty's naval press, there was no dearth of recruits. Here is a typical advertisement in the Nova Scotia *Gazette* in 1779:

> THE REVENGE
>
> *All gentlemen volunteers, seamen and able-bodied landsmen who wish to acquire riches and honour are invited to repair on board the Revenge, private ship of war, now lying in Halifax harbour, mounting 30 carriage guns, with cohorns, swivels, etc., bound for a cruise to the southward for four months against the French and all His Majesty's enemies, and then to return to this harbour.*
>
> *All volunteers will be received on board the said ship, or by Captain James Gandy at his rendezvous at Mr. Proud's Tavern near the Market House, where they will meet with all due encouragement and the best treatment. Proper advance will be given.*
>
> GOD SAVE THE KING

The records show that at least forty-eight prize ships were brought into Halifax by such privateers in a single year. The business was chancy but often lucrative, and as the Nova Scotia privateers cruised all the way from Newfoundland to the West Indies they developed during the long war a class of seagoing adventurers very much like those of Elizabethan England.

These activities and the efforts of His Majesty's fleet and armies brought to Halifax hundreds of French and American prisoners, who were confined in the Hollis Street jail and in hulks moored off the Dockyard. The prison rules were lax, the guards indifferent, and for the purchase of luxuries the prisoners were allowed to make small articles for barter about the town. Escapes were so common that they received little notice, for the surrounding forest was reckoned a prison wall in itself; but a large number of Americans made their way along the coast and eventually back to New England.

No reward was offered for the capture of an escaped prisoner of war. Negro slaves and white indentured servants were not so lucky. Advertisements for the return of such runaways remained a feature of the Nova Scotia *Gazette*. The trade in Negroes flourished more than ever, for the wealthier loyalists had brought scores in their train. The *Gazette* announced from week to week such bargains as "an able negro wench about twenty-one years of age, capable of performing both town and country work, and an exceedingly good cook." Mr. Jacob Hurd (whose name is still attached to a Halifax lane) could offer through its columns a reward of five pounds for the return of his runaway Negro Cromwell, "a short thickset strong fellow," badly marked by smallpox "especially on the nose," wearing amongst other things "a green cloth jacket and a cocked hat." Not every anguished owner was so generous. Mr. John Rock, a self-made man of fortune and a pillar of St. Paul's, offered a mere two dollars for the return of "a negro girl named Thursday, about four and a half feet high, broad-set, with a lump over her right eye. Had on a red cloth petticoat, a red baize bed-gown, and a red ribbon about her head."

The war dragged on. Yorktown really ended British hopes, and it became more and more apparent that Halifax would remain the final base of the British armies and in fact the last mooring post of His Majesty's fleet in North America.

13.
1775–1783

General Massey and his defenses. Taverns of the day. A rebel reappears. Death of Michael Francklin and the last Indian feast. Poverty and gaiety of war. The building of St. Peter's.

WHILE THE TOWN BUSTLED WITH ENGLISH AND Scots soldiers in red coats, Germans in blue, and Nova Scotians in green, with prisoners, French and American, in rags of all hues, with refugee loyalists of every grade from rich to destitute, with oddly dressed negro slaves, with tough and reckless privateersmen, with solemn "Dutch" market gardeners hawking their wares, with little knots of drunken Indians and stoical squaws, with larking jack-tars and bullying press gangs, General Massey persevered with the defenses like the cautious soldier he was. He could not forget the slender chances by which the province had been saved in 1776. In the following year the disaster at Saratoga cast an ominous shadow over the royal cause throughout America. France, and then Spain, and then Holland joined the war against Britain. The little home island was face to face with a combination of enemies far more powerful than the rebels across the sea.

So Massey kept his engineer Spry at work. The defenses on George's Island were improved and enlarged until that little green hump in the harbor bristled with forty-eight cannon. Citadel Hill was crowned with a large octagonal blockhouse and a maze of trenches and earthworks stiffened with bundles of green hardwood. Four new batteries appeared about the shore of Point Pleasant. The town itself presented a problem. Fort Needham, Fort Coote, and other blockhouses and earthworks defended the Dockyard and the north suburbs against assault from the land side, but the south suburb, "Irishtown," remained wide open to attack, and Massey's soldierly eye noted that the deep bushy ravine of the Freshwater

River offered perfect cover to an enemy approaching the south flank of Citadel Hill.

Accordingly the well-named Spry built a new work to command the ravine at what was called Windmill Hill and is now the junction of Queen and South streets. It had a central blockhouse and barracks for two hundred and fifty men and was named Fort Massey. The west slope of the fort hill eventually became the burial ground of the Halifax garrison. The approach was by way of Queen Street, then and for many years a rustic lane resounding from time to time with muffled drums and the solemn tread of military funerals. The cemetery remains, and the modern Fort Massey Church preserves the name although all trace of the old fort vanished long ago. A sharp dip in the city's face beyond South Street is all that remains of the leafy glen where Massey expected to see a rebel storming party making for the rear of Citadel Hill.

By the war's end there were fourteen forts, blockhouses, and barracks in and about the town proper, accommodating twenty-eight hundred troops, quite apart from the batteries on Point Pleasant, George's Island, and at what now is Imperoyal, and quite apart from the acres of tents on the Citadel slopes, the Common, and Camp Hill. In addition to these establishments were the garrison lumberyard, the King's Wharf and its store sheds, the town guardhouse on Hollis Street, the growing Dockyard, and sundry gun sheds, depots, and offices in the town itself. Halifax had become cluttered with military property which was a stumbling block to orderly town planning at every turn and the bane of its commercial life for generations. Indeed as time went by the military octopus tightened its grip; Halifax was a fortress, nothing more, and the civilians were interlopers. Nevertheless the civilians slowly multiplied in the shadow of the forts, grumbling at military occupation and rule but somehow proud of it, taking visitors to see the forts and barracks, flocking to every garrison sham fight and parade, and eagerly boarding the ships of the fleet on visiting days. The sound of the drum, the twitter of naval pipes, have been magic music to Haligonians all down through the years.

The American war brought the usual hectic prosperity, filling the coffers of the great merchants and government contractors and spilling over into the pockets of the town. New residences appeared, and the busy splashing of paint on the old ones—white, red, but mostly brown or yellow—was evidence of a growing civic pride. Argyle was the most fashionable street, shady with willow trees in summer. Its general appearance was marred by a ramshackle artillery gun shed above the Parade, where the muzzles of a long row of cannon frowned over the heads of the redcoats at drill.

The Golden Ball on the corner of Sackville and Hollis streets was now a serious rival of the Great Pontac for fashionable dinners and balls. The "Split Crow" at the foot of Salter Street catered to seamen and privateersmen. Country folk up for the market frequented the Crown Coffee House in Upper Water Street near the Dockyard. Every St. Patrick's Day a group of Irishmen dined together at Sutherland's Coffee House in Bedford Row, although they had not yet organized a formal society. Freemasons met sometimes at the Golden Ball but more often at the Wolfe Inn on Granville Street, opposite Government House.

Along the Windsor Road appeared a number of small wayside taverns where officers and gentry and their ladies could stop for a glass of wine or a dish of sillabub while enjoying the view of Bedford Basin. The most famous of these stood by the highway near Willow Park. This was the Blue Bell, a landmark for years with its neat painted sign, and the townsfolk fell into the habit of calling the road which led to it "the Bell road," a name which still clings to the stretch across the Common. This was the only approach to Bedford Basin until 1782, when Sir Andrew Snape Hammond became governor. The Hammonds were fond of their farm in the North End, where they lived each summer to avoid the heat and stench of the lower town, and to connect this rustic residency with the Windsor Road the governor created a new highway running across the heel of the Halifax peninsula, still called Lady Hammond Road.

In 1781 Mr. John Howe, the loyalist from Boston, printed the first issue of the Halifax *Journal*, which continued its existence until 1870. The biggest news of its first year was the surrender of Lord Cornwallis at Yorktown. Although the war was to drag on for another two years the outcome was certain now, and the trickle of refugees into Nova Scotia became a torrent.

In 1782 young Richard Uniacke turned up again, this time with a law degree from Dublin and letters from Baron George and other powerful friends in Britain. The degree and the friends got him a fat post at once. He became Solicitor General of Nova Scotia. The loyalists grumbled severely, for it was less than six years since Uniacke had been taken prisoner in the

Cumberland rebellion and the memory was still keen in certain quarters. Already the population was divided into two groups, the "old settlers" and "the Refugees." Just as the old settlers had been ruled by a coterie of office holders and wealthy merchants, so the loyalists had a greedy clique eager to establish for itself in Nova Scotia the offices and perquisites lost in the older colonies. The next two generations were to see a continual struggle for power between these groups, with the leaders gradually merging their interests against *hoi polloi*, and the middle and lower classes finally triumphant under the leadership of John Howe's son.

The year 1782 saw also the passing of Michael Francklin at the age of sixty-two. He was worn out by his struggle to keep the province under the British flag, especially that part of it which became the separate province of New Brunswick. Until 1783 the forests of the St. John and the St. Croix rivers were in the hands of the Indians. Francklin had thrown himself into a battle of wits with American agents there, both sides trying to win over the savages who controlled the great stretch of river and forest between the Bay of Fundy and the St. Lawrence. In the end Francklin won; the chiefs returned Washington's gifts and accepted the rule and bounty of King George, and eventually the St. John Valley became the home of thousands of exiled loyalists and the backbone of a new province carved out of Nova Scotia's flank. Francklin did not live to see that great migration, but his work was done. In November 1782, in his office at the north end of Granville Street, he collapsed and died in the arms of some Indian chiefs for whom he was arranging a winter supply of clothing and blankets. He was given a grand public funeral and buried in a vault under St. Paul's. Two hundred Indians followed the coffin to the church, with faces blackened, beating their breasts and uttering the weird death chant for a warrior. That was a scene—and a sound—long remembered in Halifax.

Francklin's name is commemorated in a stretch of semiwooded land adjoining Point Pleasant Park and in the street which gives access to it. Just below this spot, on the shore of the Northwest Arm, the Indians held their ancient spring feast seven months after Francklin's death. As usual the festivities were attended by a number of convivial or merely curious Haligonians. They were attended also by a group of die-hard rebel sympathizers from the town; and these, taking advantage of Francklin's passing and the presumed end of his influence with the savages, suddenly hoisted the Stars and Stripes on a pole and astonished the Indians with an inflammatory speech. It was the last flicker of a spirit once very strong in Halifax but dying fast, defeated by the events of the war itself and submerged by the inrush of loyalists. It had no effect on the Indians, who remembered their great white friend, but the authorities were alarmed and forbade any further celebration of the Indian feast. So perished the festival of St. Aspinquid which had been so long a feature of the Halifax year.

In 1783 the war ended at last; and with the evacuation of New York, the last royal stronghold, came the final hegira of the loyalists. By November more than twenty-five thousand refugees were in Nova Scotia, half of whom landed at Halifax. On their heels came a great part of the British army. "Every shed, outhouse, store and shelter was crowded with people. Thousands were under canvas on the Citadel and at Point Pleasant, everywhere indeed that tents could be pitched. St. Paul's and St. Matthew's churches were crowded, and hundreds sheltered there for months. Cabooses and cookhouses were brought ashore from the ships and the people were fed near them on Granville and Hollis streets. There were many deaths and all the miseries and unsanitary conditions of an overcrowded town. For four months the bulk of ten thousand refugees were fed on our streets, amongst them many reared and nurtured in every comfort in the homes they had to fly from."

The wealthier refugees and many war-rich merchants of Halifax at this time were buying old houses for the sake of the sites, tearing them down, and erecting mansions in their place. The poorer refugees eagerly carried off the rotten lumber from these sites and erected shacks along Albemarle (now called Market) Street and on Barrack Street, adding to the slum already there. With the refugees in flight from New York came hundreds of runaway slaves and other Negroes freed by their masters for lack of means to support them. A knot of these settled themselves in Albemarle Street, where a small Negro quarter survived into modern times. Others scattered into the northern outskirts of the town or into the province, where small Negro quarters soon appeared outside the chief country towns.

As the winter set in, the miseries of the refugees increased, and by January 1784 Governor Parr was writing to London: "I cannot better describe the wretched situation of these people than by enclosing a list of those just arrived in the transport *Clinton*, chiefly women and children, scarcely clothed, utterly destitute, still on board the transport, crowded like a sheep pen, as I am totally unable to find a place for them and we cannot move them by reason of the ice and snow."

In contrast with this vast misery, and cheek by jowl with it, flourished the gay life of the army and naval officers, the wealthier loyalists, the prosperous contractors, shipowners and others who had made money out of the war. The town swarmed with discharged soldiers and sailors dissolute in the sudden letdown after eight hard years of war. Henry Alline, the fiery and eloquent New Light evangelist, said of his visit to Halifax in 1783: "I preached in different parts of the town and have reason to believe that there were two or three souls that received the Lord Jesus Christ. But the people in general are almost as dark and vile as Sodom."

The gaiety of the postwar fever penetrated even the sober precincts of St. Paul's, where old parishioners found their services profaned by loud laughter and talking in the pews, a constant taking of snuff, sneezing in consequence, and a great flourishing of handkerchiefs. Not that sober and pious refugees were lacking—they were many. Chief of these was Philip Marchinton, who had managed to get away from New York with a fortune of £35,000. He soon established a successful mercantile business in Halifax, purchased the whole block of valuable property between Jacob Street and Bell Lane, and built a dissenting chapel in Argyle Street in which to air his own sermons. Eventually squabbles arose between the amateur preacher and his congregation and the incensed Marchinton closed the church. He was an odd man. Haligonians long remembered the death of his wife, and how the great merchant had the remains of "my dear Jane" enclosed in a coffin with a glass top, and went daily to see her until poor Jane was no longer fit to gaze upon.

One outcome of the war was a new measure of religious tolerance. There were many Roman Catholics amongst the loyalists and discharged British troops, and in 1783 they asked Governor Hammond to repeal the statute which prevented their church from owning land or erecting houses of worship. The petition was granted and they purchased the block of land running up the north side of Spring Garden Road from Barrington Street to Grafton Street. Upon this site, where the chancel of St. Mary's Basilica now stands, they erected the frame of a wooden church on July 19, 1784. It was called St. Peter's. Archbishop O'Brien wrote long afterwards: "The firebrand never flourished in the old city by the sea.

Nowhere on this continent perhaps were more stringent penal statutes enacted, and nowhere did they so quickly become obsolete; and nowhere has there been so little persecution, and so much kindly feeling between Catholics and Protestants."

14.
1784–1792

Corporal Cobbett. New ventures in sea-borne trade. Wild Prince William. Pretty Mrs. Wentworth. His Majesty's Lieutenant Governor.

NOW CAME THE AFTERMATH OF THE WAR AND THE great migration. The mass of the refugees, unable to find a living in a town stricken by the postwar slump, drifted away to take up lands elsewhere. Halifax was a sorry spectacle. "Collections of old shacks on the shores, remnants of old tents and spruce wigwams on the Common, which had been erected and subsequently abandoned... bore silent evidence of the poverty and suffering of the great multitude."

There remained many veterans of the loyalist regiments and other refugees accustomed to town life and unable to face the rigors of farming in the wilderness. These took any work they could get. William Cobbett, one day to be famous in Britain and America, arrived at Halifax in 1785 as a soldier on his way to garrison duty in New Brunswick. He wrote: "When I first beheld the barren, not to say hideous rocks at the entrance to the harbor I began to fear that the master of the vessel had mistaken his way, for I could perceive nothing of the fertility that my good recruiting captain had dwelt upon with such delight. Nova Scotia had no charm for me but novelty. Everything I saw was new: bogs, rocks, stumps, musquitoes and bull-frogs; thousands of captains and colonels without soldiers and of squires without shoes or stockings. In England I never thought of approaching a squire without a most respectful bow; but in this new world, though I was but a corporal I often ordered a squire to bring me a glass of grog, and even to take care of my knapsack."

When "squires" were reduced to such straits the state of the born poor may be imagined. The town swarmed with thieves. The law dealt harshly with those who were caught; in the year 1785 no less than twelve were hanged in public, one of them for stealing a few potatoes. The rickety slums crawled with disease and spread their germs to the well-to-do. Amongst the more notable dead were the Irish chief justice, Finucane; Lord Charles Montague, who perished miserably in a hut in the woods; and the two dashing German officers, Baron Knyphausen and Baron de Seitz. All of them were buried under St. Paul's–De Seitz in full uniform and decorations, sword at his side, spurs on his boots, and an orange in his hand, following an ancient German custom at the burial of the last of a noble house. His great ring set with eleven diamonds, his coach and horses and other property, were sold in Halifax; and the rest of his worldly goods vanished even from the grave, for thieves broke into the church and rifled the vault.

The governor, that dapper little soldier John Parr, exerted himself on behalf of the poor loyalists, at the same time rejoicing in his own fat salary and perquisites and boasting of his snug position in letters home to England. He was typical of many English officials, then and later, who did their duty conscientiously but saw that their own nests were well feathered in the process, and lived for the day when they could depart from these raw scenes and live in well nourished retirement in England.

Some well-to-do officials and merchants of Halifax now were following Spry's example and building country estates for themselves well away from the squalor of the town while keeping it well within reach. The Dartmouth side of the harbor became a popular retreat, and there the wealthy merchant Hartshorne and others built fine homes and entertained lavishly. Lieutenant Governor Fanning built a house at Point Pleasant opposite Purcell's Cove and surrounded it with gardens. It became a show place for the townsfolk, who now extended their walks past the Kissing Bridge and through the shady pines of the Point.

North of Fanning's residence the refugee printer John Howe built a more humble home where in 1804 was born the boy Joseph, who became the most famous and beloved figure in Nova Scotia history. These two houses were the first on the shore of the Northwest Arm, apart from a few hovels belonging to fishermen and smugglers hidden in the woods. As the years rolled by, the well-to-do moved towards the west until the triangle made by Tower Road, Spring Garden Road and the Northwest Arm was occupied almost exclusively by their estates, each mansion surrounded by wide acres of natural park and reached by winding and picturesque carriage drives. Quinpool Road originated as a carriage drive to an estate of that name. So did Jubilee Road, Oakland Road and other streets of the modern residential area.

For many years the track called Quinpool Road formed roughly the border between the semi-wooded estates of the gentry and the stone-walled fields of the small farmers who struggled for existence on the rest of the plateau. The town itself huddled on the harbor side, shut in by the forbidding mass of Citadel Hill and the swamps of Freshwater River. Its one bit of elbow room lay to the north, where a scatter of homes crept gradually along the slope towards the Dockyard.

Nova Scotia, cut off from the other thirteen colonies at a stroke, like an arm from a living body, was lost and alone. The old home of so many of her people, her natural market and shopping place, was now a foreign country—worse, a country with a jaundiced eye on everyone and everything British. The old trade in America was gone with the wind of 1776. But there remained the sea, a broad highway to the world. Shrewd Halifax merchants and sailors began to venture far in quest of business; to the West Indies, to Britain, to Spain, to the Mediterranean, and around the Cape of Good Hope to the Indian Ocean.

In 1785 a large group of Quaker whalers removed from Nantucket to ply their trade out of Halifax Harbor. They set up an establishment at Dartmouth and for six years their industry flourished. Then a beckoning of the imperial hand induced the whalers to remove their enterprise, lock, stock, and barrel, to Britain itself, for the benefit of British home trade, and this promising industry vanished. The British Government had laid a heavy hand on coal mining in Nova Scotia before this, fearing competition with home trade. In such ways the lone loyal colony in America was hamstrung in its efforts towards self-support. And in 1785 another attempt to incorporate the town of Halifax was thwarted by the governor and council. The townsmen held indignation meetings at the Pontac; but they were up against the old hard wall of military rule, and nothing could be done.

To deal with the rising problems of sea-borne trade the chief merchants and shipowners formed the Halifax Marine Association. On the social side, the sons of Erin formed in 1786 the Charitable Irish Society, which still flourishes after generations of noble effort in behalf of poor immigrants landing at Halifax. Mr. Secretary Bulkeley formed all sorts of social groups, including a chess club which met at the Pontac for years. The Methodists built their first church. As for the Anglicans, the numerous people of their faith amongst the loyalists had given the church in Nova Scotia a new importance and Halifax became the seat of an episcopal see. In 1788 they established a boarding school for boys, forty miles away in the quiet country air of Windsor as Lord William Campbell and Richard Bulkeley had originally planned. From this root came King's, the first college in the province.

In 1786 Nova Scotia came under the vice-regal rule of Sir Guy Carleton, newly created Governor General of Canada, and dapper Johnnie Parr stepped down to the rank of lieutenant governor. (He was thus the last Captain-General and Governor of Nova Scotia, a rank that began with Cornwallis.) When Carleton, newly elevated to the peerage as Lord Dorchester, came to visit Halifax in this year there was a round of festivities in his honor. He was the darling of the loyalists—the soldier who saved Quebec in 1775, the wise organizer of the evacuation of New York in 1783, the man to whom they looked to press their needs in London now. There were balls, dinners, and card parties; there were receptions at Government House, at the Pontac, at the Golden Ball, at Roubelot's, at Morris's, and at Mrs. Sutherland's Assembly Rooms. It was all in sharp contrast to another sort of visit from another sort of visitor.

A week before this, Halifax had received its first royal guest, Prince William of the Royal Navy, one of the scapegrace sons of George III. Prince Billy was just twenty-one, a brisk red-faced young rake whose head rose to a point. (He was known in the Navy as Coconut Head.) By his father's favor he commanded the frigate *Pegasus* and had celebrated his birthday on the voyage in a spree that involved himself, his officers, and many of his seamen in helpless drunkenness. For many hours the ship was in charge of the midshipmen, one of whom with English understatement wrote in his journal: "...altogether a strange scene...one that would have astonished the members of a temperance society."

The young captain was received with pomp at King's Wharf by Lieutenant Governor Parr, General Campbell, Admiral Byron, and a concourse of service and civilian bigwigs, who bored him with fulsome addresses until the impatient Billy begged them to give over and treat him like any other frigate commander. This was due to no democratic urge; Billy simply wished to sample the delights of Halifax unhampered by his royal rank. This he proceeded to do for a week before departing for his winter station in the West Indies. He liked what he found in Halifax and sampled it again in the following three years. One of his boon companions was a dissipated young subaltern of the garrison named Dyott, who in his more sober moments kept a diary. This remarkable document survives and gives us a picture not only of Prince William but of the raffish life led by many an officer of the Halifax garrison in the gilded squalor which followed the American war.

His Majesty's young gentlemen amused themselves with such diversions as duels, cockfighting, fishing, hunting, chowder parties on McNab's Island, and coursing hares with terriers on the Common, but chiefly with drinking and lechery. The drinking was prodigious. "We drank twenty-eight bumper toasts, by which time we were in pretty good order. At nine o'clock a *feu-de-joie* was fired by the garrison from the Citadel. Those who could walk attended. I was one of the number that got up the hill.... After supper we set to Burton ale. The Prince was in the greatest spirits, sang two or three songs and for three hours laughed incessantly. I believe our risible faculties were considerably assisted by the Burton, as seven of us, the Prince included, drank fourteen bottles; that mixed with the champagne and claret must have made a pretty fermentation in our stomachs. We all, with stumbling and fumbling, attended His Highness to the barge."

There were dangers in all this hilarity, for the townsfolk of Halifax if not for the merry young gentlemen. "His Royal Highness dines with Captain Duvernet commanding the artillery, who gave us a most excellent dinner and a good deal of wine. In the evening HRH was amused with a set of fireworks designed by Duvernet, which was very pretty. Also he ordered a number of live shells to be thrown, which had a good effect." Need we add that the convivial Duvernet's batteries overlooked the town and anchorage?

Here is an account of a regimental dinner at the Halifax barracks in 1787, with Prince Billy, the lieutenant governor, the general, and the commodore present:

"The Prince took the chair himself and ordered me to be his Vice. We had a very good dinner and he sent wine of his own, the best claret I ever tasted. We had the Grenadiers drawn up in front of the messroom windows to fire a volley in honour of the toasts. As soon as the dinner was over he began. He did not drink himself, but he took care to see that everybody filled, and he gave 23 bumpers without a halt. In the course of my experience I never saw such fair drinking. When he had finished his list of bumpers I begged leave as Vice to give the Superior, and recommended it to the society to stand up on our chairs with three times three, taking their time from the Vice. I think it was the most laughable sight I ever beheld to see our Governor, our General and the Commodore all so drunk that they could scarcely stand on the floor, hoisted up on their chairs each with a bumper in his hand; and three times three cheers was what they were afraid to attempt for fear of falling. I then proposed His Royal Highness and a good wind whenever he sailed, with the same ceremony. He stood at the head of the table during both these toasts and I never saw a man laugh so in my life. When we had drunk the last, the old Governor desired to know if we had any more, as if he once got down he would never get up again. HRH saw that we were pretty well done and walked off. There were twenty dined. We drank 63 bottles of wine."

If the prince did not drink on this occasion it was not from sobriety, for drinking and wenching were his pet diversions. Probably he had some amorous engagement for the later hours. Halifax was full of naughty women, ranging all the way from the unwashed sluts of Barrack Street to the elegant wife of Mr. John Wentworth, and Billy knew them all. His favorite evening amusement was a tour of the town's bawdyhouses accompanied by Dyott and one or two other debauched young gentlemen of the service, who made sure that the daughters of joy staged a command performance for the prince—"some very pretty scenes," as Dyott tittered in his reminiscences.

More than once William must have gone straight from these pretty scenes to the arms of pretty Mrs. Wentworth, a fact of which she was doubtless aware, although it does not seem to have offended her in the least. Frances Wentworth at this time was forty-two, a little past her bloom but still slender, vivacious, adept and experienced in the arts of the drawing room and the bedchamber—and still very much the clever and ambitious wife of plodding John. How much her liaison with Prince William was induced by passion and how much by womanly calculation it is impossible to say. Certainly she played her part well, with John's obvious knowledge and consent. Whenever the prince was in town Mr. Wentworth conveniently left for the country to pursue his duties as Surveyor-General of the King's Woods; and while John strode the forest clearings levying fees upon the reluctant settlers his lady exerted her shapely self with no less purpose for the pleasure of their royal guest.

All this made scandal in the more sober circle of Halifax society. Indeed many ladies would not call on Mrs. Wentworth, much less admit her to their drawing rooms; and Prince Billy, a snob at heart, took care not to be seen in the same carriage with her. But beauty and patience conquer all things, and Frances Wentworth had a sweet revenge. In 1791 she and John sailed for England to visit their sixteen-year-old son, a student at Westminster. While they were there, old Lieutenant Governor Parr died at Halifax in an apoplectic fit. The news sped across the sea—and Opportunity appeared at the Wentworths' lodging with a thunderous knock.

Frances had lost no time in renewing her acquaintance with Prince William, now Duke of Clarence. At forty-six this provincial Ninon de Lenclos had lost little of her charm and none of her ability to please; and for his part William, while deep in his amour with the coarse and jolly Mrs. Jordan, was not averse to re-tasting a remembered pleasure from across the sea. Always generous for favors received, he exerted himself on her behalf. In certain quarters his influence had weight. Added to the exertions of the Rockinghams and other powerful friends of the Wentworths it had the desired effect. An irreverent young Haligonian visiting in London at this time wrote home to Nova Scotia: "I wrote my friend Paine a few days back, since which inform him that his friend Wentworth has succeeded to the Government of Nova Scotia, and Madam had the honour of kissing our gracious sovereign's hand. Previous to her departure the Duke of C–e presented her with a Damask Sopha accommodated with four well-stuffed pillows, and she tried the length of it on the Queen's birthday."

With or without the sofa, but with His Majesty's commission in John's traveling case, in April 1792 the new lieutenant governor and his lady sailed for home in HMS *Hussar*, and five weeks later they were greeted by a salute of fifteen guns from the Halifax batteries and escorted to Government House by a delegation of magistrates and army officers. On the following day Wentworth was sworn into office, and the boom of the cannon ranged along the upper side of Grand Parade announced his inauguration to the harbor hills. No one realized it at the time, but these echoing salutes proclaimed as well the opening of the liveliest and gaudiest era in the history of Halifax.

15.
1784–1792

Effects of the French Revolution. "The Mall." A public hanging. Fashions of the day. The bitterness of Dr. Byles. A Negro exodus to Africa. A grand ball at Government House.

A NEW WIND WAS BLOWING THROUGH THE WORLD. The French Revolution, begun in 1789, was now well set on its tumultuous course, tearing away the cobwebs of Europe as it went. Manners, dress, art, no less than political thought, were undergoing a swift and sweeping change. Britain and the countries of Europe were on the verge of a twenty-year war which would affect them all profoundly, but they had a short time yet to enjoy old things and ways. The star of Napoleon had yet to rise. Indeed at the very time when Frances Wentworth and Duke Billy were concerned with that "sopha" in London, young Bonaparte, still an unknown lieutenant of artillery, was engaged in writing an essay for the Academy of Lyons which had for its subject, "What are the principles and institutions most likely to bring about the greatest happiness of mankind?"

Across the sea Halifax had reached the depths of the postwar slump in 1788, and things were improving. The poorer loyalists had settled somehow, the sharpers and adventurers had drifted away to greener pastures, the captains and merchants had found new channels of trade. The presence of Prince William on the Halifax station for several successive seasons had drawn to the town a following of wealthy young English rakes like Lord Montmorris and the Earl of Eglinton who, if they added nothing to the moral tone of the population, put a great deal of gold in its pockets.

Richard Bulkeley (who had a farm at Dutch Village) and other gentlemen interested in the land had formed Nova Scotia's first Agricultural

Society. A grammar school had been established at the corner of Barrington and Sackville streets. Richard Uniacke, the onetime rebel, had become speaker of the assembly. There was a new tone to the assembly itself, and William Cottnam Tonge especially was demanding changes in a voice that would be heard. The young rake Dyott, transferred upcountry with his regiment, was writing wistfully: "They were very gay at Halifax—plays, balls and assemblies; not near so much whist as usual but an abundance of good eating and drinking."

The utility of "The Mall" in all weathers had set an example to the merchants of Granville Street, who built a broad wooden walk from Buckingham Street to the corner of George, and thence down George Street to Hollis. This soon became the 'Change of Halifax, where merchants, shipowners, and financiers gathered every fine morning from eleven to twelve to discuss their affairs. In cold or wet weather they held their meetings in the Guild of Merchants' chamber of the Pontac Inn, a sort of transatlantic Lloyds'.

The public still enjoyed its military spectacles, although the garrison now was on a peacetime basis and comparatively small; and there was a good public hanging from time to time. In 1790 a woman convicted of murder provided an excellent show for young and old. The gallows were erected in stony George Street just above the Parade, where the people could gather to watch the affair; she came from the jail standing up in a horse dray, which was driven under the gallows while soldiers and constables kept back the curious throng. The rest was simple. The hangman placed the noose about her neck, the drayman lashed his horse, and away went hangman, drayman and cart, leaving the woman to kick her life out in the breeze from Citadel Hill.

But there was other entertainment. The theatre had long since made its appearance, and now there were two, the "old" Grand Theatre on Argyle Street and the "new" Grand on Grafton Street. The plays were mostly farces of the sort popular in London at the time, and the actors usually were young officers of the army and navy and young bucks of the town, giving way occasionally to a strolling company of professionals.

Theatre advertisements in 1788 requested the ladies to "dress their heads as low as possible otherwise people sitting behind cannot have a view of the stage." In a short time this admonition was needless, for the fashion in hairdressing, like every other mode, was changed by the wind from Europe. Paris set the pace. Giddy with the new freedom, the ladies of republican fashion had staged a revolution no less surprising than the storming of the Bastille. Away went the ponderous stuffs, the voluminous gowns and petticoats, the cumbersome hoops, bustles, and panniers, the agonizing stays and laces, the mountainous powdered coiffures which had reached their ultimate ridiculous height in the court of Marie Antoinette. Liberty demanded the other extreme, so that chic French women came forth in one-piece gowns of light muslin, batiste, or lawn, cut very low, divided into skirt and bodice by a ribbon tied just below the all but naked breasts—and with very little underneath. Hair was cut shorter and dressed close to the head, and hair powder was abolished. High heels had perished as well, and ladies slipped about in flat soft shoes tied sandal-fashion up the ankle.

All this was quickly aped by ladies of fashion in England and the colonies. Statesmen might thunder against the new French politics and parsons denounce the new French morals, but fashion (then as now) knew no boundaries and recognized no man-made restrictions. Thus the ladies of the gay garrison circle in Halifax in the closing years of the eighteenth century displayed their persons with far more daring than does the so-called emancipated woman of the twentieth. Indeed a fashionable young woman of 1795 caught in a sudden summer shower in Barrington Street today would be arrested on the spot by a shocked policeman.

As for the gentlemen, while doubtless enjoying these gauzy liberties in the other sex, they went yet a step farther in their own discomfort, clasping their legs in skintight breeches, stifling themselves in a multiplicity of waistcoats and in coats with enormous collars and enormous tails, and choking themselves with prodigious cravats. Only in the matter of hair did they admit a morsel of common sense. Hair powder had been going out of fashion for some time in the wake of wigs. Very soon the pigtail was to vanish as well, except in His Majesty's Navy. Young bucks of the 1790s were ordering their valets to crop the hair loosely at the nape and ears. The long familiar tricorne hat was going out of favor too, and men of fashion were wearing hats cocked high at front and back in the mode which nowadays one always associates with Napoleon.

The older generation clung to its ways, of course, and as late as 1820, when trousers had come into vogue, elderly gentlemen could be seen about the streets of Halifax in buckled shoes, stockings, breeches, embroidered waistcoats, huge square-cut coats, and wigs. The middle class and poor, always a decade behind the London (not to say Paris) fashion, continued to wear their sober hoops and gowns and mobcaps, their old-fashioned breeches, stockings, surtouts, and three-cornered hats, well into the nineteenth century.

The dangers of tight lacing had long been realized even by the women who most indulged in it, and as far back as 1786 we find Mather Byles, the loyalist parson who was chaplain to the Halifax garrison, writing about the death of his wife. "With a coolness which astonished all who heard her she deliberately sent for Doctor Almon and requested that, as her complaints were mysterious and extraordinary, her body might be opened for the benefit of Survivors, adding that she knew I was a person of too much good sense to hesitate about it. I consented and it was done. Her liver, which was supposed to be enlarged and ulcerated, was perfectly sound and in its natural state. She was in every respect formed for a long life. Her death as it appeared from the most undeniable evidence was totally owing to the pernicious practice of lacing and girdling herself too tight. Her funeral was long, a large number of American refugees being dressed in black and walking as Relations."

Dr. Byles was one of the most remarkable men of the time in Halifax, learned, witty, a keen observer, a diligent writer of letters. He had visited London after the war, preached in Westminster Abbey and watched his friend Jeffries (the former surgeon of the Halifax garrison) set off from Hyde Park in a free balloon. (His daughter Rebecca, writing from Halifax to Boston in 1785, declared: "Dr. Jeffries has since been from Dover to Calais. There for you, see what a Loyalist can do!") It was the first air crossing of the Channel.

Byles was embittered by the war and its harsh aftermath for the loyalists. Like many another refugee he had been disappointed in his hopes of preferment in Halifax and could not abide the place. "Every insignificant fop wriggles like a skinned eel...rheumatisms and rum-atisms are the two endemial diseases of Halifax...I have advertized my house for sale and shall without the least regret bid a final adieu to a place which, upon cool reflection, I must pronounce to be in every respect the most contemptible my eyes have ever beheld; and I desire never to forget that the most irreligious people I ever knew were at the same time the most ignorant, the most stupid and the most unhappy."

Yet he is said to have been the author of the following happy doggerel, recited to the customers of the *Gazette* by the printer's boy who carried the papers from door to door:

Behold another Christmas gone, our time so swiftly passeth on,
And New Year's Day is just at hand, and this our notice doth demand.
On that account the printer's boy begs leave to wish you all much joy.
Being blest with peace in Eighty-Three, its happy fruits today we see;
Commerce and trade do now increase and we have Plenty joined with Peace.
Our Yankee friends now cross the seas and bring provisions as they please;
Beef, pork, mutton, good beets and veal; corn, oats, squashes and Indian meal.
By these our tables are well spread and we again are nobly fed.
Then let us joyn in songs of praise, who live to see such happy days;
All parties with each other rhyme and live in peace to endless time.

Certainly Byles was the author of the lines his daughter Elizabeth worked into a sampler, no doubt expressing the sentiments of most young loyalist ladies in the Halifax of her time:

I, a young exile from my native shore,
Start at the flash of arms and dread the roar;
My softer soul, not form'd for scenes like these,
Flies to the arts of Innocence and Peace.
My heart exults while to the attentive eye
The curious needle spreads the enamel'd dye;
While varying shades the pleasing task beguile,
My friends approve me, and my parents smile.

All these peaceful arts and traffics were about to perish when John and Frances Wentworth arrived in such triumph and installed themselves in Government House. War was on the way and Halifax was to know neither Innocence nor Peace for twenty-two years; but there remained a breathing space, a brief time for peaceful works and at least one noble deed. The condition of the freed Negroes in Halifax and elsewhere in the province had been pitiful ever since they came north with the white refugees. This had been noticed by a humane young naval officer, John Clarkson—a friend of Wilberforce the emancipator—who brought the matter to the attention of the British Government. Clarkson was commissioned to travel over Nova Scotia and offer the Negroes free passage to Sierra Leone. He arrived at Halifax in October 1791 in a ship appropriately called the *Ark*; and four months later, with fifteen chartered ships and 1190 joyful blacks, he sailed away to Africa. As to whether or not they were better off in Sierra Leone, history remains undecided; but thousands of blacks were themselves so doubtful that they refused Clarkson's offer and remained in Nova Scotia.

John Wentworth threw himself into his role of lieutenant governor with energy. His earlier trampings about His Majesty's forests had shown him all too clearly the need of new roads into the hinterland, and for a start he was able to report within a few months "a good cart road" across the province from Halifax to the growing settlements about Pictou. His mind was alive with other notions, not least a canal to link Halifax with the Bay of Fundy by way of the old Indian war trail through the Dartmouth Lakes and down the Shubenacadie River. But that would have to wait for a time.

Halifax, as Dyott remarked, was very gay. Dyott came to town on leave in March 1792 and later recalled: "On the fifteenth I went to Halifax and on the seventeenth was admitted a member of the Society of friendly brothers in a knot belonging to the 16th Regiment. We kept the day in honour of St. Patrick by dining together at the coffee-house, and a pretty scene of drunkenness it was. I stayed in town till the 25th leading a life of debauchery."

But the great event of 1792 was a grand ball and supper at the old Government House on Hollis Street. A Halifax reporter was obviously carried away by it all:

"The company being assembled in the Levee Room at 8 o'clock, the band played God Save the King three times over, after which the country dances commenced, two sets dancing at the same time. The whole house was open, every room illuminated and elegantly decorated. There was a room set apart for cotillions above-stairs for those who chose to dance them, and a band provided on purpose. During the dancing there were refreshments of ice, orgeat, capillaire, and a variety of other things. The ladies sat down at table and the gentlemen waited on them.

"Among the ornaments which were altogether superb there were exact representations of Messrs. Hartshorne & Tremaine's new flour mill, and of the windmill on the Common. The model of the new lighthouse at Shelburne was incomparable, and the track of the new road from Pictou was delineated in the most ingenious and surprising manner, as was the representation of our fisheries, that great source of the wealth of this country. To all these inimitable arrangements mottoes were attached. The viands and wines were delectable, and mirth, grace and good humour seemed to have joined hands to grace some glorious festival. But this was only for the friends of the Governor and lady. When the ladies left the supper room the gentlemen sat down at table, when the Governor gave several loyal toasts, with 'three times three,' and an applicable tune was played after each bumper, which had an admirable effect. At 2 o'clock the dancing recommenced, and at four the company retired."

The piquant part of this is the phrase *only for the friends of the Governor and lady*. Frances Wentworth was having her revenge upon those Halifax respectables who had snubbed her six years earlier. Ladies on her black list were never invited to Government House, and their husbands found the all-important patronage of the governor sadly lacking in their business affairs. There were purse pangs and heartburnings over this, and they were to go on for another sixteen years.

16.
1793–1795

Beginning the Napoleonic Wars. Prince Edward and Madame St. Laurent. Building a new fortress. The first telegraph system in America. "Friar Lawrence's Cell."

IN 1793 THE GREAT NEW WAR WITH FRANCE CAME OUT OF the blue, and into the blue went ten years of peaceful reconstruction. Halifax was plunged again into its feverish role of fortress and naval base. The fleet came in, regiments of regulars arrived, and militia were called in from all parts of the province to work on the neglected defenses. Within a few days the first press gang was at work, and laborers, clerks and 'prentice-boys dived into cellars or hid in garrets with an alacrity that grew with practice as the war went on.

Wentworth thrust the province and himself into the war with patriotic fervor and a certain self-interest, for under the prompting of his lady he was now in urgent pursuit of a baronetcy. Without delay he formed the Nova Scotia Regiment of Foot, had himself appointed colonel at full pay, and sought His Majesty's permission to add the magic word "Royal" to the title of his corps. This having been granted, the regiment was able to wear the royal blue facings on its scarlet coats instead of the humble provincial green. These trappings did not impress General Ogilvie, commander of the Halifax garrison, who had the regular's usual contempt for provincial troops and for a time refused to recognize the Wentworth corps at all.

Nevertheless the Royal Nova Scotia Regiment became a very efficient unit, its officers chiefly loyalists and other veterans of the American Revolution who had seen more downright fighting in their time than had Ogilvie himself. The general was glad to avail himself of their labor in building a new battery in the woods of Point Pleasant. This with a becoming modesty he named after himself. Improved by successive generations and garrisons, but now abandoned, Fort Ogilvie stands in Point Pleasant Park to this day, a monument to a little man.

The worthy general's chief stroke for king and country at the time was a heavily armed expedition to St. Pierre and Miquelon, those barren French fishing posts off the south coast of Newfoundland. The islands surrendered without firing a shot and Ogilvie carried off in triumph Governor Danseville, his staff, and several hundred poor French fishermen with their women and children, as prisoners of war. The loot was small but it contained one useful thing, a bell from the church of St. Pierre, which made its way into the belfry of St. Peter's Church at Halifax.

The housing of these unfortunates presented a problem. Ogilvie placed them temporarily in the old Cornwallis Barracks, just below Royal Artillery Park. Eventually they were scattered over the town and province. Danseville, his aide Mizanseau, and one or two other officials were placed on parole and allowed to live a mile or so outside the village of Dartmouth. The governor received a generous allowance from the British Government and lived in considerable style at Brook House, where among other things he made a fishpond and laid out walks amongst the surrounding groves of birch and beech. Like many another luckless French prisoner he remained for the duration of the war—in his case twenty-one long years. His aide Mizanseau married a Nova Scotia woman and never went back to France. This was true of many others. Not a few escaped from Halifax as the years went by, and made their way to the Acadian villages at the western tip of Nova Scotia, where they married and settled peacefully for the rest of their lives. One of these, a young French privateersman captured early in the war, became a prosperous merchant and shipbuilder and eventually a member of the Nova Scotia Legislature.

For Halifax in the spring of 1794 the war took on a new and magnificent complexion with the arrival of Prince Edward, the active soldier son of King George, just returning from a brief but triumphant expedition against the French West Indies and still in hot pursuit of military glory. He had spent three years previously in Canada, commanding the garrison of Quebec, and now he was obsessed with a single idea—that sooner or later the French would send a great fleet and army across the Atlantic for the reconquest of Canada, using Halifax as a base.

His first move was to demand (and receive) the appointment of Commander in Chief, Nova Scotia. He came north on the wings of the wind—in the frigate *Blanche,* to be exact, in twelve days from St. Kitts—and landed at King's Wharf under a salute of twenty-one guns. Already his busy mind was hatching plans for the Halifax defenses. His first command had been Gibraltar and now he saw himself as another Heathfield sustaining a famous siege in the wilds of Nova Scotia. As a son of His Majesty, and with the appointment in his pocket, he was to be obeyed without question or delay. With him money was no object; he was not quite twenty-seven and his personal debts already were over £20,000.

Yet Edward was by far the most respectable of the sons of George III. He had been educated in the rigid German military system from the age of seventeen. He stood over six feet, was athletic and intelligent, and was filled with soldierly ambition. He was never drunk, for that would have been undignified; unlike his brothers, he was always acutely conscious of his dignity as a soldier and a prince. In Quebec and Halifax he kept a refined and charming mistress, of mysterious origin although definitely French, and variously believed to be a native of France, of Quebec, or of Martinique in the French West Indies. It was a case of true love. They remained devoted to each other until, when he was well past middle age, duty obliged him to put poor Julie aside, marry an authentic princess and produce an heir to the British throne.

Edward had three great faults: he had too great a sense of his own importance, he had no sense of the value of money, and he had not a spark of humanity in dealing with his soldiers. As a result wherever he held command, at Gibraltar, at Quebec, at Halifax, he left a memory of pomposity, vast expense, and mutinous troops. But he left other memories and many solid accomplishments at Halifax, where for six years he was the foremost figure in the town, energetic in civil as well as in military affairs, a stout patron of church and theatre, and a genuine if somewhat austere friend of the poor.

When he came to Halifax in 1794 he found a struggling, shabby wooden town defended by the tumbledown remains of forts hastily thrown up or repaired at the time of the American Revolution. When he left, Halifax was studded with excellent public and military buildings and surrounded by powerful batteries—it was the strongest fortress outside Europe—with a new and lofty tone to its society and a vigorous outlook on the world. For a century afterwards the Haligonians talked of Edward's time as a golden age.

Most of the gold came from Britain, a drain which worried the British Government more and more as the war and the years rolled on. First the new commander in chief required a town house suitable to his station and to the tastes of his lady, Alphonsine Thérèse Bernadine Julie de Montgenet de Saint Laurent, usually known as Madame St. Laurent. This he built on the north flank of Citadel Hill, a roomy and handsome wooden mansion with a wide Corinthian portico facing the Common and a stretch of well-kept gardens running down the slope to Cogswell Street. The entrance to the carriage drive was lighted by two ornate copper lanterns, which many years later came (appropriately enough) into the hands of Abraham Gesner, the Nova Scotian inventor of kerosene.

After this he built a block of garrison offices and a workshop for the Royal Engineers adjoining the North Barracks farther east along the Citadel slope, so that the whole south side of Cogswell Street from Brunswick Street to the Common was occupied by military property of various kinds. The old barracks were in a ruinous state, so Edward had both North and South barracks rebuilt on a more elaborate scale. He built a new barrack for the gunners on Sackville Street, at what became known as Royal Artillery Park, had the Grand Parade cut down to the level of Barrington Street and built a stone wall and railing about it, and scattered offices, store sheds and guardhouses (each of these with cells for delinquents) about the downtown streets.

But these were petty matters. From the moment when Edward cast a first speculative glance at Citadel Hill his mind was filled with memories of the rock on the St. Lawrence, and he determined to make the sugarloaf hill which dominated Halifax as strong as the citadel of Quebec. First he leveled the ruins of the old blockhouse and the trenches and earthen batteries built there during the American war. Then he cut off the whole top of the hill to a depth of fifteen feet, using the displaced earth and stone to fill hollows in the slope. Upon the plateau thus created he built a rectangular earthen fort with four bastions, all surrounded by a wide ditch ten feet deep, in which for lack of water he planted a row of sharp palisades to discourage assault.

The entrance was on the eastern side facing the harbor, and from it a road ran down the hill to the head of Buckingham Street. The center of the work was occupied by a parade ground and by a large barrack of heavy beams fitted together like the timbers of a ship. This barrack held six hundred and fifty men, and from the flat roof, like the gun deck of a warship, heavy cannon menaced the harbor and the approach across the Common. This constituted the keep of the new fortress, with the rest of the garrison barracks ranged close at hand along the upper reach of Sackville Street and all of Cogswell Street, and with the artillery park, the garrison offices and workshops, and the house of the commander in chief all within easy reach.

In attending to the heart of things, Edward did not neglect the outworks. The old defenses on George's Island he replaced with a star-shaped fort accommodating three hundred men, thirty heavy cannon, and (with his memories of Gibraltar) two furnaces for heating shot red-hot. He placed another chained boom across the Northwest Arm where Colville had placed his in 1762, fastening the end with a huge ring bolt in what has been known ever since as the Chain Rock in Point Pleasant Park. He also rebuilt Colville's old battery and placed four cannon to cover the boom.

The old Eastern Battery, at what is now Imperoyal, Edward repaired and strengthened with a battery of heavy guns. He added a crescent-shaped battery of similar cannon to Fort Ogilvie. At the far end of Bedford Basin he repaired old Fort Sackville and added a new barrack for the garrison. To defend the harbor entrance he erected a battery at Sandwich Point, looking across to Mauger's Beach—exactly where De Labat had planned the chief French fort in 1711. All of these fortifications were in the latest European mode, with such innovations as cannon on traversing platforms; these were a vast improvement on the old carriages, which had to be shifted with handspikes in the hands of the sweating gunners.

Indeed nothing was too new or too expensive for the prince and his keen engineers. In 1794 a British expedition to Corsica had suffered sharply from a small and apparently impregnable fort on Cape Mortella. When its small garrison surrendered at last the fort was found to be round and flat on top like a pillbox, with masonry walls of immense thickness; and the only means of access was a door twenty feet above ground, reached by a ladder which could be hauled up inside. The report of this affair made a profound impression in England, which was living in the constant threat of French invasion, and large numbers of "Martello" towers began to appear along the Kentish coast. News of this development reached Halifax quickly, and Edward lost no time in building Martello towers at Point Pleasant, at the Eastern Battery and on the cliff at York Redoubt.

But perhaps Edward's greatest work was a telegraph system, the first in North America. It was known that the French had invented a semaphore telegraph as early as 1793 and that by means of it Paris was able to communicate rapidly and efficiently with the armies on the borders. The British at once began to experiment with such a system and eventually adopted a Swedish invention: each station consisted of an enormous Venetian blind whose six shutters could be dropped or turned on edge in various combinations; and it was visible by telescope for miles. After much experiment a chain of these things was built between Whitehall and the Channel ports. The Admiralty continued to use the system until 1816.

In the meantime, indeed while the Admiralty was still playing with the shutters, Edward's engineers had devised a system of visual telegraphy, using a code of flags and large black wickerwork balls and drums for signaling by day, and combinations of lanterns at night. There were signal posts of this sort near Chebucto Head, at York Redoubt, on Citadel Hill, and at the Dockyard. Haligonians became accustomed to the sight of baskets and bunting running up and down the flagstaff on the hill, a constant flutter from morn to night, for Edward was pleased with his new toy and kept it busy. The outposts reported everything that happened, even the petty misdemeanors of the soldiery, and the commander in chief bombarded them with questions, orders, regulations, and punishments. His rigid discipline kept the cat-o'-nine-tails swinging in every barrack yard, and from time to time the whole garrison was marched to the Common to witness the hanging of mutineers and deserters.

His residence was admirably suited for these affairs. From the Corinthian portico he could see the gallows towards the Egg Pond and from its eastern windows he could watch the floggings in the North Barrack square. In the words of the Halifax antiquarian, Piers: "Scenes of gaiety and splendour once distinguished this historic plot of ground; formal levees, stately dinner parties, gay balls; gallant army and navy officers, loyal colonial officials, gentry of the town; infatuating ladies, glittering candles, brilliant uniforms and dresses, sparkling jewels; the ripple of light-hearted laughter and the strains of music. Just below, not a hundred yards away, was the North Barracks parade ground where too often at daybreak some poor shivering culprit stood bound to the triangle, in a hollow square of his callous comrades, to suffer hundreds of lashes by the merciless drummers of the regiment; while despite the drowning roll of drums his cries were borne upward to the peacefully sleeping household of the Commander-in-Chief."

Perhaps the prince's lady disliked these early morning sounds. Probably she disliked the conspicuity of the residence, its ease of access to a stream of fashionable visitors, the constant tramp of redcoats marching past, and the chill winter shadow of Citadel Hill. Perhaps she disliked too close a proximity to Mrs. Wentworth, for she must have heard anecdotes of Edward's brother Billy and the Circe of Government House. But she had nothing to fear. Mrs. Wentworth now was forty-nine and (with all due respect to Mr. Kipling) the charms of forty-nine are under a severe handicap when the man is a rigid soldier turning thirty and very much in love with a demure little French morsel on the sunny side of twenty-five. The clever Frances was too experienced a campaigner to risk defeat in such a contest, and she had reached at last an age when the genteel arts of the drawing room were just as effective as the hurly-burly of a damask sofa somewhere else, and much more restful.

Whatever the reason, whatever the persuasion, Edward soon decided to remove his charmer from the jostle of the town to a more secluded love nest on the wooded shore of Bedford Basin. The Wentworths, eager to oblige, suggested their summer place near Birch Cove. It was six miles or so out of town by the Windsor road, and their rustic cottage bore the charming name of "Friar Lawrence's Cell"—a very appropriate place for Edward to play Romeo to Julie's Juliet. Here on a tall wooded bluff aloof from the road the prince built his country house, a two-storey wooden building in the Italian style with a flat roof commanding a magnificent view of Bedford Basin. His soldiers cleared the undergrowth all about it and made a wide natural park with gravel paths and rides laid out in sweeping curves to spell the letters of Julie's name. A small brook was led in a series of pretty waterfalls to an artificial pond shaped like her heart.

At intervals, where a view of the Basin glittered through the birches, Edward placed little summerhouses of gilded latticework, with fantastic pagoda roofs and tiny bells and dangling strips of glass along the eaves, tinkling musically in the breeze off the water. At the foot of the slope, on a small knoll by the waterside probably occupied originally by the Wentworths' "Cell," he built a wooden rotunda where the regimental bands played on gala occasions. (This bandstand still exists.) Nearby, to guard his privacy, a whole company of the Royal Nova Scotia Regiment languished in a specially built barrack. Finally, so that Edward could remain in constant touch with the Citadel and outposts while spending pleasant hours in the company of his *chere amie*, a signal station was installed on the hill behind the lodge—a unique collaboration of Venus, Mars, and Mercury.

17.
1796–1800

The wild Maroons. Prisoners of war. Life in wartime. The telegraph enlarged. The building of a new Government House. Departure of a soldier prince.

When Clarkson sailed away with his impoverished blacks in 1792 it seemed for a time that the Negro problem in Nova Scotia had been solved. But there remained many free blacks and a great number of slaves. After 1792, through the influence of Chief Justice Strange, a stout emancipationist, the owners of runaway Negroes found it difficult and finally impossible to recover their "property" through the courts. This rang the knell of slavery in Nova Scotia; but it meant a growing number of Negroes wandering about Halifax, living by odd jobs, begging, and petty thievery. Then, in 1796, the whole problem in an aggravated form was dumped back into the town's lap. As usual with Haligonian problems it came from outside, by a twirl of the imperial machinery.

The rich and important colony of Jamaica had been gravely concerned about a tribe of runaway slaves known as the Maroons. The horrid example of Haiti, where the blacks were in bloody and successful revolt against their masters, sent a chill up the Jamaican spine, and it was decided to gather up the insurgent Maroons by military force and ship them away to the top of the world—to Nova Scotia. London gave its blessing; Nova Scotia was assured that the Jamaican Government would pay for the Maroons' support until they were settled. No doubt Prince Edward, eager to obtain fresh labor for his works, threw his powerful word into the scales.

In the summer of 1796 there arrived at Halifax five or six hundred wild black men, women, and children in charge of two Jamaican officers with names right out of a romantic novel—Mr. Ochterloney and Colonel

Quarrell. Quarrell had at his disposal a sum of £25,000 for the settlement and maintenance of his charges, and he began by purchasing land and erecting buildings at Preston, in the woods behind Dartmouth, including a mansion for himself which he called Maroon Hall. Prince Edward at once put the strongest blacks to work on the Citadel defenses, where their efforts were long commemorated by the Maroon Bastion. The rest were encouraged to clear land and plant vegetables at Preston for their own support. The British Government granted £240 a year to maintain a school for the exiles, and Governor Wentworth talked loftily of "disseminating piety, morality and loyalty amongst them."

Sad to say, the Maroons wanted none of these things. They cherished a god called Accompang, whose name they had given to their old stronghold in the distant hills of Jamaica. The worship of Accompang involved mysterious rites for the good of their souls, and in turn Accompang indulged them in all sorts of orgies for the pleasure of their flesh. For four years the nocturnal forest about Preston rang with voodoo chants and orgiastic laughter, and the townsfolk of Halifax and Dartmouth heard dreadful whispers of the rites. There were whispers also of something else.

Sir John Wentworth (he had received the coveted baronetcy in 1795) was not quite so interested in the blacks' piety and morality as he would have the home government believe. As far back as 1784, when the loyalists were selling off slaves dirt-cheap because they could no longer support them, Wentworth had gathered up nineteen, had them baptized in preparation for the next world, and shipped them off to the fever-stricken plantation of his kinsman in Guiana, which doubtless proved the last way station on the road. In this new black wave he saw a double opportunity, to secure the administration of the Jamaican fund and to use some of the blacks for his own purposes.

Upon surrendering their Bedford Basin retreat to Prince Edward, the Wentworths had bought an estate and built a summer residence on a Preston hilltop, commanding a magnificent view of lakes and streams and rolling wooded hills. Here they entertained royally, saluting the approach of distinguished guests such as the prince and Madame with the boom of a cannon on the terrace and maintaining a staff of well-trained servants, white and black. For crossing the harbor towards his country house and for stately excursions by water to the prince's lodge at Bedford Basin, Wentworth had purchased a luxurious galley, rowed by several pairs of oars, in which Lady Frances could recline and journey with all the ease of Cleopatra. In fact, as usual, John had neglected nothing in gratifying his lady's whims and as usual he was casting about in all directions to find the means of supporting them.

The Maroons offered a handy source of free labor for his Preston fields. He seized on fifty of them, male and female, without delay, lodging them on the estate. To friends who questioned his safety in the midst of these savage creatures he boasted that he was "often without a sentry and without a door or window locked, and still they did no mischief." No doubt he worked them hard, but he found them congenial in more ways than one. Lady Wentworth divided her time between the Preston estate and Government House, but during the summer Sir John stayed there for weeks on end overseeing his dusky retainers.

This led to an unexpected and subtle revenge upon the beautiful and imperious woman who so often had sent him forth from her bed to make way for other lovers. The typical Maroon girl was a magnificent creature of the kind celebrated by a Jamaican poet as "the Black Venus." When Frances was absent from her Preston bed one of these took her place beside the governor. Long after John and Frances were dead, and long after the Preston mansion was dust and the well-tilled gardens given up to pasture, the descendants of John and the handsome Negress pointed out the site of Wentworth's country seat and boasted of the "high blood" in their veins.

Most of the Maroons, untamed, unhappy, pinched by the bitter winters and the hungry land, became turbulent to the point of insurrection. In 1800 the government shipped them off to Sierra Leone—the second Negro exodus from Nova Scotia.

Meanwhile the war waxed furiously, with the French armies victorious in every European field and their warships and privateers cruising every sea. Nelson's star was rising, but so was Napoleon's. Daily, hourly, Prince Edward awaited the French invasion, while the rocky forest about Halifax rang with the exertions of his troops and engineers. At a time when England herself faced imminent invasion and needed all her strength along the Channel, Edward demanded and drew across the Atlantic a stream of troops, cannon, munitions, and gold for the fulfillment of his dream. Among other things he had determined to extend his telegraph along the Great West Road to Windsor and finally to Annapolis, the old capital of the province, where he maintained an alert garrison in Fort Anne. Engineers surveyed the route, and companies of sweating redcoats began to hack long avenues through the forest to provide a view from station to station along the way.

And the French came; but not as invaders. They came as prisoners, taken at sea or in the West Indian islands, a dozen here, a few hundred there; as the war progressed the town was full of them. Their full support meant a vast expense and they were therefore permitted to rove about the streets doing odd jobs and buying their own provisions. Among them were black soldiers of French colonial regiments taken in St. Domingue and elsewhere; a memorable figure was the majestic Negro Bellegarde in the full uniform of a brigadier general in the French service, walking the streets with his wife and family.

Many of these prisoners, white and black, were afire with the fanatical spirit which in Europe had made the French armies invincible. Before long there were frequent scuffles and riots in the streets and, what was worse, rumors that the prisoners were spreading their republican doctrines amongst the Acadian population. Edward ordered them confined henceforth under guard. Their officers were paroled and allowed to live like Danseville at Preston. The rest were confined in the new naval prison on Melville Island in the Northwest Arm, in a wooden prison at Dartmouth, and in an increasing number of dreary hulks moored off the Dockyard or in Bedford Basin. By the war's end there were thousands of prisoners in the town and province, some of whom, ignored in the brief truce of 1802, had been twenty years in captivity.

One Frenchman wounded and taken at sea had this to say of prison life in Halifax in the year 1808: "When I had recovered (in the naval hospital) they took me to Melville Island. On arrival I found all the Frenchmen at work, one knitting, others spinning, others making model warships of all kinds which they rigged with silk, and made the cannon out of *sous*. They sold some of these ships for not more than 20 piastres, and they had spent close to six months making them. Other Frenchmen made such things as snuffboxes, knives, forks, dominoes, ships—all of bone. The French prisoners bought more than a thousand ox-bones (per year) from the butchers of Halifax, paying five shillings a hundred. One made hats, others made stockings, mittens, gloves, purses. Everything we needed in Halifax we got through the jail-keeper. We advanced him money, and he kept a shop himself in which he sold bread, butter, potatoes, lime, soap, rice, pepper, thread, needles and onions, in other words everything we needed. When we asked for something he had not got, he made a note of it at once, and took the notes with him when he went to town. We got more than five thousand pounds of wool a year from Halifax. We had painters, goldsmiths, shoemakers, carpenters, schoolmasters, dancing-masters, music teachers; and each worked at his trade."

In 1799 there was a French invasion of another sort—three noble refugees from the Revolution: the Duc d'Orléans, the Duc de Montpensier, and the Comte de Beaujolais, all young, all brothers, all seeking a living in the New World. Prince Edward entertained them at Halifax, gave them money to pursue their way to the United States, and thought no more about it. But fifty years afterwards when Queen Victoria paid a state visit to France she was received with pomp and circumstance by Louis Philippe, King of the French, who once had been glad to borrow £200 from her father on the far side of the Atlantic.

The provincial privateers were busy and successful, notably in the West Indies and along the Spanish Main, and French and Spanish prizes with queer rigs and lovely names came sailing into Halifax for adjudication by the Vice-Admiralty courts. The booty taken in these vessels ranged all the way from cacao to church regalia. In 1802 Father Burke of St. Peter's Church was able to write this to his bishop: "I am sending you some vestments...some privateers from here stole them from the poor Spaniards, and not knowing what to do with them made a present of them to us. You see, my lord, how the misfortune of some becomes the good fortune of others!" On the other hand the painfully built foreign trade of Halifax had all but vanished in the new tide of war; many of her merchant ships had been captured by enemy warships and privateers, and Nova Scotian seamen were languishing in French and Spanish prisons all the way from Caracas to Calais.

But money was plentiful because of war expenditures, and the times were gay. There was a round of genteel entertainment led by Sir John and Lady Wentworth at Government House and patronized by Prince Edward and Madame. Edward also dined with the national societies, danced at the balls, and attended the plays, though he always retired soon after ten in order to rise at daybreak for the morning parade. What his hard-drinking, wenching, and gaming officers suffered from this rigid schedule may be guessed, and at least one of them chose a bold way out. In 1798 a dashing lieutenant colonel on Edward's staff eloped with pretty Mrs. Munto, leading lady of the theatre—the choicest scandal of the year.

The winters were as cold as ever. The officers and gentry and their ladies indulged in lively sleigh drives along the Windsor road on sunny afternoons, a practice made easy by the fact that Prince Edward, who drove back and forth from his Basin lodge, turned out his troops to shovel the way whenever a snowstorm blocked the road. Skating was the popular pastime. Crowds went to the Northwest Arm, where "judges, lawyers, high officials, rectors, curates and the dignified Bishop Inglis himself joined hands with the crowd. Colonels, majors, captains, middies were all on skates, and the fair sex were out in full force."

The large garrison, the fleet, the multitude of prisoners, the swelling population made a heavy demand on supplies of all kinds, and when winter set in food was scarce and fuel was dear. The common fuel was wood, brought by coasting vessels from Lunenburg and other settlements. The price of labor in Halifax had risen so high with the war that no one cared to hire men to cut fuel in the woods behind the town; it was cheaper to buy firewood fifty or sixty miles down the coast than to cut and haul it from the woods of Dutch Village. And coals from Cape Breton were growing in popularity with the increasing cost of wood.

Until this time the churches had been heated chiefly by the warmth of piety. Worshippers sat wrapped in their heaviest cloaks and greatcoats, many with hot bricks and portable charcoal heaters at their feet, and until 1790 it was common to see young fops, as well as the ladies and old gentlemen, carrying muffs. In 1795 the good folk of St. Matthew's bought a stove and the next year the parishioners of St. Paul's followed suit. The Anglican church was larger and more difficult to heat, and at last Prince Edward's staff came to the rescue with a pair of army stoves.

Press gangs harried the town, searching taverns, brothels, and frequently the homes of townsmen. Old Mr. Bulkeley, now Judge of Admiralty and crippled with rheumatism, held court in a large chamber of his house on Argyle Street, a fact which made a *cause célèbre* in 1798 when the press gangs were especially bold. Bulkeley called nine captains of the Royal Navy before him and censured them severely for their persistent flouting of the law. They retaliated with a letter to Admiral Vandeput, charging that the judge was incompetent and that in any case the Admiralty Court should not be held in a private house. There was a storm, but Bulkeley rode it out serenely. It was not the first clash between naval officers and the civil power and it would not be the last.

Sir John and Lady Wentworth now were urging the provincial government to build them a new official residence. The old wooden one between Hollis and Granville streets was surrounded by shops and taverns, with the fish and green markets only a few steps away. Fashion had moved up the hill. The presence of a prince of the blood and his swarm of well-to-do officers had set a new and opulent scale of entertainment, and Lady Frances was determined to lead the field. In a single year at her frequent balls, assemblies and dinners she entertained twenty-five hundred guests; and always she complained of the inconvenience, the cold and other failings of the old residency built by Governor Lawrence. She was a perfect snob, reveling in her title and her intimate contact with royalty, and she wanted a perfect setting for herself.

In the summer of 1798 Prince Edward's horse stumbled and threw him. He was not badly hurt, but the agitated Julie sent for a doctor. It was well known that Edward's long-standing quarrel with his father was the reason for these posts abroad, and that he was forbidden to return to England without good excuse. Hence when the doctor found a wrenched leg he tactfully suggested the waters of Bath. Edward was delighted. He was eager to visit London and press his claims for a parliamentary grant, a title in the peerage, and the rank of Commander in Chief for North America instead of merely for Nova Scotia.

He had to wait until October for official leave, and then he sailed with Madame at once, leaving orders enough to keep the garrison scurrying for the next twelve months and graciously permitting Sir John (in view of the discomforts of Government House) to move into the Bedford Basin lodge, where he could keep in touch with the town by the military telegraph. In the meantime Lady Wentworth, hearing another loud knock of opportunity, had herself sailed in haste for England, ostensibly to visit her grown-up son.

In Britain all went well. Frances hunted up her powerful allies the Rockinghams, Duke William, and the rest, and she was on hand to welcome Prince Edward and his lady when they set foot on English soil. With such friends at court her success was certain. Upon a day she was received by Queen Charlotte and granted the coveted (and not inappropriate) title of lady in waiting, with permission to reside abroad. The appointment carried with it £500 a year, a bagatelle to one of her expensive tastes but not to be despised in view of Sir John's financial straits. Meanwhile Sir John was playing his part with a typical apple for teacher. Among the Halifax commissaries and others who depended on government patronage he raised a subscription of five hundred guineas for a token of good will towards the absent commander in chief, and sent it overseas by the diligent merchant Hartshorne. In January 1799 Lady Wentworth saw that the token, a diamond star of the Order of the Garter, was presented to Edward at Kensington Palace by Charles-Mary, her handsome son.

In the summer of 1799 all came back to Halifax in triumph—Lady Wentworth with her new mark of royal favor; her son, a graduate of Oxford, for whom an appointment to His Majesty's Council in Nova Scotia followed as a matter of course; and Prince Edward with his Julie and his peerage (he was to be known henceforth as the Duke of Kent) plus a parliamentary grant of £12,000 a year and the command of all British forces in North America.

In his absence the telegraph system had been extended to the Annapolis Valley as he had directed, and when he arrived off Chebucto Head in the frigate *Arethusa* in September the news was signaled fifty miles to Windsor in something like twenty minutes. The duke was bursting with his new importance and with new ideas. The joyful Wentworth wrote: "The Duke of Kent has entered upon his command with infinite activity and ideas extremely enlarged since his departure. The arrangement in contemplation promises a plenteous circulation of money and improvement to this province. He is now residing chiefly at my house near town (i.e., the Bedford Basin lodge) which he has requested to reoccupy."

One of the duke's new ideas was the enlargement of his telegraph system beyond all previous imagination. In view of his new responsibilities as Commander in Chief of North America he had determined to carry it around the Bay of Fundy to St. John, thence up the St. John Valley to Fredericton, and eventually to Quebec. The engineers and the ax-wielding redcoats fell to work at once. Edward's enthusiasm had taken no account of the Bay of Fundy fogs, which prevented visual signaling for weeks on end, and although the chain was completed as far as Fredericton it does not seem to have been operated beyond Nova Scotia. There, however, he enjoyed it thoroughly. To test it on one occasion he made a midwinter journey to Annapolis and stayed some time at Fort Anne, receiving a stream of reports from Halifax and sending a stream of orders in return.

A visitor to a Halifax barrack in the snowy January of 1800 was surprised to see preparations for a flogging—the troops drawn up in the barrack yard, the naked culprits fastened to the triangles and shivering in the bitter air, the tallest drummers in place with their long-tailed cats, the others waiting to drown the cries with the roll of their drums, the officers and the surgeon standing by. He was surprised because he knew that the duke, who insisted on confirming all courts-martial and allotting the punishments, was at the moment in Fort Anne one hundred and thirty wintry miles away. But the explanation was simple. The commander in chief was about to flog his men "by telegraph"!

Edward's new siphon into the British Treasury poured money into his hands. He commenced new barracks on George's Island, built a mansion called Bellevue on Spring Garden Road for his general's residence, and bought Navy Island, in Bedford Basin, to be used as the site of a hospital for infectious diseases. He had a passion for punctuality and another for mechanical toys. Wherever he went in the world his quarters were cluttered with music boxes, artificial singing birds, toy organs with dancing horses, and watches and clocks of all kinds, especially those that rang chimes or played a tune. These mingled passions led to another structure in Halifax, a clock tower on the town side of Citadel Hill with a dial on each of its four sides and bells ringing to remind the idle citizen or soldier of the passing hour. The clock did not arrive until long after Edward's departure. It was installed in 1803 and it remains today the chief memento of the royal martinet and perhaps the best known feature of the city.

The duke's example created a new flurry of building activity in the town. Merchants were building finer homes and bigger stores; even common folk were improving their tenements, and the inevitable fires in a compact wooden town from time to time swept away acres of old hovels and made space for something better. In the year 1800 the duke, always in demand for these occasions, laid cornerstones for the "Round Church" (St. George's) on Brunswick Street, a Freemason's Hall, and—not least—Government House, the new residency of Sir John and Lady Wentworth.

Thus the Wentworths won again, and the Nova Scotia Legislature which had hoped to use its money for a decent House of Assembly had to go on meeting in a rented wooden building near the site of the present post office. The new Government House was situated much farther south, facing Hollis Street, with its rear towards the old town burial ground. There it stands today (but with its main entrance changed to Barrington Street), a handsome example of Georgian architecture and one of the show places of the city.

It was supposed to cost £10,500—that was the figure voted by the reluctant assembly—but canny John and ambitious Frances revealed more extravagant ideas as the building rose, indeed long after it was supposedly finished, and the final cost including furniture and equipment was little short of £30,000, a very large sum in the Nova Scotia of their time. Into its construction went "free-stone from Cape Breton, Antigonish and Pictou, cut-stone from Lunenburg and Lockeport, red flagstone from Antigonish, blue rubble stone from Bedford Basin, flat stone from Northwest Arm; red pine timber from Annapolis and Tatamagouche, white and yellow pine from Cornwallis, sand from Shelburne and Eastern Passage, great quantities of small brick from Dartmouth, of large brick and lead from England, slate from Scotland and lime from New Brunswick." Thus if every Bluenose taxpayer found Sir John's powerful fingers in his pocket there was at least one compensation: practically every part of the province was represented in the structure.

But long before Government House was finished, in fact soon after that ceremonious laying of the cornerstone, the great friend of the Wentworths took his departure. The duke's ambitions had strayed across the sea, where the union of Britain and Ireland was about to take place. Fancying the post of commander in chief in the emerald isle, Edward demanded another leave to England, this time pleading a bilious illness. The recall came in August 1800 and away he went with Madame St. Laurent, never to return, leaving eleven of his soldiers under sentence of death for mutiny and desertion.

Three days after he sailed, these unfortunates, dressed in white and accompanied by the garrison chaplain, a Roman Catholic priest and a wagon full of coffins, were paraded with the whole garrison to the Common. Eight of the men were reprieved in the very shadow of the gallows; the others swung in the summer sun, a grim reminder of the princely martinet who so shortly before had gone down smiling to his boat through a throng of cheering townsfolk. Thus opened the nineteenth century for Halifax.

18.
1800–1807

Fires and fire companies. Judge Croke. Captain Marryat. A visit from Tom Moore. Indiscipline in the fleet. The Rockingham Club. The Leopard–Chesapeake *affair.*

THE DUKE OF KENT DID NOT GET HIS APPOINTMENT to Ireland. Instead, after cooling his ambitious heels in the shadow of his father's displeasure for many months, he was ordered to his old post at Gibraltar; and the king told him sourly, "Now, sir, when you go to Gibraltar do not make such a trade of it as when you went to Halifax!" Edward's expenditures in Nova Scotia had appalled the British Government no less than his father, and when they patched up a brief uneasy peace with Napoleon in 1801 they made haste to cut to the bone their commitments across the sea. The fleet was withdrawn, the garrison reduced, and the great telegraph system abandoned, all but the stations along Halifax harbor.

Halifax celebrated the peace with an illumination of its windows and turned to pick up the pieces of prewar trade, a matter of great difficulty at a time when Napoleon obviously was planning new conquests and when the trading nations—even the neutral United States—had felt only too recently the scourge of his privateers. Halifax town and countryside were full of discharged and penniless soldiers and seamen, the great merchants tightened the strings of their moneybags, and to cap all there was an epidemic of smallpox and an outbreak of destructive fires.

A succession of such fires in the lower town in 1801 caused the chief townsmen to form the Sun Fire Company, probably the first volunteer company in Halifax. Hitherto fire fighting had been done chiefly by the soldiers and engines of the garrison. As time went on it became fashionable to belong to a volunteer company; the Phoenix, the Hand-in-Hand, and the Heart-in-Hand companies were formed, and every gentleman kept in readiness his leather cap and bucket. They fought the fires with their buckets, their quaint hand-pumped engines, and their leaky leather hose, while the troops of the garrison formed lines to keep back the crowd and prevent looting.

The population in 1802 was over eighty-five hundred, living in something like one thousand dwellings in Halifax town and peninsula, and most of them wondering whence their next shilling was to come. During the six years of Prince Edward's reign every available man and boy had been drawn from his normal occupation to the military works. Now all was at an end. But the golden crust of Halifax, the circle of well-salaried officials and the war-enriched merchants and speculators still managed to do themselves well. Some already had copied the prince and built villas along the Bedford Basin shore. Others, like the Wentworths, had country estates on the Dartmouth side; one of these was the wealthy and popular Jewish merchant Samuel Hart, who purchased Maroon Hall and its thousand acres after Quarrell's departure and entertained there on a kingly scale.

Still others were purchasing or extending estates on the peninsula itself, in the fields and copses towards the Northwest Arm. One such was Judge (later Sir Alexander) Croke, the brilliant, grasping, and cynical Englishman whose influence had procured him the Court of Vice-Admiralty at Halifax at a time when prizes were blowing into the port on almost every wind. He purchased a thirty-acre estate which he called Studley after his English home, a fine spot commanding a view of the Northwest Arm and dotted with beautiful bowers in which the judge spent his spare time painting and composing essays in verse.

Croke soon had a seat on the council, and for the duration of the Napoleonic Wars he wielded a powerful and sinister influence in the affairs of the province. His most notable effort was the ordinance which made the government-subsidized King's College a preserve of the established church, shutting out all students who would not subscribe to the Thirty-nine Articles. This bit of bigotry outraged even the ultra-Tory Bishop Inglis, who protested in vain, and for his pains was lampooned in one of Croke's privately circulated "poems." Entitled "The Cure for Love," it portrayed the good bishop (an elderly gentleman of impeccable repute) engaged in making amorous advances to a young Halifax lady on a horseback ride. The girl rejected him with such spirit that he fell off his horse into a muddy pool—this was the "cure." There was said to be some foundation for the gibe; but foundation or none it went the rounds of the drawing rooms and aroused a storm of mingled laughter and indignation.

The indignation Croke did not mind. He despised Halifax society and made this known in a long and indelicate string of verses setting forth (with names thinly disguised) the real or imagined peccadilloes of its most prominent ladies and gentlemen. This also went the rounds, and was copied carefully for reference; it did not improve his popularity. However, Croke had powerful connections in England, his position was secure, and he went on drawing his salary and fees at the rate of £4000 or so a year for fourteen years, and then departed, unwept, unhonored, and unsung—but rich—like many another official before him. His bigotry had forced King's College into an unfortunate position from which it did not emerge for many years, and in the long run he made possible the very thing he was trying to prevent—a college (Dalhousie) open to students of all faiths and creeds. By a twist of fate both colleges live today in harmony upon the grounds of his old estate. The liaison must give his ghost some very uneasy moments.

In the spring of 1803 the brief unhappy Peace of Amiens came to an end and again Halifax knew the turmoil of the great war, which was to go on with increasing range and violence for another twelve years. In the light of sad experience with Napoleon's vigorous forces the British army changed its drill, its tactics, and its dress—and cut its hair. Away went the long-familiar breeches, gaiters, cocked hats, and pigtails. The regiments in garrison at Halifax appeared in trousers, red tunics, and tall shakos, cumbersome enough in modern eyes but a vast improvement in 1805. A new regiment of provincial troops, the Nova Scotia Fencibles, was raised and equipped to replace the disbanded Royal Nova Scotia Regiment; and for the first time the militia was placed on a solid footing with new arms and equipment and a system of regular training and inspection throughout the province.

The Duke of Kent's town residence became a military hospital. Fort Needham, covering the Dockyard and the Narrows, was patched up anew. A barrack for the Royal Military Artificers went up on Sackville Street. To cover the town's approach by the Windsor road a large new blockhouse appeared on the spur overlooking the hamlet of Fairview. One McAlpine, an old loyalist soldier, kept a wayside tavern near this spot called "Edward's Valley Inn," and the post became known as Fort McAlpine.

But these were petty works compared with the duke's vast schemes. In truth the British Government had seen the absurdity of a serious French attempt on Halifax so long as Nelson and his immortal "band of brothers" kept the sea, and after 1803 all attention was given to its function as a naval base. Halifax was practically given over to the Royal Navy. The streets were thronged with lively tars, the ballroom floors with gallant officers in blue. Captain Marryat was on the Halifax station during these wars and the town has notable mention in his books. It was here that exuberant young "Frank Mildmay" (who was Marryat himself) reported his meeting with "Sir Hurricane Humbug" and his biological notions, and here that the Philadelphia damsels visited the man-o'-war and "Miss Jemima" suffered a smear of paint on "the western side of her gown."

"Mildmay" described as follows a common experience in the fleet:

> *The frigate I was to join came into the harbour soon after I reached Halifax. This I was sorry for, as I found myself in very good quarters. I had letters of introduction to the best families. The place is proverbial for hospitality; and the society of the young ladies, who are both virtuous and lovely, tended in some degree to polish the rough and libertine manners which I had contracted in my career. I was a great flirt among them and would willingly have spent more time in their company. When the ship was ordered to Quebec I ran around to say adieu to all my dear Acadian friends. A tearful eye, a lock of hair, a hearty shake of a fair hand were all the spoils…and I cast many a longing, lingering look behind as the ship glided out of the harbour. I dispensed my usual quantum of vows of eternal love and my departure was marked in the calendar of Halifax as a black day by at least seven or eight pairs of blue eyes.*

Not all the girls were left to languish in this manner. Wedding bells rang merrily in Halifax steeples throughout these wars, and many a dashing young man in blue carried off an "Acadian" bride with the blessing of her proud parents and, not infrequently, a handsome allowance from the parental money chest. The young men in blue were not averse to marrying money as well as good looks in a town where all the nice girls loved the sailor, and one of the phenomena of Halifax for a hundred years was the number of daughters of the well to do who married naval husbands and followed them across the seas. In this way many a Halifax fortune, carefully acquired in Britain's wars, departed at last to the land of its source like the waters of same golden fountain returning to the basin at its foot.

Not every visitor was so pleasantly impressed as Marryat. In 1804 young Tam Moore, at the end of his long tour of America, paused at Halifax on the way home. Governor Wentworth entertained him handsomely and took him for a carriage drive to Windsor, where the Irish bard inspected King's College and left an inscribed copy of Lucian for the library. He was pleased with the countryside but like a good many others found the rocky coast oppressive. On leaving for England in HMS *Boston* he dashed off these uncomplimentary lines:

With triumph this morning, o Boston, I hail
The stir of thy deck and the spread of thy sail,
For they tell me I soon shall be wafted in thee
To the flourishing isle of the brave and the free,
And that chill Nova Scotia's unpromising strand
Is the last I shall tread of American land.

As always, the pleasant and profitable bustle created by the fleet had its sting. Under the rule of Admiral Mitchell the press gangs reached a new height of impudence and violence. The townsmen armed themselves in self-defense; heads were cracked, and sometimes there was pistol play. The magistrates tried to assert the civil law and on one occasion laid a heavy fine upon the high-handed admiral. But Mitchell had married a daughter of R. J. Uniacke, Attorney General of Nova Scotia and a power in the Court of Vice-Admiralty. The press went on, not only in the town but in and outside the harbor, where merchant ships were robbed of their ablest seamen and many a luckless fisherman was taken out of his boat and carried off in His Majesty's ships.

The bad food, the miserable pay, the harsh discipline, the presence of so many impressed men in the lower decks, all produced a spirit of incipient mutiny which flamed from time to time on warships in the port. Always it was crushed without mercy. The savage custom of "flogging round the fleet" was frequently employed, and more than one offender was flogged to death in the process. Luckier were those condemned to death outright. On these occasions the Halifax waterfront witnessed seamen hoisted to the yardarm with the fatal noose about their necks, amid the roll of drums and with the whole ship's company perched in the rigging and ranged along the decks by order, to watch their shipmates die. The bodies of these poor fellows, daubed with tar to hold off the crows, later dangled and ratted in chains slung from the gibbets on Mauger's Beach as a warning to all seamen passing in or out of the port.

But if the discipline aboard ship was harsh there was little or none ashore. After long weeks at sea the men were like uncaged animals as soon as they set foot to the quay. Some found vent for their pent-up spirits in jolly parties touring the town from tavern to tavern; others more strenuous found a savage satisfaction in tearing down fences, gates, shutters, and shop signs and smashing the few feeble lanterns perched on poles about the streets. Some, having exhausted the delights of the bawdyhouses, proceeded to beat the harpies and destroy their premises, a sport which frequently involved tussles with the firemen and fighting it out at last with the garrison's town-guard.

The practice of emptying jails in England and elsewhere to supply short-handed men-o'-war put an evil leaven in many a crew. The port suffered the attentions of groups and sometimes whole ships' companies of toughs and thugs in naval dress. Rape, theft, and assault by His Majesty's seamen were so common as to become accepted evils of the war. The only naval personnel on duty in the streets were the press gangs, who liked a riot themselves. The sober middle-class Haligonian made his way to church or countinghouse in the midst of all this brawling and brotheldom, and kept his womenfolk off the streets after dark. The well to do, aloof behind the high walls of their town houses or upon their peaceful suburban estates, remained oblivious of it all. Secure in the presence of naval officers in their drawing rooms, they held their teas, card parties, and routs as if on another planet. One chronicler wrote: "Balls were almost a daily occurrence with such a show of beauty as hardly any other town could exhibit. The dazzling white shoulders of the Archdeacon's daughters, the bright eyes and elegant figures of the four Miss Cunards, the fair complexions and sweet expressions of the four Miss Uniackes all whirled before one, happy with the arm of a red or blue-coated gallant incircling their waists."

In 1805, the year of Trafalgar, Sir John and Lady Wentworth moved into their handsome new residency from the lodge at Bedford Basin. The empty barracks of the prince's guard at that rustic retreat then became the seat of the exclusive Rockingham Club, composed of Wentworth, the members of His Majesty's Council, the admiral, the commander of the garrison, several well-connected army and navy officers, and a number of Halifax gentry. It was a partly literary but largely social affair, and on summer afternoons and evenings the members and their ladies sat on the long piazza beside the water, enjoying the music, the refreshments, and the view. The artist Robert Field, who flourished in Halifax from 1808 to 1818, painted many of the Rockingham members, whose portraits hung in the long assembly room of the clubhouse after the fashion of the famous Kit-cat Club in London.

The Wentworths now were at their zenith, holding court at Government House with regal display and almost regal power. The control of appointments and privileges in the public service of Halifax and the province was largely in the hands of Sir John and he made the most of it from the start, filling the council with his personal friends (including his own son), finding lucrative posts for others (including his brother-in-law), and seeing that all manner of officials—from the judge of oyer and terminer to Phoebe Moody, the poor widow who looked after the Sambro lighthouse—regarded his government with favor.

The impotent House of Assembly was growing restive under this regime. Its spokesman was the fiery Cottnam Tonge, "the first tribune of Nova Scotia," the man who paved the way for Joseph Howe. The old wooden assembly room on Hollis Street rang with his bitter eloquence. The little political world of Halifax was divided into two parties; the reactionaries led by Sir John, who ruled the town and province for their own advantage in His Majesty's name, and the townsmen and farmers who were slowly groping their way towards responsible government with Tonge (pronounced "tongue") at their head. The struggle became a personal war between Wentworth and Tonge that went on for years and formed the perennial topic in kitchens and drawing rooms—and in Wentworth's dispatches to London.

Wentworth labored according to his light, which was the light of an exiled loyalist who had seen revolution triumphant in the other colonies and had a genuine interest in the loyalty and welfare of Nova Scotia, but who also was weak, a tool in the hands of his mercenary friends and especially in the hands of his clever and expensive wife. Yet if he blinded himself to the rights of common folk at home he had at least a clear eye abroad, and he was one of the first to see the thundercloud arising from the south.

The captains of His Majesty's fleet, not content with robbing provincial merchantmen of their crews, had begun overhauling American ships and treating them in the same way. The excuse was that many seamen in American vessels were deserters from the Royal Navy. This was true, for impressed men escaped at any chance, and the Americans, doing a thriving trade with all the belligerents, were able to offer high wages as well as the supposed protection of their flag. But British captains were none too scrupulous when short of hands, and as early as 1805 Admiral Mitchell's ships were seizing American citizens on the high seas and carrying them into Halifax as seamen in the lower decks. Wentworth, seeing where this led, protested to London and urged Mitchell to release the men—but all in vain.

The fleet persisted in its fatuous policy, and in 1807 there was an act of supreme folly when HMS *Leopard* actually fired upon the United States warship *Chesapeake* and seized a number of her men. The *Leopard* carried these into Halifax, where two were found to be British and still rebellious against a forced service in the Royal Navy. They were tried at a court-martial aboard the flagship *Belle Isle*, a seventy-four-gun warship still bearing scars from Trafalgar. Both men were convicted of "mutiny, desertion and contempt." One was sentenced to death by hanging, from a yardarm of His Majesty's sloop of war *Halifax*. The other died more slowly and painfully. His sentence was "flogging thro' the fleet." This meant hundreds of lashes, apportioned to the number of His Majesty's ships in the harbor. The victim was taken by boat from one to another, to receive the allotted strokes of a cat-o'-nine-tails. Usually he fainted or perished long before the round was complete, and his senseless body was hoisted aboard the remaining ships, tied to a grating, and lashed according to the sentence. All of this took place in full sight of the people along the harborside on a bright summer morning, none of them aware that they were seeing history in the making. This *Chesapeake* affair, above all other incidents, pointed straight to the War of 1812.

19.
1807–1812

Decline and fall of the Wentworths. The intrigue of Aaron Burr. Smuggling supplies to Wellington. The money-makers and the poor. The Columbine *mutineers. Jordan the Pirate. The building of Province House. The state of fleet and garrison. The problem of explosives.* Shannon *and* Chesapeake.

THE OMINOUS ECHOES OF THE *CHESAPEAKE* INCIDENT were not lost upon the authorities in Britain. Downing Street counted heavily on the self-interest of the New England merchants who were busy making money out of American neutrality, but was aware of the rising power of the "war hawk" party at Washington who were all for seizing Canada while Britain was locked in the struggle with Napoleon. It was decided that a show of British force should be made on the west side of the Atlantic, using Halifax as a base. Warships, troops, and transports arrived from Britain; and, as it seemed wise to have a soldier in the governor's seat at Halifax, Prevost brought with him a blunt notice of dismissal to the aging Sir John. This was tempered by a recommendation to the Provincial Assembly that Wentworth be pensioned for the rest of his life.

Reluctantly the Assembly granted £500 a year, to which the home government added £600 later on. Thus ended the florid reign of the Wentworths. In the spring of 1808 Sir John and his lady withdrew to the Bedford Basin lodge and the soldier Prevost moved into Government House, which he described as "an edifice out of all proportion to the situation and the cause of my predecessor's reduced circumstances, notwithstanding his income derived from his situation of Surveyor of Woods."

The new commander at once began to reorganize the provincial militia and dispatched Postmaster John Howe, the old loyalist, to travel secretly through the American seaboard states and report on the sentiment and preparation for war. Prevost received a secret traveler himself—none other than Aaron Burr—who came to Halifax in June 1808 under the alias of "Mr. Edwards." Government House has seen some odd characters and heard some queer conversations in its time, but its very stones must have crackled with astonishment when Burr, the dashing hero of the American Revolution, the adroit politician, the former Vice-President of the United States, the man who had killed Alexander Hamilton in a duel, sat in a chair and unfolded to Prevost and Admiral Warren a fantastic scheme for the seizure of Florida and other Spanish possessions on the southern border of the American republic.

The details of the scheme remain a mystery, for Prevost and Warren promptly bundled Burr off to London with an introduction to the great Castlereagh, and if his ideas were committed to paper that paper is lost, or buried in the Foreign Office archives. Prevost himself seems actually to have contemplated a descent on Florida with his troops and ships, but London did not approve. Late in 1808 the expedition sailed down the American seaboard to the West Indies, concluded its show of force with an attack on the French island of Martinique, and returned to Halifax in the spring of 1809.

To Sir John Wentworth, nursing his self-esteem and his ailing lady in the Basin lodge, the expedition had an ironic note; for his old political enemy Tonge went off with Prevost, accepted a post in fever-haunted Demerara, and never came back to Nova Scotia. There was another bit of irony. In the absence of the new lieutenant governor in the West Indies the affairs of Nova Scotia were in the hands of the senior justice—the detestable Dr. Croke—who made full use of his brief authority to advance his reactionary theories and measures and eventually to claim half the lieutenant governor's salary. To the long-suffering Haligonians the short leap from Wentworth (whom they despised) to Croke (whom they hated) was a leap from frying pan to fire. Fortunately the fire soon went out.

Britain was now engaged in the long and arduous campaign in Portugal and Spain which was to place the name of Wellington on everybody's lips as Nelson's had been a few years before. This produced a queer anomaly in British affairs. For while the British troops in Spain depended heavily on supplies purchased in the United States, the Royal Navy (flushed with success since Trafalgar and swollen to an enormous size) was flouting American rights on the high seas and steering a direct course to war. The first result of this was an American embargo on supplies to Europe—a blow aimed straight at the British army's stomach.

And so began a strange and prosperous trade out of Halifax, the transshipment of American supplies to Wellington. New England merchants loaded cargoes ostensibly for non-European ports and transferred them at sea to Nova Scotian bottoms, which then ran Napoleon's "blockade" (a multitude of nimble privateers) to Spain. A leader in this business was the Halifax merchant Enos Collins, whose career was a romance in itself.

Collins was of the Yankee stock that settled in Nova Scotia before the Revolution. He had begun his career as a privateersman raiding the French West Indies and the Spanish Main in the closing years of the eighteenth century. A man of keen insight and ruthless energy, he soon commanded a ship of his own in the West Indies trade and before long moved to Halifax, operating a shipping business and taking an increasing hand in the financial affairs of the port. The great war provided first-rate opportunities for the amassing of wealth. Such a torrent of specie came into Collins' coffers through his swiftly growing enterprises that long before Waterloo he and his partners virtually controlled the finances of Halifax and the province.

They were not alone in money-making, however. The war was pouring a golden river into Halifax and there was room for many a diligent bucket. In the Vice-Admiralty Court, as we have seen, Judge Croke was doing extremely well on his salary and fees. So was Richard Uniacke, the one-time rebel, now a sedate conservative holding the post of advocate general to this court. Ships and cargoes of many nations, taken prize by the navy and the busy Bluenose privateers, came under their jurisdiction. In one three-year period of the war Uniacke's fees alone amounted to £50,000. So it went down the scale through the army and navy contractors and the host of petty officials and other land sharks to the busy dramsellers and prostitutes. (Dramsellers' licenses were £6 each, and the town collected £1400 in a single year.)

A Committee on Trade functioned busily, for the trade of Halifax was now the war itself, the greatest business in the world. In 1809 the Fire Insurance Association was formed. So was the Marine Insurance Company. Even the churches were prosperous. St. Peter's was enlarged and equipped with a fine new organ all the way from England. St. Paul's received an addition to the north end, including a new steeple and the bells whose sound is so familiar to the Haligonian of today. The "Round Church" (St. George's), begun in 1799, was completed in 1811; and in the following year St. Matthew's was enlarged.

But all this prosperity was poorly shared. At the top of the human scale twenty or thirty officials and merchants made enormous fortunes. Lesser officials and the middle class were comfortable enough. Yet in the year ending February 9, 1811, in the midst of war prosperity, one in every four Haligonians subsisted on the firewood, sugar, tea, rice, flour and bread distributed by a society for the relief of the poor. These were indeed days when "the world was for the few—and the very few."

Prevost's redcoats turned the town scarlet for a time and then thinned away. Even the Duke of Kent's old regiment, the 7th Fusiliers, stationed so long in Halifax that they were part of it, went off to fight with Wellington. Many had Halifax wives and children, who departed with the regiment to follow the drum through Portugal and Spain. The duke's great defenses, neglected for years, were sloughing to ruin under the successive frosts and thaws. Britain was staking the defense of Halifax, her lone naval base north of Bermuda, upon the strength of the fleet itself. The press gangs were busier than ever, and fishermen and coasters were afraid to come to town. Gay Halifax yachting parties passing McNab's Island could see the bodies of the mutineers of HMS *Columbine* rotting on the gibbets, and one of the sights of the Point Pleasant walk was the sun-bleached skeleton of Jordan the pirate, dangling in chains a few rods past the Kissing Bridge.

Gangs of French prisoners could be seen working on the Sambro road, the St. Margaret's Bay road, the road to Preston, and the road to Truro, guarded by squads of bored redcoats. Haligonians young and old visited the prison on Melville Island frequently to see the foreigners at work, to purchase the little bone ship models and souvenirs which at one time graced every Halifax mantelpiece, to take music or dancing lessons, or to polish their drawing-room French. The old habit of flinging slops and garbage into the Halifax streets was now curbed by an act: "All persons in the town are bound to keep the gutters and streets before the houses and land occupied by them clear and free from nuisances, under a penalty of twenty shillings for each and every offence." And the act was evidently enforced, for tavern keepers complained that farmers and countrymen were under the absolute necessity of leaving their sleds and teams in the streets before the premises of petitioners.

In 1810 the Wentworths departed for England, leaving a multitude of debts and memories. England always had been the spiritual home of Lady Wentworth and the actual home of her exquisite son, who had gone back there after a brief brush with the crudities of life in Nova Scotia as a member of the council. All her adult life Frances had delighted in the aura of royalty, and when Sir John found a country house at £400 a year in the shadow of Windsor Castle (Sunning Hill) she was content there to end her days.

The soldier-governor Prevost had been too busy soldiering to govern very much, and in 1811 off he went to govern Lower Canada and eventually to bury his sorry military reputation by the shore of Lake Champlain. His last act before leaving Halifax was to lay the cornerstone of Province House, the long-delayed home of the legislature, amid a great throng of troops and townsfolk and to the boom of cannon, the rattle of muskets, and the blare of bands. The name of the architect remains uncertain—according to one source it was "Richard Scott, Esquire"—but whoever he was he achieved a miracle of proportion and design. Estimated to cost £20,000, Province House was eight years a-building amid the rising costs of war and the final bill was over £52,000, a horrid extravagance to the taxpayers. But it stands today a thing of beauty and a joy for centuries if not forever, dwarfed by the taller modern buildings all about it, a little gray gem in the heart of Mammon.

In Prevost's place came Sir John Coape Sherbrooke, a capable man and the one to see Nova Scotia through the War of 1812. When he arrived in 1811 the smell of powder was already in the air, for in May the United States frigate *President* had encountered the British sloop *Little Belt* at sea and without warning fired a broadside that killed sixteen and wounded twenty-one of her men. The attack was said to have resulted from a misunderstanding, but clearly it was an act of revenge for the *Leopard–Chesapeake* affair. To the more superstitious townsmen other signs of trouble were not wanting. Early in September a mysterious comet was seen in the sky. A few weeks later the whole coast was ravaged by a hurricane. But a real cause for alarm was the ancient truth that weakness invites attack. Canada looked an easy prize while Britain was heavily engaged in Europe, and all the gossip from the United States was of preparations for attack by land and sea.

With this threat staring him in the face, the startled Sherbrooke found himself in charge of a "fortress" whose defenses had been neglected for a decade and were in fact tumbling down. The Duke of Kent's great telegraph chain, abandoned outside Halifax in 1802, had fallen to pieces, and the long avenue cut through the forest towards Quebec was choked with another growth of trees and bush. The corps of expert signalers had vanished. Indeed the whole garrison of Halifax was barely enough to fill St. Paul's at a church parade. As for the fleet on which so much depended, it was customary for His Majesty's ships on the Halifax station to depart for the more delightful air of Bermuda in late November, not to return until the following June. Occasionally one or two wintered at Halifax or arrived in early spring. For months on end the sole upholder of Britannia's trident at Halifax was *Centurion,* the famous old ship in which Lord Anson circumnavigated the globe in 1741-44. She had long since been condemned for sea service, and was in fact anchored and "aground on her own beef bones" off the Dockyard, where she acted as receiving ship for the station. In these circumstances opened the War of 1812.

President Madison chose his moment in June. American armies promptly marched over the border of Upper Canada and a host of Yankee privateers put out into the Atlantic. The first news of the war for many a British merchant skipper was the capture of his ship and cargo on the high seas. For Nova Scotia it was the sudden attack on HMS *Belvedere,* a frigate of the Halifax station, by an American squadron under Commodore Rodgers. By good luck and seamanship Captain Richard Byron of the *Belevedere* managed to get away to Halifax, bringing with him three American merchant ships he had picked up on the run.

At once there was a furious stir. Kent's old earthworks and bastions on Citadel Hill were hastily repaired, the Martello tower at Point Pleasant was improved and armed with new cannon, a Martello tower with walls five to six feet thick was completed on George's Island. And now came to light for the first time the problem which has plagued the life of Halifax ever since 1749, that of storing explosives for the garrison and fleet.

For many years the King's ships entering port had anchored off George's Island and stored their powder in a wooden magazine outside the rampart of the island fort, "a very improper situation" as one officer mildly pointed out. This flimsy building, which held twelve hundred barrels of gunpowder, not to mention shells, bombs, rockets, and other explosive munitions of the time, stood less than eighty yards from the rampart with several guns pointing over it—a giant firecracker in the heart of the anchorage.

This arrangement was altered when the *Belvedere* brought her damaged hull and alarming news into port, but the change was no improvement.

An engineer who inspected the defenses in July 1812 concluded his report with the ominous remark that the greater part of the powder now was stored in the old hulk *Inflexible* (dignified by the title of "floating magazine") and the rest in a wooden shed at Fort Massey, the blockhouse at the south end of Queen Street. This would not do, of course! Sherbrooke built at once a big stone magazine inside the earthworks of the Citadel, capable of holding 1344 barrels of powder. For generations this remained the garrison's powder store, and for generations the squat green cone of Citadel Hill loomed over the town like Vesuvius over Pompeii, a smiling monster with havoc in its bowels.

The population of Halifax in 1812 was about ten thousand, most of whom firmly believed that the Royal Navy was invincible. For fifteen years or more the British world had been glutted with naval victory. The magic of Nelson's name still hung in the sea air. If anyone had told them in the spring of 1812 that Britain had far more ships than she could maintain, that the ships on the North American station in particular were undergunned and seriously undermanned, that many were rotten, that few had enjoyed a home refit in years, and that none was fit to fight against an American ship of comparable size, he would in all probability have been hanged or confined as a seditious traitor.

On the other hand if he had pointed out that the American men-o'-war, though few, were mostly well-found and speedy frigates, each carrying more and heavier guns than British ships of the same rate, each fully manned by volunteers—bold and skillful seamen all—and that in single combat, ship to ship, the odds were all on the American, they would have laughed in his face. The first lesson came quickly.

In August 1812, HM frigate *Guerriere* of thirty-eight guns, on her way to Halifax for a refit, encountered the US frigate *Constitution* of forty-four guns and promptly closed to fight. In two hours *Guerriere* was a gutted wreck, with seventy-eight of her crew of three hundred killed or wounded, including her captain and first lieutenant. She surrendered, the first of several British frigates to undergo this melancholy experience. The Royal Navy was thunderstruck—and so was Halifax.

Young Captain Dacres, wounded and released on parole, underwent court-martial for the loss of his ship. The court-martial took place in Halifax Harbor aboard HMS *Africa*, one of Nelson's ships at Trafalgar. Among the officers who heard Dacres' evidence was Captain Broke of

HMS *Shannon*, a zealous officer who came away eager to avenge *Guerriere*. He wrote his wife: "We must catch one of those great American ships and send her home for a show." One day he walked into the bookshop of William Minns, opposite Grand Parade, and cheerfully declared: "Well, Minns, I'm going to Boston to challenge the *Constitution*." Like most Haligonians of his time, Minns knew something of fighting ships; and the fate of young Dacres was fresh in his mind. He ventured a notion that *Shannon*'s eighteen-pounders had no chance against *Constitution*'s twenty-fours. "Ah," said Broke, "but I intend to close with her quickly—and board!" Off he went, a confident figure, to his destiny.

Broke had a private fortune and a patriotic heart. He treated his men humanely; when *Shannon* took American merchant ships, his share of the prize money went to the lower deck. But he drilled them very hard, especially in gunnery. It was not his fate to meet *Constitution*, and for months he cruised without result. Then he learned that the US frigate *Chesapeake* was just completing a refit in Boston Harbor and sent in a challenge to her captain. *Chesapeake* came out accompanied by a flotilla of Boston pleasure craft eager to watch the fight. The world knows what happened.

On a fine Halifax Sunday, June 6, 1813, someone slipped into morning service at St. Paul's and whispered to a friend. The friend departed swiftly with him. So did others within earshot, and as the whisper spread, almost the entire congregation. All Halifax was running down the steep streets to the wharves. Two ships were coming up the harbor. One girl of thirteen recalled the sight long afterwards: "The first was a little dirty black ship and the other was a fine big ship." The first was *Shannon*, worn by a three-months' cruise. The second was *Chesapeake*, with the fresh paint of her refit shining in the sun. The tall corpse of her Captain Lawrence lay on the deck covered by the folds of the surrendered Stars and Stripes. His last gallant words—"Don't give up the ship!"—are the motto of the United States Navy to this day.

The ships came slowly into the roadstead. The garrison bands marched down to the waterfront to greet them with brass and drums. The troops and people cheered. One venerable Halifax merchant was seen at the end of his wharf playing "Rule Britannia" on a vast 'cello, and capering as he played. Handkerchiefs waved. Ships in the anchorage manned their yards. Young Tom Haliburton, some day to be famous as the creator of

"Sam Slick," was one of the boys who swarmed aboard the prize; and he never forgot what he saw:

> *The coils and folds of rope were steeped in gore as if in a slaughter-house. She was a fir-built ship and her splinters had wounded nearly as many as the Shannon's shot. Pieces of skin and pendant hair were adhering to the sides of the ship, and in one place I noticed fingers protruding as if thrust through the outer wall of the frigate; while several sailors, to whom liquor had evidently been handed through the ports by visitors in boats, were lying asleep on the bloody floor as if they had fallen in action and expired where they lay.*

Broke had suffered a severe scalp wound in the scrimmage on *Chesapeake*'s deck and it was some time before he was able to walk along Barrington Street with a handkerchief bound about his head. The merchants presented him with an address and a piece of plate. The home government gave him a baronetcy. Meanwhile honor was paid to the vanquished. Lawrence's body was landed at King's Wharf under the solemn boom of minute guns from Grand Parade. The procession wound slowly up the hill and along Barrington Street with the surviving officers of *Chesapeake* behind the coffin, then officers of the garrison and Royal Navy, and a column of Halifax gentry bringing up the rear. The Stars and Stripes covered the coffin, and upon it lay Lawrence's sword and hat. Six captains of the Royal Navy carried the pall.

The burial took place in the town cemetery at the corner of Spring Garden Road and Barrington Street, with an army band playing the funeral music, the rector of St. Paul's conducting the rites, and three hundred redcoats of the 64th Regiment firing a salute over the grave. Lawrence himself was the son of a loyalist; and when, a few weeks later, the coffin was exhumed and shipped to New York for final burial in Trinity churchyard, his body passed from British to United States soil for the second and last time.

20.
1813–1815

The trident of Britannia. Moral conditions. Pushing the war with the United States. The conqueror of Washington. The Negro problem again. The Castine expedition. News of Waterloo. The first police court and constables.

FOR HALIFAX THE CAPTURE OF THE *CHESAPEAKE* WAS the great event of 1813—an exciting year. Britain, aware now of the great danger to Canada, sent out what troops she could spare for its defense. Some of these, after a long wintry voyage in the teeth of the westerlies, landed at Halifax in January and February. They marched away along the snowy road to Annapolis, took ship over the Bay of Fundy to St. John, and proceeded on snowshoes up the St. John Valley and through the forests of Quebec. It was an epic journey, deserving a better place than it has been given in histories of the war. When the snow was off the ground in May, these troops were followed by De Watteville's regiment of Germans.

But Britain had no intention of fighting a large-scale war in the interior of the continent, where the Americans had the advantage of short communications and the Royal Navy could not make itself felt. Twenty years of struggle with republican France had taught Britannia how to exert her sea power to the full, and the enormous fleet built up to strangle a continent on one side of the Atlantic could be moved easily to the other.

And so Britannia shifted the trident to the other hand. A multitude of British naval craft, large and small, appeared in the western Atlantic, using the bases of Halifax and Bermuda. The eastern seaboard of the United States came under stiff and stiffer blockade, and finally under attack. For as Napoleon's armies faded away on the plains of Russia and in the fields of Germany, Spain, and Austria, it became possible to shift whole brigades of British veteran troops across the sea.

Thus from 1813 onwards Halifax became the rendezvous of fleets and troops on a scale hitherto unimagined. The harbor was alive with men-o'-war and transports, American prizes gathered by the Royal Navy, and the bold and skillful Nova Scotia privateers. (One small privateer schooner alone sent in thirty-three American ships.) And to the swarm of French prisoners at Melville Island and in the hulks there was added such a multitude of captured Americans that at one time Lord Bathurst seriously advocated their removal up the coast to Louisburg for the safety of the fortress.

By 1814 the long war-borne prosperity of Halifax had reached a golden peak that cast its reflected gleams into every part of the province. Farmer, fisherman, woodsman, artisan, all had a fat and constant market for their produce in this fabulous town. The coterie of leading merchants and officials, rich as rajahs, entertained officers of the fleet and army with almost oriental lavishness. There was the usual sorry side. If prosperity had reached its height, dissipation had found the depths. Day and night drunken redcoats and seamen reeled about the streets with shrieking trollops from Barrack Street and "the Beach." Fighting between the navy's press gangs and the townsmen was barely noticed in the general hubbub; but one cold day in January 1813 there was a brawl on the Market Wharf between soldiers and civilians that went from fists to bayonets and ended with blood on the snow. Five civilians were stabbed, one fatally. A civil court found one soldier guilty of murder, but once again the townsmen were reminded that a civilian had no rights. Sherbrooke obtained a royal pardon for the murderer, and that was that.

"The upper streets were full of brothels. Grog-shops and dancing-houses were to be seen in every part of the town. A portion of Grafton Street was known as Hogg Street from a house of ill fame kept by a person of that name. The upper street (i.e., Brunswick or 'Barrack' Street) was known as 'Knock Him Down Street' in consequence of the affrays and even murders committed there. No person of character ventured to reside there; nearly all the buildings were occupied as brothels for the soldiers and sailors. The streets of this part of the town presented continually the disgusting sight of abandoned females of the lowest class in a state of drunkenness, bare-headed, without shoes, and in the most filthy and abominable condition."

All this, be it noted, was within a good bottle-throw of Argyle Street with its fine mansions and shady willows, within a shout of St. Peter's and St. Paul's. And all the seepage of that wallowing slum known as "the Hill"—enclosed by Brunswick, Albemarle (now called Market) and Grafton streets—came down with the rains into the ornate gardens and spotless cellar kitchens of Argyle and Barrington and the busy counting-houses of Granville and Hollis, to mingle at last with the fetid mud of Water Street. The town was not so much a whited sepulcher as a gilded chamber pot. Disease, many-faced and many-armed, stalked and slew. As a climax, the smallpox turned up again in the winter of 1814-15 and soldier, sailor, tinker, tailor perished by scores.

Still, the churches and the society for the relief of the poor went quietly about their work. The noble-hearted former soldier Bromley established his Acadian School for poor whites, Negroes, and Indians. The printer Holland founded a newspaper, the *Acadian Recorder*, which lived for more than a century. The building of Province House went on steadily. So did a fine stone residence for the admiral, still known as Admiralty House, which stands in the naval grounds facing Gottingen Street. Afar in England, Frances Wentworth died; and old Sir John came back like a ghost, almost unknown in this roaring mob of strangers, to end his days boarding here and there in the scene of his royal triumphs and his royal cuckoldom.

The late spring of 1814 brought tremendous news. Napoleon had fallen and was banished to Elba, and the allied armies were in Paris. The twenty-year war with France was at an end. The news came, on a Sunday and the celebration was postponed to the next day—a grand military review, much firing of cannon in the anchorage and forts, a regimental band blaring patriotic airs from the flat roof of the market house, vast dinners and windy speeches in the Exchange Coffee House and other inns, and in the evening every house lit from cellar to garret as part of the general "illumination." Crowds milled in the streets until a late hour, feeling pleased but doubtless wondering what would happen next. It was astonishing to think that a whole generation of Haligonians had grown from birth to maturity knowing only a time and state of war.

An exchange of prisoners commenced at once. Hundreds of French captives had melted away into the countryside during the years; but there remained a homesick multitude at Melville Island and in the hulks seeking transport to a France changed beyond anything they remembered. Governor Danseville of St. Pierre had spent twenty-one years on parole at Brook House amid his flower beds and wooded walks. Here through the slowly changing seasons he had entertained his fellow Frenchmen and many a Halifax merchant and official; and here he had enjoyed a liaison with the mysterious Margaret Floyer, said to have been the daughter of a British officer, who for fourteen years had eased the loneliness of Brook House. Now she was dead, the Bourbons were back in Paris, and the aging aristocrat went home.

And now homeward straggled scores of Haligonians, most of them seamen long captive in French prisons, some of them grown old behind the bars, leaving a melancholy list of others buried in foreign soil.

There remained a war to finish—the struggle with the United States. It would not last long now. The seaboard states had been half-hearted from the first. At one time a mysterious delegation had turned up in Halifax proposing that New England secede from the Union and join the British American colonies. And the war hawk party again and again had seen their country's armies thrown out of Canada or taken into camp as prisoners by a few brigades of redcoats and militia. Now they saw something else, the movement of Wellington's veteran regiments across the sea. It was plain that they and Madison had bet on the wrong horse in the war.

In the summer of 1814 the British began their carefully planned sea and land attacks upon the American coast. Most notable was the expedition to the Chesapeake, which defeated an American army, sent President Madison and his Cabinet scuttling into the country for their lives, seized Washington, and burnt the Capitol. This British force also took Alexandria and came within an ace of taking Baltimore, where Francis Scott Key watched "the rocket's red glare, the bombs bursting in air" and conceived the national anthem of his people. General Ross, the daring and able commander of the British forces, the first man into Washington, was killed three weeks later in the attack on Baltimore. His body was brought to Halifax and buried with military honors in the old town cemetery opposite Government House. There his bones lie all but forgotten—the man whose sword inspired not only "The Star-Spangled Banner" but that wicked little twist of *Marmion*:

> *Fly, Monroe, fly! Run, Armstrong, run!*
> *Were the last words of Madison.*

The fleet brought something else back to Halifax—the Negro problem. Several hundred slaves, men, women, and children, had escaped from the Chesapeake plantations and flocked down to the British ships, entreating the sailors to take them away to freedom. The admiral gave his consent and in September these refugees were put ashore in Halifax. The lieutenant governor found quarters for them in and about the town, where their descendants remain to this day. They were placed in charge of the commissioners of the poor, who clothed them against the coming cold weather in captured American uniforms and the regimentals of a disbanded provincial corps. The memory of these Africans cavorting about the streets in the blue and buff of the United States Army and the green and scarlet of the York Rangers was long cherished in the town.

However, the military operation which chiefly affected Halifax in the long run was a descent on Maine in September 1814 made by troops from the Halifax garrison and led by Sir John Sherbrooke in person. The invaders captured Machias, Hampden, Bangor, and Castine; indeed the whole of eastern Maine remained in their possession until the war's end. These outports of the United States had long been centers of the secret transshipment trade with Britain. And the trade not only went on uninterrupted, but grew as the months went by, the difference being that it went on openly under British occupation, with all goods solemnly cleared in and out of the Castine customhouse precisely as if Maine were a British possession.

The volume of this trade was such that, when the British troops withdrew, the collected revenue ran to thousands of pounds sterling, a tidy sum which was carried off to Halifax. By a gesture of the imperial government this "Castine Fund" was turned over to the Lieutenant Governor of Nova Scotia to be used as he saw fit for the benefit of the province. Out of it eventually came Dalhousie College.

The momentous year 1815 opened in severe cold and deep snow, with smallpox raging in the town. Peace with the United States was signed in Ghent on Christmas Eve, 1814, but it was not proclaimed in Halifax until March 3, 1815—such were the delays of the westward Atlantic passage in winter. So, too, the news of Napoleon's escape from Elba failed to reach Nova Scotia until the Little Corporal had fanned into one last fatal flame the embers of the old French war.

The news of Waterloo reached Halifax in the merchant ship *Trial*, thirty-three days after the last shot was fired on that famous field. There was another celebration, another town illumination. Subscriptions for the families of soldiers killed or wounded in the battle quickly reached £3800. There was the inevitable public dinner at Mason's Hall, with tall old Richard Uniacke in the chair. The list of toasts was long—there were exactly one hundred and one—and the affair went on far into the next morning. A friend of Uniacke's, up betimes, met the Irish giant in the street and inquired if the Waterloo dinner was over. "Not at all," laughed Uniacke. "I'm away home for my snuffbox and then back to finish the toasts!"

Perhaps the most poignant feelings about the war were those of the old loyalists and their sons and daughters, whose bitterness had been softened by the passing years until 1812, and who then found themselves for the second time at strife with the old home to the south. One of them, old Mather Byles' daughter Becky, wrote to a relative in Massachusetts in the spring of 1815: "You have, I am certain, joined me in blessings to a merciful God for once more granting us the blessing of peace. The papers of my father have given me the first thorough information I ever had of my own family. I glory in the pious and learned race from whence I sprang, and cannot help regretting that I lived at a time when it pleased an infinitely wise God to scatter us over the face of the earth." That is a cry from the heart.

And now, at the very end of the great war, when behind its prosperous façade the town had become a ceaseless Donnybrook Fair combined with all the worst features of Whitechapel and Portsmouth Hard, when no man's liberty was safe and no woman's person secure in the streets, when merchants lined their shutters with sheet iron, when housewives took in their washing if a soldier or sailor loitered nearby, when the war and its spoils had drawn to the port the scum of two continents—now at last a town police force, court, and jail were established.

The delay was no fault of the townsmen, who had suffered long. Services of this kind in a town of any size require incorporation for efficiency, and the military governors and their obedient councils persistently refused the incorporation of Halifax as if it meant the downfall of the fortress. But in 1815 the townsmen were enabled to set up a "Bridewell or House of Correction," complete with cells, in the building formerly used as a poorhouse. And a regular town police court began to function with three magistrates, chief of whom was John George Pyke.

"Mr. Pyke was allowed eleven shillings and eightpence a day, and had three police constables at his command, with the assistance of Hawkins, a coloured gentleman who, dressed in an old military uniform with cap and feathers, escorted the criminals to and from the workhouse, and when occasion required inflicted his thirty-nine lashes on juvenile offenders at the old whipping post."

These were pitiful measures, in view of the moral condition of Halifax in 1815, but at least they were a start. It should be noted that Pyke's constables were under separate authority and quite distinct from the "night watch" which had been in existence since very early days. To the passing visitor the town seemed fair enough with its well-kept main streets, its handsome new public buildings and the elegant mansions of those who had prospered in the wars. Such a visitor was Bishop Plessis of Quebec, who caught a glimpse of Halifax in the summer of Waterloo. This is what he saw, as his boat approached:

> *The most striking edifice is that containing the town clock. It is a square tower and its ground flat is occupied as a guardhouse. Its situation is extremely well chosen. Soon after this the barracks of the troops came into view, and then those of the artillery, both situated in the upper part of the town. The citadel with its flag and signal staff is visible at the same time. After this we see the steeples of the various churches and then other buildings, public as well as private, which seem to vie with each other in the beauty of their situation and the variety of their style. At last the whole city displays itself in the most advantageous manner.*
>
> *It has the form of a parallelogram placed upon the slope of a hill. Six large streets run parallel with the water; these are intersected by ten cross streets. Water Street is half a mile in length and is bordered with houses from one end to the other. The remaining streets are being built up rapidly. One could not believe it possible that such noble houses as those in the upper part of the town could be built of wood. A great number of houses are finished with a flat roof, others have flat roofs on the wings and a sloping one on the main building. One must come to Halifax to find handsome porticos, superb entrance doors and steps, broad stairways, and noble and well-furnished apartments.*

The only public building up to the present built of stone is the Governor's house. The stone is grey, is easily cut, and is here held in great repute. Some private individuals have used it to make columns from eight to ten feet in height to finish off the railings in front of their houses. With this stone they are now building a hall which will accommodate both houses of the Provincial Parliament, also another house above the dockyard for the Admiral of this station, and a third one for some officers of the Marine Department. These three edifices, now well advanced towards completion, cannot fail to greatly embellish the town.

Excepting the sidewalks the streets are not paved but are covered with a kind of gravel or coarse sand, which dries as soon as the rain ceases to fall. They are generally kept extremely clean, and in many places are ornamented on both sides by willows, from which the tops are lopped off from time to time, causing them to spread out, and thus affording as much shade as the linden and limes of Canada.

21.
1815–1820

Halifax at the time of Waterloo. Stagecoach and "team boat." Soldier settlements. "Agricola." The Earl of Dalhousie and his college. The end of an era.

HALIFAX HAD LIVED SIXTY-SIX YEARS, OF WHICH forty-four were years of war, beginning with Indian raids and ending with the news of Waterloo. Its foundation as a fortress had been justified repeatedly as the wars went on, reaching a final vindication in the clash with the United States, when almost the whole British power in North America by land and sea had turned upon this single pivot. All this had made great changes in the town and its people. The old tie with New England, so strong from 1750 to 1783, and emphasized somehow by the ingress of loyalists at the close of the Revolution, had been weakened steadily by the American attitude during the Napoleonic Wars and finally snapped by the events of 1812.

Moreover there was now a second generation of adult native-born, in whom the blood of the early Yankees, "Dutch," and loyalists was intermingled. Many of them had fought His Majesty's enemies on land and sea in the course of the past ten years, some in high rank. Townsmen took pride in the fact that such men as Provo Wallis, who brought *Shannon* into port after her fight with *Chesapeake,* and John Charles Beckwith, one of Wellington's generals at Waterloo, were native Haligonians.

The change could be marked on the religious side in the vanishing Congregational faith amongst the Protestants and the rise of strong Presbyterian, Methodist, and Baptist churches. The Anglican section too had grown in strength, and as the established church it retained its power in the community. The Roman Catholics had increased from a mere handful to six hundred communicants; in 1817 Nova Scotia was made a vicariate apostolic under Bishop Burke, the wise and esteemed priest who had labored at Halifax since 1801.

The old Yankee customs had gone one by one. Almost the last to go was the day of prayer and fasting solemnly proclaimed each spring by the governor; the last regular observance was in 1814. The corresponding feast of Thanksgiving, celebrated in late autumn, hung on and survives as a general phenomenon—the only remaining mark of the Pilgrims on the calendar of North America.

The face of the town had changed enormously from the first straggle of huts and tents about the landing cove. True, there were miserable huts and shanties still in the slums of Water Street and "the Hill," but there were admirable streets between, as Bishop Plessis saw, and the counting-house district about Province House contained some first-rate commercial buildings. The rising walls of Province House and Admiralty House, and the finished dignity of Government House—all in stone—gave the town a look of permanence that it lacked before. And in place of the rabble of doubtful cockneys there was now a population of more than eleven thousand, the majority Nova Scotia born, busily employed, some of them rich, and all convinced of the town's eternal prosperity.

Only the fogies could remember the hungry times after the American Revolution. The late war had gone on so long, the fountain of guineas had splashed so steadily, that few Haligonians could imagine it drying up at the source or even picture the hard facts of life in a fortress town in time of peace. With few exceptions they looked upon the future in the golden glow of 1815. The exceptions were shrewd hard men like Enos Collins, Hezekiah Cogswell, and William Pryor who had accumulated vast fortunes—Collins in shipping, Cogswell at the law, Pryor in the West Indies trade—and turned those fortunes into specie before the golden glow began to fade. They and their friends, a group of twenty at most, held in their hands the actual working capital not only of Halifax but of the province, and when the depression came one jerk tightened the moneybags of all.

But all this was in the unknown future when 1816 brought the first full year of peace. The momentum of war prosperity carried the town along busily for two years after Waterloo. Water Street, worn to a chain of mud holes by the constant traffic of wartime, was now paved with cobbles and furnished with flagstone sidewalks, a vast improvement to the business of the waterfront. The numerous vessels taken prize during the war and sold at auction in the port now provided a surplus of bottoms for the shipping trade. The old traffic with the West Indies, maintained in a jerky fashion during the war by ships running the gantlet of French and American privateers, resumed its prewar regularity. A great fire swept away the sprawling rookery of old wooden shops and warehouses between Sackville Street, Hollis Street, and Bedford Row, and these were replaced very rapidly with new and better structures, often in brick or stone.

The town was still dependent for its water supply on wells, public and private, which were always a menace to health and usually a failure in time of fire. Now some enterprising souls proposed a Halifax Water Company to build and operate a reservoir on the Common. But this scheme had to be given up for lack of funds.

A stagecoach line was established between Halifax and Windsor. The coaches, for many years a familiar sight on the road, were described as "ponderous machines with three seats inside and a carriage board suspended from the roof behind the stage, on which a ton or two of baggage sat with several sailors' chests. Eighteen passengers were stowed away, driven by six horses; and so began the journey up the road past the garrison chapel and out to Bedford Basin."

Some adventurers proposed one of the newfangled steamboats to supplant the old slow ferries to Dartmouth—a pair of shallops moved by sail and oars. But this scheme fell through. Instead the ferry company built what it ingeniously called a "Team boat," consisting of two hulls joined by a large platform, and a paddlewheel moving between. The motive power was supplied by eight or nine horses harnessed to an enormous windlass amidships, which was connected with the paddles. This floating merry-go-round, often with a large square sail (and sometimes a topsail) hoisted to the harbor breeze, made the voyage to Dartmouth in something like twenty minutes.

In the midst of such signs of progress the town was able to ignore the first sure signs of a great financial frost—the disbandment of the garrison, the reduction of the fleet, the suspension of military building and repair, and the steady homeward flitting of wartime officials, speculators, and camp followers, amongst them the egregious Dr. Croke with his family and fortune. Sherbrooke, the brisk efficient soldier, went off to govern Canada, and in his place came the Earl of Dalhousie, another soldier, full of Waterloo honors. Dalhousie was a fortunate choice, for he was interested in plowshares as well as in swords, and foresaw the dilemma facing Halifax and the province.

The resumption of foreign trade was all very well, but, in the carry-over from the tremendous war, the trade of the world was in a strange flighty state which might collapse at any moment, and it would take a long time to recover. The solution as Dalhousie saw it was the development of the inland trade of the province itself. That meant a new and strenuous cultivation of the soil, the making of a hinterland of farms with Halifax as the market place. To this end he encouraged agricultural societies, annual fairs, and plowing matches, urged every jobless man to take up land, and settled whole regiments of disbanded troops along a new road slashed through the woods from Halifax (via Hammond's Plain) to Annapolis.

From Great Britain, which was already feeling the severe pinch of postwar times, a stream of emigration began to pour across the Atlantic. Many of the emigrants, English, Irish, Scots, and Welsh, landed at Halifax, where Dalhousie promptly sent them off into the forest to hew out farms and add to his great scheme. The discharged soldiers were fed for months (some for years) with army rations to encourage their efforts on the land. The civilians had to fend for themselves. All this had a familiar echo in Halifax; it was precisely what Cornwallis had tried to do in 1749, Wilmot in 1763, and Parr in 1783. And it had the same result.

Some of the civilians took root and flourished; others drifted off to the United States or to Upper Canada. The military settlements fell flat. The soldiers, many of them veterans of Wellington's campaigns, ceased "farming" as soon as the rations were stopped or at best when the government issue tools wore out. One of them, a former sergeant in the 3rd Dragoon Guards, set up shop in Water Street with the bird of peace and the following doggerel painted above his door:

My name is Pat Love, at the sign of the Dove.
I made my money in France and Spain—
And spent it all on Hammond's Plain.

By 1820 Halifax seemed full of Sergeant Loves.

All this stress on agriculture was a far reflection of the popular movement in Britain, blessed by "Farmer George," fanned to a steady heat by

Arthur Young in his monthly "Annals of Agriculture," and manifest in the growth and influence of such groups as the Highland Agricultural Society. Coming from old Scotland to the new, where the landscape and climate seemed much the same, Dalhousie naturally urged the same policies. He was aided powerfully by a series of letters, full of keen advice on the better cultivation of the Nova Scotia soil, which now began to appear in a Halifax newspaper. They were signed "Agricola" and there was much speculation about the author, who proved to be the proprietor of a Halifax grocery shop but knew, nevertheless, what he was writing about. He was John Young, a Scotsman who talked as well as he wrote; for years he continued to be the *vates sacer* of the Bluenose farmers.

In 1819 Young built his celebrated farmhouse "Willow Park" on Windsor Street near what is now the corner of Almon Street, then an area of open fields, and there put his intensive-farming theories into practice. It is difficult to realize nowadays the fervor his letters created, not only in the countryside but in the town; for in those days many a Halifax smallholder (not to speak of the landed merchant aristocracy) was a diligent gardener, and flowers, vegetables and small orchards flourished behind the shops and tenements of the downtown streets as well as in the fields beyond the Common. Much of Young's advice and Dalhousie's dream perished in the unkind soil of the Atlantic slope; but from this time provincial agriculture went forward on a scientific basis out of which eventually, as the trading center, Halifax received due benefit. Today Agricola Street commemorates that age of urgent husbandry.

But Dalhousie's best exertion was in quite another field—the cultivation of the mind. Coming from the free and vigorous atmosphere of the Scottish universities he was dismayed to find the higher education in Nova Scotia in the hands of the established church and limited to young men who were of that faith or willing to subscribe to its tenets. The bigoted Croke had departed, but his long shadow still darkened the door of King's College. Old Bishop Inglis, whose voice had been raised against Croke's policy, had died soon after Croke's departure. His body had been brought by sleigh to Halifax and buried under St. Paul's. Dead men tell no tales and lift no barriers.

And so Dalhousie founded the college which still bears his name, to provide education for students of all faiths. For a site he chose the north end of Grand Parade, where in Cornwallis' original plan a courthouse was supposed to stand, and where the city hall stands today. He laid the cornerstone on May 22, 1820, in the presence of a great gathering of public dignitaries, troops, and citizens, and paid the cost of a building from the Castine Fund, that useful trophy of the War of 1812. The college was a simple, solid Georgian structure of stone. The early students wore scarlet gowns like those of some Scottish universities.

Unfortunately, within a few weeks Dalhousie went to govern Canada. His place was taken by Lieutenant Governor Kempt, another soldier, whose recipe for progress was neither agriculture nor learning but the building of roads. For many years the college had a precarious existence, and there were times when it ceased struggling altogether. The stately Georgian edifice at times housed all sorts of alien activities—"a museum, a debating club, a Mechanics' Institute, a post office, an infants' school, a painting club and a pastry-cooks' establishment"—not to mention a fever hospital and a beer bottlery. The building itself has disappeared long since. But Dalhousie University survived and flourished in the time to come. It stands today on the Studley campus, a monument to the wisdom of the Scottish nobleman not only in its many fine buildings but in the long list of Nova Scotians and others who have found wisdom within its walls.

In the period just after Waterloo there was also a great improvement in the common education. For boys and girls of the more prosperous class there had always been various small private schools. In 1816, evidently under a wartime appropriation, the garrison completed a school for children of the Royal Artillery and the Royal Sappers and Miners. In this year, too, Walter Bromley's Acadian School had four hundred poor children in attendance. Bishop Burke had arranged a school for Roman Catholic girls, and was teaching classes of boys in the glebe house. The Church of England had established what was called the National School, operated on the Madras System, in a three-storey building erected for the purpose on Argyle Street facing the Parade.

In 1818 Halifax was made a free port, an important step in its trade march to the world. The town itself demanded elbow room, and Spring Garden Road was extended across the old South Common with building lots laid out on both sides. At its lower end in 1820 Bishop Burke laid the cornerstone of St. Mary's, but the post-war slump was just setting in and the construction of the big ironstone structure went on slowly for years, while the upper stretch of Spring Garden Road beyond "Bellevue" remained a stretch of fields.

Fields, pastures, walled and tree-masked estates, and the occasional hut of a cowherd or truck gardener filled the whole long reach running between Queen Street and Tower Road. "The Mall," that famous planked walk from the Parade to the Kissing Bridge, had fallen into disrepair and there were no funds to replace it. The area about the Kissing Bridge (now partly occupied by the sprawling railway yard) was then known as Smith's Fields. It was owned by two or three old German bachelors named Schmidt who ran a tannery beside the brook, and were fond of schnapps. One of them provided the town and himself with a horrid sensation by falling head first into the hearth one winter night. His headless trunk was discovered in the morning, and for many years young Haligonians pointed out the spot with awe.

As always with postwar depressions, the ultimate solution was in the hands of the young. There was some famous young stuff stirring in Halifax in these days. Young Joe Howe and Larry Doyle were playing ball in the streets, and in winter probably taking the "team boat" across the harbor for a game of ice hockey on the Dartmouth lakes. Tom Haliburton had just been admitted to the Nova Scotia Bar. James Gordon Bennett, the future founder of the New York *Herald*, was teaching a small school near Dartmouth. Sam Cunard was a rising young merchant, dealing in lumber and sailing ships, and dreaming of steam. A quiet young lieutenant of the Royal Navy, William Edward Parry, was sitting for a portrait by the Halifax artist Field, and dreaming of the Northwest Passage. Anthony Holland, the restless editor of the *Acadian Recorder*, was building a paper mill on Bedford Basin, the first in the Maritime Provinces and one of the first in Canada. Handsome young Richard Uniacke, son of the old attorney general, had killed handsome young Mr. Bowie in a pistol duel at Fort Needham and was standing trial for his life in what is now the library of Province House—with his own father the prosecutor. Abraham Gesner, that brilliant young student and Jack-of-all-trades from the country, one day to be famous as an inventor of coal oil, was trying to make up his mind whether to be a surgeon or a geologist.

It was the beginning of a new era, and the close of one whose end was clearly marked by the deaths of three old men early in the year 1820. On January 22 the Duke of Kent passed away in England. The martinet who had done so much to put Halifax on the imperial map had faded in his latter years to a querulous pauper, burdened with debt, subscribing small sums to charitable societies, and dabbling in socialism. His last and greatest call to duty had required him to put aside his beloved Madame St. Laurent (who died in a Belgian convent) in order to marry a German princess and father a legitimate child. All this he had accomplished. Now he laid his peculiar burdens down, and his German father-in-law paid the funeral expenses. Kent died a failure; but his infant daughter was to become the greatest queen who ever sat on the British throne, and within a century his descendants were to sit on the thrones of Russia, Germany, Norway, Rumania, and Spain. His early dreams of glory had never aspired so far.

On January 29—just a week later—old George III perished at last. He had been blind and mad for years. He had come to the throne in 1760 when Halifax was a small and struggling outpost on the wild shore of Nova Scotia; and his reign had covered a succession of tremendous events, each of which had a vital part in the city's story. His life had been embittered by continual quarrels with his scapegrace sons, one of whom now stepped blithely to the throne. The double tidings of death reached Halifax many weeks later by sailing ship, and the accession of George IV was celebrated with all due ceremony on April 7. The royal standard was hoisted on the Citadel and then lowered to half-mast, minute guns boomed from George's Island, and the town went into official mourning.

All this was too much for poor old Sir John Wentworth, who died the very next day in his chamber at Mrs. Flieger's boarding house on Hollis Street. The Duke of Kent had been his friend and patron, just as rollicking Prince Billy had been his wife's, and Kent's years at Halifax had coincided with the Wentworths' rise to power and luxury. For George III, John Wentworth had sacrificed a fortune and a governorship in the rebellious colonies, and under George III he had retrieved his rank and made and spent another fortune in Nova Scotia. Now all that fighting, striving, conniving, wining, dining time was past.

Wentworth's ambitious lady was dead and buried in England. For years he had crept about the streets of the town he had seen become a city, an almost forgotten figure, and no doubt at the age of eighty-three he was glad to go and be buried under St. Paul's. At Preston his country farm was in the hands of strangers. Kent had given him the Bedford Basin lodge, which by Wentworth's will now passed to his relative Mrs. Gore, the novelist. Already that famous love nest was in sad repair, and in a few years more it was to fall in utter ruin like a symbol of all the worldly vanity that glitters for a time and then perishes forever. With it went almost the last trace of the most romantic age in Halifax. Three notable things remain today: Government House, the funeral hatchment of Wentworth hanging in St. Paul's, and Kent's clock tower, still grimly ticking off the hours on the slope of "the Hill."

22.
1820–1837

Peace and depression. A son of Benedict Arnold. Rebuilding the fortress. The Shubenacadie Canal. The battle of the banks. Joe Howe's great libel case.

THE CITY, ALL UNKNOWING, FACED A CENTURY OF PEACE after Waterloo. There would be war in that time, to be sure, and some would touch her, but Halifax was not to know again the turmoil and glamor of a great war until 1914. After the almost incessant fighting since 1749 such a prospect was beyond imagination, and for ten years after Waterloo the port was like Othello, mourning an occupation gone and groping half-heartedly for another. Hundreds of houses were for sale or to let. Streets which had been improved on the new Macadam principle in the afterglow of war prosperity sank in mud once more. The ordinance for enforcing the cleanliness of the town was permitted to lapse. Garbage and rubbish cluttered all but the chief thoroughfares and grass grew in the outlying lanes, even in bawdy Barrack Street.

The tight clutch of the private bankers kept all specie out of sight. Gone were the familiar Spanish dollars of the prewar days, gone the British guineas of wartime. The town and province were bedeviled not only with the paper currency issued so blithely by their government during the war but with the doubtful paper notes and copper tokens issued by many a Halifax merchant. One unfortunate Haligonian went armed with a twenty-shilling provincial note to buy carrots, turnips, a squash, and two cabbages in the "green market" above the ferry dock. Several farmers refused to change the note at all, but at last he emerged with his vegetables and a ponderous amount of change in local notes and tokens. He complained to the press: "I thus had eight paper notes, one silver piece and 84 coppers—in all 93 separate things before I could get vegetables for my family's dinner. For God's sake, gentlemen, let us get back our DOLLARS!"

In 1819 the British Government's economies made their final pinch at Halifax with the breaking-up of famous old *Centurion*, the dismantling of the lofty mast-sheers which had been so long a landmark, and the virtual closing of the Dockyard itself. Most of its employees were discharged and the rest removed to Bermuda. This was a sad blow, for the yard had been a valuable feature of the town's employment ever since 1758. As for the army, only a shadow of the garrison remained. The town was dotted and surrounded by empty barracks and silent depots and offices, rusting batteries and crumbling forts. It looked as if Britannia had written the fortress off her books forever. But appearances are deceptive in the letdown after a great war. Nothing was farther from Britannia's mind.

The unrelenting hostility of the United States ever since the Revolution, and their open ambition (as evidenced by the pounce of 1812) to rule the continent, had persuaded the British that they must not be caught again with their Canadian defenses down. And since Halifax had proved a key not merely to the North Atlantic but to the eastern seaboard of that bellicose republic it was sure to be the prime object of the next American attempt. Such an attempt was not likely within twenty years—the republic still had wounds to lick. After that, who could say? The threat, if not the execution, certainly would appear the first time Britain became engaged in a major war elsewhere. So reasoned Downing Street.

In view of all this the gods must have chuckled when Britannia decided to rebuild the Halifax fortress on a greater scale than ever with the Americans in mind. For the man on the spot, the man who drew up the initial plans, was a son of that famous and much-abused American, Benedict Arnold. Colonel James Robertson Arnold, a child at the time of his father's flight, was one of the first students admitted to King's College at Windsor, Nova Scotia, in 1788. Ten years later he entered the British Army and served in Egypt and elsewhere. From 1818 to 1825 he commanded the Royal Engineers at Halifax—a small energetic man with keen eyes, a walking replica of Benedict himself, popular and respected by his officers. It would be interesting to know something of his inner thoughts as he planned those massive works which were to make Halifax proof against American ambitions in the years to come. All we know is that at one time in his seven years' duty at Halifax he made a pilgrimage to the old Arnold house in St. John, New Brunswick, where the family had lived for five embittered years after the Revolutionary War. Colonel James walked about the rooms in silence, and emerged in tears.

Arnold's plans were general in scope. Detail and execution fell to his successor, Colonel Gustavus Nicolls, who in 1829 began to make the Citadel an impregnable keep for the whole defense system of the port. This time the great central fort was to be made proof against the frosts and thaws of the Nova Scotia climate as well as against shot and shell; a solid thing of masonry with deep and roomy casemates, an arsenal of cannon, and a forbidding moat. A meticulous man, Nicolls estimated the cost at exactly £115,999 16s. 3-3/4d. (one wonders what the three farthings covered!) and the work was to be done chiefly by civilian contractors, with the garrison supplying some of the labor.

The work went on, and on. It went on every spring, summer, and autumn for more than thirty years. The whole hill was "made over," or as Piers puts it: "The remains of the Duke of Kent's old fort were demolished and the top of the hill cut down to a height of 225 feet above sea level—33 feet lower than the original height. The material year by year excavated from the ditches, the interior and elsewhere was carted outside and spread to form the symmetrical glacis we now see, every foot of which could be swept by gun and musketry from the ramparts. Tens of thousands of tons of squared granite and ironstone were brought from the King's quarries northwest of Purcell's Cove, a property of 204 acres acquired for this purpose in 1828. This excellent stone was used in the high revetments of the escarp and counterscarp, the interior retaining walls, the buildings and other parts of the work."

A popular Halifax superstition insists on an underground passage for troops between the Citadel and the harborside, and even George's Island. Let the precise Piers demolish it: "There is a large and carefully built brick sewer leading from the bottom of the ditch at the redan salient, down the glacis to the head of Buckingham Street, where it connects with a large stone drain on the site of an ancient stream and passes downhill till it reaches the harbour in the Ordnance Yard. The existence of this drain has given rise to the fallacious idea which has always been current and which former officers used to delight their lady friends. A man, by stooping, can pass through this conduit, but it was not constructed for the passage of troops."

And so Halifax in 1829 was furnished with what amounted to a major local industry, good for a generation, employing hundreds of men and paying them in coin of the British Realm. It was a satisfying stay in years of trouble. There was another. A private industry of much the same sort had opened in 1826 when Wentworth's old dream, the Shubenacadie Canal, was actually begun. Its purpose was to link the port of Halifax with the farming districts of the Bay of Fundy by a waterway across the province, following exactly the old warpath of the Micmacs. Like the Citadel, this work went on for more than thirty years, distributing great sums for labor and material. And, like the Citadel, the Shubenacadie Canal was obsolete when finished; the one was made useless by the invention of rifled cannon and the other by steam railways.

Trade began to pick up steadily. Shipbuilding, a thriving provincial industry in the early stages of the Napoleonic Wars, had been crushed by the tumble of prizes taken from the enemy and sold at auction on the Halifax waterfront; but by 1825 this surplus of cheap bottoms had disappeared and the Nova Scotia yards began to build more and larger ships than before.

The chief handicap to business was the lack of a general-purpose bank. The lone existing bank was anything but that. In 1825 Enos Collins and his associates had formed the Halifax Banking Company, with offices in his grim ironstone building on Water Street, thus incorporating their private monopoly of finance. More than this, five of Collins' partners were members of His Majesty's Council for the province, and the rest of that body of twelve were friends or relatives of the bankers. So the Halifax Banking Company dominated not only the finance but the very Government of Nova Scotia. The situation stank in the nostrils of all but the successive military governors, who continued fatuously to regard these merchant princes of the council as the one group of reliable men in the country—a notion carefully fostered by The Twelve. They kept the occupant of Government House so busy sniffing the rabble for sedition that the peculiar reek in the upper chamber of Province House passed unnoticed or at any rate was ignored.

But change was on the way. The great movement for parliamentary reform, already in full march in Britain, was gathering momentum in the colonies across the sea, and nowhere more than in Nova Scotia. The voice of Cottnam Tonge had been lost in the swamps of Demerara; but there were other tongues now, and one in particular, that of Joseph Howe. Early in 1828 the young printer had become sole proprietor of the *Nova Scotian* newspaper. He was twenty-four, a plain man with a long straight nose, craggy eyebrows, a firm mouth, and a shock of receding dark hair that stood out from his skull as if electrified by the energy within. On warm summer evenings, after the long day's work at the printing shop, he would trot down George Street to the Market Slip, hurl off his clothes, and plunge into the harbor for a swim by the light of the stars. In just such a fashion he threw himself into the deep and murky waters of provincial politics.

Strangely enough, the opening gun against the Rule of Twelve was fired by a group of the lesser capitalists, who were determined to start a general-purpose bank in opposition to the Halifax Banking Company. The need was obvious, and as the shares of the proposed bank were open to public subscription the sponsors had no difficulty in getting 184 signatures (including Joe Howe's) to their petition for incorporation. The bill of incorporation was keenly examined in the assembly and passed, with several provisions which are now fundamental to the Canadian banking system, notably the double liability of shareholders for the protection of the public.

The bill then went to the council, who invariably held their meetings behind the closed doors of the upper chamber. Exactly what was said there no one ever knew—but all could guess. The bill for the incorporation of the new public bank was in effect being considered by the board of the Halifax Banking Company. Finally the council announced that the bill had been passed "with amendments." At once there was a storm. The assembly demanded the amendments, debated them—even accepted some—and threw out the rest with scorn. The temper of the lower house was such that The Twelve, fearing to arouse sleeping dogs in other directions, wisely decided to give in. The bill passed. The subscribers held a meeting in the Exchange Coffee House, and some weeks later the new institution opened for business in a few rented rooms in John Roman's stone building at the corner of Granville and Duke streets. The year was 1832, and thus was born the Bank of Nova Scotia, which has since outgrown its swaddling clothes and indeed its native province, but still holds its head office at Halifax.

The first shot had gone home, but The Twelve were well entrenched in other ways and in 1835 Howe launched his own attack. His immediate target was the clique of magistrates appointed by the Crown (i.e., by The Twelve) to the rule or misrule the city itself. In the columns of the *Nova Scotian* he accused them of corruption and neglect, and there was a furor. The obvious remedy for such evils—the incorporation of Halifax—had been refused by successive governors-in-council. Now that the cry for incorporation had broken out anew, The Twelve decided on a counter-stroke. Prodded from above, the magistrates sued Howe for libel.

Lawyer after lawyer told Howe his case was hopeless. Finally the young editor borrowed a few books of law, studied libel with care, and prepared his own defense. The defense was thin from a legal point of view; but the clear ringing voice, the flow of apt phrase and smiling anecdote, the impressive array of figures at which he was so adept, the courage of his convictions, the homeliness of his eager face and stocky figure which made him one of them, his very presence there before the powerful magistrates like a shock-haired warrior defying the lightning, not only won the jury but served notice to the crowded court and the mass of townsfolk in the street outside that here was a champion of the people, thrown up by the very need, and armed with strong and shining weapons.

From that moment Howe never looked back—and Privilege never looked comfortable. The fight for the incorporation of Halifax became one with the fight for responsible government of the province, which raged with great sound and fury for the next five years. It is a great and fascinating story, too long to narrate here. The principle of responsible government was granted in 1840 and came into full effect in 1848, when the first responsible government in the British Empire took office in the gray stone Province House—a fact of which Nova Scotians are properly proud. The incorporation of Halifax had been conceded in 1841. By that time a great change had come upon the city.

23.
1820–1837

The Shea murder case. Moral recovery. The end of Negro slavery and King Rum. Costumes of the period. The Mechanics' Institute. The cholera. A flood of immigration.

THE CHANGE THAT CAME OVER HALIFAX WAS NOT SO much a physical as a moral one. As we have seen, the long wars had left it a sink of depravity notorious in every cantonment and dockyard of the empire. The ten years following Waterloo were the sober morning after. Of course there remained a garrison, and the squadron came in each summer as before; indeed before long the Dockyard was re-opened, and in place of the old *Centurion* came another famous ship, *Pyramus*, one of Nelson's prizes at Copenhagen. His Majesty's young naval and military gentlemen continued to kick up their heels in the manner of the times, and common tars and redcoats continued to seek diversion in Water Street and Barrack Street. But they were not so obstreperous as in time of war. For the first time in a generation they were far outnumbered by the townsmen, and their antics came under a more searching light.

Some of the antics were merely amusing, like the ride of young Viscount Jocelyn, a subaltern of the Rifle Brigade, from Halifax to Windsor and back—ninety-two miles—for a wager against time. It was a famous wager and a famous ride, and a whole generation of Haligonians talked about the daredevil horseman and his two mounts, "Naughty Tommy" and "Swap."

Not so amusing was an affair at the officers' quarters on Cogswell Street just after Christmas 1824, when Ensign Richard Cross of the 96th Regiment killed an old schoolmaster named Shea by running him through with a sword. These quarters were the scene of much debauchery. Shea had gone there in search of his daughter—a not uncommon errand in those days. The seducer found himself on trial for murder, with strong circumstantial evidence against him. But his companions swore his innocence like officers and gentlemen, and he was acquitted.

A change in garrison morals began soon after, when Sir Peregrine Maitland arrived in Halifax as lieutenant governor. Every governor had his *idée fixe*. Those who came during the wars naturally were obsessed with war. Dalhousie believed in learning and the soil. Kempt doted on roads and pretty women. Maitland (1828-34) was a moralist of a puritanical sort not seen in Halifax since the days of the Yankee pioneers. The gambling, cockfighting, wenching, dueling, and carousing habits of the garrison and fleet came under his heavy displeasure. He frowned on ostentation as he frowned on sin, walked to church with his lady (thus putting a blight on the Sabbath procession of carriages to St. Paul's), forbade the time-honored pageantry of a garrison parade on the Common every Sunday afternoon, and in person fell upon the Sunday market (an outgrowth of the wars) like a wrathful prophet.

The viceroy's attitude was odd when one considers that his sovereign during much of this time was none other than William IV—that very Prince Billy of the old wild days when Frances Wentworth was scheming her way to Government House and playing a lively second fiddle to the ladies of Barrack Street. But those days were gone with Frances herself; and Billy had changed. He had become not only a king but a faithful husband, of all things; and in a few years he would pass to his eternal reward murmuring (of all things), "The church! The church!"

All this was part of a post-Regency wave of respectability now sweeping over Britain and across the sea. It was reflected in feminine dress. Vanished were those flimsy peep-bo gowns of the 1790s, gone the jouncing hips and bosoms, the turbans, the Wellington bonnets, the Wellington mantles, the Wellington jackets, froggings, and epaulets with which the ladies had endeared themselves to military hearts in the Napoleonic years. Fashion and ultramodesty, enemies for decades, joined hands at last in a marriage that lasted seventy years.

Stays and tight-lacing were back with a vengeance; indeed the corset was soon to be a veritable suit of armor in itself. It became not only proper but chic, even in summer, to wear drawers—hitherto chiefly the property of old ladies and the inelegant poor—and to wear them in a cascade of ruffles right down to the ankles, a sight that would have thrown the all but bare charmers of Kent's day into hysterics. Over these things, as the years rolled by, went increasingly numerous and formidable petticoats, gowns, bodices, pelisses, jackets, and shawls, so that by 1850 a well-dressed woman on her way to St. Paul's was like nothing so much as a perambulating cabbage with a whalebone core. The female body had gone into hiding and was not to emerge or even to reveal its shape for half a century.

As for the townsmen, those vain and contrary creatures were now displaying their manly figures to all possible advantage in skintight trousers that strapped under the instep, in snug-waisted frock coats with flaring skirts and padded hips, and balancing on their heads those enormous top hats which threatened to snuff them like candles at any moment. But they had begun to curb their drinking habits. Temperance societies were appearing. The four, five, or six bottle man was no longer a hero but a bore. Even the laborer began to curb his ancient thirst for rum, not so much from virtue as from necessity. For one thing, he had less money for drink in these pinching times of peace. For another, the supply and price of rum had undergone violent change.

It is strange to reflect that the abolition of Negro slavery in parts of the Caribbees had changed the lives of a province of free whites two thousand miles to the north. Abolition in the British West Indies in 1833 ruined the old system of vast sugar plantations with their ever-busy distilleries, and dried up the Gulf Stream of cheap rum which for nearly a century had flowed to Nova Scotia in the holds of the fish and lumber traders. Of course rum, sugar, and molasses remained the staples of the West India trade; but the planters never recovered their old mass production, and the demon in the Nova Scotian's jug was never again "as cheap as water and a sight more plentiful." The Halifax custom of paying wages partly in rum was ended at last. Merchants no longer stood a cask of right Jamaica in mid-floor, complete with spigot and mug, for the refreshment of their customers. The household keg became a luxury.

In place of the old thirst there appeared a sudden parch for knowledge. That poor man's university the Mechanics' Institute was springing up all over Britain, and as early as 1829 Joseph Howe was urging one for Halifax. An Institute was duly organized and on January 11, 1832, Howe had the pleasure of making the inaugural address. He spoke there again on many occasions, preaching always the gospel of faith in Nova Scotia and the intelligent use of her resources. Others, expert in particular fields, lectured on history, architecture, music, agriculture—everything from hydraulics to comparative anatomy. Men of every sort crowded the Institute to the doors. It was astonishing. Their interest remained, and grew. Dr. D.C. Harvey has truly said that "during the next quarter of a century the Institute might well be called the University of Halifax."

Thus, twenty years after Waterloo, the Haligonians with the rest of the British world were well embarked upon an age of respectable progress and progressive respectability which needed nothing but a name. This was supplied, curiously enough, by a daughter of that former Haligonian the Duke of Kent. She came to the British throne in 1837 and her name was, of course, Victoria.

Outwardly the town was little changed except in one notable respect. In 1829 and 1830 the commissioners of streets in an excess of zeal decided that the sidewalks must be cleared of all obstructions great and small. Axes fell, and down crashed all those fine old willows and poplars which for decades had shaded the residential streets and lent even Barrack Street in summer an air of rustic charm. In a stroke the town stood naked on the harbor slope—naked and ashamed, if Akins' is any witness. In later years attempts were made to replace these trees in the downtown streets and they flourished again, only to perish when electric light and the telephone made their supreme contribution to progress and ugliness and changed every city in the world to a deadwood forest of poles, wires, and bars.

The road from Halifax to St. Margaret's Bay and the south coast was still very bad. Dalhousie's military road, straight as a sword cut through the woods from Hammond's Plain to Annapolis, remained unfinished and impassable. The chief route from Halifax to the country was still the Windsor road, with a branch beyond Bedford running through the forest to Truro. Since the approaches to this main exit from the city—the old Bell Road running between the Citadel and Camp Hill, and the Lady Hammond Road leading from the distant northern suburbs—were awkward and circuitous, Sir James Kempt in 1824 made a short cut, via Robie Street to Fairview, which still bears his name and remains the chief highway from the city.

There was still no adequate water supply, no sewage disposal system, no street lighting beyond a scatter of whale oil and seal oil lamps maintained by merchants outside their premises for the benefit of the town watch. There was no decent hostelry in the town. Audubon, that bird-loving artist, visited Halifax in 1833 and found a very poor nest indeed. "The coach drew up to the house of Mr. Paul, the best hotel, where with difficulty we obtained one room with four beds for six persons. With a population of 18,000 souls and 2,000 more of soldiers, Halifax has not one good hotel, and only two very indifferent private boarding houses where the attendance is miserable and the table by no means good. The card of an Italian was sent to our room, telling us that he had fine baths of all sorts; and we went off to his room and found one tin tub and a hole underground into which sea water filtered, about the size of a hogshead. I plumped into this with Ingalls and Shattuck, then rubbed ourselves dry with coarse towels, and paid six cents for the accommodation."

An attempt to enforce fireproof building in the lower town had been given over. Nevertheless by 1827 Halifax could boast thirty-seven brick buildings and seventy-three of stone. The latest of these was St. Mary's, finished in durable ironstone to replace the small red wooden church of St. Peter's, now far too small for the growing Catholic population. (In 1829 the timbers of St. Peter's were dragged away to the waterfront, floated across the harbor, and set up again in Dartmouth by the enterprising priest and members of that parish.)

The graveyards were still receiving far too many of the people before their time. The old insanitary conditions were largely responsible, and there was no excuse for the great smallpox epidemics of 1827 and 1828 when Doctor Jenner's discovery had been known in Nova Scotia for a generation. Death wore its old familiar forms—"putrid fever" (typhus), "bloody flux" (dysentery), "putrid sore throat" (diphtheria)—and, for the young especially, there was always scarlet fever. There was always consumption, too, for young and old. But in 1834 the Reaper appeared in a new and fearful guise, Asiatic cholera, which had crept out of India into Europe and now crossed the sea in the emigrant ships.

This disease struck its victims down with little or no warning, turned their living bodies a horrible bluish purple, reduced the voice to a harsh rattling whisper, and tortured the limbs with such agonizing cramps that muscular contractions and twitchings continued for some time after death—an awesome spectacle to the ignorant hospital attendants. Forewarned from London and Quebec, the Halifax authorities made some preparation, including the conversion of Dalhousie College into a plague hospital and the establishment of a rigid medical inspection and quarantine for emigrant ships.

In the harbor quarantine the poor emigrants died like flies. In the city itself on September 4, 1834, the *Acadian Recorder* noted a daily average of 35 new cases and 17 or 18 deaths a day. (In the first six weeks there were at least 762 cases in Halifax, and 284 deaths.) When the garrison barracks became infected the troops were moved out, some to Bedford, the rest under canvas on Camp Hill. Wagons made the rounds of the town each morning and conveyed the dead to Fort Massey cemetery, where the crude coffins were dropped into long trenches and hastily covered with earth. The worst of the epidemic passed with the cool winds of autumn; but Halifax had suffered a violent experience and the government now turned a baleful eye on the business of emigration.

Ever since the fall of Napoleon and the end of the wars a horde of people had poured across the Atlantic. Some were English, many were Scots, most were Irish, and nearly all were poor, driven across the sea by the hard times at home and filled with dreams of rich lands in the new world to be had for the asking. Such folk, ready and eager to sell their very bedding for passage money, became the prey of a class of shipowners and masters compared with whom the seventeenth-century buccaneers were a company of philanthropists.

These scoundrels crammed their dupes into foul and often unseaworthy ships, sailed with scanty stores into the North Atlantic on a passage that at best took twenty or thirty days and at worst might take six months, and dumped their surviving human freight ashore at the first landfall. Too often the drunken or incompetent masters wrecked their vessels on the coast or the outlying islands with frightful suffering and loss of life. There were rich lands to be had in the middle west of the United States or of Canada, but willy-nilly thousands upon thousands of poor Irish and Scots found themselves ashore in Nova Scotia or Newfoundland without a penny in their pockets, many of them diseased or ill, and only the Highlanders knowing how to make a living in these gaunt regions of rocks and forest.

In Halifax, the Charitable Irish Society, the North British Society and many other kindly souls tried to provide in some fashion for the locust swarm of human beings from across the sea. At first the emigrants were welcomed as reinforcements in the struggle towards prosperity; but as the times grew harder and year succeeded year with the same endless flow of destitutes to be fed, clothed, and nursed to health—most of them would drift away, later, to Upper Canada or the United States—the burden became oppressive. Even Newfoundland began to discharge its horde of Irish newcomers into Nova Scotia.

The last straw came in 1834, the year of the cholera, when the British Government shipped to Halifax a considerable group of outpatients of Chelsea Hospital (the home for old or disabled soldiers), many with their families, with a bland request that they be established on the land. Some perished of cholera before they had been many days ashore. Lieutenant Governor Sir Colin Campbell gathered up the rest and sent them back to England at the expense of His Majesty's Government and to the sharp annoyance of His Majesty's treasury. By this time there was an outcry from both sides of the Atlantic for regulation of the emigrant ships. The sad tales of poor folk dumped in Newfoundland or Nova Scotia were having their effect amongst friends and relatives at home. After 1835, while the comparatively short journey and low fare to Halifax continued to attract a certain number, the great body of the migrants went to the Canadas, Upper and Lower, or on to the United States.

These vicissitudes for the Haligonians—the postwar depression, the great epidemics, the collapse of the rich West Indies trade, the cataract of poor folk from across the sea—came to a head in the year Victoria came to the throne, when a financial panic in the United States stunned the whole trade of North America. These were the birth pangs of the Victorian age in Nova Scotia and, as it proved, of the greatest chapters in Nova Scotian history. Already the age had produced the man, for in 1837 Joe Howe walked into Province House as a member of the legislature.

24.
1837–1849

The first steamships. Halifax incorporated. Mr. Dickens pays a call. Gaslights and sailing ships. The Saladin *Piracy. The first water system. The electric telegraph and the "pony express." The first hundred years.*

THE SHUBENACADIE CANAL COMPANY WAS SLOWLY extending its ditch towards the Bay of Fundy. But already it was obsolete; Howe had begun to talk about a railway. Dalhousie's agricultural societies were very much alive, but his college was sickly and his notion of a province of farmers was dead. The clairvoyant Howe had observed in 1834: "Agricultural production may be restrained by our narrow limits and by the character of our soil and climate; there are no such formidable obstacles to the rapid growth of a commercial marine and to the almost indefinite extension of domestic and foreign trade." The next thirty years were to see the truth of that.

The province was covered with good timber, easily floated to the coast by the short rushing rivers—and the same rivers turned the sawmills. Immigration had filled the country towns with cheap labor for the lumber camps and mills; and the coast was inhabited by an amphibious folk who knew how to build ships and how to sail them. The growth of world trade after 1840, with its inevitable demand for ships and seamen, provided Nova Scotia with the opportunity for which she might have been created.

The strange thing is that Howe, having envisioned the industry which in his own time was to make Nova Scotia the wealthiest and busiest of the Canadian provinces, was unable to foresee its eventual ruin by iron and steam. The first ocean-going steamers were built of wood. The pioneer *Royal William* had been turned out by an ordinary Canadian shipyard and there seemed no reason why Nova Scotia could not launch these things as fast as she was launching wind-ships. Indeed the first steam ferry in Halifax Harbor, the *Sir Charles Ogle*, had been launched from a Dartmouth yard as far back as 1830.

In 1838 Howe and Thomas Haliburton went off to tour Europe (where Haliburton's "Sam Slick" was the latest literary sensation) and their sailing ship encountered in mid-ocean the new steamship *Sirius*. "On she came," said Howe, "in gallant style with the speed of a hunter while we were moving with the rapidity of an ox cart.... Never did we feel so forcibly the contrast between the steamer and the sailing vessel." At once his vivid mind conjured lines of steamers connecting Europe with the obvious (because it was the nearest) port on the North American mainland—Halifax—and as soon as he reached London he made for the Colonial Office to present a memorandum on the subject. Within a few weeks the British Government issued its famous call for tenders for a line of steamships to carry Her Majesty's Mail between Britain and New York via Halifax. None of the British shipping firms would undertake it alone, but it remained for another Haligonian, the shrewd, thrifty, energetic Samuel Cunard, already a millionaire in lumber and sailing ships, to secure the contract, form a company, and carry the plan into effect.

When Cunard returned to Halifax in 1839 he was fêted by his fellow townsfolk at a monster picnic on McNab's Island. In the same summer Haliburton, fresh from his European triumphs, received a public banquet in Halifax. In this summer, too, the Haligonians for the first time celebrated the founding of their town, marking its ninetieth birthday with a mass picnic held beside the ruins of "Prince's Lodge" on Bedford Basin as if to remind themselves of the emptiness of a purely military prosperity. Already Howe's leaven was at work in the Bluenoses. They believed in themselves, in their port and province, with a passionate faith that was to see itself fulfilled.

In May 1840 the first trans-ocean experiment of the Cunard steamships, the oak-hulled *Unicorn*, arrived at Halifax in fourteen days from Liverpool. The wharves were jammed with people cheering as if at a great victory; guns fired, flags waved, and during the ship's brief stop at Halifax no less than three thousand Haligonians went aboard for an inspection of this marvel of the age. Two months later she was followed by *Britannia*, the first steamer on the regular Cunard run, which Halifax received with similar enthusiasm.

This, be it remembered, was the year in which Nova Scotia won the principle of responsible government. It was an enthusiastic time. The colony had come a long and difficult way since the other thirteen plumped for complete self-rule in 1776, and John Quincy Adams, former President of the United States, must have thought upon it as he stepped ashore and made his way through the Halifax streets. He was going to call upon his father's old friend and political enemy Sampson Salter Blowers, the venerable loyalist judge, born seven years before Halifax was founded, a resident of the town since the Revolution, and destined to live a full century. Blowers was in himself a rugged example of the hardy Bluenose spirit which had refused to sacrifice its principles and flourished now in spite of climate and adversity. When he died in 1842 Haligonians recalled curiously that the old man had never worn an overcoat in his hundred years of life.

In 1841 Halifax was incorporated and—shade of Audubon!—the new Halifax Hotel opened its doors. The city police, a little band of constables in plain clothes and tall beaver hats, walked solemnly about the streets. The night watch, a separate organization, wore similar clothes and carried staves and lanterns, as well as noisy iron rattles for scaring thieves and summoning assistance. The night watch were paid one dollar for each night's work, which consisted of patrolling the streets—two men to each ward—and crying the hour in stentorian tones for the peace and comfort of the burghers.

The Horticultural Society chose for its labors a part of the old South Common facing on Spring Garden Road, the beginning of the present Public Gardens. The temperance movement, led by J.S. Thompson, was in full crusade. Joe Howe was everywhere, writing lively topical editorials, winning devotees, fighting enemies (even to a duel at pistol point with J.C. Halliburton), preaching the need of a railway, a fleet of steamships, a native literature, and practicing his speeches in a loud voice in the seclusion of Steel's Pond at the edge of the Point Pleasant woods. On a winter day in 1842 he hustled down to the Cunard wharf to meet that distinguished passenger Mr. Charles Dickens and show him the town.

The creator of Pickwick had this to say of his visit:

> *It happened to be the opening of the Legislative Council and General Assembly, at which ceremonial the forms observed on the*

commencement of a new sessions of Parliament were so closely copied, and so gravely presented on a small scale, that it was like looking at Westminster through the wrong end of a telescope. The Governor, as Her Majesty's representative, delivered what may be called the Speech from the Throne. He said what he had to say manfully and well. The military band outside the building struck up God Save The Queen with great vigor before His Excellency had quite finished; the people shouted; the in's rubbed their hands; the out's shook their heads; the Government party said there never was such a good speech; the Opposition declared there never was such a bad one; the Speaker and the members of the House of Assembly withdrew from the Bar to say a good deal among themselves and to do a little; and in short everything went on and promised to go on just as it does at home on like occasions.

The town is built on the side of a hill, the highest point being commanded by a strong fortress not yet finished. The houses are chiefly of wood. The market is abundantly supplied and provisions are exceedingly cheap. The weather being mild for that season of the year there was no sleighing; but there were plenty of those vehicles in yards and by-places, and some of them, from the gorgeous quality of their decorations, might have "gone on" without alteration as triumphal cars in a melodrama at Astley's. The day was uncommonly fine, the air bracing and healthful, the whole aspect of the town cheerful, thriving and industrious. I carried away with me a most pleasant impression of the town and its inhabitants and have preserved it to this hour.

Year followed crowded year. In 1843 the newly formed Gas Company lit the first homes. The Bluenoses were building ships and sending them off to the world laden with lumber, fish, coal and plaster; they were even sending shiploads of ice, packed in sawdust, from the Dartmouth Lakes to the West Indies. Some shipbuilding was done on the shores of Halifax Harbor—the Dartmouth firm of Lyle & Chappell were especially busy—but no elaborate plant was needed for the business. A shipyard could be set up almost anywhere along the coast near to timber, in fact wherever there was a stream to turn a sawmill and tide to float a ship. The whole rugged shore of Nova Scotia rang with the sounds of ship carpentry; and Halifax supplied the hardware, the canvas and rigging, the finance, the insurance and the agencies for foreign trade.

A romantic time, indeed. Sometimes the romance became sheer melodrama, as in 1844 when the *Saladin* piracy case set all Halifax agog. The ship was wrecked on the coast east of Halifax and HMS *Fair Rosamund* brought the pirates to port for trial and punishment. Upon a summer's day the whole city turned out and gathered about a grassy knoll between Tower Road and South Park Street, just opposite Holy Cross Cemetery in what then was the South Common. There stood the scaffold, surrounded by a red-coated company of Her Majesty's 52nd Foot. Up Tower Road from the prison at Northwest Arm came the sheriff in a gig, followed by the condemned seamen in a pair of carriages with four priests, all escorted by a strong detachment of the 1st Royals, their muskets and long bayonets glittering like the bars of a cage. On the scaffold the prisoners confessed their crimes. One made a speech to the crowd which delighted the hearts of the balladmongers. The priests prayed, the drops fell, the four seamen swung in the hot July sun—and Halifax went home to its dinner.

The *Saladin* affair far overshadowed other events of a year in which the old town cemetery was closed to burials at last, Valentine the portrait painter began to take daguerreotypes, the ingenious Fenerty produced paper from wood pulp in Holland's old mill by the Basin shore, the garrison began to build a large chapel (later known as Trinity Church) on the site of one of Cornwallis' old forts, the ferry steamer *Micmac* was launched at Dartmouth, and Lieutenant Governor Falkland ended the time-honored custom of marking royal birthdays and other public holidays with a grand review of the troops on the Common.

Falkland, a handsome young nobleman with lofty ideals but little political experience and no tact at all in dealing with "colonials," had the misfortune to cross pens and opinions with the ebullient Joe Howe. His self-importance was not diminished by the fact that his lady was a daughter of Prince Billy on the wrong side of the royal blanket, and his hauteur was such that he thought nothing of sending a servant to represent him at a public concert. He was in fact the last of a long list of governors (with notable exceptions like Dalhousie) whose attitude had been similar if not always so obvious.

The "colonists," proud in their own new right and itching to rid themselves of all trace of the old subservience, were not the people to take this sort of thing mildly. Halifax, remembering Prince Billy, was inclined to ribald laughter which Howe increased with pasquinades in prose and verse. He literally laughed Lord Falkland out of office, for in 1846 the lieutenant governor secured an appointment in Bombay and went off with his lady in a huff—and with one final gesture of contempt. Rather than sell his beautiful horses to be straddled by provincial legs he had them taken to the Common and shot.

In the twenty years since 1826 the population of Nova Scotia had more than doubled. There was plenty of labor for railway construction, and the government began a survey from Halifax to Windsor. At the same time Howe began to urge the merits of that new invention the electric telegraph, so superior to the old and nearly forgotten system of the Duke of Kent. As the first port of westbound Cunarders and the last port of the eastbound, Halifax could become a clearinghouse for news of the world, its name in every journal, on everybody's lips. It sounded like another of Howe's dreams.

More practical was the problem of the city's water supply, now solved at last. In 1847 a new water company carried a pipeline from Long Lake, in the woods at the head of the Northwest Arm, to the corner of Bell Road and Robie Street. Its original intent was to keep filled a large reservoir that was to be dug on Camp Hill; but, having got so far, the company went on with it and carried the pipes into town.

Meanwhile Morse's electric telegraph was swiftly spinning its metallic web along the eastern seaboard of the United States. One thread reached up to Boston and went on to St. John. New York financiers and newspapers suddenly saw a light. Howe's talk of quick transatlantic news via Cunard Line and telegraph made sense—money sense. The Nova Scotia Government, at Howe's urging, agreed to build the link from St. John to Halifax; but this would take another year, and meanwhile the impatient New Yorkers sought a means to fill the gap. The great newspaper men Bennett, Greeley, Dana, Hallock, and others—but especially Bennett, who knew Halifax from his youth, and whose New York *Herald* was the first to print financial news from Wall Street and first to obtain an important political speech by telegraph—formed the Associated Press. Its objects were to secure a special news packet from Cunarders coming into Halifax, to encourage the building of the Nova Scotia telegraph, and in the meantime to arrange quick passage of the precious news to the telegraph at St. John.

So in 1849 Halifax became the starting point of a "pony express." The news packet was dropped over the side of each incoming Cunarder to a boat at the harbor entrance, passed to a rider on the shore, and carried at a gallop through the city and across the province. The distance to Digby was 144 miles, with a fresh horse waiting at each 12-mile stage and a fresh rider at the halfway point. At Digby a small steamer rushed the packet over the Bay of Fundy to St. John and the marvelous telegraph.

The first packet was dropped early on the wintry morning of February 21, 1849, from the Cunarder *Europa,* eleven days out of Liverpool. It was published in New York on the following day. The advantages of the scheme, especially to Wall Street (the packet naturally included the latest figures on the London Stock Exchange) were enormous, and before long a rival pony express was running neck and neck with the other. The toughest and most daring horsemen in the province were hired at fat wages and the finest horses procured. The sight of these riders dashing through the streets of Halifax, and on past the villages along the route, created the greatest excitement; wagers were laid on the rival carriers. It was not without regret that the sporting Bluenoses saw the telegraph completed in the late autumn of 1849.

The telegraph was denounced by Howe's opponents as a waste of public money; but within a year the line was paying 5 per cent on the investment, Halifax was being advertised as never before, and the great and growing shipping interests of the port were finding in the humming wires a facility beyond price. Halifax was just a century old, and enjoying its first permanent outdoor lighting—eighty gas lamps hissing and popping at the corners of the downtown streets. The city celebrated its centenary with a holiday. A great public gathering was addressed by Murdoch the historian and, of course, by Joe Howe, so that the city's past was discussed with thoroughness and its future with imaginative passion.

25.
1849–1860

The first railway. Effects of the Crimean War and Indian Mutiny. The great industrial exhibition. The boom in sailing ships. Nova Scotia's first VC. The dollar supreme.

On its one-hundredth birthday Halifax was woefully deficient in many important respects, despite gas, water, the telegraph and such other signs of progress as a piano factory, a zoological garden, an art exhibition, and a public library. Dalhousie College remained in the doldrums for lack of funds. The Halifax Hotel, built in the enthusiasm following the foundation of the Cunard Line, had not received the expected rush of European tourists and was bankrupt. There was not a decent carriage for hire in the city, and no means of transportation out of it except in the lumbering stagecoaches or the small and crowded cabins of the coastal packets.

The Annapolis Valley, the city's best source of fresh meats, poultry, fruit, and vegetables, was separated from it by forty or fifty miles of road so bad that (lacking the horse relays of the stagecoaches) farmers came to market only in summer and early autumn when the way was dry and practicable, and for a month or two in winter when the snow made sleighing possible. The alternative was a voyage of something like four hundred miles by schooner around Cape Sable; for the Shubenacadie Canal seemed as far from completion as ever.

Howe had suggested a railway to Windsor as far back as 1835. Now he looked again. The Durham Report of 1839 had recommended a railway line linking Upper Canada with the Maritime Provinces as a means of promoting intercolonial trade and defense. So far nothing had been done about it. Away went Howe to London as a delegate of his government to urge the railway upon the imperial authorities. He proposed that the provinces build the line and finance it with their own bonds under guarantee by the imperial government, so that a low interest rate could be secured.

All the provinces were ready to do their part but the imperial government blew hot and then cold on the scheme. Finally the Nova Scotia Government undertook to build a line from Halifax to Windsor at its own expense (borrowing the money from English capitalists at a thumping 6 per cent) and Howe resigned from the cabinet to become chairman of the railway board and see the thing through. On June 13, 1854, the first sod was turned.

That was a momentous year. The drums of the 76th Regiment, quartered in the Citadel, had ushered it in at midnight on New Year's Eve by a march around the frosty ramparts. The great work on the hill was nearly complete—just in time for the contingency foreseen in 1825. Britain was about to engage in a great European war for the first time since Waterloo, and once again the traditional hostility of the United States had to be reckoned with. Far from abating in the peaceful interlude, the spirit of 1776 and 1812 was very much alive; in fact it had a fresh virulence, for the enormous Irish immigration of the past ten years had filled the American cities and introduced into American politics a new and fanatical hatred of everything British.

The mass of the American people wanted peace, for they were gravely concerned with an internal problem, slavery, which threatened to tear them apart. Indeed in 1854 they showed a friendly attitude towards the Canadian provinces in the signing of the Reciprocity Treaty, which leveled the customs barriers across the continent and permitted trade to flow in its natural channels. But a friendly mass had been pushed into an attempted conquest of Canada in 1812, and it could be pushed again. Already the Hannibal Chollops of all the states were uttering loud cries of love for the Russians, the newest enemies of the arrogant British. The Haligonians sat under the powerful cannon of the Citadel, regarded the rising brick walls of the biggest barracks (Wellington Barracks) yet seen in the city, inspected the fleet in the harbor, and waited to see what would happen.

What happened was a vindication of the basic good sense of the American people. During the Crimean War the United States maintained a strict neutrality, if its jingo newspapers did not. There were incidents and provocations, of course. One occurred when Joseph Howe, at a request from London, left his railway for a month or two and went to New York to recruit a legion of Germans and Irish for the war against Russia. He secured nine hundred men and, to satisfy the United States law, shipped them to Halifax as "labourers for the railway." His further efforts were defeated by an Irishman in Halifax who telegraphed New York and aroused to fury the very numerous Anglophobes of that city. A mob surrounded Howe's hotel and he barely escaped with his life.

Before going on to Britain and the Crimea, Howe's recruits were quartered in the fortress, the Irish on Melville Island and the Germans in the Citadel. Haligonians long remembered the deep harmonious voices of the Germans as they gathered on the ramparts on calm evenings and sent the songs of the fatherland ringing over the town. Another thing long remembered occurred when one of the regiments in garrison, the 72nd Highlanders, formed up on the Grand Parade and heard their colonel demand in a ringing voice "All volunteers for active service—one pace forward, march!" The regiment stepped forward as one man. And away it went soon afterwards, kilts swinging, pipes wailing, to the waiting steamer and the grim hills of the Crimea.

In a sudden gush of martial spirit the officers of the Halifax militia held their first regimental meeting in many years. But the war was remote, and most Haligonians held the even tenor of their way. The Freemasons had a fancy-dress ball. The Fire Engine Company had their annual sleigh drive. The townsfolk took their Sunday walks, towards "Richmond," the terminus of the new railway at the north end of Barrington Street—a stretch then known as Campbell Road. The gentry went for sleigh drives along the Basin shore to John Butler's wayside inn, rode in their carriages in the summer weather to Point Pleasant, sailed on merry fishing trips and to picnics at McNab's Island, and attended fashionable weddings at St. Mary's and St. Paul's.

The great event of the year was the Industrial Exhibition, something entirely new. A huge marquee on the lawn at each end of Province House displayed dairy and vegetable products and the more bulky industrial wares. The building itself was filled with exhibits of Nova Scotian art and enterprise; oil paintings, water color and drawings in chalk, pencil, and crayon were on view in the Council Chamber, saddlery, hardware, gold and silver ware and jewelry in the Judges' Robing Room, and so on through the other chambers. There was everything, from embroidery and chenille work to musical instruments and fine furniture.

Altogether there were 1260 exhibitors and over 3000 exhibits; the list makes astonishing reading in the light of modern times, when so many of these skills and manufactures have vanished from Nova Scotia. It reflects a busy and thriving time when the Bluenoses were self-sufficient at home and pushing their sails and products into every sea, a little nation of 300,000 with their backs to the continent, flying their own ancient flag beside the Union Jack, sure of themselves and their future.

Within a few months the first section of railroad was finished from the Richmond terminus to Three Mile House at Fairview. Passenger cars full of eager Haligonians went for the jaunt, all drawn by an engine named of course the *Mayflower*. And now appeared the incomparable Fishwick, a transatlantic Thomas Cook with a genius for transportation. When the line reached Bedford, Fishwick undertook to forward goods by cart into the interior. When it reached Windsor he made connection between that port and St. John with his own steamers *Emperor* and *Empress*. When it reached Truro, Fishwick's Express was there to carry the freight in enormous horsedrawn wagons to Amherst, Pictou, and New Glasgow. Fishwick would tackle anything at any time, on land or water, and for a generation he was in his way the most remarkable man in Halifax.

In 1855 the redoubtable Howe was defeated at the polls by a redoubtable country doctor entering politics for the first time, Charles Tupper, another man of destiny. With Tupper appeared the first faint shadow of a cloud which was to change the whole outlook of Nova Scotia—confederation, twelve years away.

Nothing marred the sunshine of 1856, however. The Crimean War was at its height, shipping boomed, money was plentiful. The Union Bank opened its doors to take care of some of this prosperity. Howe found another seat. The city built a stout new stone wall and iron fence about the old cemetery, as if to keep its ghosts where they belonged. A hospital for the insane was rising on the Dartmouth side at a spot appropriately called Mount Hope, and some quick soul in full possession of his wits had already stolen the coins out of the cornerstone. A new city prison appeared on Rock Head with a marvelous view of the Narrows and Bedford Basin; later generations of law-abiding home builders were to regard that site with envy and despair. The Citadel was finished at last, and the Admiralty transferred Melville Island to the garrison for the discomfort of army defaulters.

The war ended suddenly, and in the pleasant month of June 1856 Her Majesty's 76th Regiment marched out of the Citadel to encamp at Point Pleasant, making room on "the Hill" for the bronzed and bearded 63rd, just arrived from the Crimea. But the last shots had barely died away at Sebastopol when rebellious sepoys fired the first ones of the Indian Mutiny and another war began. Every British soldier bound for India and every ounce of his equipment and supplies had to make the long voyage around South Africa. Apart from this, the great gold rush to California was now at its height, with a multitude of adventurers going around the Horn, while the new gold rush to Australia carried every digger and his duffle halfway around the world.

All this meant ships, and ships were Nova Scotia's business. The steamer was not yet a serious competitor on the ocean routes or even in coastal shipping. The long deep-sea runs about the world required big sailing ships—bigger than most Bluenose craft at this time; but the demand dragged the big windjammers off the North Atlantic and West Indies charter markets and so made way for the stout and handy Nova Scotia craft. Every bottom built in Nova Scotia carried a Bluenose skipper, Bluenose mates, and usually a Bluenose crew on its business about the seas. Joe Howe was predicting firmly that a time would come—and that not far—when half a million Nova Scotians would make their living on the sea.

These were the days when sailing ships, flank to flank at the wharves, raised a thicket of spars along the Halifax waterfront, and their long sharply steeved bowsprits and jib booms literally made a roof above the sheds of Water Street. Water Street was a small boy's paradise with its ship forest, its lively sailormen with tales of all the world, its smell of hemp and tar and strange cargoes, its endless procession of laden horse drays rattling over the cobbles, its busy sailmakers, spar makers, carpenters, riggers and calkers, and its general air of belonging to the sea and having nothing to do with the land. Indeed it was the haunt of many a staid townsman in his leisure hours. An American visitor, the great Rufus Choate, taken ill and dying in a house overlooking Halifax Harbor, murmured to the attendants: "If a schooner or sloop goes by, don't disturb me; but if there is a square-rigged ship, wake me up."

The wars touched Halifax lightly but with a thrill of local pride. Two Haligonians, officers in British regiments, perished gallantly at Sebastopol, and the townsmen erected in their honor the somewhat ugly brownstone arch, surmounted by a lion, which still stands over the gateway of the old cemetery on Barrington Street. Sir John Inglis, the courageous defender of Lucknow, was a Halifax man; as there was already an Inglis Street, Lucknow Street was named in his honor. In the column fighting for his relief was a Nova Scotia Negro, William Hall, a son of escaped slaves from the *Chesapeake*. He had joined the Royal Navy at Halifax and served as a gunner in Peel's detachment from HMS *Shannon* when Sir Colin Campbell made his famous dash. For his courage in the storming party, Hall was awarded the Victoria Cross—Nova Scotia's first VC, and the second in all Canada.

In 1857 a huge fire swept a great part of Hollis Street and destroyed old Mather's Church, that relic of the Yankee pioneers. Two years later, another fire destroyed much of Granville Street. The two fires made a great clearance in the heart of the town, and modern structures went up to replace the old. In truth, fire was a benefactor in the old crowded wooden city, whatever the momentary suffering. The irony of later days was that twentieth-century alarm systems and fire-fighting apparatus perpetuated the wooden slum which in the old days was swept away at least once in each generation, and which long defied the efforts of hopeful committees dedicated to slum clearance.

In 1861 the city turned out loyally to welcome Edward, Prince of Wales, a lively young man of nineteen who was busy seeing the world. When he passed on to Canada, the invaluable Fishwick took full charge of the arrangements for his staff and baggage. More exciting was the new gold rush to Nova Scotia, of all places! In 1858 one L'Estrange discovered gold to the eastward of Halifax, at Tangier. Soon it was found elsewhere in the province, and every Halifax shop clerk had visions of sudden wealth. A city newspaper complained humorously that the "Gone to Tangier" sign was hanging everywhere. The rush petered out, however, like others in Nova Scotia since. There is gold to be found in many parts of the province—even under the streets of Halifax, in certain places—but with few exceptions the veins are too thin for profitable mining.

At this time the dollar became officially what it had been so long in practice, the recognized currency of the province. Hitherto the merchants had done their business in dollars and cents and written their accounts in pounds, shillings, and pence, to the acute discomfort of their clerks. The Reciprocity Treaty of 1854 had brought a great increase in trade with the United States, where the dollar was supreme, at a time when the British Government's sterling expenditure on the Halifax fortress had come to an end and the garrison was sharply reduced for service in the Crimea. The change was inevitable. Still, the public accounts continued to show parallel columns of pounds and the dollar equivalents; and the old habit of reckoning in "Halifax currency" pounds and shillings persisted many years. As late as 1915 bank notes payable in "Halifax currency" turned up to puzzle the tellers, and an investment banker who took over some old trusts in that year found that he was supposed to pay an annuity in it.

As the last echoes of the Indian Mutiny died away there was a lull in the shipping business. Then came the storm that blew it to the greatest prosperity it had ever known—the American Civil War.

26.
1861–1865

The American Civil War. The Trent *affair. British troops for Canada. A steam navy. Again rebuilding the fortress. Blockade-running. The police reorganized. The affairs of* Chesapeake *and* Tallahassee.

THE GROWING TENSION BETWEEN THE NORTHERN and Southern States had aroused a natural and very lively discussion in Nova Scotia because of the proximity of New England, the heart and soul of abolition. Trade relations with New England were very strong since the Reciprocity Treaty, the Bluenoses still regarded Boston as the business center of the universe, and high wages had attracted thousands of Nova Scotian young men and girls to the factories of Massachusetts. The influence of Henry Ward Beecher was felt by preachers in Nova Scotia no less than in the States, so that there was a tendency to combine denunciation of sin at home with thunders upon the iniquity of slavery a thousand miles away. More important still, everybody had read or was reading *Uncle Tom's Cabin*, by Mr. Beecher's sister.

Thus at the beginning of hostilities in 1861 there was a general sympathy in Nova Scotia for the North and a rush of young adventurers to join the Union army. One "Highland" regiment raised in Boston in 1861 consisted almost wholly of Nova Scotians, some of whom were members of the Halifax militia; and their tales of battle appearing in letters to home newspapers were followed with all the avidity of a people actually at war.

But the gathering of large armies across the border aroused misgivings in old men who remembered 1812, and their misgivings were increased by an astounding rumor from the States. It was said that Washington politicians were planning to unify their nation by a deliberately provoked war with a European nation or nations, preferably the British. The rumor was true. In April 1861 the United States Secretary of State, Seward, had made this cool proposal to President Lincoln, and suggested himself as the man to conduct the provocation and the war. Lincoln quietly put it aside. But the impression was abroad and it was not lessened when Seward ordered the governors of the Northern States to take "military precautions" on the Canadian frontier and the adjacent coasts. Then came the *Trent* affair.

There was a sensation in Halifax when the telegraph told how a United States warship had fired upon the Royal Mail steamer *Trent* in Bahamian waters and forcibly removed the emissaries of the Confederate Government who were on their way to Britain. Here to all appearances was the deliberate spark in the gunpowder. Excitement was just as tense in London, and throughout the empire. The British Government demanded prompt return of the captured Southerners, meanwhile rushing off transports packed with troops and war material for the defense of Canada. Some of these were landed near Rimouski, before winter closed the St. Lawrence, and the rest came to Halifax and St. John.

While this was going on the Northern newspapers were in full cry, approving the *Trent* seizures and twisting the lion's tail with all their might. The Secretary of the US Navy declared full approval of his warship's action; indeed the whole Cabinet was belligerent with the exception of the Postmaster and Lincoln himself, who insisted that the *Trent* passengers must be restored. Fortunately the President had his way. His clinching argument is said to have been: "Boys, I reckon we'll give them up. It's what we fought for in 1812—and we'll drink our own tea, won't we?"

Late in December HMS *Rinaldo* of the Halifax squadron went into Provincetown, Massachusetts, and there received the liberated Confederate ambassadors. And that apparently was that. A succession of Confederate victories in the field kept all eyes in Washington towards the south for some time to come. In the end, of course, the North was bound to win, with its overwhelming forces; and what would happen then was anybody's guess. In the meantime the British and colonial governments took no chances with the security of Canada.

In January 1862 Halifax swarmed with five thousand newly landed British troops, and the whole city turned out to watch the Grenadier Guards in their red tunics and black greatcoats, the veterans of Alma and Inkerman, marching through the streets to the Richmond railway station. Most of these troops were bound for the upper provinces; they and their artillery and stores had to be taken over the new railway line as far as it went, and thence by sled and afoot through the snowy forest to Quebec. And who had charge of these arrangements? Fishwick, of course! He got the columns there in record time.

When the fleet came in, the Haligonians rubbed their eyes. Only a year or so ago the station squadron had consisted of thirteen ships, an odd assortment of steam and sailing craft, and the flagship was the huge old wooden three-decker *Indus* with her Nelsonian masts and spars and her seventy-eight smooth-bore cannon. Now, presto!—the harbor was alive with twenty-four men-o'-war, Britannia's latest, every one a steamship. There was a significance in this that had nothing to do with war but a great deal to do with Nova Scotia's future. The twilight of the windjammer had begun.

And now the irony which dogs the footsteps of all fortress engineers caught up with those of Halifax. The rifled cannon had been perfected, and by its mere existence the defenses begun in 1829 and built at such cost in thirty years of incessant labor were rendered obsolete in a twinkling. There was no time to be lost. The whole defense system of the port had to be recast, and the work commenced at once. The garrison did part, but most of the transformation fell to John Brookfield, the able engineer and contractor whose firm did so much government and private building in Halifax in after years.

The work went on throughout and long after the American Civil War. In the pinewoods of Point Pleasant, Fort Ogilvie was rebuilt entirely and enlarged, the Martello tower repaired, and a new fort (Cambridge Battery) constructed between the Martello tower and the point itself. York Redoubt on its steep bluff was completely remodeled. So was Fort Charlotte on George's Island. Old Fort Clarence of the Dartmouth shore, scarcely changed in design since 1784, was rebuilt entirely. On the northwest tip of McNab's Island a new battery appeared at Ives Point. All these works were of massive masonry deeply banked with earth and armed with the latest rifled cannon, ranging from 7-inch guns weighing seven tons to lo-inch monsters weighing eighteen tons each. Finally, to replace the old gunpowder store in the Citadel (or rather to supplement it, for it was no longer sufficient for the garrison, let alone the fleet) a large bombproof magazine was constructed just below Wellington Barracks in the north end of the city, adjoining the Admiralty grounds.

Besides strong detachments of artillery, engineers, and other fortress troops, two crack British regiments were in garrison throughout the war, one quartered in Wellington Barracks, the other in the Citadel and Glacis Barracks. At regular intervals these regiments exchanged quarters, marching in column with their bands, and when they met in Gottingen Street the junior opened its ranks with British Army punctilio so that the senior could pass through.

To support the regulars in case of attack there were five battalions of Halifax militia. Each of these had an additional "volunteer company," a *corps d' elite* with a uniform of its own design and hue. When the Chebucto Greys, the Scottish Rifles, the Mayflower Rifles, the Halifax Rifles, and the Irish Volunteer Rifles paraded on the Common the effect was not merely martial but magnificent. The ladies who flocked there in billowing crinolines and ruffled pantalets, twirling absurd little parasols aloft, found themselves gazing upon a human rainbow.

Behind this gaudy show the core was hard enough. Training was vigorous under tough veteran sergeant majors of the British Army, and every man in the city between the ages of sixteen and sixty took his part. The aging Joe Howe observed, in 1862: "Half the members of the legislature last winter earned an appetite for breakfast in the drill-room, and used to pass my window on the coldest mornings with their rifles over their shoulders. The crack of the rifle is as common a sound as the note of the bobolink, and inter-colonial shooting matches are becoming an institution." And this was going on all over the province. By 1865 the Bluenoses could boast a force of nearly 60,000 trained men, the largest in the British American provinces.

The contradictory human thing about all these precautions against American attack was the fact that the Nova Scotians continued to take sides in the strife below the border. Every village smithy, every corner store rang and thumped with argument. The general sentiment against slavery gave a majority for the North and young men continued to join the Union regiments. This sentiment was thoroughly exploited by Union recruiting agents operating from Boston, who offered bounties as high as three hundred dollars to every man who would enlist. It was said that by the war's end not less than ten thousand Nova Scotians had fought in the blue ranks of the North.

One was a son of Joe Howe himself, a trooper in Sheridan's famous cavalry. Another was Dr. Brown Gesner (a son of the Nova Scotia geologist), surgeon to the 10th New York Infantry, who came to Halifax on leave in 1863 and married Miss Frances Field at the altar of St. George's. Every great battle of the war brought melancholy little obituaries in the Halifax newspapers. When the end came there were Nova Scotian graves all the way from Bull Run to Appomattox and from Vicksburg to Wilmington; and there were crippled veterans in almost every town and village of the province. The stone lion facing Government House commemorates a pair of Nova Scotians who fell in the Crimea; but only the files of dead Halifax newspapers mark this great American struggle in which Nova Scotians were engaged on a scale hitherto unknown in their history and not repeated until 1914.

The proportion of Bluenoses fighting for the South was small; Howe estimated it at one to every fifty for the North, but the barriers of distance and the Union blockade had much to do with that. A tendency to side with the underdog in the fight was natural, even in many who disliked slavery. In Halifax itself the pro-South sentiment was strong, and was increased by two unexpected developments of the war. One was the destruction of a large part of the American merchant marine by bold and active Confederate cruisers, and the absorption of the rest in moving huge Union armies up and down the coast. The other was the Union blockade of Southern ports, which created chances for smuggling at enormous profit. The first sent ocean freights soaring and spurred the Nova Scotia shipyards to a new frenzy of activity. The second brought an entire new industry to Halifax—the business of blockade-running—and with it an invasion of Confederate agents and of adventurers from half the world.

A great part of this business was paid in gold, but the early victories of the Southern armies were so impressive that many a Halifax merchant accepted large sums in Confederate paper currency, all worthless by 1865. The demand for goods was various and astonishing. The Southern forces wanted arms and munitions of all kinds, and blankets, saddles, boots, and medical supplies. The Southern ladies demanded bonnets, gowns, shoes, stockings, stays, ribbons—everything a woman wants, especially in time of war, to make herself pleasing to her men. In Halifax the agents of this risky but lucrative trade bought everything they could lay their hands on, and the price was no object.

Said one eyewitness: "I have seen a man go into a large wholesale dry goods store in Halifax and ask the proprietor in the most matter-of-fact way what he would take for his whole establishment—spot cash. The town was filled with Southern agents. Hesslein of the Halifax Hotel could hardly buy champagne fast enough; for the Southerners, with old-fashioned notions of hospitality and with the official classes and the military and navy to win over, put no restraint on their lavishness. I have held a million dollars in my hand when a Southern agent, temporarily in hiding, entrusted notes of the Confederacy to that amount in my care."

The station ships of the Royal Navy, sweeping in and out of the harbor on their lawful occasions, screws churning, paddles thundering, were an impressive sight, especially when a favorable wind enabled them to hoist their auxiliary sails for extra speed. But far more interesting was the fleet of blockade-runners. All were steamships, screw-propelled or paddle wheelers—and if "paddle" sounds clumsy, be it remembered that some of these ships could make up to twenty knots. Most were designed and built for this exciting game, and photographs taken in Halifax Harbor in 1864 show long sleek hulls with streamlined paddle boxes and a minimum of superstructure, all marking a sharp advance in steamship architecture in a few short years.

In contrast, the sailing ships of Nova Scotia flocked out of the harbor carrying cargoes to the world and especially to the Northern States, where the provincial staples, lumber, fish, and coal, were all in great demand. By 1862 one third of the ships entering the port of Boston were windjammers from Nova Scotia. Two years later there was a freight-steamer line as well.

Halifax was prosperous as never before in all her boom and bust history. The city was glutted with money. In 1864 the Merchants' Bank was founded on the strength of it, and, for complete coverage, so was the People's Bank. The semiweekly auctions of stocks and bonds in the Merchants' Exchange Reading Room were lively affairs. The weather had a quaint effect on the market. "On stormy days the attendance would be limited and stocks would be 'slaughtered'. A few days afterward a sale would take place on a fine day with a room full of buyers and better prices would be obtained." Picture a speculator of 1864 consulting not a ticker tape but a barometer!

The excitement and hubbub as usual brought trouble for the town watch. That strange restlessness which always appears in garrisons and fleets in a time of war, and which breaks forth in riot on the smallest excuse, showed itself notably in the so-called "Greasy Pole Riot" of 1863. Apparently dissatisfied with the award of prizes in a greased-pole competition held in Grand Parade the day before, the soldiers of the 16th Regiment broke out of barracks and indulged in an orgy of fisticuffs and window smashing which set the whole city in an uproar.

A force of special constables armed with short batons went into action, and eventually order was restored. On October 1, 1864, the police force was reorganized completely. The day and night watches were brought under one command and dressed in uniforms, each man wearing a round copper badge bearing the words Halifax Police. The whole force consisted of five sergeants and twenty-eight constables, sufficient for civic needs but still hopelessly inadequate in case of "trouble with the military"—a condition which Halifax has had to face again and again in her long story.

Behind this hustle and bustle certain other interesting things were going on. For one thing the Shubenacadie Canal, begun in 1826, was finished in 1861. A small steamer made the passage from Halifax Harbor to Maitland on the Bay of Fundy and returned in triumph. Dalhousie College, after years in the doldrums, was reorganized as a provincial university in 1863. But most important, if much less noticed, was the progress of a great idea—the confederation of the British colonies in North America.

The notion was old, of course. It had been suggested in Halifax and elsewhere as far back as the 1790s. But the threat of a modern war with the United States brought the matter to a head. Two weeks after Seward made his astounding proposal to President Lincoln, Joseph Howe stood up in the Nova Scotia Legislature and moved that the British Government and the governments of the Canadian provinces be approached "on the subject of a union of the North American provinces, or of the Maritime provinces." He won his resolution.

The machinery of discussion was slow (the transatlantic cable laid in 1858 had proved a failure) and most Haligonians had forgotten the matter within twelve months. But Howe was to remember it bitterly in the days to come. Already fate was setting the stage for the great quarrel. In 1863, after a defeat at the polls, Howe took a post with the Fisheries Commission, a British Government appointment. In 1864 his great political rival Tupper himself proposed a union of the Maritime Provinces; and in September of that year came the first conference at

Charlottetown, where the Maritime delegates found their meeting invaded by a delegation from Canada proposing a larger union. Howe was invited, but he was away on his duties in Newfoundland. He had little to say when the combined delegations came on to Halifax and suave John A. Macdonald announced their agreement on the principle of a complete confederation.

The Canadians made a good impression in Halifax, although there was some sarcastic comment on the way they had taken over the Maritime conference. Most popular was D'Arcy McGee, with his ready wit and smile. His wit never deserted him, even in his cups. One evening as he and Tupper were walking along Barrington Street, McGee gave vent to his noisy spirits outside St. Mary's glebe house. Said Tupper, urgently: "McGee, be careful—the Archbishop will hear you!" Archbishop Connolly, much beloved in Halifax, was a strong believer in confederation. McGee replied: "Don't call me McGee—call me Jones!" Mr. A.G. Jones was (next to Howe) Tupper's most bitter opponent on confederation.

D'Arcy McGee had been first in the Canadian provinces to see the danger arising from the quarrel between the States, and his memorable "The first gun fired at Fort Sumter had a message for us" rings like a bell after all these years. The alarm of 1861 had faded away in the later thunders of the American struggle, but Northern newspapers continued to beat the anti-British drum and there was much talk of "driving the French out of Mexico and the British out of Canada" as soon as the Confederacy was crushed. Indeed it was suggested that the United States might not wait so long, for by 1863 its armies were enormous and the American development of ironclad warships had rendered the other navies of the world as obsolete as the prewar Halifax forts.

The most likely *casus belli* was the use of British ports by Confederate naval raiders, and Halifax twice witnessed a touchy situation. In December 1863 the steamer *Chesapeake* (a name which pops up with curious frequency in the city's story) left New York for Portland, Maine, having on board a number of passengers who were in fact Confederate sailors in disguise. As darkness fell, the Confederates seized the ship at pistol point, shooting one or two of the officers and putting the rest of the crew in irons. They then made for Halifax; but a shortage of coal forced them into a small bay near the harbor mouth, where *Chesapeake* was boarded and seized by one of the United States cruisers watching the port.

This procedure was as highhanded as the Confederates' own, for *Chesapeake* lay well inside Nova Scotia territorial waters; and the situation was explosive, for Vice-Admiral Sir James Hope and his powerful British naval squadron lay at anchor just around the corner. Wisely, the commander. of USS *Dacotah* sent *Chesapeake* into Halifax for disposal by the Court of Vice-Admiralty, and at once there was a furore in the United States and a battle of wits in Halifax. The Confederate chief agent at Halifax, Benjamin Wier, had an office on Brown's Wharf where he and his staff labored ardently to forward the blockade-running and other matters important to the Southern cause. The United States consul, Mortimer M. Jackson, was a zealous and vigilant man with a staff naturally busy making all possible difficulties for Mr. Wier; and Jackson was in secret communication with the Union cruisers hovering off the port, reporting to them every move of ships and cargoes bound to the South. Thus there was a little War between the States in Halifax itself, each with its ardent group of Haligonian supporters.

The North struck the first blow; a charge of attempted murder was laid in the Halifax courts against the three captured Confederate officers, and an officer and boat's crew from *Dacotah* brought the trio ashore to be turned over to the sheriff for trial. But the South won the round, for two prominent Halifax doctors and the son of a wealthy brewer staged an adroit scuffle on the wharf, under cover of which the prisoners dived into the crowd and were spirited back to Dixie.

The matter of *Chesapeake* herself was thrashed out in the Court of Vice-Admiralty under an able Halifax judge, Alexander Stewart. The Confederates claimed *Chesapeake* as a legitimate prize of war. The Union maintained that her seizure was piracy. The two sides secured the most brilliant lawyers in the city for the case and the argument was long. Stewart's judgment was cold and correct; the ship and her cargo were to be restored to their owners at once. It aroused much recrimination between the rival parties in the city and there was a memorable scene in the sedate chambers of the Halifax Club, where the judge was upbraided and insulted by what the record mysteriously calls "a gentleman of high position." There was even some dissatisfaction in Washington, where the Secretary of the Navy (the backer if not the author of the *Trent* affair) declared unblushingly that "the delivery of the *Chesapeake* ought to have been made promptly and unconditionally by executive authority"; but the egregious Seward had the good grace to add his government's appreciation of "the enlightened and impartial spirit by which the Vice-Admiralty Court has been guided."

More famous is the affair of the *Tallahassee*, the Confederate raider which slipped out of Wilmington in the summer of 1864, appeared off New York turning away foreign shipping with a magnificent warning that the port had been closed "by order of the Board of Admiralty at Richmond," sank fifty Northern merchant vessels between Sandy Hook and Cape Cod, and at last fled into Halifax with the Union cruisers *Huron* and *Nansemond* in hot pursuit. Under the British neutrality laws Captain John Taylor Wood of *Tallahassee* had exactly forty-eight hours in which to coal, repair his damages, and go out to face the Union music. As the time drew near, the whole city was agog.

The story has been told a good many times; how the Union cruisers waited off Chebucto Head, watching the main harbor channel, and how in utter darkness a local pilot named Jock Fleming guided *Tallahassee* through the shallow and dangerous Eastern Passage—a winding channel considered impassable to all but small fishing craft—while a boat ahead took soundings here and there. *Tallahassee's* engines turned slowly as she used first one and then the other of her twin screws to twist her nimble way among the shoals, until at last she gained the open sea and slipped away to safety. It would be hard to say which heaved the biggest sigh of relief: Captain Wood, Jock Fleming, the "Southern" Haligonians, or Britannia in the person of Admiral Hope, K.C.B., who was spared the embarrassment of watching his friend Wood hammered to bits by a pair of Yankees under the noses of the British fleet and fortress.

When the war came to its inevitable end in 1865 a number of Confederate officers removed with their families to Halifax and formed a little colony of "un-Reconstructed rebels" in the port. Notable amongst them were Commodore Josiah Tatnall, the man who made famous the phrase "Blood is thicker than water," and Captain John T. Wood of the Confederate Navy. Others were Colonel Bennet Hornsby, the Kentucky cavalryman, and Richard Fielden Armstrong, late lieutenant of the famous *Alabama*. Hornsby went into the real estate business, developed the Willow Park section of Halifax as a residential area, and for many years was one of the most successful land speculators in the city. Wood, the hero of *Tallahassee*, who had fought with his sailors ashore as infantrymen in the last dying struggles of the Confederacy, was a grandson of Zachary Taylor, twelfth President of the United States, and a nephew of Jefferson Davis, President of the Confederacy. He lived the rest of his days in Morris Street, where his neighbors long remembered the upright figure, the quiet courtesy, the broad hat, the white hair and trim goatee of a typical Southern gentleman of the old school. His son Charles, a graduate of the Royal Military College at Kingston, Ontario, was the first Canadian officer to fall in South Africa during the Boer War. His grandson S.T. Wood joined the Royal Canadian Mounted Police, rose through the ranks and became one of the most notable commissioners in the history of that noted force.

27.
1865–1875

The decline of sail. Fenian alarms and excursions. The horsecars. Confederation. A visit from Prince Arthur. Death of Joseph Howe.

LEE'S SURRENDER AT APPOMATTOX ENDED NOT ONLY the American Civil War but the whole series of unrelated wars and world migrations, beginning with the California gold rush in 1850, which in fifteen years had carried the business of ship building and operation to a dizzy peak of prosperity. Now came the slump, and Nova Scotia was hard hit. But worse was in store. The steamship had emerged from the wars triumphant over sail in all departments—as a man-o'-war, as a troop transport, and as a freight carrier. The blockade-runners especially had proved the ability of a steamship to carry a cargo quickly and surely to its destination, regardless of weather, and to maintain a regular schedule on that basis. When these ships (most of them British built and owned) turned to compete for the shrunken freights of a postwar world, the tramp steamer was born and the doom of the sailing ship was sealed.

Lacking cheap and plentiful iron, Nova Scotia was not equipped to fall in with the trend. In any case the Bluenoses were wedded to sail and clung to it, building fewer but bigger hulls to catch the long-haul trade about the world where time was not so important, and where for some years yet the steamers could not compete for lack of bunker space and adequate coaling stations. Depending on their know-how, on the sheer ability of their hard-driving captains not only to move their ships about the seven seas but to smell a freight in any out-of-the-way port and make a sharp bargain for it, the Bluenoses went down slowly, fighting to the end.

The death of sail took many years, but the great profits of the fifties and sixties shrank to a trickle in the seventies, and by 1880 grass had begun to grow in many a once-busy shipyard. Iron hulls, even for sailing ships, were stronger, tighter, more enduring. They were cheap to build and easy to maintain, their cargo capacity was greater for a given size, and their insurance rate was much less. Hence the shipping firms of Nova Scotia in the 1880s began to buy iron or steel hulled windjammers built in Great Britain, in a last attempt to get costs down and outbid steamers on the ocean routes. It was the twilight of the old sea-gods, descending at a time when the surviving Bluenose yards actually were turning out their finest handiwork.

The great shipping slump coincided with the end of the Reciprocity Treaty with the United States, under which Nova Scotia had built up a great and profitable trade with New England, her neighbor and natural market. The Americans, flushed with victory over the rebels and more belligerent than ever, were in no mood for extending trade concessions. On the contrary there was much talk of "annexation" of the Canadian provinces, and thousands of wild Irish veterans of the Union army were gathering on the border for the "invasion."

They called themselves Fenians, of course, and declared that the conquest of Canada was to secure the liberty of Ireland—a piece of Hibernian logic that did not impress the Canadian provinces, which had spent the past five years preparing to resist an invasion made on any pretext whatever. The Fenians who eventually crossed the border in force at half a dozen points found the Canadian woods and pastures full of determined men who shot remarkably straight and used the bayonet with a zeal that reminded the intruders uncomfortably of Johnny Reb. They ran back across the border, and then—and not till then—the United States Government stepped in and put an end to their antics.

The wet width of the Bay of Fundy spared Nova Scotia any incursions of this sort, but the Bluenoses mustered their army of sixty thousand and for many months kept it on a day's notice footing.

These alarms and excursions in a trade-fallen time created the atmosphere in which Nova Scotia greeted the confederation of Canada in 1867. Charles Tupper, who believed that ends justify means, had led the province into what most Bluenoses called its "chains" without consulting the people. Howe, the old war horse, objected violently to the means and carried his attack to confederation itself. The uproar lasted five years.

The provincial constituencies were strongly against confederation. Halifax itself was divided into two camps, roughly half-and-half. Those who saw the advantages of union in matters of defense, in the prospect of a great Canadian market by way of the promised intercolonial railway, and the immediate benefit of new wharves, breakwaters, and other public works in Halifax itself were all for confederation. Those who were proud of Nova Scotian independence, who distrusted Canadian—especially Upper Canadian—motives, who looked at the map and compared the trade advantages of the broad ocean with that of a narrow and problematical ribbon of steel, who knew that whatever happened in the other colonies the British Navy alone could guarantee the security of Nova Scotia, and that Britain must maintain the Halifax fortress for its own security in the North Atlantic—all these were opposed.

Unfortunately for the latter the British Government, while determined to keep Halifax as a North Atlantic base and Esquimalt as a North Pacific base, was anxious to shed the burden of defending the enormous stretch between. And as Nova Scotia was the stumbling block to a confederacy willing to assume this burden the Bluenoses found themselves under strong pressure, not merely from the upper provinces but from the imperial power itself. This manifested itself in many ways.

To begin with, the lieutenant governor, Sir R.G. Macdonnell, an outspoken anti-confederate, was replaced at Halifax by a strong confederate in the person of Sir Fenwick Williams, the Nova Scotian hero of Kars. The commander of the Nova Scotia militia (an imperial appointment) was General J.W. Laurie, an ardent confederate. He was determined to take no chances in the event of a clash, for the Bluenose temper was running high. Militiamen of anti-confederate views were given short shrift in the matter of appointments and even in the patriotic privilege of training for defense. "Them's as for Canada may drill. Them's as for Nova Scotia may sit on the fence," was the order given by a sergeant major at one general inspection; and the general approved. So it went in other matters.

In Halifax things were still fairly prosperous in the carryover from the Civil War; in many ways all seemed right with the world, despite another cholera scare in 1866, when the steamer *England* arrived with the plague on board. She was held in the harbor mouth and the disease did not reach the city, although in the quarantine on McNab's Island many of her passengers and the heroic port health officer, Dr. Slayter, perished.

In May, at the height of the Fenian scare, the US monitor *Mainitomah* arrived in port for a visit, accompanied by the unarmored *Augusta*. All eyes were on the monitor, the first Halifax had seen of the new American ironclads which had changed the face of naval warfare. But on the following day HMS *Favourite* arrived from England, the first British ironclad on the North American station; and while the two crews looked each other over in the succeeding days a pair of big troopships passed down the harbor, one carrying a regiment of redcoats to Barbados for garrison duty, the other taking a regiment to Quebec for service against the Fenians. Britannia was still in business.

In June of the same year Halifax opened its first street railway, running the whole length of Barrington Street (which in those days bore different names for its various sections: Pleasant Street, Barrington Street, Lockman Street, and Campbell Road) from south to north. These were the famous old horsecars, of course. The whole city turned out to watch the inaugural trip—five passenger cars containing Lieutenant Governor Doyle and other important folk, and two truck cars for the band of Her Majesty's 4th Regiment, tootling bravely all the way from the Kissing Bridge to Richmond Depot. The cars were a tremendous success; everybody wanted a ride. Within a few weeks a solemn deputation of the unco guid called upon Mayor Richey to stop the horsecars on the Sabbath. The people were having altogether too much fun.

Warships continued to flit in and out. In April 1867 a French squadron—*Magenta* flying the flag of Vice-Admiral de la Roncière, *Magnanime*, and *Flandre*—arrived from Vera Cruz. They were the last of the French getting out of Mexico and leaving Emperor Maximilian to his fate. If the British were slow in getting out of Canada, at least one half of the American newspaper prophecy had been fulfilled.

In 1867 Halifax became a city of the Dominion of Canada, amid more groans than cheers. Howe was demanding repeal of the act of confederation already, and that famous voice had lost none of its magic. The young bloods of the anti-confederation party were setting the city aroar with their lively newspaper, the *Gunboat*; and the young bloods of the other side were plotting their most dastardly trick, a fake edition of *Gunboat* hailing the new Dominion.

The city's social and business life proceeded calmly enough, nevertheless, in the first summer of its new state. Sunday schools held picnics at Downs' Zoological Gardens on the Dutch Village Road or cruised along the harbor and Bedford Basin to Prince's Lodge in a chartered ferryboat.

Sir William Young, the chief justice, formally opened two new acres of flowers about Griffin's Pond, adjoining the Horticultural Gardens. Engines with enormous cone funnels chuffed out of the Richmond depot dragging trains to Windsor, Truro, or Pictou, and a new private company had begun to lay rails from Windsor to Annapolis. Shipping men were sending hopeful charter offers to Britain over the transatlantic cable, laid finally and successfully by the *Great Eastern* in the previous year.

The remodeling of the fortress, begun in 1861, was nearly complete, the new Pavilion Barracks were going up on Brunswick Street, the new Glacis Barracks would be finished next year, and, to make all complete, the imperial authorities were about to build on Cogswell Street "the finest military hospital in America." Fashionable Anglican wedding parties drove out to the little "Three Mile Church" at Fairview; and when the snow came the Halifax Club, the Chebucto Greys and scores of other clubs, regiments, schools, and associations went tinkling along the Basin road in the starlight on their annual sleigh drives.

Howe had triumphed in the first Dominion election, held just eighty days after confederation came into effect. Of the confederates in Nova Scotia only Tupper won his seat, and Howe went to Ottawa heading a phalanx of stem Bluenoses dedicated to repeal. That could be granted only by the imperial government. In February 1868, Howe sailed from Halifax for London with a little group of supporters. But Tupper turned up in London. The British Government (with Tupper playing devil's advocate) refused to consider repeal on any account, and Howe came home in June reciting alternatives ranging all the way from "We may confess to final defeat and accept the best terms we can get from the Canadians" to the grim "We may be driven by-and-by, despairing of all other redress...to take up arms."

In this atmosphere Halifax greeted the first anniversary of confederation. It was tense. On June 29 the Haligonians held their customary holiday to celebrate the Queen's coronation. All provincial government offices in the city were closed. All Dominion public offices in the city remained open. Two days later, Dominion Day, all the provincial offices were pointedly open, while the dominion offices were closed. Indeed all the signs seemed ominous. When the Citadel fired a salute in honor of Canada's first birthday, one of the guns went off prematurely, killed two artillerymen, and wounded several others. And when Sir John Macdonald came to Halifax in August with a delegation to iron out the differences, one editor openly advocated assault. But Howe quashed any such rudeness in a prompt and trenchant letter to the press.

All that autumn and winter, letters passed between Howe and Macdonald on the subject of better terms for Nova Scotia; for Howe had given up repeal as hopeless. By November he was comparing the continued outcry for it to "the screams of seagulls round the grave of a dead Indian on the coast of Labrador," a simile difficult to improve upon. In another two months the new terms were settled, Howe accepted a post in the dominion cabinet, and the great fight was over; but its echoes were to go on rumbling for generations.

In 1869 the city received a royal visitor, Prince Arthur. The Governor General of Canada came down for the occasion, the admiral arrived in HMS *Revenge*, and the prince landed under a salute of cannon and proceeded to Government House through streets lined with redcoats of the garrison, Royal Marines, local militia and volunteer companies in all the hues of the prism, and all the various societies. It was like old eighteenth-century days. In the evening the public buildings were illuminated, every loyal citizen kept his house lights burning to a late hour, and crowds of soldiers, sailors, and townsfolk strolled under the gas lights of Barrington Street.

The prince spent a busy week. He was entertained by Archbishop Walsh at a luncheon, attended a band concert in the Horticultural Gardens, reviewed the troops, the seamen, and marines on the Common—a tremendous display, for the fleet was in—and he inspected the warships, attended the Highland Society's picnic on McNab's Island, was enrolled as an honorary member of the Halifax Club, and attended a military ball in Province House, a citizens' picnic at Prince's Lodge and a torchlight parade by the Halifax firemen. The city was highly pleased with itself as well as with the prince, and talked about the show for months.

These pleasant memories obscured a significant bit of news from across the sea, the opening of the Suez Canal—another nail in the coffin of the wind ships. Steamers now could make the short run to India with easy coaling stages; and the long ocean run around the Cape, where the sailing ship had the advantage, had lost at once its importance and its profit. In the same year the canny Fishwick opened a steam-packet service from Halifax along the south shore of Nova Scotia, where there was no railway and where for a century a fleet of schooners and brigantines had carried all the trade. Even the sailing coaster was doomed.

In 1870 the directors of the Bank of Nova Scotia, meeting in their institution on Hollis Street, discovered that their manager James Forman had been falsifying the books for years. His defalcations came to $315,000. This revelation startled the city and rocked the bank to its granite foundations. No less startling in its way was a rude disturbance some months later in the dim recesses of the Halifax Club where the steward, yielding to an impulse that must have assailed him many times before, brought the members out of their chairs by stabbing himself repeatedly with a knife and jumping out of a window. The wretched man died; but fortunately the club recovered.

In the same year, with an almost audible sigh of relief, the British Government withdrew its troops and responsibilities from all of Canada except Esquimalt and Halifax. Joe Howe, old and crotchety, could not resist a blast at the new imperial policy "which strips Canada of every soldier, gathers up every old sentry-box and guncarriage…and ships them off to England." He was getting feeble now. He had never been happy at Ottawa where, though he was too proud to admit it, his position was essentially false.

In 1873 Howe came home to accept the greatest honor in his native town and province, the post of lieutenant governor. Within three weeks he was dead. On June 4, to the boom of minute guns on the Citadel, the long funeral cortege wound its way from Government House to Camp Hill Cemetery and the whole province mourned. In the time to come men boasted if they had passed a word with him or held his horse, women if he had kissed them—and he usually had. Howe, with his human strengths and weaknesses, not always right but always the bonnie fighter right or wrong, was to be remembered and beloved as the gallant knight in shining armor who rescued Nova Scotia from the twelve greedy uncles only to see her swallowed by the dragon.

28.
1876

The Intercolonial Railway. Decline of trade and prosperity. The evolution of the Halifax Brahmin.

ON DOMINION DAY, 1876—NINE YEARS AFTER CONfederation—the promised Intercolonial Railway was opened for traffic from the Great Lakes to the sea at Halifax. And that was just the trouble with it. The traffic seemed to flow in that single direction by an inexorable law of gravity, like the waters of the great St. Lawrence itself. Nova Scotia's products remained chiefly fish, coal, and lumber; but Ontario had no taste for codfish, got its coal cheaply across Lake Erie from the Pennsylvania mines, and had lumber (and a good many other things) to sell.

In the nine years past, Halifax had lost a good deal of its international trade by the decline of wooden shipping and the rising tariff walls of the United States; but there remained a solid and profitable trade within the Maritime Provinces. The city and province had many small factories catering to this market, and their products were supplemented by large quantities of European goods imported through the old-established Halifax mercantile houses. Business was conducted in the stately fashion which had grown up in colonial times, with the provincial merchants coming to town once or twice a year to look over stocks, place their orders, and arrange for shipment. Their merchant hosts entertained them handsomely but decorously and they went away to their towns and villages with pleasant memories and a renewed supply of goods.

All these affairs were rudely upset when the Intercolonial Railway poured into the province not the promised and expected army of eager Canadian customers but a flying column of sharp and thrusting drummers from the factories and great mercantile houses of Toronto and

Montreal. Complained a survey of Halifax business published at this time: "The importers here purchased from these drummers on the understanding that their customers in the country would not be 'drummed' also. But these enterprising drummers would rush over the whole land and sell to customers in any smaller quantities at prices as low as those offered to the wholesale trade; and thus, with their warehouses filled and the outlets stopped, the Halifax merchants found themselves suffering all the evils of a business overdone."

An army engineer, drawing up plans for the defense of Halifax in the early days, had stated that his first design was "to protect the Inhabitants of the Town from the sudden incursions of Canadians & Indians." It was sad to think that the huge defenses erected since had succeeded only in keeping out the Indians.

The 1876 survey went on to say, with dignity but with flair: "The solid people of this racy and unique community, prudent, homelike and accumulative as they are—for the fortunes here have been saved rather than made—naturally object to the mode of selling goods by drummers on the ground that it is too expensive for healthy business; but while they have been obliged in a measure to accept the situation, their stubborn struggle against the inevitable has allowed considerable encroachment upon their proper territory, and much of the traffic thus snatched from their immediate grasp will not soon be called back...This old-fashioned dignity in business...is hardly sufficient to the present emergency...It is for the wholesale merchants of Halifax to study carefully the situation and to take promptly such steps as shall retrieve for them the relative position occupied by their fair city years ago."

But alas, the "relative position" was not to be retrieved by the mere hire of drummers. The large and growing industries of central Canada with their cheap power and rich resources were too much for their small counterparts in the outlying provinces. Also the saddle of the Dominion, like any other, was placed in the middle; and he who sat there rode the horse, commercially and politically. When Sir John Macdonald applied his National Policy in 1878 the Halifax importers found that a bridle went with the saddle—and the bit was very painful in their teeth.

It was of no use to cry like Joe Howe's seagulls over the grave of repeal. Free Trade was doomed in the world, and repeal could not revive it any more than repeal could revive the wooden ship or the Shubenacadie Canal, or stop the Canadians from harnessing the power of Niagara. What the Halifax diehards were fighting was no longer merely confederation but the law of economics, a battle they were bound to lose. The only hope for Halifax lay in that same law; for, with the industrialization of central Canada and the settlement of the West, eventually there must arise a flow of goods and products seeking outlet to the world. And since the St. Lawrence was ice-locked five or six months in the year, inevitably Halifax and St. John must become not merely the perennial ports of the Maritimes but the winter ports of the whole Dominion east of Winnipeg.

No one could foresee this with any clarity in 1876, not even that father of confederation Dr. Tupper, although he lived to see it coming true. And so in 1876 Halifax stood on a crest, glancing back with a sigh upon fifty years of phenomenal progress and facing a long and indefinite decline. The city had a population of about thirty-one thousand, who lived in four thousand houses, worshiped in thirty-three churches, sent their children to half a dozen free schools, patronized a free library, subscribed to several reading rooms, and maintained three homes for orphans, an asylum for the deaf and dumb, another for the blind, a convent, a YMCA., a temperance hall, a sixty-bed civic hospital, a courthouse and jail, a Home for Aged Ladies, a fine new Masonic Hall, an industrial school for boys, another for girls, and on the Dartmouth side an insane asylum and a Home for Inebriates.

The city had at last an adequate theatre, the Academy of Music. Built of brick faced with stucco, it stood opposite the corner of Barrington Street and Spring Garden Road near the site once occupied by Horsman's Fort, that vanished defense of the old south gate. St. Mary's Basilica had a new granite façade and steeple, replacing the old brownstone tower. Dalhousie College had about a hundred students and, one hopes, a stern power of concentration, for the lecturer's voice was accompanied by a certain clink and gurgle coming from the basement, where Oland's brewery had its office and bottling department. There was a Medical School, housed in a modest wooden building in the angle of Robie and Morris streets. The Roman Catholics had established St. Mary's College, and the Presbyterians had a college of their own on Gerrish Street in the north end.

There were other institutions, not so uplifting, described in a brochure of the time as "the City Market and the Police Court, ugly buildings near the heart of the city; the City Prison, a granite structure occupying far too fine and prominent a spot a mile north of the city; and the Provincial Penitentiary in a cosy secluded nook [beside the Northwest Arm] a mile south of the city. Happily the latter will soon be removed. The Poor House is...unwisely situated on the [South] Common. This palace of brick is free to the poor at all times and the inmates sometimes number over 500."

Brunswick Street, still known by the sobriquet of "Barrack Street," had a Soldiers' and Sailors' Home not far from the Home for Fallen Women, a juxtaposition which doubtless seemed appropriate at the time. "The Hill," if somewhat more subdued, like Water Street had lost none of its old-time flavor. A ballad of the day relates the familiar adventures of a sailor who comes ashore with thirty pounds and a gold watch in his pockets, and awakens the next morning stripped of everything and obliged to creep back aboard in borrowed garb:

I might have got a better suit if I'd a' had the chance.
I met a girl in Water Street, she asked me to a dance.
I danced my own destruction, I'm stripped from head to feet;
I take my oath I'll go no more to a dance on Barrack Street.

Come all you young sailor lads, a warning take by me,
Be sure and choose your company when you go on a spree;
Be sure keep out of Barrack Street or else you'll rue the day-
With a woman's shirt and apron they will rig you out for sea.

In 1874 the Horticultural Society sold their gardens to the city for $15,000—a bargain—and these, with the area about Griffin's Pond acquired in 1867, made the solid block which is now the Public Gardens. Two thousand trees were planted on the central walk and along the Sackville Street and Summer Street sides, and croquet, archery, and later tennis courts were laid out in a playground at the northeast end.

There were two railways out of the city, the Intercolonial and the Windsor & Annapolis (the latter soon to be open as far as Yarmouth), and nine steamship services including a fortnightly sailing to Great Britain by the Allan Line and a monthly service to the West Indies by the Royal Mail Steamship Line. But Sam Cunard's great line was now too big and too important to call.

Two of the old stagecoach lines survived, one lumbering down the south shore to Yarmouth, and the other up the eastern shore to Sheet Harbour. Fishwick was operating all along the Nova Scotia railways in the role now played by the Canadian Express; and his steamers carried passengers and goods from Halifax to Charlottetown with stops at Arichat and Pictou, and from Halifax to Yarmouth, stopping at all the south shore ports.

The Bank of Nova Scotia was flourishing, and to a lesser extent so were the Union Bank, the Merchants' Bank, the People's Bank and the old Halifax Banking Company; the chief stockholder in the last-named, Enos Collins, had died in 1871 aged ninety-nine, probably the richest man in the whole of the new Dominion. A newcomer, the Bank of Montreal, had opened a branch in Halifax soon after confederation.

There were several private investment banking firms and in 1874 the Halifax Stock Exchange opened its doors, taking the place of Mr. John D. Nash, the celebrated stock auctioneer. Meetings were held on Monday, Wednesday, and Friday of each week "at ten minutes after the firing of the noon gun from the Citadel." A seat on the Exchange cost $200. At first the list of stocks called included nine banks and two fire insurance, three marine insurance, and six miscellaneous companies, besides dealings in government, city, school, and municipal bonds. The annual transactions in these ran to about two million dollars.

The Halifax fire department was equipped with three steam fire engines and several of the old hand engines, which now were rarely used. The firemen were still volunteers, although with one exception all the old private "fire companies" had vanished. The exception was the Union Protection Company, founded in 1768 and by this time manned chiefly by elderly veterans of the fire brigade and devoted to salvage work.

The city's manufactures included furniture and woodenware of various kinds. Several firms made pianos; there were two large and busy boot and shoe factories, two tobacco factories, several carriage factories, a brush factory, several busy flour mills using Nova Scotia grain, the large steam bakery and flour mill of enterprising Mr. Moir, several foundries, steam and gas fitting establishments, and of course a multitude of industries catering to the shipping trade. On the Dartmouth side of the harbor were a flourishing ropeworks and the iron and steel works of the Starr Company, one of whose products, the "spring" skate, was in demand wherever there was ice in the world.

All of these had begun to feel the pinch of the times and the sharp thrust of competition from central Canada. Already the Nova Scotia Iron Works had closed its gates forever, and one by one nearly all the rest were to go as the years rolled by. Those which could not compete with Ontario went by the road of bankruptcy. Those which could compete were quietly purchased by Ontario concerns and as quietly closed at the first opportunity. The end was the same. And the end was the same for one after another of the great mercantile houses which were the mainstay of the city's business. Jerked by the bridle of the national policy they turned to central Canada for their stock in trade, and soon became merely commission agencies for the Ontario factories.

Worst of all was the freezing and, in effect, the departure of the rich capital acquired during half a century of booming prosperity. Until about 1825 the dream of the average merchant or official in Halifax was to gather enough wealth to retire in England; and all through the colonial period there was a steady departure of capital across the Atlantic as fast as it accumulated. The sinister Mauger was one of the earliest and richest men in this procession, and Thomas Haliburton ("Sam Slick") the last official of prominence. The movement was increased by a tendency of the sons of wealthy merchants to seek commissions in His Majesty's forces, and of their daughters to marry British army and naval officers, nearly all of whom eventually retired in England with the family fortune.

With the end of the Napoleonic Wars and during the exhilarating material and intellectual rise of Nova Scotia the old trend vanished, and for fifty years Halifax was the repository of a vast and increasing capital, much of it invested in shipbuilding, shipping, and the associated trades. In 1866 this capital began to withdraw from ships, and by 1876 the withdrawal had become a flight. The prospects of reinvestment in Nova Scotia were doubtful. Stocks of Canadian banks seemed safe (especially of banks run by hardheaded Bluenoses), and for the rest the booming industries of central Canada and the railways and other prospects in the opening West offered the best chance of increment.

Thus after confederation the funds of Nova Scotia began to go inland, and there appeared in Halifax a whole class of *rentiers*, rich or merely well to do, who had ceased to take an active part in commerce and were content to leave their money in the hands of solid investment trusts. Their quiet mansions, concentrated chiefly in the rectangle bounded by South

Street, Tower Road, Inglis Street, and Barrington Street, made the South End an equivalent of Boston's Back Bay.

The South End Haligonian became, in fact, very much a Brahmin of the Boston sort, urbane, well educated, generous in many ways but prone to haggle over ten cents with the grocer, familiar with London, New York, Boston, or Montreal but puzzled on Gottingen Street and lost on Chebucto Road. Marriage was always within the tight little circle or a matter of finding a wife or husband among the right sort of people somewhere else, bringing up the children in the paths of righteousness and gilt-edged bonds, with summers at Chester and now and again a winter in Bermuda, but finding real contentment only in town behind their own trees and lawns or their bulky brick or brownstone fronts. With her treasure locked and guarded by these charming and well-feathered griffins Halifax went into an unhappy trance for forty years.

29.
1877–1897

The fortress again. A naval dry dock. Lafcadio Hearn and the Cambridge Library. Garrison life. A carnival of '89. The last romantic days of Tommy Atkins. The harbor bridges. The resurgence of Dalhousie College.

WHILE THE COMMERCIAL SIDE OF HALIFAX languished, the military side remained very much awake. A new and ominous force was astir in the world. Germany's three aggressive wars in twenty years, and especially the speed and force with which she had crushed France in 1871, aroused uneasiness in Britain. When the wily Bismarck concluded a non-aggression pact with Austria and Russia in 1881 the British unease changed to alarm, for it meant that future German adventures must be aimed towards the west—and Germany had begun to hanker for a colonial empire. Quietly the British Government appointed a royal commission to examine the defenses of naval bases and coaling stations abroad, especially the "marine quadrilateral of England," Malta–Gibraltar–Bermuda–Halifax.

What the commission found was an old story; the advance of heavily armored warships, breech-loading cannon, and new explosives had made the defenses obsolete. The commission made strong recommendations but nothing much was done until 1884, when Germany suddenly hoisted her flag in four parts of Africa, rolled an acquisitive eye elsewhere, and announced that she had come to stay as a world empire. That meant a German navy. Navies cannot be built in a day—but neither can fortresses.

Lord Carnarvon arose in the Parliament to ask what had been done about the report of 1881. He was assured that the "marine quadrilateral" was "fairly safe from attack," but the anxiety of the Commons was such that the government hastened to put the recommendations into effect.

This had been foreseen at Halifax by the garrison engineers, who had just completed a close and very accurate survey of the city peninsula and its environs, the bench marks of which are still to be seen about the city.

Thus in 1885 there began another rebuilding of the fortress which went on quietly and persistently for twenty years. Point Pleasant Battery was equipped with searchlights and a steam-driven plant for the electrical supply. (Despite the incorporation of the Halifax Electric Light Company in 1881, the city was still largely gas-lit.) George's Island received a guncotton tank and store for the newfangled floating mines, and test rooms for the mines were built there and at York Redoubt.

A powerful new fort was begun on the old McNab estate on the south side of McNab's Island. The cost of this was estimated at £24,000, and by an adroit twist of imperial finance the sum was charged against the fat profits from the Suez Canal. As the small family cemetery of the McNabs lay on the crest of the chosen hill, the engineers carefully built the fort around it, so that the bones of old Peter McNab and his folk rest in what is probably the world's best guarded graveyard.

Fort McNab was equipped with 10-inch and 6-inch breech-loading cannon designed to sweep the whole harbor approach between Chebucto Head and Lawrencetown, and was sheltered by concrete casemates deeply banked with earth. As it drew near completion in 1894 the contractors began another new work on the opposite side of the main harbor entrance, Sandwich Battery, sited on a steep granite bluff south of York Redoubt. In 1899 Fort Hugonin was built on the island, between Fort McNab and Ives Point Battery. Like the others it had concrete casemates and earth ramparts, but it was armed with quick-firing guns to stop torpedo-boat raids into the harbor.

In 1889 the busy contractor S.M. Brookfield built just north of the Dockyard a large dry dock, primarily for the use of the Royal Navy but later much used for the repair of merchant ships as well. The first ship to enter it was a British cruiser, HMS *Canada*, an omen of a time to come when Canada would have a fleet of her own.

As a more restful but no less useful appanage to the fortress the imperial authorities erected a brick structure to house the garrison library and provide a social center for the officers. This building, later known as Cambridge Library, was in the Royal Artillery ground facing Queen Street. The garrison library was begun by that wise Scot the Earl of

Dalhousie, with a grant from the useful Castine Fund, sometime between 1816 and 1820. At first it was housed in a grim ironstone building at the corner of Water Street and Bell Lane, a noisy evening quarter of grog-shops and sailors' brothels. Later it was transferred to Glacis Barracks, where in 1864 it was enriched by an unexpected windfall, the garrison library of Corfu, just evacuated by British troops after a half century of occupation. This accession made the old quarters very cramped, and cramped they remained until the books were moved into the newly built Cambridge Library in 1886.

It is an oddly moving experience nowadays to go into the quiet reading room at Cambridge Library, turn the pages of well-worn English classics bearing the stamp of the Corfu military library, and realize that most of them must have passed through the hands of eager young Lafcadio Hearn. And it was in the old library at Glacis Barracks, and later within the walls of this room, that George F. Henderson, then an unnoticed subaltern of the Yorks and Lane, made those careful studies of the American Civil War which resulted first in *The Campaign of Fredericksburg* and finally in his famous *Stonewall Jackson*. Henderson's works and teachings, adopted in the British and United States staff colleges, profoundly influenced a generation of young officers who found themselves in positions of command when the first German gun was fired in 1914.

Life was quiet and pleasant in the Halifax garrison in the eighties and nineties, especially for young officers, who could enjoy some of the world's finest shooting and fishing within an easy buggy ride of the barracks, skim about the harbor in yachts built to their own design, or (dressed in smart breeches, riding boots, open shirts, and pillbox caps) gallop their sleek ponies over the slopes of old Fort Needham in strenuous chukkers of polo. They still indulged in cockfighting, usually in the seclusion of Standford's Pond near Dutch Village or at an inn on the St. Margaret's Bay road, and their birds were raised and trained by sporting characters, usually Irish who catered to the fancy.

However, they gambled (and drank) much less than their predecessors of the early part of the century, and dueling had perished in the 1850s. Indeed the last military duel at Halifax was a hilarious affair in which, all unknown to the hotheaded principals their seconds loaded the pistols with powder and mashed cranberries. The shots produced a horrid red splatter that left the duelists aghast and set the whole garrison laughing.

There was still plenty of scope for fun in the service. One officer insisted on keeping a bear, which finally ran amok and set the barracks in an uproar until the gate sentry killed it with a bayonet thrust. On another occasion in the nineties some merry subalterns turned loose a wildcat in the artillery barracks on Sackville Street and engaged in a furious chase with a pack of hounds—the talk of the city for months.

In March 1889 the city had a reminder of the more sober facts of garrison life when the Cavalier Barracks in the Citadel caught fire and blazed high in the wintry night. Several hundred tons of explosives were stored in the magazine, and the only fire-fighting apparatus was an old-fashioned hand pump. The city fire brigade rushed up the hill and joined with the troops in a manful struggle while thousands of people, at first attracted by the blaze, scattered for safety as it grew. When the Citadel water tanks were pumped dry, the fire had to be fought with water pumped up from the city mains by an engine on Brunswick Street. Fortunately there was no worse damage than the destruction of the barracks.

That summer the Haligonians held a grand carnival to mark their city's 140th birthday. The celebration opened with a street parade of decorated floats and marching groups, military, naval, and civil. The city firemen trudged along in stout blue uniforms, hip boots, and American helmets, carrying axes and fire hooks, driving their highly polished brass steam engines or the more prosaic ladder carts behind teams of well-groomed horses. The trade unions manned a big float, brandishing hammers, hods, trowels, shovels, and saws. A canoe club float held, of course, a "war canoe" with a crew of energetic young men paddling gaily in the empty air. The snowshoe clubs—the famous Red Caps in their white blanket coats and scarlet tuques, the others all in blue—sweated along under a hot sun in all their winter gear. The baseball clubs, cool in tight breeches, stockings, striped shirts, and round peaked caps, marched with bats shouldered in a military manner as became the sportsmen of a garrison town. (One Negro ball club marched behind a float labeled "Preston Delegation.") And the century-old suspicion of Uncle Sam, lately revived in the fisheries controversy, was apparent in a float exhibiting that gentleman complete with top hat, goatee, tail coat, and striped trousers; he fished busily over the stern, looked from time to time at a string of big codfish at his side, and turned a sly glance at a Canadian sign that bore the words "No Trespassing."

It was all good fun, and the program went on with sports on the Common and in the waters of the harbor. But the great event of the day was a combined exercise of the armed forces, a "battle" for the fortress. The warships of the North American squadron steamed into the harbor with launches ahead busily exploding mines. The forts thundered away, all to no purpose. The fleet thundered back and finally anchored boldly inside George's Island, booming away at the Citadel and landing a brigade of armed sailors and marines. Reinforced by the Duke of Wellington's (West Riding) Regiment the invaders marched gallantly through the south end, defeated the Halifax Rifles and the Princess Louise Fusiliers on Camp Hill and the north Common, and went on to storm the Citadel in column of companies, pouring up the hill like blue and scarlet rivers, defying the law of gravity as well as a hot fire of blank ammunition from the defending Royal Artillery and Halifax Garrison Artillery.

As a spectacle it was magnificent, but some of the naval officers must have wondered what would have happened if the forts had been firing shell, and George Henderson, looking up from his battle studies, would have sickened to perceive that British military thought was so far behind its fine new quick-firing cannon and magazine rifles. Perhaps it was here that he first saw himself as a man with a mission, for in this year he went to Sandhurst to teach tactics and military history. In fact, the color and romance had gone out of warfare with the development of modern firearms, and the British Army staff were to suffer a severe shock in South Africa a few years hence. The Navy had no such experience, and as late as 1915 found itself attempting at the Dardanelles what it had carried out with such aplomb as an exercise at Halifax in 1889.

Meanwhile the garrison continued to wear its red coats and tall dress helmets, to cherish its traditions of Waterloo and Inkerman, to tend its sick in Cogswell Street Hospital and to bury its dead at Fort Massey. Tommy Atkins strolled with housemaids in the Public Gardens and dallied in the summer dusk on the Citadel slopes or in the cool pine shadows of Point Pleasant; young officers went about their sports in the field, enjoyed their yachting on the harbor, or fenced adroitly with matchmaking mamas in Halifax drawing rooms. Nobody realized that these colorful days were drawing to a close.

When the West Riding Regiment departed on a routine transfer in 1891 the farewell was fully in the tradition of the past—the old trooper

Orontes at the quay with her quaint stem galleries, her twin funnels, her three masts fitted with yards and sails; the redcoats filing slowly up one gangway, their wives and children up another; the mass of friendly Haligonians, male and female, old and young, waving hats and handkerchiefs; the bands of the Halifax militia battalions and of the relieving regiment (the Leicesters) playing solemnly in turn, "Far Away," "Will Ye No' Come Back Again?" "Goodbye at the Door," "The Girl I Left Behind Me," "Goodbye, Sweetheart, Goodbye," and "We May Not Meet Again."

It was a scene long familiar to British garrison towns about the world. Indeed at this very time Mr. Kipling was putting it into words:

> *Troopin', troopin', troopin' to the sea:*
> *'Ere's September come again—the six-year men are free.*
> *O leave the dead be'ind us, for they cannot come away*
> *To where the ship's a-coalin' up that takes us 'ome to-day.*

But for Halifax the troopin' days were numbered. The machinery of imperial policy was turning once again. The ghost of Napoleon had returned to the grave at last, and the Russian menace was largely a figment of the after-dinner port in the messes of Peshawar. The rising and obvious enemy of Briton, Frenchman, and Muscovite alike was the new belligerent Germany, busy with armies and battleships. Sooner or later the British legions must go home. For that matter it would soon be time to gather the strength of the fleet in European waters. No one saw this more clearly than Vice-Admiral "Jackie" Fisher, who commanded on the Halifax station from 1897 to 1899.

These decisions were still fluid in the early nineties, awaiting the catalysis that was to come with the Kaiser's famous telegram to Kruger in 1896 and the attitude of his country in the Boer War. In the meantime the Haligonians went on blissfully with the only considerable industry left to them by confederation, that of supplying the needs of the British garrison and fleet. There was, indeed, one new industry, a sugar refinery; for there was still a West Indian trade. But the old manufactures which once kept the city humming and clanging were gone, and the steady decline of prosperity made itself felt on every hand.

The telephone was still a novelty. Electricity was coming slowly into general use. As late as 1892 the YMCA debated solemnly whether to lighten their darkness with gas or with the newfangled bulbs. In 1896 the old horse cars vanished, giving place to electric trams, which not only covered the old route from north to south along Barrington Street but extended a track as far as Willow Park in the same year.

Meanwhile, in 1885 the first railway train had reached Dartmouth by way of the Narrows, crossing the harbor on a bridge designed and manufactured by the Starr Company of that town—the first steel swing bridge built entirely in Canada. It stood on piers of rock and crib-work in water ranging from 50 to 75 feet in depth, and lasted just six years. Then it was swept away in a September hurricane. In 1892 the railway engineers completed another bridge at the same spot, built on piles driven into the harbor bottom. This one lived eighteen months and then, in the early hours of a calm summer morning, gave up the ghost and dropped into the Narrows. The engineers gave up as well, and built a railway loop through the rocky hills about Bedford Basin. But the memory of the harbor bridge lingered on. By 1920 the dream of every citizen of Halifax and Dartmouth was a highway bridge across the strait which the ancient Micmacs had called *Kebek*.

While the commercial life of Halifax sank into apathy after 1876, and while military life blazed up in a last display of imperial power, the spiritual life of the city experienced an astonishing rebirth. By now the citizenry had reached the height of Victorian respectability; sobriety and godliness went hand in hand, the barrooms had a muted note, and even the naughty ladies of Water Street and "the Hill" no longer flaunted their profession in the streets but hid themselves like guilty Eves behind the red blinds of their establishments.

It was not a religious revival but rather an awakening of culture, of the sort that Dalhousie began with his hopeful college and Joe Howe fanned to a flame through the Mechanics' Institute in the ardent thirties and forties. Art, music, and literature came to the fore once more. Perhaps the first sign was the building of the Academy of Music in 1876, and the resultant attraction of good repertory companies and an occasional opera, not to mention the encouragement of local theatricals. It certainly was manifest in 1887, the year of the Queen's golden jubilee, when the Victoria School of Art and Design was founded, and when the city built an ornate bandstand in the Public Gardens and arranged weekly concerts by the excellent bands of garrison regiments and visiting warships, as well as civic orchestral groups. To supply the proper keynote Sir William Young, the bewhiskered and benevolent chief justice, presented the Gardens with chaste statues of Ceres, goddess of autumn, Flora, goddess of flowers, and Diana at the bath, so that John Halifax and his wife, seated on green benches under the trees, could enjoy the strains of music amid the scent of flowers and the sight of Greek and Roman curves.

But the chief and truly magnificent expression of the new urge was the flowering of Dalhousie College beyond the dreams of its founder. Sir William Young, chairman of the college governors since 1848, was the prime mover in this as in many other things that were good for the city. As far back as 1856 he had confided to a friend: "Let me lay the foundations broad and deep in a system of free schools, and a provincial university may be our next move. To accomplish these ends, although it would be ridiculous to say so in public, I assure you I would willingly sacrifice place and power." From 1863 onwards he proved it, not only with his works but with his purse—his contributions to Dalhousie alone are said to have totaled $68,000.

This was true munificence in days when a dollar could buy so much; but it was only a beginning. In 1879 the Reverend John Forrest interested his brother-in-law George Munro in the struggling university. Munro, a Nova Scotian who had achieved wealth as a publisher in New York, began at once by endowing a chair of physics at $2000 a year. In succeeding years his interest and bounty grew until his benefactions totaled $350,000, a great sum even today, an emperor's gift in the 1880s. His example inspired others, including Alexander Macleod of Halifax who in 1882 bequeathed $65,000 to the university.

With these powerful transfusions in its veins, Dalhousie at last achieved independence of the meager provincial grants and a chance of full stature in the world. Already it had outgrown the ancient building on Grand Parade, an unsatisfactory site in any case, in the noisy heart of the city, with army bands blaring at every change of guard and the boys of the National School on Argyle Street hurling stones at the building and the students.

In 1886 under Young's wise guidance the governors made an agreement with the city by which the university gave up the building and its rights in the Parade site in exchange for a sum of $25,000 and a new site in the green fields of Carleton Street in the city's west end. There the cornerstone of a new brick structure was laid in April of the next year, and in the autumn the faculty and students moved into the still unfinished building. In honor of the Reverend John, who had done so much to bring it about, and who now became Dalhousie's president, the new home was called the Forrest Building. The old college on Grand Parade was torn down in the following year, and the city hall stands on its site.

30.
1898–1913

The war in South Africa. The Halifax Golf Club. "Jackie" Fisher. The imperial troops depart. HMCS Niobe. *The naval college. Population trends. Planning a great seaport. Halifax on the verge of the First World War.*

At Christmas, 1898, Canada issued her noted postage stamp showing the world with the British Empire in flaring red and Halifax in the center. The legend ran, "We Hold a Vaster Empire than Has Been." A proud boast and true; but the shadows of great wars and greater change were coming, and in another half century the boast would not be worth the two cents that most people paid for the stamp. It was time for Kipling's "Recessional."

The wars and changes began in the very next year, when the Boers set South Africa aflame and revealed to the world (and especially to the watchful Germans) the empire's fatal weakness. A major war in any part of it absorbed the energies of the whole and left it open to a deadly stab elsewhere.

Halifax at the time was looking the other way, for many of her citizens had joined the gold rush to the Klondike and two of them had struck it rich to the tune of $83,000. The city newspapers, even to their advertisements, were full of the new Eldorado (Stairs, Son and Morrow were advertising "our new water-closet, the Klondyke") and there was so much talk of Hunker Creek, Gold Hill, Chechako Hill, and Bonanza Creek that at first no one paid much attention to the news from Kimberley and Ladysmith.

Suddenly the full meaning of the South African troubles dawned upon the city, for the Tommies in her forts and barracks were needed far to the south. Off they went, and the Canadian Government raised a regiment to garrison the fortress in their place. But this was not enough. The empire's need of showing a united front to the world—especially to Europe—

demanded the presence of Canadian, Australian, and other colonial troops in battle on the veldt. And so the Royal Canadian Regiment went off to Africa, including the company of Nova Scotians who later bore the brunt of the regiment's famous fight at Paardeberg.

Foreseeing further contingents for Africa (and future responsibilities at home) the Dominion Government built at Halifax in 1899 the big brownstone Armouries, with their quaint candle-snuffer turrets and vast drill hall, facing the Common from the corner of Cunard and North Park streets. This building (eventually the home of the Halifax militia) was used as headquarters for the South Africa volunteers, many of whom (and all of their horses) were quartered in the Exhibition buildings far out on Windsor Street at Willow Park.

Haligonians followed the war with keen interest, for most of the British regiments fighting on the veldt had lain in the city barracks at some time or other and the casualty lists were filled with the names of friends. This interest became more personal when the Canadians reached the front, for the martial-minded townsmen had flocked to enlist in the first and second contingents. When the Canadian Mounted Rifles boarded the transport *Milwaukee* at the old Deep Water Terminal in February 1900 the whole city went down to see them off; and when the RCR returned full of honors later on, all Halifax was there to welcome them.

The city was full of veldt talk. The Halifax militia at summer maneuvers in the hills behind Dartmouth rejoiced in battles at "Preston Kopje" and "Woodlawn Kopje"; Sandwich Battery on its rugged knoll received the name of "Spion Kop" by which it was known for decades; and the city's smartest milliner advertised the latest thing in ladies' felt hats, "in Baden-Powell, Ladysmith, Yeomanry and Queensland styles." The star turn at the Exhibition in the summer of 1900 was a grand military spectacle—the battle of Paardeberg, complete with Boers, trenches, artillery, and Canadian troops "including several men of H Company RCR who have returned from South Africa."

To be sure there were other things to think about that summer. The male habit of chewing tobacco, fashionable in the sixties and still going strong, had at last drawn the concentrated ire and fire of the ladies. The Halifax and Dartmouth Council of Women passed a resolution against "the dangerous and unclean habit of expectorating in public places"; and they had a point, for their modest hems still swept the floors and sidewalks.

At the Academy of Music, the Richards Stock Company was playing in *The Queen's Money, The Village Blacksmith, Led Astray,* and (yes!) *Faust.* There were patriotic concerts in the Public Gardens with music by militia bands, with water sports on the big duck pond, and hundreds of couples dancing on the lawns to the sedate tunes of Buchanan's Orchestra.

Each afternoon an excursion steamer sailed around the harbor and Bedford Basin to give visitors a view of the fleet or the merchant steamers and sailing ships. The 63rd Band gave concerts at Greenbank, the Chebucto Club held regattas on Banook Lake, white-clad gentlemen of Halifax and of the army and navy played interminable games of cricket on the Wanderers' Grounds or the Garrison Grounds at the southwest foot of the Citadel, and *hoi polloi* played baseball on the Common.

Dartmouth folk complained of "furious driving" on Windmill Road, where the young bloods liked to test their horses. The Canadian Garrison Regiment had seventy-five deserters in its first year, one of whom was the best pitcher on the regimental baseball team—a sad loss. "Harrow House," a day and boarding school for boys, caught fire one night in the summer holidays, and the proprietor, Mr. G.M. Acklom, MA, aroused the Brahmins of Tower Road by firing a revolver from the roof.

The Dominion Atlantic Railway was operating the "Flying Bluenose" all the way from Halifax to Yarmouth. The Halifax & South Western went as far as Bridgewater, where a stage coach trundled on down the south shore. The Intercolonial still brought salesmen from Ontario, hauled immigrants towards the glittering West, and was not above running special trains from the city to the Florence Hotel on Bedford Basin, where the dances were very popular if not quite the proper thing.

In the spring of 1900 the Halifax Golf Club secured part of the Enos Collins estate, "Gorsebrook," and prepared a course. Membership was limited to fifty ladies and fifty gentlemen, and the playing guests included officers of the Royal Naval squadron, who brought the band of HMS *Crescent* to discourse sweet music on sunny afternoons. The shade of the old privateersman, stalking his ancient grounds, must have wondered what Halifax and the world were coming to.

They were coming to something far beyond the realms of golf. With the signing of peace with the Boers in 1902 and the announcement of an alliance between Britain and France in 1904 the new trend in imperial policy became sharply apparent. The growth of Germany's forces and ambitions was about to change the face of the British world, for, like Rome beset in ancient days, Britain began to call home her legions and her fleet.

Admiral "Jackie" Fisher was now First Sea Lord, and one of his first moves was to reduce the North American squadron to a shadow. For their part the British army authorities, having replaced the ill-disciplined Canadian Garrison Regiment with imperial troops at the close of the Boer War, prepared now to turn the entire Halifax fortress over to the Dominion. Having made this decision Britannia determined to hand it over in first-class condition. The renovation and rearming of the forts, begun in 1885, were now complete, and it only remained to modernize and extend the barrack accommodation in the city.

To this end between 1901 and 1906 the imperial government equipped Royal Artillery Park with new quarters for engineer and artillery officers, new quarters for married "other ranks," and new quarters for single men—all built of brick and completely furnished. A new military gymnasium appeared at Glacis Barracks on Cogswell Street, on the site of the officers' old fives court. New quarters for married soldiers, known as Churchfield Barracks, went up on Brunswick Street just north of the Garrison Chapel—these to supplement the existing married quarters in Pavilion Barracks on the farther side of Cogswell Street.

Manual training workshops and new married quarters appeared at Wellington Barracks. The old wooden school for soldiers' children on Brunswick Street had a brick addition. Even the military prison on Melville Island received new wardens' quarters and a block of stone cells to supplement the long wooden building originally built for French prisoners in 1809. In various other parts of the city there arose substantial army residences, offices, stables, and supply depots. In short, Britannia spared neither thought nor expense in making sure that her daughter took over a going concern.

On November 15, 1905, most of the garrison sailed for England. Two months later the fortress was turned over with ceremony to the Canadian Department of Militia and Defence. The last imperial troops left Halifax in February 1906 ending an occupation of nearly 157 years. At the same time the Royal Navy handed over the Dockyard. The departing troops took with them a few portable stores, including one curious item, a number of "cats, punishment" from Melville Island—the last relics of the flogging days. Everything else was left as it stood, clean, efficient, ready for use, an example of the imperial power at its shining best. The same thing had happened at Esquimalt. Our Lady of the Snows was on her own from coast to coast.

It was a shock to Halifax business and to Halifax sentiment, for with the last departing Tommy went the life and color of the fortress. The new mistress, breathing the rarefied air of the Gatineau hills, busy populating the prairies and seeing no larger water than the Great Lakes, regarded this sudden responsibility with a vast indifference if not distaste. She had no navy, and no intention of building one. The notion of a standing army distressed her and she cut her requirements to the bone.

The Royal Canadian Regiment she left in Wellington Barracks as her chief concession to the port's defense. She raised a small force of Garrison Artillery and auxiliary fortress units (recruiting them chiefly among ex-soldiers of the imperial force who had taken their discharge in Halifax) to act as caretakers of the sprawling barracks, depots, and forts. The Dockyard became a place of rust and ghosts. Admiralty House was closed and the furniture sold. The outer forts were manned for brief gunnery exercises in summer and left in the hands of military janitors the rest of the year. The inner forts were carefully locked against thieves and abandoned to time and weather.

Enthusiastic Mr. Kipling, entering Halifax in the nineties, had found in her mouth immortal words:

Into the mist my guardian prows put forth,
Behind the mist my virgin ramparts lie;
The Warden of the Honour of the North,
Sleepless and veiled am I.

By 1910 he could have found her muttering something like:

Into the west Canadian brows look forth,
Not to the east. My virgin ramparts lie
Green-rotten like the Honour of the North—
Naked, imperilled, I.

True, there was some agitation in Canada for an Atlantic squadron of sorts, if not an adequate garrison. In 1911, yielding to pressure, the

Dominion Government found a guardian prow to put forth. The cruiser *Niobe*, formerly of the Royal Navy, arrived in Halifax in the autumn of that year amid much fanfare, and after a few short excursions settled down to a comfortable berth at the Dockyard. Canada was making other nautical gestures, of course; there was some eloquent talk of an Atlantic fleet of cruisers and destroyers, of which *Niobe* was the forerunner or, as one might say, the mother. Alas, these infants were strangled at birth by the politicians. *Niobe* remained alone and forlorn at Halifax, saving on bunker bills, slowly going aground on her own beer bottles, and doubtless weeping for her children like Niobe of old. The Royal Canadian Naval College, which set up classes in an old red sandstone building behind Admiralty House in 1911, went on in a small but excellent way turning out young officers for a navy that did not exist, and sending them home to Britannia for a chance to go to sea.

When the *Titanic* disaster of 1912 aroused the shipping nations to demand an ice patrol in Canadian waters and off Newfoundland, the work had to be undertaken by ships of the United States Coast Guard, *operating out of Halifax*. Such was the state of the Warden, and such was the Honour of the North, twenty years after Kipling wrote his glowing lines.

Commercially, the city was emerging from the long trance which began in 1876. The awakening was to a large extent due to a hardy revival of provincial prosperity. The farmers of the fruit belt along the Annapolis Valley had discovered a market in Great Britain. The fishery had vastly increased in value and the Bluenoses were shipping salt cod to Spain and Italy, to the West Indies, and to Brazil, and making money in the process. (By 1913 one thrifty fishing town, Lunenburg, was reputed to have more wealth per capita than any other east of Montreal—including Halifax.) The discovery of large and cheaply mined iron deposits on the coast of Newfoundland had led to a swiftly growing steel industry at Sydney and New Glasgow and a new use for Nova Scotia coal.

The booming days up to the early 1870s, the decline after 1876, and the revival of the 1900s are reflected in the Halifax census figures:

1851 population	20,749
1861 population	25,126—an increase of 21%
1871 population	29,582—an increase of 19.3%
1881 population	36,100—an increase of 22%

1891 population 38,437—an increase of 6.5%
1901 population 40,832—an increase of 6.2%
1911 population 46,619—an increase of 14.1%

The promised markets in central Canada had never materialized. However, a kind of transit freight was pouring inland over the rails from Halifax—a multitude of European immigrants heading for the prairies. There was something wry about this spectacle to the Haligonians, watching a world go by. In 1913 when the hegira reached its peak, no less than 96,000 immigrants passed through the old Deep Water Terminal and vanished into the West. The shipping involved in this movement boosted the port figures for the year to 185 steamships of about two million tons—the largest steam tonnage yet seen at Halifax in a twelve-month period. It was an unexpected sidelight on the old confederation promise that Halifax should become the busy eastern gate of Canada.

Nor was the traffic all one way; for the great industries erected in Ontario under the national policy had begun to reach out to world markets by way of the St. Lawrence and the wharves of Halifax and St. John. It dawned upon Ottawa suddenly that the gateways on the east had at last a national importance, especially that of Halifax, with its vital naval role to play in case of trouble. The port facilities of Halifax, money-starved for forty years, were chiefly relics of the sailing days, a straggle of small decrepit wharves and sheds along Water Street. Only the Intercolonial Railway terminal on Water Street, reached by a spur line from Richmond, had rail connections or adequate berthing for steamships of even medium size. The huge new liners on the North Atlantic run could not be berthed at all.

Something extensive—and expensive—had to be done at Canada's front door, and there was no time to be lost. To leave the job to private interests would mean delays, conflict, and a patchwork result; and it would ignore the whole conception of the port as a national asset and responsibility. Working through the Department of Railways and Canals, the Canadian Government drew up its plan and announced its purpose. It was breath-taking to the Halifax of 1913, so long accustomed to federal indifference.

The Department already owned the Richmond and the Deep Water terminals. Now it proposed a whole new system of concrete piers and quays, equipped with fireproof sheds, modern machinery, and railway lines. The obvious place for these was adjoining the Deep Water terminal, with an extension of the railway along Water Street; but that meant taking over most of the existing waterfront and buying its owners out of business. In the long run it was the proper course, but the cost looked tremendous in 1913, and so it was decided to build the new terminals in the south end of the city towards Point Pleasant, where there was plenty of room. This involved a deep railway cutting in the slate rock around the western flank of the city and through the south end, an ugly necessity which marred the suburbs with a sort of volcanic fissure, miles long, filled with deep rumblings and wild whistle whoops, and emitting smoke and steam.

All in all it meant the greatest change in Halifax since the cockneys cut their clearings on the shore in 1749; but it was not the only change. A big new sugar refinery was in prospect for the Dartmouth side, and many new business structures in Halifax itself. Dalhousie University, having purchased the Studley estate for a campus, planned now to build itself extensively and in stone, in a manner befitting its place in the world. The Department of Militia and Defence actually proposed to spend a million dollars on the fortress. The city had determined to put an end to the old Green Market, so long a feature of Halifax life, which cluttered Cheapside and the sidewalks about the Post Office every Saturday with country carts parked wheel to wheel, baskets of eggs, butter, cheese, fruit and vegetables, and filled the air with a clamor of hucksters, live poultry, and the jangling bells of tramcars trying to get past. Instead there was to be a new Market Building on Albemarle Street, under the shoulder of Citadel Hill.

Haligonians, setting down the works planned, proposed, or actually under construction in 1913, figured as follows:

New railways terminals and station	$35,000,000
Railway hotel	500,000
New railway piers at old Deep Water terminal	3,500,000
Extension to Richmond railway yards	170,000
Extension to dry dock and plant	1,000,000
Halifax & Eastern Railway, equipment	5,500,000
Acadia Sugar Refinery at Woodside	3,000,000

New public market building	150,000
Dalhousie University buildings	500,000
New business structures	980,000
City reservoir, water tower, pipe extension	150,000
Extension of sewage system, western slope	100,000
New buildings at Quarantine, new ferry terminal, etc.	105,000
Fortifications, Department of Militia and Defence	1,000,000
	$51,655,000

It was a surprising prospect; and it came to pass—not in entirety, of course, for the million dollars for the Halifax forts proved to be merely a dream; and not all at once, for construction of the new railway terminals took several years, and such matters as the big quay wall and docks and the railway hotel had to wait fifteen to twenty years. But it meant that Halifax had resumed the march so rudely interrupted in 1867. It was just forty-six years since confederation.

The streets were still unpaved except in the tramcar tracks, muddy in spring and autumn, swirling with dust in the summer winds. The business section and some of the residential streets had flagstone or concrete sidewalks and the old genteel south end of Barrington ("Pleasant") Street still had its worn red-brick walks and cobbled gutters; but everywhere else the townsfolk strolled on paths of household cinders, dumped by the city's collection wagons and casually raked level. The automobile had made its appearance, but it was still a minor factor in the traffic. There were no motor trucks at all. The city fire apparatus was still horse-drawn, and the alarm was sounded over the city by bells in the fire-hall towers, ringing the location by a code which every housewife kept pasted on her kitchen door.

In the dry weeks of summer the city sprinkling carts made their slow rounds to lay the dust. For the sake of economy these frequently were drawn by fire horses so that when the bells rang an alarm the drivers had to lash their steeds in the direction of the stations, with the carts swaying dangerously and spraying furiously regardless of the traffic.

The sailors of *Niobe* and the soldiers of the garrison made thin threads of blue and khaki in the streets. (The red coats had gone out of use with the opening shots of the Boer War, except for dress occasions, and the last of them vanished from Halifax with the imperial garrison in 1906.) The city was still cluttered with army property, much of it not in actual use, the brick buildings shabby and the more numerous wooden ones daubed with hideous red paint. Once a year, to remind the citizens of the facts of life, the convenient paths across Camp Hill and the Citadel were barred by military sentinels, compelling the hurrying clerks and shopgirls on their way to work to walk all the way around.

The militia drilled in winter in the Armouries, and in summer encamped for a fortnight on McNab's Island or at Bedford, clad in khaki shirts and slacks and straw "cow's breakfast" hats, exerting their skill with the Ross rifle on the ranges and practicing Boer War tactics in the neighboring woods and pastures. Every school had its cadet corps, some in khaki, some in gray, with .22-caliber rifles on the army model for practice in the school basements. The old town clock was usually out of order (alas for the Duke of Kent) but every citizen set his watch and every housewife her clock by the noon gun from the Citadel, and skippers checking their chronometers in the harbor watched the Citadel ramparts for the drop of the gilded time ball. Every evening when dusk had fallen in the streets and all good citizens were yawning their way to bed, the bugles in the Citadel and Wellington Barracks sounded "Last Post" over the downtown roofs, the clear notes rising and falling and echoing faintly in the Dartmouth hills.

Although radio broadcasting belonged to the future there were a few experimental wireless sets owned by enthusiastic amateurs. These picked up dots and dashes from the ships, or from the Camperdown station at the harbor mouth, which began to operate in 1905. Moving pictures had appeared about 1908, and already there were two or three theatres devoted to them. Acker's Theatre on Sackville Street catered to vaudeville and roving girl and music shows, and the Academy of Music had its repertory company.

The favorite winter sport was skating on Northwest Arm or Chocolate Lake, but sleigh drives along the Basin road remained popular. The imperishable Red Cap Snowshoe Club still held its annual race, and there was a regular ice hockey schedule in the Arena. In summer, group picnics went by the little steamer *Dufferin* to McNab's Island or Prince's Lodge, where nothing remained of Prince Edward's old love nest except the rotunda for his band. Sometimes there were club and Sunday-school excursions to Cow Bay (now Silver Sands, forsooth!) but Northwest Arm was the great resort in hot weather, easily reached by tramcar or on foot, and covered on Saturday afternoons and Sundays by a floating carpet of trim varnished skiffs and gaudy canoes.

In 1908 Sir Sandford Fleming, that fine old Scot who built the Intercolonial Railway and much of the Canadian Pacific Railway, presented the city with one hundred acres of natural park, known as the Dingle, on the west side of the Arm. And here in 1912, through the energy of the local Canadian Club, appeared the fine campanile tower in granite and ironstone which commemorates the first legislative assembly in Halifax in 1758. Panels in native stone from all parts of the world were contributed by the various dominions and colonies of the empire, by the provinces and universities of Canada and by the chief cities of Britain; and the ladies of Bristol, England, presented a silken replica of the flag given John Cabot by King Henry VII.

Within the city, hucksters made their way about the streets in small carts uttering those peculiar yells, unintelligible to the outsider, which meant "Fresh mackerel!" "Fresh strawberries!" and so on; and in winter in the poorer streets arose the weird wail of the itinerant coal vender, "Co! Cao! Co! Cao!" Countrywomen hawked mayflowers in the downtown streets, and on Saturdays in the market place one could buy baskets made in the peculiar African style of the Preston Negroes' ancestors, or the typical Micmac baskets of maple splints, dyed in various colors, which Cornwallis must have noticed back in 1749.

In the harbor the steamship now was supreme, yet many fishing schooners flitted in and out, and sometimes a big square-rigger was still to be seen at the Richmond pier loading lumber for the West Indies. The airplane was a curiosity, although as far back as 1907 Alexander Graham Bell, Glen Curtiss, J.A.D. McCurdy, and others had met in the Halifax Hotel and organized a flying club. Their experiments and triumphant flights—the first in the British Empire—took place over the frozen surface of Bras D'Or in Cape Breton, in 1909. In 1913 the Exhibition in the grounds on Windsor Street was enlivened by a daredevil Yankee aviator and his companion, who went up daily from the racecourse and took turns at jumping with a parachute—a very early demonstration of that perilous outdoor sport.

Townsmen wore the sack suit, usually with the tall narrow-brimmed bowler which looks so quaint in the family album nowadays, and always with a heavy watch chain draped across the waistcoat front. Women were slowly emerging from the chrysalis in which their grandmothers had wrapped the sex in Joe Howe's salad days. The crinoline had marked this Victorian fashion at its most voluminous and worst, but that had disappeared soon after confederation; and slowly, since then, the gown had crept closer to the body and lifted a little from the dust of the street. Now the petticoats were down to one, and the skirt clung to the legs in a fashionable hobble; some daring young things were wearing theirs with a slit, calf-high, which enabled them to get on and off the tramcars with *éclat*.

King Edward, so like the sons of George III, so very unlike his austere mother, had died in 1910. Halifax remembered him as a casual visitor in 1861, traveling as "Lord Renfrew" and casting a roguish eye on the scene of his grandfather's amour at Rockingham. The new king was George V, a very different monarch. Haligonians remembered him as the keen young officer who commanded the gunboat *Thrush* on the station in 1890. Many remembered also his fondness for fishing, and how he used to hire a horse and Concord wagon at Tom Robinson's livery stable and lumber off happily into the woods in search of likely streams. In May 1913, his son Albert, a quiet young man with a stutter, arrived on his father's old station as a middy in HMS *Cumberland* and attended a dance at Government House. It was a long time since Prince Billy had danced in Halifax, and the gulf between the two young men was fully as wide.

Very soon the Haligonians could tear another sheet from the calendar and contemplate a miracle—one hundred years of peace. By the following summer it was just a happy memory.

31.
1914–1918

Ending one hundred years of peace. Alarms and humors of war. A seaplane base at Eastern Passage. The Common commandeered. Prohibition. Blind pigs and prostitutes.

IN THE SUMMER of 1914, THE HALIFAX MILITIA INFANTRY held their annual camp on McNab's Island, popping away on the rifle range, skirmishing with blank cartridges—a great lark—in the dark spruce woods, or watching the small garrison steamers *Alfreda* and *Armstrong* tow targets for gun practice in the forts. Far up the harbor the "guardian prow" *Niobe* lay out of commission at the Dockyard, her tall masts holding a tracery of radio aerials towards the summer sky. The Halifax *Herald* was busy promoting its second great "automobile endurance contest"—five hundred miles over the rough dirt roads of western Nova Scotia. The Queen Hotel, that favorite haunt of Nova Scotia politicians (where according to popular belief more government business was transacted than in Province House itself), was busy installing a telephone in every room.

All through the western suburbs and the South End, railway contractors were at work with earth-shaking blasts and snorting steam shovels; a polyglot swarm of Canadian, Russian, Galician, and Italian laborers was busy filling the swamps behind Fairview and obliterating Stanford's Pond, tearing a narrow canyon through the deep bedrock from Dutch Village to Greenbank, dumping the spoil in the harbor to form a breakwater, and demolishing houses and sheds to make way for the railway station and the proposed docks running all the way from Greenbank to the very foot of South Street. Farther along the old waterfront at the Deep Water Terminal a new concrete Pier Two gleamed white in the sun.

All Halifax was flocking to the Academy of Music to see and hear Mr. Edison's wonderful talking pictures, which showed actors singing and dancing and the great John McGraw discussing baseball. One of the reels was actually entitled *Talkie!* There was another popular spectacle elsewhere—the body of the murderer Cook, who had just been hanged for killing a Syrian peddler. Men, women, and children jammed the undertaker's rooms, the last trace of an eighteenth-century custom; the hanging was no longer public, but one might still peep at its fruit. It was a curious but understandable survival—the undertakers' parlors were only a few yards from the spot where the George Street gallows once stood.

Thus Halifax spent Dominion Day, 1914. Then, with a bang, came war again. The big noise was in Europe, but Halifax had a private and personal bang to announce the new state of affairs, for a shell from Fort McNab, practicing in sudden earnest, ricocheted into a wooden house on Lucknow Street. Fortunately no one was hurt.

The news from Europe filled the city with excitement. Crowds watched the bulletin boards outside the newspaper offices far into each night. Army officers looked wise. The cadets of the Naval College (twenty-one in all) looked wiser still, for on a sudden alarm from the wireless station at Glace Bay the maintenance crew of *Niobe* (one petty officer, a carpenter, a gunner, and a seaman) had been rushed off to defend that place against "a meditated attack by Austrian warships." These were followed in a special train the next day by forty-three naval volunteers in case they needed support. This sounds hilarious now, but it was all deadly serious in 1914. Who could ever forget how the other half of Canada's navy, the poor old *Rainbow*, with most of *Niobe*'s crew and all of *Niobe*'s torpedoes (hastily railed across the dominion) was sent out from Esquimalt in search of Von Spee's cruisers, anyone of which could have sunk her in twenty minutes? Or the gallant and comforting message she received from Ottawa: "Remember Nelson and the British Navy. All Canada is watching."

At Halifax, *Niobe* had been out of commission ever since she grounded on Cape Sable in the summer of 1911. At the outbreak of war she had no ammunition and she had no crew—and she was Canada's entire Atlantic fleet. Somehow the Navy got her commissioned and to sea, with ammunition from England and a scraped-up crew of Royal Navy officers and ratings, Newfoundland reservists, and Canadian "temporary service volunteers." In September the Royal Canadian Regiment marched out of Wellington Barracks and down to the transport *Canada*, bound for Bermuda to relieve the Lincoln Regiment, much to their disgust. *Niobe* escorted this first mild expeditionary force and continued in active service for a year as part of the North American squadron, with time out here and there for engine trouble, and once because her funnels threatened to collapse. Then she returned to her Dockyard jetty and remained, acting as depot ship for the port. She did not stir again until she was towed away for breaking up after the war.

Henceforth the role of the Royal Canadian Navy operating out of Halifax was the rugged if ignominious one of patrolling the Nova Scotia coast and keeping the Halifax harbor approaches mine-swept every day. For this purpose there was assembled a weird collection of armed steamers, converted yachts, drifters, trawlers, and motorboats which plodded their way in and out of the port throughout the war. But to all deep-sea intents and purposes Halifax became, as in the old wars, a Royal Navy base. Here for four years the loungers on the Citadel slopes and the picnickers at Point Pleasant watched Britannia's lean gray ships come and go.

There was a censorship of cablegrams and newspapers, but it was naïve. For months the city dailies continued to print in all innocence the names of His Majesty's ships in port. During the first two years the German and Austrian embassies in Washington conducted a busy espionage and sabotage campaign against Canada. While the saboteurs got no nearer Halifax than the international railway bridge at Vanceboro, New Brunswick (which that curious man Werner Van Horn tried to blow up), undoubtedly there were spies in Halifax. There was nothing to stop them and there was plenty of opportunity to get information.

Even after the Halifax newspapers ceased publishing such things, the identification of warships in the harbor was no puzzle even to an amateur. Royal Navy ratings continued to wear the names of their ships on their cap ribbons, and a stroll along Barrington Street any fine afternoon provided the most casual observer with a list of those in port. The very schoolboys (I was one) prided themselves on their ability to spot and recognize warships in the roadstead. (But I remember that we measured the fighting power of a man-o'war by the number of funnels she had. Thus we admired Admiral Cradock's *Good Hope* as she lay in the anchorage one day in the autumn of 1914, and were shocked when a few weeks later Von Spee sank her with all on board—including two Halifax cadets—at the other end of the world.)

There were other ships to admire, however. The first was *Mauretania*, which fled into Halifax soon after war was declared. The German cruiser *Karlsruhe*, which subsequently disappeared from the face of the earth, mysteriously, forever, was rumored to have been on *Mauretania*'s tail. The big liner was the first top-notch Cunarder to call at Halifax since the days of old Sam Cunard himself. As the war went on, with troop convoys assembling in the Basin and harbor, the sight of the biggest Cunard and White Star liners was a commonplace. The first Canadian contingent sailed to Britain from Quebec; but after that most of the Canadian troops passed through Halifax, and it is safe to say that of the half-million Canadians who went overseas in all services between 1914 and 1918 at least three out of four boarded their transports at Pier Two.

Halifax also became the examining point for neutral ships bound to countries bordering Germany. Bedford Basin was dotted with them, awaiting clearance; and the fine Swedish barque *Svithiod*, suspected of carrying contraband of war, lay at anchor in the Northwest Arm a whole winter. She was one of the last big square-riggers seen in Halifax.

When German submarines began to reach across the Atlantic and shipping losses became very grave, the convoy system was extended even to the grimy little tramps, so that Bedford Basin was at times filled with freighters and tankers being marshaled for the next move across the sea. By this time the Canadian anti-submarine patrol was inadequate for its task, and it was a distinct help when the United States came into the war in 1917 and established at Halifax a flotilla of fast motor "subchasers" and gunboats. Also the value of aircraft for anti-submarine work was now well recognized; but Canada had no air force. In the summer of 1918 the Canadian Government built at Eastern Passage a base for the use of American naval aircraft.

The site of this first Halifax air station comprised about twenty acres on the shore of the harbor a mile or so east of Imperoyal, and included an old store, a wharf, and various smokehouses for fish. The Canadian contractors built offices, store sheds, two barracks, a large steel hangar, slipways, and a workshop. The staff of the United States Naval Air Service numbered about two hundred officers and men, including a handsome and pleasant young lieutenant who afterwards distinguished himself in the Antarctic and became the famous Admiral Richard E. Byrd. The Americans patrolled the harbor approaches and the adjacent coastline with Curtiss flying boats and blimp aircraft until the end of the war.

So much for the sea and air part of the picture. Now for the town and fortress. As soon as war broke out the garrison cadre of artillery and auxiliary units was brought up to strength and the forts were manned. Since taking over the fortress in 1906 the Department of Militia and Defence had done little to keep it up—and nothing to keep it up to date. A small new battery (Connaught Battery) between York Redoubt and Purcell's Cove had been begun in 1912, but very little had been done even with this when the war broke out, and Connaught Battery was not finished until 1917.

The Halifax militia battalions (63rd Halifax Rifles and 66th Princess Louise Fusiliers) were called out for active service in the defense of the port. Their first concern was the water supply of the city and fortress, drawn from the Chain Lakes beyond the Northwest Arm and exposed by several roads running through the woods from the coast. Infantry were posted in rough blockhouses of timber and stones hastily thrown up at the junction of the Spryfield and Herring Cove roads and at the junction of the Sambro and Spryfield roads. A machine-gun post with shelter trenches and barbed wire appeared at the junction of the Prospect and St. Margaret's Bay roads. Three companies of infantry were established in huts at the main Chain Lake dam, with a detachment at the Spruce Hill Lake intake.

Facing the harbor, an infantry post supported by a light field gun appeared at Herring Cove and a rifle company was established in huts at the Camperdown radio and visual signal station near the harbor mouth—exactly where the Duke of Kent had maintained such a post to guard *his* signal station in 1798. Other blockhouses and trenches were constructed on McNab's Island, and here more troops were posted, first under canvas and eventually in huts.

To guard the waterfront and the town itself, a force drawn from various provincial militia units and known as the Composite Battalion was stationed at Wellington Barracks. These men, most of whom had been rejected as physically unfit for overseas service, remained at Halifax throughout the war performing useful work but subject to the usual insult thrown at home-defense troops in a time of foreign war. Carping folk called them the "Safety-First Regiment," and it was the delight of small boys to hurl snowballs after their street patrols, cocking snooks, and chanting:

Com-po-zite!
They won't fight!

Minefields were laid between McNab's Island and Point Pleasant, leaving a war channel covered by searchlights and quick-firing batteries. These were supplemented later on by an anti-submarine net of steel cable suspended from booms across the harbor from the New Terminals breakwater to Ives Point, and another running east and west from George's Island. It was the habit of German submarines in the North Atlantic to surface at night in order to charge their batteries and to communicate by radio with each other and with Germany. For their detection the Royal Canadian Navy set up radio direction—finding stations in 1918 at Chebucto Head and elsewhere along the coast. The Germans soon learned to keep radio silence, but the Canadian D.F. stations proved useful after the war as aids to navigation, especially in foggy weather, and the Chebucto Head station remained a feature of the port for many years.

The great military role of the city from 1915 onwards was as an embarkation center for overseas-bound troops. The existing barracks and depots, numerous though they were, proved insufficient for the khaki hordes decanted from troop trains as a convoy movement approached. Gradually at first and then rapidly, a camp of long wooden huts, covered with gray roofing paper, spread over the entire North Common, surrounded by a tall fence of barbed wire. Other gray huts appeared along Cogswell Street on the Citadel slope west of Glacis Barracks, on the west slope facing what now is called Ahern Avenue, and on the small bit of the South Common east of the Egg Pond.

By the summer of 1917 all that remained of the city's great central breathing space was the rough knoll of Camp Hill. Even that was to go, for now the authorities were faced with another problem—a stream of severely wounded soldiers coming back from the Western Front. The old army hospital on Cogswell Street was hopelessly inadequate. In 1917 there spread over Camp Hill, wing after wing, a large new hospital in white stucco. It was intended to be torn down after the war like the gray hut camps, but it had come to stay. There was something very terrible about that. It brought the grim and lasting side of the war to the city's heart.

There was another and more familiar, if long forgotten side, not seen in Halifax since the Napoleonic Wars—the moral blight. The long drag of the war and the presence of bored thousands of troops and naval and merchant seamen produced the old result. The natural hospitality of the Haligonians, increased by the knowledge that their own sons were in service abroad, could not cope with such numbers. The YMCA erected a large recreation hut on Barrington Street opposite Government House, but the problem was too big and too complex for local resources and the dominion authorities made no attempt to deal with it.

The provincial government, urged on by zealous reformers, took the only step it could—the total prohibition of the sale of intoxicants. For years Halifax had been exempt from the various provincial and dominion Temperance Acts, and there was an outcry against this final closure. It was remarked in the legislature that 150 liquor wholesalers and retailers in Halifax would be deprived of their business, and their employees thrown out of work. It was argued that the existing licenses would not expire until March 1917 and that the licensed shops and bars had $350,000 worth of liquor which ought to be disposed of first. The government was inexorable. The law went into effect on Dominion Day, 1916; every bar in the city was closed.

Experience proved the law a mistake. There sprang up a vast litter of "blind pigs," usually in the mean streets and often in association with brothels, selling all sorts of vile brews. These were easy to find but difficult to catch *flagrante delicto*. So were the brothels. Before the war, prostitution in Halifax had been confined to a veteran troupe of streetwalkers and to certain small establishments which operated behind drawn blinds on Water Street and in the old quarter on "the Hill"—Grafton, Market, Brunswick, and the upper parts of Prince and George streets. The war brought a great change.

The local drabs were not enough for this male swarm. Into the city poured a stream of eager prostitutes from every part of Canada, but especially from Montreal. These professionals set themselves up, in squads of three or four, in small "cigarette shops"—they had a stock of honest tobacco and matches, but the windows were obscured by large cardboard cigarette advertisements, and there were always two or three narrow inner dens furnished each with a red lamp, a couch, and a bowl of disinfectant. These opened for business in the old naughty quarters, but soon appeared along the northern ends of Gottingen and Barrington streets towards the old north railway station and about the Dockyard and the sidings where the troop trains lay.

Streetwalkers in growing numbers added their lively presence to the nightly throngs of servicemen in the shopping and theatre district, and were not above joining the Sunday parade along Lover's Walk in the Public Gardens or even the stroll to Point Pleasant. Nymphs of a more exquisite type frequented the hotels and the better restaurants, and set themselves up in discreet little flats in the south and west ends of the city. Many a respectable residential neighborhood awakened slowly to the fact that the patriotic young ladies next door, so busy entertaining army and naval officers, were in fact plying the world's oldest trade.

Police raids merely drove the trollops to other quarters, the quiet little cigarette shops closed only to reappear somewhere else in the guise of a rooming house, a café, or merely in the old way. It was like trying to catch quicksilver. The police perspired and blundered, the gay little ladies laughed behind their "Bon Tabac" signs, and the game went on and on.

32.
1914–1918

Prisoners of war. Leon Trotsky. A flood of khaki. The wartime boom. The great disaster of '17 and its aftermath.

THE WAR BROUGHT ANOTHER OLD FAMILIAR FEATURE, enemy prisoners in the Citadel and at Melville Island. Most of them were merchant seamen or army and navy reservists plucked from homeward bound ships in the early days of hostilities, and they included a number of German and Austrian officers, charming fellows who spoke English with a perfect American accent. In the chivalrous early days of the war the officers were permitted a certain amount of freedom, tramping about the suburban roads for exercise under the eye of a fat militia officer with a revolver or reclining on the cool lawn of the Waegwoltic Club watching the swimmers and the bright parasols of girls in skiffs and canoes—a much more pleasant viewpoint than the barred windows of the grim red prison across the water in Melville Cove.

Tales of German behavior in Europe soon put an end to this courteous treatment. However, the guards were inclined to be lax, and during the war there were several daring escapes from the Citadel and from Melville Island. One of the nondescripts confined in the Citadel was a mysterious Jew whose real name was Bronstein but who chose to call himself Leon Trotsky. On his way from New York to Russia in March 1917 he was taken out of a ship at Halifax and confined in the Citadel as a suspected person traveling with dubious passports. He made no attempt to escape. The Russian revolution had just begun. Within a few weeks the new Russian Government asked the British authorities for his release, and the beady-eyed man with the spectacles and the shock of dark hair walked out of the Citadel gate into history. The Allied governments never knew until too late what sort of creature they had held under their Halifax thumb.

With their old sea traditions it was to be expected that the young men of Halifax would enlist in the navy, and a good many did. But the garrison tradition seemed stronger, for most of them joined the army headed overseas. Probably the desire for a complete change of environment had something to do with it; all over the Maritime Provinces the urge was the same. Indeed in this war, as in the Second World War a generation later, the Maritime regiments were full of sailors and fishermen while the Canadian Navy was manned largely by freshwater men from Ontario and farm boys from the prairies.

The enlistment rate in Halifax, as in Nova Scotia generally, was one of the highest in Canada. Consequently whenever a Bluenose regiment departed for the war the whole city flocked to the waterfront to see it off. There were memorable scenes when the 25th Battalion sailed from Halifax in the *Saxonia* in May 1915, when the 6th Mounted Rifles departed in the following July, and when the familiar Royal Canadian Regiment came up from Bermuda in August and sailed for the front. These scenes were repeated when the 64th Battalion sailed in April 1916; but the greatest mass sendoff came when the Nova Scotia Highlanders boarded the huge *Olympic* at Pier Two in the following month.

The Highlanders were themselves a phenomenon. In the autumn of 1915 Colonel A.H. Borden was authorized to mobilize the 85th Highland Battalion at Halifax. The regiment with its jaunty bonnet and red feather caught the imagination of a province with strong Highland traditions, and such a flood of recruits poured into the Halifax Armouries that Borden asked permission to form another battalion, the 185th; then the 193rd; and finally the 219th. What started as a single battalion ended as a whole brigade, and the brigade marched aboard the transport amid the cheers—and tears—of a vast crowd from every part of Nova Scotia, jamming Water Street and the adjacent wharves for hours.

Halifax was filled with enterprising wartime strangers and booming with wartime business. The port that had been so pleased to find itself handling two million tons of shipping in 1913 took in its stride a tonnage of over seventeen millions in 1917. Exports of $19,157,170 in 1915 went to

$78,843,487 in 1916, and to $142,000,000 in 1917. Halifax bank clearings, which had reached a healthy total of $95,000,000 in 1913, swelled to $152,000,000 in 1917.

Lumber was plentiful and comparatively cheap before the great wave of inflation began in 1918, and the outcry for housing in the overcrowded city kept the building contractors busy in the north and west ends. In 1913 the city's built-up area had begun to spill across Windsor Street towards the west, with a trickle of middle-class homes along the hither ends of Chebucto Road and Quinpool Road; and the old estates of the well to do along the western reach of Quinpool Road towards the Arm were being purchased and divided by hopeful real-estate operators.

By 1918 the built-up area had passed over Oxford Street and was pressing towards the Arm Bridge by way of Quinpool and Chebucto roads, and the village of Armdale had become a thriving suburb. Construction of the new railway and ocean terminals, going on steadily throughout the war, created a sad flutter in the dovecotes of the Brahmins; there was a general exodus of the well to do away from the old aristocratic quarter of the South End, particularly in the region of Union Station with its growing maze of railway yards. Here too the trek was towards the west, especially along the shore of the Arm.

Across the harbor, Dartmouth with its excellent residential prospects had been growing rapidly since 1900. The town had already a long-established ropeworks, an iron and steel works, a sugar refinery, a brewery, and a supply base for ships of the Department of Marine and Fisheries. There was an enormous increase of industry in 1916 when the Imperial Oil Company began to construct its big refinery beside old Fort Clarence, and the homes of its employees formed the busy suburb of Imperoyal.

During the war there came to Halifax, to stay, a number of small foreign colonies—Italians, Galicians, Russians brought in by the railway contractors, and Greek fruit merchants and others attracted by the wartime boom. The small Jewish colony, dating all the way back to colonial times, received a sharp increase from elsewhere. Chinese who had set up small laundries here and there about the city during the 1900s were now joined in force by their brothers the restaurant keepers. A rash of Chinese restaurants broke over the City's face during the war. These, too, had come to stay, and before long a small Chinese quarter had come into being on Granville Street. All of these restaurants appeared at the same time, evidently financed if not operated by a single hand; and a city newspaper astonished its readers by stating flatly that the richest man in Halifax—at the moment, anyhow—was a Chinaman living quietly at the Queen Hotel.

The hustle and prosperity of the times brought a great increase in motor traffic. The army set the pace. In 1914 the garrison transport was entirely horse-drawn. By 1918 it was almost completely motorized. In 1914 civilian motorcars were few. By 1918 they were everywhere, the mixture of horse and motor traffic in the downtown area had brought the traffic policeman into existence, and already it was sadly apparent that the streets laid out by Cornwallis in 1749 were utterly inadequate for the traffic of 1919.

Women's dress leaped out of the horse and buggy era, too. The peekaboo blouse was a beginning. Skirts became shorter and fuller with each passing year of the war until by 1918 they were swinging jauntily at the knees; but as a concession to modesty the legs were still partly covered by laced boots in soft leathers reaching the top of the calf. And now the lavish use of powder, rouge, and lip paint, hitherto confined to ladies of the *demi-monde*, actresses, and society girls in search of publicity, became the preoccupation of every typist and shopgirl in the city and the world.

In 1917 occurred a catastrophe which had been privately feared and officially ignored ever since the foundation of the fortress, the explosion of a large quantity of munitions. On December 6, 1917, the naval authorities permitted the French steamship *Mont Blanc* to enter the harbor and pass the city in order to join a convoy being assembled in Bedford Basin. She had a devil's brew aboard: 2300 tons of picric acid, 10 tons of guncotton, 200 tons of the touchy TNT—a perfect detonator for the rest of the cargo—and for good measure 35 tons of benzol, an easily inflammable liquid, in thin steel drums which were placed on deck about the hatches.

It was a fine cold winter morning with a thin coat of snow on the harbor slopes. Shortly after eight o'clock as *Mont Blanc* drew abreast of the Richmond terminal she was struck by the Belgian Relief steamer *Imo*, which was coming out of the Narrows. The ships drew apart without much damage but the collision had punctured some of the drums on the Frenchman's deck and at once the benzol flared. The captain and crew promptly took to their boats and fled into the woods on the Dartmouth side. Their ship, burning furiously, drifted in to one of the Richmond piers. Someone rang an alarm to the Halifax fire department, which sent its new pumper *Patricia* (the first motor fire apparatus purchased by the city) towards the scene at once.

Meanwhile HMCS *Niobe* at the Dockyard sent off a boat party to board the ship and fight the fire. These heroic men were aboard, working furiously, and a second boat from HMS *Highflyer* was just arriving alongside, when the catastrophe came. About five minutes past nine, as most of the city schools were finishing the morning hymn, *Mont Blanc* exploded and vanished in a pillar of white smoke reaching a mile into the sky and unfolding at the top in greasy gray convolutions like an incredible toadstool. The blast rattled windows in Truro sixty miles away, and the sound traveled more than a hundred.

In Halifax and Dartmouth the explosion killed more than fourteen hundred men, women, and children outright or buried them in the ruins of their homes, where they burned to death before help could reach them. An estimated six hundred others died later of their injuries. The whole Richmond district, about one square mile in area and comprising mainly wooden structures, was smashed to flinders. Over the rest of the city as far south as Cogswell Street and Quinpool Road, doors blew off the hinges and plaster tumbled from walls and ceilings; windows facing the blast sprang inwards in jagged arrows of glass, and others vanished into the outdoors. The broad bulk of Citadel Hill spared the south end from anything worse than shattered windows, but the downtown streets, catching the blast along the harbor, were a shambles of smashed plate glass and tumbled shop displays.

In the harbor itself a great surge of water broke the moorings of ships in the anchorage and snapped the lines of those at the wharves. The steamer *Imo*, stripped clean of her superstructure, was flung up on the Dartmouth foreshore where, not far away, the French Cable Company's wharf and warehouse were demolished and a smashed brewery poured a river of beer into the harbor. *Mont Blanc* was blown to fragments of steel plate that fell like hail on the North End long after the blast had died away. The only recognizable parts of the ship ever found were a cannon, which dropped into Albro's Lake behind Dartmouth with its barrel bent like soft wax, and an anchor shank weighing half a ton which fell into the woods across Northwest Arm (well over two miles from Richmond) after an enormous toss into the sky.

The glass and iron roof of North Street Depot, the city's only railway station, dropped in upon the platforms and tracks. The Richmond freight terminus, its sidings and marshaling yards were a mass of shattered railway cars and debris. The Dockyard and Wellington Barracks were smashed. The tall brick bulk of the Acadian Sugar Refinery was snapped off like a carrot and the whole upper portion tumbled into the nearby dock. The factory of the Dominion Textile Company was burned to a shell. The Exhibition buildings were demolished. In the Richmond Printing Company's establishment practically everyone was killed, including thirty girls, and only three men escaped alive from the Hillis foundry. St. Joseph's (Roman Catholic), St. John's (Presbyterian), St. Mark's (Anglican), and other churches were demolished. So were St. Joseph's School and the Roome Street (Richmond) school, where many children perished. The north end of Dartmouth, including Emmanuel (Anglican) Church, suffered much the same fate.

The explosion came at a time when most householders were stoking their fires against the morning cold, and as their houses went to matchwood the flames broke out at once. The evil pillar of the *Mont Blanc* blew away on the light breeze, but very soon the black smoke of burning Richmond rolled up to the winter sky. For a few minutes the whole city was stunned, not only by the blast but by the terrific jar of the great slate bed on which it stands. Then the work of rescue began. The garrison sent troops, and British and United States warships in the harbor sent landing parties, to search the ruins for living and dead. The city firemen struggled manfully against fires too many to count, in as bloody a scene as any on the Western Front. (Their lone motor-pumper *Patricia* was found utterly wrecked near the scene of the blast, with the entire crew killed. Fire Chief Condon and his deputy, speeding towards the Richmond pier, were killed and their car was blown clean off the road and demolished.)

Army ambulances, trucks, cars, and wagons brought a host of injured southward. Cogswell Street Hospital, full of garrison sick and wounded from overseas, could take no more. Camp Hill Hospital, just built and not yet fully equipped, was soon choked to the doors, with the injured lying on the beds, under the beds and along the corridors. Victoria General Hospital, itself inadequate for the city's normal sick list, took in as much of the new flow as it could hold.

Two thousand were seriously injured, many of them mutilated or blind. Thousands of others, slashed by the flying glass, patched up their wounds and suffered stoically in the gaping shells of their homes. These untreated wounds, by some peculiarity of the explosion or the subsequent exposure, left ugly blue scars that in many cases disfigured the bearers for life. Six thousand people were homeless. Many more made shift in houses without windows or doors and with every scrap of plaster tumbled on the floors; and this in the depth of a Canadian winter, with a snowstorm in the offing.

Shortly after noon on the day of the explosion, army trucks appeared in the North End moving slowly along the streets with soldiers shouting, warning everyone into the open. The main garrison magazine below Wellington Barracks was in danger from nearby fires. Men, women, and children emerged from the shattered houses with hastily gathered food and belongings. Chebucto Road, Kempt Road and Quinpool Road became rivers of bloody and smudged humanity hurrying westward to the safety of open fields. Thousands did not stop until they reached the woods beyond Armdale and Fairview. And through the long afternoon hours they stood in the snow watching the smoke pall over the burning North End, waiting for a blast that never came. At some time about noon a mixed party of soldiers and sailors had made the magazine safe against fire.

As the afternoon waned, with a gray scud coming in from the sea and rapidly covering the sky, the army trucks made the rounds with this news, telling the refugees to go back to their homes. Back they went, and labored feverishly to nail carpets, blankets, odd boards—anything—over the gaping window and door frames to fend off the coming storm. All that night a blizzard howled over the city, burying the ruins with their imprisoned living and dead in a pall of snow, while in hundreds of shattered but still standing homes the people of the North End crouched over their stoves, muffled in blankets, nursing their wounds.

Since Indian days no foe had dared attack the town. The strength of the fleet and fortress for six generations had made the place too formidable. Yet here was all the slaughter and destruction of a modern bombardment concentrated in a single blast; and now in the most populous part of the city the survivors lay besieged by the winter weather, not merely for this night but for many days and nights to come. In nearly every home husband, brother, or father was away on service overseas, for the war was well into its fourth year and the drain of the Western Front had been terrific. From 1914 to 1918 no fewer than 1360 Haligonians were killed, died of wounds or perished of disease on service overseas, of an estimated 6000 enlistments—and this out of a prewar population less than 50,000. And so it was largely a population of women, boys, girls, and men too old or physically unfit for military service who bore the blow and endured the aftermath.

For many days the searchers found mangled but still living victims in the ruins of Richmond. For weeks a steady procession of wagons and sleighs carried the dead to Chebucto School, the emergency morgue, where a daylong file of bereft friends and relatives passed from corpse to corpse in search of a familiar face. In the burned zone the soldiers shoveled charred human remains into wash tubs and other handy receptacles found among the ruins, and a corps of undertakers drawn from all the eastern Canadian cities searched these grisly things for rings, dentures, and other means of identification. In the end the still unclaimed dead were gathered in rows of coffins outside the school, and Protestant and Roman Catholic clergy held a mass funeral service in the presence of a crowd of citizens standing in the snow along Chebucto Road. For some inexplicable reason, or for no reason but the hurry and turmoil of the time, the last of these unfortunates, charred beyond all recognition, were buried in the potter's field of Halifax on Bayers Road, where a single granite monument marks their common grave.

The ruins of the sugar refinery had to be removed brick by brick. The work took many months, and far into the following summer the workmen continued to find human remains. The tumbled Exhibition buildings, supposedly empty, were tackled last; and there in one of the cattle sheds a year after the disaster lay the crushed remains of a solitary tramp, the last body to be found.

The immediate task on December 6 was care of the injured and relief of the homeless and foodless—for the destruction of the railway terminal and of so many warehouses and shops left the city seriously short of supplies. The new south terminal was hastily put into service, and a day after the explosion the first hospital train left the city for Truro laden with injured survivors. Doctors and nurses arrived from outlying provincial towns and substantial help was on the way from Montreal and

Toronto; but the first and most valuable assistance came from the ancient foe beyond the Bay of Fundy.

With splendid heart and quick efficiency the State of Massachusetts sent by sea a complete relief expedition—food, clothing, bedding, medical supplies, doctors, nurses, trained welfare workers, together with a fleet of motor trucks complete with drivers and gasoline and loaded with carefully selected supplies—all ready to move off as soon as the ship came alongside. It was a perfect example of American generosity and quick-wittedness, and the city greeted it with a gasp of relief. And this was only the beginning. Financed entirely by American funds, the Massachusetts Relief Commission continued its clinics and its housing and welfare work in Halifax long after the disaster, a memory cherished by Haligonians to this day.

Meanwhile substantial funds were raised elsewhere for relief and reconstruction. The Canadian Government voted $12,000,000 and another $7,000,000 later on. The British Government voted $5,000,000. The Lord Mayor of London started a fund which reached $600,000. The Winnipeg Free Press gathered $85,000. Chicago sent $130,000, New York $75,000, Massachusetts $500,000. Australia sent $250,000, New Zealand $50,000. The British Columbia Government sent $50,000, to which the citizens of Vancouver added $56,000. The British Red Cross sent $125,000, the Province of Ontario $100,000. The Royal Bank of Canada gave $50,000, the Bank of Nova Scotia $100,000. The Dominion Iron & Steel Company gave $50,000. Altogether the contributions ran close to $30,000,000.

Most of these funds were administered by the Halifax Relief Commission, which set about its enormous task at once. Reconstruction had to wait upon temporary relief, and in the midst of a great war even that was difficult. Lumber was at a premium; glass was not to be had; the available carpenters, masons, and glaziers were lost in the enormous demand. For months the people of the North End lived like cavemen, with black tarpaper in place of windows, with patched-up doors, with the heat of their stoves escaping through cracks and slashes in the walls and roofs. The Halifax Relief Commission imported labor from as far away as Montreal, and all through the winter and spring four thousand men worked steadily to make homes weatherproof and to provide enough glass for a little blessed daylight.

Temporary shelter for the homeless began with rows of tents pitched in the snow on the North Common, in the narrow strip between the military huts and Cunard Street. Then came rows of board-and-tarpaper tenements on the South Common near the Egg Pond and the adjacent foot of Citadel Hill. But the greatest number of refugees found shelter in the more fortunate districts, and remained there until rehousing was possible. Eventually the Halifax Relief Commission took over the whole business of rehabilitation, and amongst other activities built in the devastated area west of Fort Needham a well-planned housing development which unfortunately became known (from its stucco exteriors) as the Hydrostone District. The Commission continued to rent and administer many houses in this area for more than thirty years.

33.
1918–1928

The servicemen's riot of '18. Rebirth of shipbuilding. The slump of '21. The fortress abandoned. "Maritime Rights." Completing the port. Dalhousie and King's. The automobile supreme.

In the spring of 1918, with Russia torn by revolution and the Germans fighting with renewed hope, peace seemed as far away as ever. Up to this time, the off-duty discipline of garrison and naval personnel had been generally good. The Halifax police had the usual instructions to "go easy" on service personnel, and the army and navy street patrols looked after their own. But in this final stage of the war, the restlessness of servicemen bored with long discipline and the monotony of garrison duty and coastal patrols—a state of mind sadly familiar in the history of Halifax—came to a head.

It followed a definite pattern that goes all the way back to the eighteenth century. The first signs appeared in 1917 with an ugly undertone to the usual skylarking; there was more brawling between civilians and servicemen, and more theft and robbery by men in uniform. In May 1918 a simple incident set off an explosion of violence. A sailor caught shoplifting on Barrington Street was denounced by a girl employee and arrested by the policeman on the beat. The seaman appealed to some of his comrades, who promptly attacked the policeman. The policeman blew his whistle for help, more police arrived, more sailors arrived, soldiers joined in, and in twenty minutes Barrington Street was in an uproar.

A shouting mob of soldiers and sailors beat every policeman in sight and drove the rest into the police station under City Hall, where the rioters were joined by an assortment of merchant seamen, longshoremen, and the queer denizens of "the Hill" who came flocking to join the fun. The new market place, nearing completion at the upper side of Market Street, provided a supply of bricks; and soldiers, seamen, waterfront toughs and shrieking prostitutes hurled these missiles through the police station windows and into the offices of City Hall.

Every attempt of the police to break out was driven back with a flying barrage of stones. Part of the mob broke into City Hall, smashed everything breakable in sight, and attempted to set the building on fire over the heads of the police by piling documents in a heap in the lower corridor and applying the ever-ready match. Fortunately the attempt did not succeed and the mob spent its fury on the City Hall windows. It is an illuminating commentary on the discipline of the services at this time that the mob broke up only upon the appearance of a column of armed sailors and marines landed by a British cruiser in the harbor.

That was the end of it, and the battered city comforted itself with the thought that it might have been much worse. The depressing aspect of the riot was that it could happen at all, and that the local authorities, army, navy, and civil, could be so impotent in the face of it.

In June 1918 an old industry reappeared with new strong sinews, in response to the demand for shipping. The Halifax Shipyards Limited set up a large plant for building steamships in the area flattened by the great explosion, just north of the Dockyard. It was a good thing for the city in many ways, not least because it employed a large number of skilled men and because these men and their families began to build homes in the frightful desolation about Fort Needham where so many people had been killed and where none of the survivors wished to return. Even so, much of this region long remained a little desert of coarse grass and gaping cellars, and Richmond was not thoroughly built up again until thirty years had passed.

The war ended in the following autumn, and in 1919 the troops came home. The colors of Nova Scotia's famous regiments, the 25th and 85th, were deposited with ceremony in Government House. (They were removed later to Province House.) The Royal Canadian Regiment returned full of strange faces, for few of the men who left Halifax with the regiment remained alive and unwounded; and the wartime garrison departed. The Royal Navy went back to its old role as a casual peacetime visitor. The Canadian Navy was practically disbanded. In January 1919 the United States Naval Air Service turned over the Eastern Passage station to the Canadian Government and about twenty former Royal Flying Corps and

Royal Air Force personnel took charge of the station and its equipment under supervision of the Department of Naval Service, Ottawa.

The city erected a cenotaph in Grand Parade to the memory of its 1360 sons and daughters who gave up their lives on service during the war, but only a small bronze plaque on the site of old Fort Needham marks the 2000 men, women, and children who perished as a result of the great explosion. In truth the city, shattered and shabby, was anxious to look forward and not back.

A worldwide inflation was now in full swing. The Halifax Shipyards turned out a succession of steel freighters of 8390 and 10,500 tons. The great Imperial Oil refinery expanded its buildings, tanks, and equipment. The new terminal railway was completed and the first docks begun. The city's swiftly growing demand for electric power was now too much for the existing steam plant, and in 1919 the Nova Scotia Power Commission completed a hydroelectric development on the Indian River at St. Margaret's Bay and carried transmission lines to Halifax. The census of 1921 showed Halifax with a population of 58,372; it had increased by 25 per cent since 1911. Dartmouth had grown to 7899. The future had never looked as rosy as it did in the fatal year 1921, when the whole fabric of postwar inflation collapsed through the world.

The results were immediate. The Department of Railways and Canals ceased all work on the new docks; gaunt steel skeletons of unfinished sheds, daubed with red lead, for years made a grisly spectacle for ships passing in and out of the port. A "temporary" wooden railway station at South Terminal, built in the winter of 1918-19 to replace the shattered old North Depot, remained for ten years the shabby and unlovely gateway to the city. The government shipbuilding contracts ran their course, and then the shipyards were cast upon small marine repairs to keep their plants going.

The Canadian naval force at Halifax was reduced to a pair of minesweepers, to which later on the government cautiously added one or two destroyers from Britain. The newly constituted Canadian Air Force continued to operate the Eastern Passage station on a small scale, using seaplanes to make a gradual air survey of Nova Scotia for mapping purposes, and in 1922 making experimental airmail flights to the Magdalen Islands. But in December 1925 the station was closed for more than a year, and thereafter operated only on a maintenance basis in the summer months, with fitful air-survey and anti-smuggling operations (the latter in co-operation with the Royal Canadian Mounted Police) until 1934.

The fate of old-style fixed fortresses like Liége and Namur, and the experience at the Dardanelles, where fixed forts were proved more vulnerable and less effective than mobile batteries, had a profound effect on military thought. To all intents and purposes, the Department of Militia and Defence quietly wrote the Halifax fortress off its books. Wellington Barracks, badly shaken by the great explosion, remained a semiruin. The Royal Canadian Regiment was withdrawn to Ontario, leaving only one company, with a detachment of gunners, in the Citadel. Even the old signal station at Camperdown, built by the Duke of Kent and carefully maintained, was abandoned to ruin at, last.

By 1928 the onetime fortress was nothing but a military mausoleum in which the khaki caretakers walked like specters of the past. In the garrison headquarters on Spring Garden Road a skeleton staff of officers and military clerks maintained a bored existence in looking after the Defence Department's real estate scattered about the city and suburbs. (One visitor to Cambridge Library in the early 1930s found three garrison officers, all of field rank, all wearing the ribbons of distinguished service in the late war, discussing for a solid hour the tint and texture of some proposed new curtains for the lower rooms. He seemed to hear Cornwallis, Gorham, Wolfe, and the Duke of Kent turning in their graves.)

This abandonment of the fortress would have been an excellent thing for the city if the national defense authorities had been willing to turn over at least some of their now useless properties to civic use and assessment. The haphazard acquisition of land within the business section since 1749 had left the Crown with a legacy of valuable real estate on which it paid no tax and made no grant for the maintenance of the adjacent streets, sewers, water pipes and other expensive facilities. The city fathers, contemplating the increasing hardships of the taxpayers, were faced with the doleful fact that (counting church property) about half the potential assessment of Halifax was tax-exempt. Apart from this, the extension of certain streets and the widening of others to ease the growing traffic problem were stopped on every hand by the forbidding little boundary stones marked with the broad arrow and W.D. The national defense authorities (quite properly in their own view) sat doggedly in the manger.

City or fortress? Port or naval base? The old problems that had bedeviled the townsmen from the beginning remained unsolved after 180 years. But the city's experiences in the war had made the grievance bitter. If Halifax was to be considered a weapon for the general use and benefit of the nation in time of war, then the nation owed something to the city in time of peace. It was all very well for politicians and editors far inland to declare in polite phrases that the nation owed Halifax nothing but a soldier's farewell—in the ribald army sense of the term.

What would Toronto (for instance) have said if her business district were checkered with obsolete and tax-free military property; if there were three forts in her favorite park and several more on her cherished island and the adjacent shores, all unused, but all under strong federal taboos; if she were obliged to suffer, year in, year out, the storage of dangerous explosives in her very heart; if once in every generation her whole life and economy were taken over by an invasion of uniformed strangers, forbidding her citizens to do this or do that, crowding them out of hotels, theatres, and restaurants, covering her breathing spaces with huts and barracks, hurling brickbats at her windows on departure, and saying in effect, "Kindly pick up the pieces and continue to exist, for we shall want to do all this again by-and-by"?

These postwar business and financial problems were aggravated tenfold by the alarming depression which fell upon the whole Province of Nova Scotia in the 1920s. A drift of population to the United States set in at once. By 1925 it was an exodus. A large and significant proportion of these departing people were young veterans of the war. A typical country municipality in Nova Scotia which welcomed over 450 soldiers and sailors home in 1919 was able to count no more than 200 in 1931; the rest had crossed over the mouth of Fundy and had become citizens of the United States.

Ever since the 1850s there had been a drift in that direction because of the higher wages and opportunities, but in spite of it the local population had increased. Even in the hard thirty years after confederation, when the rate of increase in Halifax shrank by two thirds, still there was growth. But in 1931 when the census takers finished their rounds Halifax found that, despite a substantial birth rate following the war, the net increase since 1921 was only 903 souls. In short, the city's population figure had stood still for a decade. Nothing like this had befallen the city since early colonial times.

All through the 1920s the Haligonians labored grimly to "pick up the pieces," not only of their city but of their trade. But poverty increased and showed itself in the increasing shabbiness of the slums between Argyle Street and the Citadel, and between Upper Water and North Park streets. There was an ominous spread of shabbiness along the upper stretch of Gottingen Street, between Gottingen and Robie streets, and about the new railway terminal in what, a few years back, had been the ornate South End.

In the province itself the unrest over hard times was very great, and suddenly the ghost of repeal walked and gibbered, for the people could not help comparing their condition with that of New England, where so many of their sons and daughters had gone and prospered, and where after all the climate and resources were much the same. The trouble seemed to lie in being hitched to the wrong wagon. In the election of 1925 a blizzard of votes swept a Conservative government into Province House after nearly forty years of Liberal rule, and in the following federal election a bloc of Conservatives from Nova Scotia, along with others from New Brunswick and Prince Edward Island, went to Ottawa demanding "Maritime Rights."

It was as if the Carolinas and Georgia had sent to Washington a bloc of Republicans demanding Southern rights, with the old ominous word Secession on their minds if not on their tongues. The apostasy shocked Ottawa into appointing a commission headed by a distinguished British engineer and economist, Sir Andrew Rae Duncan, to examine conditions in the Maritime Provinces and to make suggestions for their improvement. The commission's inspection was searching and competent, and the recommendations of the subsequent Duncan Report were many. Among other things the Report strongly advised national development of the ports of Halifax and St. John, to be carried out by local harbor commissions each with a free hand to build docks and warehouses and administer port affairs.

There was nothing new in this, except its application. In 1928 the Halifax Harbor Commission came into being, with federal funds to complete the port facilities planned in 1913 and halted in 1921. The Commission proceeded at once with docks, piers, sheds, a grain elevator, and a cold storage plant, all on the south waterfront in conjunction with the new railway terminal. Especially valuable was the new Quay Wall, one of the finest in the world, 2007 feet long, with 45 feet of water alongside at low tide, continuous steel-frame transit sheds, and five lines of railway along the whole length. Here the biggest warships and liners in the world could dock with ease, by day or night, at any stage of tide, at any season of the year. In the time to come most of them did, and on one occasion in 1939 the United States battleships *New York, Texas,* and *Arkansas* were all berthed in line along the quay.

A feature of the revival of Halifax business in the later 1920s was the erection of a modern hotel, the Lord Nelson, soon followed by The Nova Scotian, which was built in connection with Union Station by the Canadian National Railways. These filled a sad want, for the older hotels had been swamped by the needs of a national port, especially during the late war. Another feature of the times was the change in entertainment. Vaudeville, after a last parade of song and dance at Acker's and the Strand during the war, disappeared shortly afterwards. The motion picture was supreme. In 1929 the old Academy of Music was torn down to make way for a temple devoted to the new and exciting talking pictures. So perished the last legitimate theatre in Halifax after years of shabby gentility and spasmodic flirtation with the movies. The last performance in the old building was Victor Herbert's *The Fortune Teller*, sung by the Halifax Dramatic and Musical Club in June 1929.

Dalhousie University had completed its new buildings on the Studley campus during the war, just in time to receive a rush of young men getting out of the armed services. Soon afterwards the main structure of old King's College at Windsor was destroyed by fire. The faculty and students moved to Halifax, setting up temporary quarters in the wooden Birchdale Hotel near Northwest Arm. Time had removed the old animosities, and King's College decided to rebuild on the Studley campus in association with Dalhousie. In 1929 the cornerstone of the new King's was laid, and in the following year the college moved into the handsome Italian Renaissance buildings which now adorn the northwest portion of the campus. At this time also, through the generosity of Mr. W.H. Chase, the campus received a fine Georgian building to house the archives of Nova Scotia.

Mass production of automobiles after the war changed not only the traffic but the habits of North America. In Halifax the narrow hilly streets laid out in 1749 presented sharp and peculiar problems, not yet solved. Motorbus lines appeared, and extended farther each year into the province in competition with the railways. So did freight transit by lines of motor vans. The street and fire departments of the city were completely motorized. The spread of the motorcar to general use brought extensive paving of the city streets, and that itch of the modern city dweller for "a place in the country." A rash of summer cottages broke over the face of the landscape about Bedford Basin, along the outer reaches of the harbor and along the St. Margaret's Bay road. The family skiff or canoe fell into disuse, and membership in one of the Northwest Arm boat clubs, once the duty and joy of every right-minded Haligonian, was left to a few enthusiasts. The old aquatic spectacles of the nineties and the Edwardian years, the smart military bands playing at the Waegwoltic, and the whole Arm covered with energetic young men in flannels and girls with parasols—these were a thing of the past.

By 1935 the only horses to be seen in the city were those of the Riding Club, the milk dealers, a handful of old-fashioned teamsters, and of course the country wagons at the Market. But in the fine new buildings of the Exhibition every autumn the Haligonian could indulge his curiosity about these vanishing beasts among the farm exhibits or on the racecourse.

Nearby, at the Forum, he could indulge his sporting instincts in winter with ice hockey, a very old occupation in Halifax and Dartmouth. It is a fact little known in Canada, but a fact none the less, that ice hockey, Canada's national game, began on the Dartmouth Lakes in the eighteenth century. Here the garrison officers found the Indians playing a primitive form of hurley on the ice, adopted and adapted it, and later put the game on skates. When they were transferred to military posts along the St. Lawrence and the Great Lakes they took the game with them and for some time afterwards continued to send to the Dartmouth Indians for the necessary sticks.

34.
1919–1939

The years between the wars. Radio broadcasting. The Flying Club. Chebucto Field. Eastern Passage. A national port. The death of Prohibition. Another magazine. The miracles of asphalt and gasoline. The royal visit.

THE NEEDS OF FLEETS AND ARMIES DURING THE 1914–18 war had brought about a great advance in radio, and as soon as the war ended the world had a new toy and a powerful new medium of expression. Experimental broadcasting stations like the American KDKA (Pittsburgh) and WGY (Schenectady) began to fill the air with words and music, and all over the continent enthusiastic amateurs were busy making apparatus for reception. The first symptom of the new fad in Halifax was the appearance of a few radio parts offered for sale in the window of the Marconi Wireless Telegraph Company's small office on Granville Street in the autumn of 1919. In the next five years the side line became a major part of that company's business from coast to coast, and there sprang into existence a host of independent shops devoted to the sale of parts and, before long, of complete reception sets made by a score of manufacturers.

Halifax heard its first music over the air as far back as 1909, when the Prince of Monaco's yacht *Hirondelle* astonished the operators of the Camperdown wireless station with tunes from an ingeniously contrived "wireless piano." But this was not true radiotelephony, which first appeared in the American subchasers and blimp aircraft operating out of Halifax in 1918. In 1920 the manager of the local Marconi office, Ralph Letts, with the co-operation of Phinney's musical instrument firm, set up a small broadcasting station in the cupola of the Marble Building on Barrington Street. The transmitter was contrived from an army radiotelephone set of the type developed for field use during the war. The call letters of this pioneer Halifax station were CFCE.

The station's irregular broadcasts included gramophone music, and impromptu talks by such notables as the mayor of Halifax; wireless operators on ships leaving the harbor were asked to listen and report on the distance achieved. At this time other enthusiastic Haligonians were experimenting with the new medium, among them W.C. Borrett, who in May 1926 opened the first regular broadcasting station in the city. For several years his station CHNS, with which the Halifax *Herald* was closely associated, operated from the top floor of the Lord Nelson Hotel with its aerials on the roof. Eventually the aerials were set up on tall steel masts far outside the city beyond Bedford, and the studios were removed to Broadcasting House in Tobin Street. By 1928 the radio had become a household necessity, the city's rooftops were a maze of small aerials slung from chimneys and poles, and every townsman had a seat in the whispering gallery of the world.

The war also had brought an astounding development of aircraft. In 1909 Louis Bleriot flew across the Channel from Calais to Dover, twenty-one miles. Within ten years a pair of RAF officers, Alcock and Brown, had flown the Atlantic and changed the future of the world. The training of so many fliers during the war had provided every community with young men eager to use their skill and to teach others. Unfortunately Halifax had no airfield, but by 1928 members of the Halifax Flying Club were buzzing over the city in small float-equipped planes, using the RCAF base at Eastern Passage. By 1930 the city had acquired a stretch of fields on the north side of Chebucto Road between Mumford Road and Connaught Avenue, and leveled a pair of runways. For ten years this was the city's only airport for wheeled planes. It was too small for anything much larger than the Flying Club's light Moths; the RCAF pilot who landed a trimotored Ford aircraft on the field in the early 1930s found it a soul-shaking experience.

The rapidly increasing size of commercial aircraft left Halifax in a dilemma. There was not room for a suitable landing field on the peninsula, and without enormous expense there was no way to make one in the rugged hills beyond. Yet Lindberg, by his epic flight from New York to Paris in 1926, and his flock of imitators in the next five years, made plain the need of large airports in Nova Scotia and Newfoundland if the transatlantic flight was to become a commercial success. It was clear that if Halifax was to retain its importance as a strategic key to the North Atlantic, such an airport must be built.

It involved millions, an expense far beyond the city's resources in the "Hungry Thirties" and, for that matter, beyond the means of Canada's own peacetime budget. However, the news from Europe after 1934, especially the resurgence of German militarism under Hitler and the ominous growth and reach of Germany's air force, made a Halifax airport not merely desirable but a necessity. This had a peculiar emphasis in 1937 when the German airship *Hindenburg,* ostensibly on a routine trip to New York, cruised slowly over Halifax with several experts busy photographing the Dockyard, the harbor, the city, and the forts. It was the first time in history that a hostile foreign power had got a close and accurate view of them. For Germany was definitely a hostile power in 1937. Munich was only a year away; and after that, the deluge.

In August 1934 the Eastern Passage air station went into permanent operation under the RCAF after sixteen years of semi-idleness and "maintenance basis" existence. It still had little more than the plant and equipment that had been installed for the Americans in 1918, existing purely as a seaplane base. The RCAF went on with its aerial map-photograph work, its anti-smuggling patrols, and the training of seaplane pilots, using Montreal-made Fairchild aircraft. The need for runways and hangars for wheeled planes was very great, but of course these were hard times and the Air Force had to get along on limited funds. However, a relief camp for unemployed Halifax and Dartmouth workmen was set up at Eastern Passage under Air Force supervision at this time, and under the direction of the station commander, Squadron Leader H. Edwards, a very energetic and resourceful officer, the first preparations for a land runway were made.

This relief work continued for two or three years. The men received a small wage in addition to their board and lodging, and were not inclined to do much work of any sort; nevertheless Edwards accomplished a good deal. During the period 1934-38 the government provided additional funds to purchase another twenty acres of land and to build a large fireproof workshop and a combination barracks and mess hall for Air Force personnel, as well as paved roads, a water system, and various other improvements. In the autumn of 1938 a number of twin-engined Stranraer flying boats were received at Eastern Passage, and intensive training of pilots and crews began at once. During this year several hundred acres of rough land were procured, across the main highway from the old seaplane base, and the construction of a first-class airfield was begun. There was not much time for the enormous work that had to be done; the new base was still under construction when "the years between the wars" came to an end.

The life of Halifax during the second decade of the years between the wars was one of solid if slow and unspectacular progress. The city was just recovering from its long postwar depression when the American financial crash of 1929 shook the world; but, having shared little of the American boom, Halifax had nothing new to suffer.

The new dock facilities constructed between 1928 and 1931 drew a steadily increasing amount of business to the port. In 1936 the Canadian Government abolished the local harbor commissions in all national ports and set up a system of local managers under the control of a central board at Ottawa. There followed a good deal of controversy over the merits of the two systems. Under a local commission the Halifax harbor facilities had been immensely improved; but certain features of this carte blanche expenditure of federal funds were definitely objectionable. Also in the general scramble for business by local harbor commissions there was cut-throat competition, which resulted in reduced rates, concealed rebates in port charges, and loss all round. Under the "central board, local manager" system the rates were fixed and above board, and each port was forced to stand on its own feet.

The rivalry of Halifax and St. John as the winter ports of central Canada changed its character after 1919. Prior to that time St. John, although three hundred rail miles nearer the heart of things, suffered a nautical disadvantage in the strong tidal currents and dense fogs of the Bay of Fundy. Since then radio beacons, sonic sounding apparatus, radar, and other modern aids to navigation have abolished those old bugbears of the shipmaster, and today Halifax must compete on a straight basis of port efficiency with her rival up the Bay. It is a healthy competition, from which Halifax emerges with its full share despite the fact that St. John, as the Atlantic terminus of the Canadian Pacific Railway, has all the powerful resources of that company in the collection and routing of freight, while the Canadian National Railways as a truly public utility cannot be quite so single-minded about its terminus at Halifax.

The noble experiment with prohibition came to an end in 1930, none too soon for public morals in the postwar era. It had proved nothing except that human beings cannot be legislated into continence. Indeed it had undone much of the good accomplished by the temperance movement in the half century before the First World War, for under official ban the drinking of spirits once more became popular and even fashionable in all classes of society, and there sprang up a wide and intricate system of smuggling, illegal distilling and sale which made a mockery of law in general.

In Halifax as elsewhere this was apparent in the great number of successful bootleggers and "blind pigs," and a busy smuggling trade which defied the efforts of temperance inspectors, police, and customs officers alike. A fleet of fast rumrunners, operating up and down the North American coast from Jamaica to St. Pierre, played a merry and triumphant game with Canadian and United States coastal patrols all through the 1920s. The innumerable lonely inlets in the coast of the Maritime Provinces made smuggling easy and profitable. In 1929 a plebiscite in Nova Scotia showed a strong majority in favor of ending the farce, and in the following year the provincial government opened its own liquor stores.

In the 1930s, alarmed at their own unemployment problem, the United States for the first time in their history reduced immigration by setting up a rigid quota system. This had a profound effect upon Nova Scotia, from which for generations (and especially during the 1920s) there had been a drain of young men and women to New England. In late Victorian and Edwardian times the Canadian West had diverted some of this stream, but now the West was settled to a point where the old glittering opportunities were gone.

Thus after 1930 the ambitious youth of Nova Scotia had to stay at home on the farm, in the shop, in the mine or the fishing boat, and the home population for the first time since confederation retained its natural increase. As the 1930s rolled on through the great depression this phenomenon created serious unemployment problems in Halifax and the province; but it resulted in the spread of towns and villages, a progressive increase in the shore fishery, a more intensive cultivation of the soil, and the growth of pulp and paper mills and other wood-using industries.

In 1935 the Haligonians had a sudden reminder of their city's function as the national powder-keg, for the Department of National Defence decided to build a new magazine at Burnside, three miles across Bedford Basin from the northern tip of Halifax. Designed as a joint explosives store for the three armed services, it was to consist of small brick structures each surrounded by a thick rampart of concrete and earth, and all served by a jetty on the Basin shore. In theory a dangerous explosion was impossible with this arrangement; no single building could hold a large quantity, and its circular rampart would confine the blast.

Construction went on quietly through the later 1930s. The separated storage buildings spread slowly along the green face of the Basin slope, until by 1939 the magazine was like a small town in itself, in a desirable situation, facing across the broad anchorage towards the city and Rockingham, with every fine sunset flashing on its windows and bringing out the warm color of the bricks. Many a tourist regarding this idyllic scene across the water from the train or a car on the Bedford highway must have wondered what unromantic architect had designed the grim "houses" that looked out on such a view.

The popularity of motor transport had made the gravel roads of the province an anachronism by 1935, when Nova Scotia began to widen and straighten her main highways and to pave them with asphalt. The next step came in 1938 when the Department of Highways undertook for the first time to keep the trunk roads open throughout the winter season. As all roads in Nova Scotia lead to Halifax the city's trade derived immense benefit, for countryfolk wishing to shop now had a simple run by bus or motorcar at any season of the year. By 1939, through the magic of asphalt and gasoline the province had become a parish.

In the summer of that year the British Overseas Airways began regular mail and passenger flights across the Atlantic to Montreal, an event as momentous as Sam Cunard's steamship contract just a century before. At the same time Trans-Canada Air Lines began regular mail and passenger flights across the country from coast to coast. In truth the whole dominion had become a parish, with Europe practically on its doorstep. Unfortunately the peaceful advantages of all this were overshadowed by the black news of German aggression leading up to war.

The shadows were lightened for a moment by the visit of King George and Queen Elizabeth in the early summer of 1939. They reached Halifax at the close of their Canadian tour, and at noon on June 15 the whole city turned out to watch their special blue and silver train pull into Union

Station. In the early afternoon the royal pair made a tour of the city in an open motorcar, along a route lined by cheering crowds. It was just twenty-six years since the Haligonians had first seen their King, then simply "Prince Albert," a carefree young middy ashore from the *Cumberland*. Now they regarded a lean and somber man in the uniform of an admiral of the fleet. His smiling Queen held all eyes; she was wearing her favorite powder-blue costume and the "off the face" hat which fashion everywhere was copying, and her graceful gesture of greeting, a little turn of the hand, was repeated again and again along the way.

The royal drive through the city was followed by a pageant on the garrison sports ground with the King and Queen as guests of honor and an immense crowd spread over the southern slopes of Citadel Hill. The weather was perfect; it was a hot June day with a light breeze from the sea. In the harbor lay the destroyers *Skeena* and *Saguenay* (nearly half the Canadian Navy at this time!), the British cruisers *Southampton* and *Glasgow*, and the liner *Empress of Britain*, waiting to escort the distinguished guests to sea. At the crest of the green hill the Citadel was in semiruin. The granite walls were bulging into the moat; some had been torn down, and others propped with timbers, as a "relief project" for unemployed veterans of the first German war. It was symbolic of the whole fortress and of the old empire which built it.

Every handful of earth here was crumbled history. The very ground on which the visitors stood, and on which the carefully rehearsed pageant of welcome unfolded its show, was part of the fatal scene where Loudon, Wolfe, Howe, Kent and others in the long military succession had shot or hanged their defaulters. From the top of the hill Cornwallis, Horatio Gates, Rogers of the Rangers, Jeffrey Amherst, John Moore, Colin Campbell, Williams of Kars, Inglis of Lucknow and many another famous soldier had once surveyed the defenses of the town, and a succession of fighting sailors from Boscawen to Cradock had gazed down upon their ships at anchor in the harbor. Hereabouts, or in the town below, had walked William Cobbett, Tom Moore, Aaron Burr, William Cullen Bryant, Rufus Choate, Joe Howe, Charles Tupper, Sam Cunard, James Gordon Bennett, Captain Marryat, Charles Dickens, John Quincy Adams, Leon Trotsky, and many another person of note in the world's affairs. And here had been a succession of princes, five of whom (including the present visitor) became Kings of England, and one an Emperor of France.

Indeed the greater part of the pageant on that memorable June day in 1939 was invisible. Already the old empire was vanishing. Canada, Australia, New Zealand, South Africa were sovereign nations in their own right; Ireland was a republic in all but name. Egypt, India, and Burma were clamoring for independence. The Protectorates of Iraq and Palestine were soon to become a burden beyond endurance. The old homeland herself was about to suffer destruction such as she had never known in all her history, for in another twelve months the barbarians would be at her gates. But the shape and temper of the new commonwealth were emerging as the imperial rule withdrew. The coming war would merely speed a process which began in Canada in 1870 and reached its first milestone at Halifax and Esquimalt in 1906; and the strength of the new association was to prove itself in the six-year struggle ahead.

When the visitors departed at the end of the day, Premier Angus Macdonald of Nova Scotia bade farewell to his Queen in the old courtly Highland way by bending a knee and kissing her hand, a gesture that delighted every Bluenose with a drop of Highland blood. The squadron left the harbor just as the sun was going down, with *Skeena* and *Saguenay* leading, then *Empress of Britain* with the flush of the sunset on her fresh white hull and golden-tinted funnels, and finally *Southampton* and *Glasgow*, all in line. They steamed slowly down to Chebucto Head and turned towards the east in the last of the afterglow, in a sea smooth and shimmering like mother-of-pearl, a departure almost theatrical in its perfection.

The sun was indeed going down on them and on the world; for within nine weeks the Russo–German pact was announced. Hitler followed quickly with his famous demands on Poland, Britain gave her solemn warning, and the long night fell.

35. 1939–1945

War precautions. The new airfield. Departure of Canada's 1st Division. The lifeline to Britain. Camps and barracks. The astonishing Canadian navy.

On September 1, 1939, when German forces crossed into Poland, the Halifax militia received orders to mobilize; the forts were manned, and the Dockyard was a scene of great bustle far into the night. On September 3, Britain declared war. As the Haligonians listened to their radios they heard the deep slow voice of their recent royal guest making a solemn appeal to the peoples of the commonwealth, and later the voice of Mr. Mackenzie King declaring that Canada placed herself at Britain's side in the struggle. Late that night came the first news of the war: the liner *Athenia* with fourteen hundred passengers, many of them Canadian men, women, and children, had been torpedoed without warning and sunk with great loss of life two hundred miles west of the Hebrides. The Battle of the Atlantic had begun.

For Halifax the Second World War began really six months earlier, in February 1939, when the staff of "H" Division, Royal Canadian Mounted Police, set up a security survey and conferred with officials of the Nova Scotia Light & Power Company, whose plant and distribution system were the very nerves and sinews of the port's defense. Together they drew up a plan of precautions against sabotage, and as a beginning the company built a flood-lit steel fence around its main steam-electric plant on Water Street. Other measures were to go into effect on advice from RCMP headquarters, but as an extra precaution a radio receiving set was installed in the power station itself with operators listening constantly for news from London. At five o'clock in the morning of September 1 they picked up the first report that German troops had crossed into Poland, and within an hour every vital point in the city's gas and electric system was under watch by armed guards drawn from the company's staff. When the day shift arrived for work at eight o'clock they found new fencing everywhere. Instructions for all employees were on the notice boards; all parcels were inspected before being passed inside, all incoming vehicles—even the company's own tramcars—were searched for explosives or incendiaries, and there were special precautions against fire.

When Britain actually declared war two days later the whole system was closely guarded, even to the distant sources of the company's hydro-electric supply, where dams and powerhouses in the forest were patrolled by armed woodsmen and hunters, all crack shots, hired for the purpose. This went on for six years. In Halifax itself the company built heavy steel housings around many of the main transformers to shield them against bomb or shell fragments, and surrounded others with cribwork and a two-foot thickness of sand and gravel. As the war progressed the company's skilled personnel were engaged in many other tasks at the urgent request of the armed services.

The new war brought back to Halifax familiar scenes. At first it was much like 1914—the boom of guns at practice in the forts; the queues of young men at the recruiting offices; the warships coming and going; merchant ships assembling in the safe anchorage of Bedford Basin; the rumors of spies and saboteurs; the soldiers of city militia battalions with their 1914 model flat-topped caps, brass buttons and badges, long tunics, and trouser legs bound in puttees, standing guard over the city's water supply and the government docks.

The resemblance soon changed. Batteries of anti-aircraft guns and searchlights sprang up like a fairy toadstool ring in the wooded hills about the port, and were placed on the roofs of downtown stores and elsewhere in the city; there were numerous and prominent signs saying "Military Zone: Photography Forbidden"; a ban was placed on outdoor lighting displays; aircraft throbbed overhead by day and by night; the radio programs were interrupted by a few bars of "Rule Britannia" and a mysterious voice calling "Attention, all light-keepers in the East Coast area! Instructions A—A for Apples—will be carried out!"

Work was rushed on the great runways, the barracks, mess halls, hangars, and workshops at Eastern Passage, and in the meantime the city was thronged with young men in Air Force blue seeking billets and lodgings until there was accommodation at the field. The Royal Canadian Navy also, with a view to its coming immense role in the North Atlantic, recruited rapidly and poured a host of officers and men into Halifax. The garrison artillery and other fortress troops were all at their posts towards the harbor mouth, or manning the anti-aircraft stations. The only regular infantry in Halifax itself, "A" Company of the Royal Canadian Regiment, left for Valcartier in November; so that through the first winter of war the streets were largely a study in two shades of blue.

Canada's handful of destroyers (the Pacific force had made a quick trip to Halifax via the Panama Canal) whisked in and out of the harbor. A flock of launches and motor yachts of all shapes and sizes commenced coastal patrols. (Most of them had been hastily purchased in the United States, brought north by civilian crews, daubed with gray paint and manned by the RCN) Battleships and cruisers of the Royal Navy appeared and vanished; but soon their duties in the western Atlantic were taken over by armed merchant cruisers, the famous "AMC's"—liners with well-known names, scarcely recognizable in coats of gray, flying the white ensign and manned by the Royal Navy.

All through November and early December 1939 contractors under navy supervision were busy making a submarine-defense net across the harbor entrance from Mauger's Beach to York Redoubt. The net was of steel cable, supported by many buoys of special design, and its entrance was guarded by two gate-ships, one painted bottle green, the other a flaring scarlet. It was a long and intricate job—apart from the gate-ships, it cost $300,000—and the defense was still incomplete when Canada's immortal 1st Division embarked for Britain. Their transports, including such fine ships as *Aquitania*, *Alaunia*, and *Monarch of Bermuda*, made a fat and tempting target in the harbor, and although the garrison and navy took every possible precaution there was unavoidable risk. Fortunately the German submarines at this early stage were too busy around the British Isles to venture across the Atlantic.

Most Haligonians were unaware of the passage of the 1st Division until the ships were well at sea; but those who lived near the railway saw an endless procession of troop trains clacking through the suburbs towards the middle of December and drew their own conclusions. As each train pulled into the dock sidings the troops jumped out and marched straight aboard the ships. Exceptions were made in the case of the West Nova Scotia Regiment and "A" Company, RCR, some of whom were permitted to say good-by to their families in one of the terminal sheds—each relative having first obtained a pass from the garrison headquarters on Spring Garden Road. The division sailed in two convoys, the first on December 10 and the other on December 22. The Bluenose unit, the "West Novas," sailed in the Polish liner *Chrobry* with the second convoy, its band playing "O Canada" and the regimental march "Wenosco" as the ship pulled away from the quay. It was a bleak day with a thin snow blowing like mist from the sea, and the transports soon vanished in the murk towards the east.

The first wartime Christmas in Halifax was one of confidence and good cheer. Food, drink, clothing, fuel, everything was cheap and abundant. Every home in the city invited young servicemen to share its dinner and fun; the Egg Pond, Chocolate Lake, Banook Lake, and every other sheet of ice about the port were crowded with skaters, and the theatres were jammed. One thing was missing. During the 1930s Halifax like many another city and town in Canada had made a custom of outdoor decoration at Christmas time—each house with an arch of fir boughs over the door, small spruce trees lining the front walk, sometimes a stuffed figure of Santa Claus by the door or perched on the roof against the chimney, all illuminated with colored electric lights. The port ban on outdoor lighting displays put an end to all this for the duration of the war.

Spring came, and Dartmouth was enlivened by the presence of the Prince Edward Island Highlanders guarding the huge new air-drome behind Eastern Passage. In April 1940 there was thunderous news from Europe—the German invasion of Denmark and Norway. This was followed in May by the German thrust into Holland, Belgium, and France. By June 18 Britain stood alone in Europe against the whole might of Hitler's war machine, and Winston Churchill was making his greatest speech. With all the ports of western Europe, short of Spain and Portugal, in their hands the Germans began to carry the war into the North Atlantic with aircraft, surface raiders, and submarines. Thus by the summer of 1940 Britain like a diver in deep waters was dependent for life upon a slender and fragile line stretching across the sea, and that line began at Halifax.

Here came the Americans' "every aid short of war"; here came the products of the Canadian forests and fields and factories; here came the

Canadian troops bound overseas; here the convoys assembled; here the escorting warships were refueled, provisioned, and refitted for the long and dangerous ocean passage; here the gray merchantmen damaged by enemy action, by storm, or by collision in the dark thick nights, were repaired and sent back into the struggle.

Here in October 1940 came the famous fifty American destroyers, "traded" to Britain in the moment of her greatest need. The destroyers—all First World War types—steamed into the harbor in groups of eight or ten, several days apart, and moored at South Terminal. Their US Navy crews made a last check to see that everything was shipshape, lowered their flags, quietly marched across the quay, and entered the waiting railway trains which sped them back across the border. Two hours after the last American sailor left the quay the British crews appeared, marching down past the Nova Scotian Hotel. Each crew lined up opposite its allotted ship while flag parties went aboard and with a brief ceremony hoisted the white ensign. The crews then filed aboard and took up their duties. Under cover of these official gestures, however, there had been some unofficial and very business-like activity. During the two-hour interval when the destroyers were crewless, flagless, and apparently nobody's property, specially trained electricians from the nearby plant of the Nova Scotia Light & Power Company had slipped aboard and begun to install degaussing gear, that ingenious British invention which protected iron and steel hulls against the Germans' new magnetic mine.

There was a queer twist of history in all this. It was the first time the British naval colors had been seen flying over a United States warship since the War of 1812—and with what a difference!

At this time, also, Halifax witnessed another nautical transformation. The German invasion of Norway had left homeless a great number of Norwegian ships, among them two whaling fleets just steaming north from a season in the Antarctic. Each fleet consisted of a large "factory ship" whose storage capacity rendered her easily convertible to an oil tanker, and a number of small fast whale-hunting steamers which, with certain changes and equipment, made ideal minesweepers. They proceeded to Halifax, where for a time the streets and cafés were lively with muscular young whalermen out for a spree. Then Norwegian naval officers arrived and made arrangements to refit the ships for war in two small ports west of Halifax; the crews donned Norwegian naval uniforms and departed down the coast to train at "Camp Norway."

The year 1940 closed in anxiety and grim resolution. The war in the North Atlantic had reached a new and terrific intensity, and every convoy that left Halifax had its tale of disaster and heroism to tell on its return. The city's part in the new German war was much like its part in the war of 1914-18; once again Halifax was a naval and air base, a loading and assembly point for merchant convoys, an embarkation point for troops, and a fortress. But there was a vast difference in the scale of all these functions, and in the equipment and technique employed.

To take them in reverse order, the fortress itself in the modern manner depended largely on the strength of its air squadrons for active defense, and for passive defense upon the searchlight and anti-aircraft batteries. The outer forts, increased by a heavy battery behind Devil's Island, were in effect powerfully armed sentry boxes watching the harbor mouth.

As an embarkation point Halifax had the same importance as before, but this time the army erected large assembly camps at Debert and Windsor in the hinterland of Nova Scotia, whence troops could be railed into the port and marched at once aboard the transports. The troops within the urban area were kept at a minimum, the Common remained an open space in the city, and with the exception of a tent camp erected one summer in the Wanderers Grounds there were no soldiers quartered in Halifax except those engaged in garrison and port operation duties. Various Canadian regiments awaiting shipment overseas sent detachments for a tour of duty in the Halifax forts, but these of course were quartered there.

The activities of the garrison, the army recruiting services, and embarkation personnel now required a depot camp, and this was built on the obsolete Halifax airport on Chebucto Road in 1941. It consisted of gray wooden single-storey barracks which eventually spread over the entire field and were known as Chebucto Camp. In the same year the RCAF built an embarkation camp at Willow Park, in the hollow of pasture land west of Windsor Street and opposite the old roundhouse and workshops of the Canadian Nations Railways.

This large wooden camp of long, green-roofed, single-story barracks, mess halls and offices was known as Y Depot. Its ultimate capacity was five thousand men, and here were gathered graduates of the Empire

Training Scheme from all the air schools in Canada on their way overseas—Britishers, Canadians, Australians, New Zealanders, and men from all the various colonies. From it as many as twenty-five hundred airmen at a time passed through the Halifax streets to embark. While awaiting a convoy, the young airmen strolled about Halifax and were welcome guests in the homes. The Australians in their darker blue were especially popular, and an Anzac Club came into being downtown for their benefit.

In November 1943 when the bulk of the great force trained under the Empire Scheme had passed overseas, Y Depot was turned over to the Royal Canadian Navy, which renamed it HMCS *Peregrine* and quartered there large numbers of personnel including women of the "Wren" division.

As a convoy loading and assembly point Halifax became literally the crossroads of the world. The congestion at docks and wharves was so great at times that many ships had to be loaded or discharged in Bedford Basin. For this purpose a large fleet of lighters was built at Liverpool, Nova Scotia, with gangs of men working day and night, and using timbers of British Columbia fir hastily railed across the Dominion. The merchant fleets of Norway, Denmark, Holland, France, Belgium, and Greece, rendered homeless by German invasion, made their headquarters here, and as the strain of the sea war increased, most of the governments-in-exile purchased buildings in and about Halifax and equipped them as clubs or rest homes for their merchant seamen.

The British and the rapidly expanding Canadian merchant marine soon discarded the old easy-going system by which a shipmaster in need of men picked them up casually at the local shipping office. All British merchant seamen "on the beach" in eastern Canada were collected at Halifax in what was known as the Manning Pool, where they could be drawn upon according to the needs of the ships in port. Thus in the streets and in the various seamen's clubs in Halifax by the summer of 1941 there could be heard the tongues of almost every branch of the white race, and of Chinese, Lascars, Arabs, Negroes, and others from the stokeholds and forecastles of ships gathered from every part of the world. The ships to be seen at the wharves were of all types from smart motor ships of up-to-date British and Scandinavian lines to queer tall-funneled, spar-decked craft from the Mediterranean Sea and the Oriental coasts and rivers.

When troop trains made their periodical shuttling movements into the port the huge silhouettes of the *Queen Mary*, *Queen Elizabeth*, and

Aquitania and such famous smaller liners as the *Empress of Britain, Empress of Australia, Monarch of Bermuda,* and *Duchess of York,* the fine new Polish ships *Pilsudski, Batory,* and *Chrobry,* the French *Pasteur,* and the Dutch *Nieuw Amsterdam* could be seen towering over the sheds along the Quay Wall and the other closely guarded piers of South Terminal. The 85,000 ton *Queen Elizabeth* and her companion *Queen Mary,* with their luxurious passenger accommodation ripped out and narrow steel-and-canvas bunks thrust into every possible space, carried as many as 15,000 troops each.

A maid-of-all-work was the Furness liner *Nerissa,* which frequently ran the North Atlantic gauntlet without escort (although she was of medium size and not particularly fast) carrying odd lots of troops between convoys. She had amazing luck for many months, and when finally she was torpedoed and sunk in the western Atlantic her place on the "milk run" was taken by the Royal Mail liner *Andes,* which also had phenomenal luck at a time when the submarine wolf packs roved almost at will between the British Isles and Thirty West.

But the feature of the war which chiefly absorbed the life of Halifax was the role of the Royal Canadian Navy as custodian of the West Atlantic. The growth of the Navy from 1939 to 1945 is a book-length romance in itself. Starting practically from scratch with 1800 personnel, a handful of destroyers and minesweepers, and meager and obsolete shore establishments at Halifax and Esquimalt, Canada's navy by the spring of 1945 possessed 370 fighting ships besides a multitude of auxiliary craft and had on its rolls 95,000 officers and men. For most of these Halifax was the chief base and nerve center, and for many it was the training school as well.

At first the RCN barely had strength enough to patrol the Halifax harbor approaches and the Royal Navy bore the whole burden of the Atlantic battle. (But it should not be forgotten that the Canadian destroyers performed strenuous service then and later in the cut and dash fighting off the French coast.) Much of the early work in the North Atlantic was done by sloop-class patrol craft and former passenger liners armed and manned by the Royal Navy. The commander of the 3rd Battle Squadron, Rear-Admiral S.S. Bonham-Carter, R.N., established himself and his operations staff in the former yacht *Seaborne,* anchored off Halifax Dockyard; the administrative and pay staffs took over the old King Edward Hotel at the corner of Barrington and North streets, which was named HMS *Canada*.

When the Canadian Navy was able to assume the chief burden of the North Atlantic patrols and convoys in 1941, Rear-Admiral Bonham-Carter and his staff withdrew to Britain, where subsequently the gallant admiral distinguished himself on the hazardous Murmansk convoy run. However, for troop convoys out of Halifax the Royal Navy provided cruiser and battleship escort throughout the war; and throughout the war the quirks of naval strategy (such as the *Bismarck* chase) brought many of Britain's famous "battlewagons" into port.

At various times the battle cruiser *Renown*, the battleships *Warspite, Malaya, Rodney, Ramillies, Revenge, Barham, Queen Elizabeth* and *King George Fifth* (usually known as "K.G. Five"), the aircraft carrier *Furious* and many a cruiser and smaller craft of the Royal Navy were to be seen in the anchorage or moored at South Terminal, and their crews ashore filled the streets, the parks, and the walks about Northwest Arm with animated blue. For the service of these ships and for fleet Air Arm detachments at Eastern Passage and elsewhere in Nova Scotia, the Royal Navy maintained its HMS *Canada* offices and staff all through the war.

Before the fall of France in the summer of 1940, units of the French fleet took part in the North Atlantic escort work and frequently refueled and victualed at Halifax. The battleships *Jeanne d'Arc* and *Dunkerque* were familiar visitors. The French aircraft carrier *Bearn* lay in Halifax Harbor laden with brand-new American planes when her country surrendered and the invidious Pétain government ordered all French naval craft to make for "friendly" ports. This created a touchy situation at Halifax, as at Alexandria and elsewhere, but eventually *Bearn* was permitted to sail for Martinique in the West Indies, there to lie ignominiously at anchor until the war's end.

The outstanding French naval craft in the memory of Halifax, however, is the huge submarine *Surcouf*, which was seized by the Royal Navy in an English port when France collapsed. Later she was taken over by the Free French forces and for two years she engaged in escort work in the Atlantic, operating chiefly out of Halifax, where everyone came to know her bulky form in the anchorage or sliding past Point Pleasant. A hostel equipped and maintained by a group of Halifax citizens for the entertainment of French personnel was named *Maison Surcouf* in her honor. Poor *Surcouf* came to a sad end eventually in a convoy to the West Indies, when she was accidentally rammed and sunk with all on board by one of the escorting warships.

A Dutch submarine was attached to the RCN establishment at Halifax during most of the war. Designed for service in the North Sea, she was unsuitable for Atlantic escort work; but she proved very useful in training maneuvers with Canadian frigates and corvettes off the Nova Scotia coast.

In January 1943 a pair of Russian submarines turned up at Halifax, stayed for a time, and vanished as mysteriously as they came. Her officers had that curious secretive air which marks the Soviet service, even among allies. Her seamen, a picked lot, were less inhibited when ashore. They demanded wine and women, and a Royal Navy petty officer who was told off to see that they were entertained in any way they chose had a merry tale to tell when the last of his charges went singing back aboard.

After the United States came into the war in December 1941 American warships were frequently in Halifax, and a growing preponderance of American merchant ships in the convoys entailed a busy office of the US War Shipping Administration in the city. For the use of their crews a well-equipped "Yanks' Reading and Recreation Club" came into being on Hollis Street.

All of these ships were conspicuous by reason of size, shape, or flag. They attracted attention by their difference. In comparison the destroyers, frigates, corvettes, minesweepers and other craft of the Royal Canadian Navy were commonplace. Yet this host of small Canadian ships fought the main battle of the Atlantic, in all sorts of weather, under the toughest conditions—and in a silence like that of the grave, for a dense fog of censorship masked their doings and muffled their story throughout the war. To paraphrase Mr. Churchill, never in the history of human conflict was so little of it told. The people of Halifax learned some of it, as mentioned casually and with due regard to Security (that god of the censors) by men on shore leave. The rest of the world knew little, knows little even today.

It is not a subject for this book; the Canadian Navy waged its struggle all the way from Halifax to Newfoundland, to the bitter seas of Greenland and Iceland, to the British Isles, and south to Bermuda and the Caribbean. It is a saga of brilliant courage and stark endurance, of patient labor, of skill, of wit in out-guessing a wily and largely invisible enemy, and of an unshakable determination in all ranks from admiral to seaman. Today on the Citadel, facing toward the harbor mouth, a modest white memorial reminds the visitor of the many Canadians, including merchant mariners, who perished in the long battle, some of them within sight of the harbor lightship.

36.
1939–1945

The old Dockyard vanishes. HMCS Kings. *Maintaining the lifeline.*

ON THE EVE OF THIS WAR THE HALIFAX DOCKYARD still retained a distinct air of the eighteenth century. Even some of the long grim buildings erected between 1759 and 1815, with their ironstone lower stories and gray wooden lofts, remained untouched by time and circumstance and still in use. During the 1914-18 war some temporary wooden structures had been added but most of these had disappeared soon after. The new war brought a cataclysmic change. All of the ancient buildings were swept away ruthlessly, giving place to the multifarious stores and workshops required by a base for the world's third largest fleet, with a brick block of administration offices towering over all.

Old docks and cambers were filled, old jetties extended, new jetties built. The work went on through the war, and by 1945 the familiar and picturesque dockyard had vanished. In its place was a great factory buzzing with more than three thousand civilian employees, not to mention thousands of naval personnel. Ignoring the men in blue, and ignoring the warcraft moored three and four abreast at the jetties, it might have been a large modern industrial plant plucked from some Ontario city and set down on the shore of Halifax harbor for the manufacture of radios or refrigerators.

From 1939 onward the naval force at Halifax increased to nearly 20,000 men and women, and the navy reached through the city for barracks and training grounds. First the Exhibition buildings were taken over, then Wellington Barracks, and finally the embarkation camp at Willow Park—Y Depot—which was renamed HMCS *Peregrine*. King's

College was taken over for the training of naval officers, renamed HMCS *Kings*, and populated with men in blue. It was strange to hear a seaman stroking ship time upon a large brass bell on the portico, and to see companies of young officers and sometimes "Wrens" marching up and down the campus to the blare of band music from a loud-speaker apparatus on the grounds. Meanwhile the faculty and students of King's College removed to hospitable Pine Hill, whose classrooms they shared for the duration of the war.

At Camperdown near the harbor mouth, where the Duke of Kent had built the outermost station of his telegraph system in 1798, and where the Marconi Wireless Telegraph Company had operated a station from 1905 to 1924, a large naval radio station now appeared, covering the entire knoll with its accompanying barracks and stores. In the city itself the combined command of the naval and air forces operating out of Halifax took over a building at the corner of South and Barrington streets, with windows looking towards the harbor past the railway station square and the statue of Cornwallis. Here was the famous Operations Room, from which the combined command directed the war in the western Atlantic.

The long and bitter struggle on the sea presented from the first a problem in the refitting and repair of ships. The effects of the modern explosives in German mines, torpedoes, and air bombs were terrific. The Atlantic itself, especially in winter, inflicted crushing blows on the deep-laden merchant ships and the lightly constructed destroyers, frigates, and corvettes. The convoy system, which meant large numbers of ships steaming without navigation lights or radio transmission in the long winter nights and in the summer fogs, brought many a collision and a straggle of lame ducks.

The burden of repairs fell upon ports in the Maritime Provinces, for the ship-fitting plants up the St. Lawrence were far away and in any case shut off by ice five months in the year. Chiefly it fell upon Halifax. By design the plant of Halifax Shipyards Limited (established in 1918 to build ships for the Canadian Government) included the dry dock built for the Royal Navy in 1889, and so lay cheek by jowl with Dockyard itself. This provided a very useful partnership in the Battle of the Atlantic, for the Dockyard facilities, great as they became, could handle only a portion of the naval repairs, let alone the repair of merchant ships.

To meet the enormous demand, the Halifax Shipyards Company expanded on both sides of the harbor. At the main plant next to the

Dockyard, the old 568-foot dry dock was augmented by a 600-foot floating dock built and launched within the plant and capable of lifting 25,000 tons. In the Halifax plant every sort of equipment for the repair or refitting of ships was at hand; and eventually the company began to build destroyers for the Canadian Navy as well. Warships and merchantmen of all sizes down to 3000 tons were repaired here. Ships of less than 3000 tons went to the plant at Dartmouth Cove, where they were hauled up high and dry on 5 marine railways.

The two ship-repair plants of this company worked day and night throughout the war, and from 1939 to 1945 repaired and refitted more than seven thousand vessels ranging all the way from battleships to small tramp steamers. The repair of decks and hulls—all outdoor work—went on without ceasing, often in snow and bitter temperatures, with a winter wind whistling out of Bedford Basin and forming ice on everything touched by the harbor lop.

Damage from torpedoes was severe. Many a hull in dry dock resembled nothing so much as a burst paper bag. Sometimes a ship was blown in half, and the two halves—or perhaps only one half—were held afloat by the grace of a watertight compartment and towed into the harbor by salvage tugs. The German acoustic torpedoes, which found their target by following up the thrash of a ship's propellers, blew the rudder and propeller to smithereens and usually smashed the whole stern. Many a ship was struck by more than one torpedo, yet by miracles of courage and seamanship lived to reach Halifax, there to be restored and sent forth again into the battle. It detracts nothing from the magnificent record of the navy and of the merchant marine to say that a significant part of the Battle of the Atlantic was fought and won in the workshops of Halifax harbor.

In fact all the resources of the city were drawn into the long sea war, which tested the energy and ingenuity of the people of Halifax to the utmost. The experiences of the Nova Scotia Light & Power Company are typical. In the summer of 1939 the company, foreseeing its needs, had under construction a hydroelectric plant at Black River in the interior of Nova Scotia. The generator had been ordered from a Swedish firm; but the war broke out before it could be delivered; and then, of course, Sweden was cut off in the Baltic.

As the generator was needed urgently for the swiftly growing Halifax load, the Swedes determined to ship it by rail across Russia to Vladivostok, and thence by sea to Vancouver and by rail across the Dominion. But in their calculations for this enormous journey they forgot that certain tunnels on the trans-Siberia railway had a very small overhead clearance. The generator for Halifax became stalled at the entrance to one of these tunnels and nothing was heard of it again. Presumably the acquisitive Russians found a use for it.

As a precaution the Halifax company had ordered another generator in Canada at the outbreak of war, and this arrived just in time to take up the added wartime load. But the load was increasing so fast that the company had to undertake still another development on Black River, and finally a large new steam electric plant within the city itself. These were urgent matters, for a shortage of electricity would have hampered severely the war activities of the port and fortress. All installations were completed and put into operation in time to serve the ever-growing demand, in spite of a drastic labor shortage, scarcity of materials, and the disorganization of an area turned upside down by the activities of the armed services.

This company also had the task of installing electric distribution systems in the various camps, forts, signal stations, and barracks about Halifax (the system required for the Eastern Passage air station alone was that of a good-sized town) and to each of the antiaircraft searchlights and batteries hidden in the wooded hills. All this was in addition to the demands of the sprawling wartime housing developments and of a civil population suddenly swollen from less than 70,000 to something well over 100,000.

The same company operated the Halifax electric tramways, using a type of car—the "Birney"—adapted to the narrow streets and steep grades of the city. The multitude of service personnel and civilian war workers of all kinds demanded more and more trams, and the whole continent was explored. Many cities using Birney cars refused to part with even one, but eventually the Halifax tramways received and operated cars from places as widely separated as Cape Breton, Toronto, Thetford Mines (Quebec), and Bakersfield, California. At the same time, to serve the busy host at the Dockyard and the adjacent shipyards, an additional tram line had to be laid. No rails were to be had in the Dominion, and so the line to Point Pleasant Park was torn up and laid down at the other end of the city on the old-fashioned principle of duty before pleasure. All this required extra power, and as tramcars operated on 550-volt direct current the company had to ransack Canada and the United States for the necessary equipment. Eventually it was found available in faraway Tennessee, and was hurriedly shipped north to Halifax.

No less vital—and even more interesting—were the duties thrust upon the company's skilled personnel by the emergencies of the sea war. The magnetic mine for a time threatened the existence of every warship and merchantman on both sides of the Atlantic. Then the degaussing invention robbed the Germans of what had promised to be the outstanding naval weapon of the war. But it meant that every ship had to be fitted with miles of wire slung in bound coils about the bulwarks and, as the enemy made his mines more sensitive, by special coils in the forward and after ends of the ship, sometimes in the engine room, and even on the rudder!

The Navy asked the Nova Scotia Light & Power Company to train a special marine department and undertake this work without delay. Among the first ships they fitted with degaussing gear were the battleship *Ramillies* and the cruiser *Emerald,* both of which later took part in the chase of the *Bismarck.* Next came the armed merchant cruisers, the "AMC's" of Bonham-Carter's command. The most famous of these was *Jervis Bay* whose heroic crew under the immortal Fogarty Fegan later sacrificed themselves to save a convoy from a German battleship. Others were well-known liners such as *Ascania, Laconia,* and *Voltaire.* Transports of many flags carrying Canadian troops overseas were degaussed at Halifax, including the big French *Pasteur,* which required more than thirty miles of wire.

On one occasion the former Canada–West Indies liner *Lady Rodney* had to be fitted with degaussing gear before she could proceed to sea. The matter was urgent, and the notice very short; and most of the available electricians were engaged in important naval work which could not be put aside. Where could they get the men? Somebody had a bright idea: Why not enlist the students of the Nova Scotia Technical College on Spring Garden Road? As soon as the matter was put before the college president, Dr. F.H. Sexton, he suspended all classes and lectures and the students were whisked away in trucks to the waterfront. For three days, working around the clock under the supervision of a few electrical experts, they labored to install the lifesaving coils—and *Lady Rodney* sailed on time.

Out of these problems and adventures came the custom of presenting each ship "degaussed" with a framed quotation from Homer:

"This magic circle round thy bosom bind,
Live on—and cast thy terrors to the wind."

Each inscription was prepared in the language of the ship's crew—a job for the interpreters—for during the war Halifax electricians installed degaussing gear in ships belonging to nineteen nations.

Before long the company's marine department was tackling all sorts of electrical problems. It installed in Canadian minesweepers the special apparatus for detecting and exploding magnetic mines. It worked in secret with Navy experts to adjust the "radar" apparatus in many a warship, installed crew alarm and ship telephone systems in others, and repaired the elevator motors of aircraft carriers. But the heaviest part of its work lay in the continual repair and adjustment of electrical equipment aboard merchantmen awaiting convoy—dynamos, motors, "zigzag" clocks, telephones, radio apparatus, sounding gear, and a dozen other matters of modern nautical importance. It installed or repaired generators, added new lighting, rewired engine rooms, and overhauled electrical steering gear and gyro compasses.

On one occasion in the early months of 1944 an American convoy bound for Murmansk ran into heavy weather off the Nova Scotia coast and received such a buffeting that it had to put into Halifax for repairs. A wit suggested naming the harbor "Cripple Creek," for in this one convoy there were twenty-eight damaged ships. In the words of a company bulletin—"What a picture they presented! Forward guns were buried in ice, telephones for gun control were water-soaked and out of commission, navigation lights broken and torn away, railings and other steel work twisted and bent, steampipes on deck frozen tight. In many cases the cargo had shifted, with army tanks and trucks running loose in the holds…and everything generally in a mess. Every ship-repair firm in Halifax was called in to put the ships in shape at the earliest possible moment. Rush calls went to New York for replacement parts—but there was no time to wait for parts. Almost everything from electric generators to steel braces had to be borrowed from other ships berthed in the harbour and Bedford Basin. The task was speeded day and night to meet the date for the next eastbound convoy, and every ship sailed on time."

37.
1939–1945

The Atlantic convoys. Overcrowding and its consequences. Dangers of fire and explosion. Emergency precautions. The enemy outside the gates. The passing of prisoners. Mr. Churchill. The voyage of the St. Roch.

AN ODD FEATURE OF THE WAR IN ITS FIRST TWO years, while the United States remained neutral, was the curiosity of American tourists. Eager for a glimpse of the struggle in the Atlantic, they flocked to Halifax. The *pièce de résistance* was of course the departure of a convoy. At such times the vicinity of the Yacht Club and the pine-shaded shores of Point Pleasant were alive with people watching the steady procession of warships, transports, or merchantmen from Bedford Basin steaming slowly hour after hour past the city, past the park with the pleasant name, and thence through the net defense opposite York Redoubt, to vanish at last in a smudge of smoke towards the east.

After the summer of 1941 the shortage of gasoline, the scarcity of train and hotel accommodation, and finally the entry of the United States into the war, shut off these visitors; but the sea pageant at the harbor mouth held its fascination for the Haligonians until the very end. From 1942, when German submarines began their sustained warfare along the whole coast, through 1943, 1944, and the early months of 1945, when ships were mined or torpedoed sometimes within gunshot of the outer Halifax forts, when gunfire and the distant thud of depth charges could be heard through the open windows of the Nova Scotian Hotel, the sight of the gray ships plodding out to face such music all the way to Britain or Murmansk was something to catch the heart. No one could watch it unmoved.

The city was crowded as never before. The huge expansion of port activities added thousands of workmen and their families. The presence of

3500 airmen at Eastern Passage brought many wives and families. But the growth of the Halifax naval establishment from a few hundred to nearly 20,000 provided the greatest housing problem. For the skilled civilian labor brought in from every part of the dominion the government built masses of prefabricated cottages, which spread over the vacant parts of the Richmond suburb above the shipyards, along the western slope of the plateau from Chebucto Camp to Windsor Street, and from the north end of Dartmouth towards the Narrows.

But the government made no provision for the families of servicemen, taking the view that since men in the armed forces overseas had to leave their families at home no exception could be made in the case of naval and other personnel posted at Halifax. Advertisements in newspapers across Canada suggested, urged, and finally commanded that people who had no business in Halifax should stay where they belonged. All this was blithely ignored. From 1939 onwards every train arriving in the city decanted women and children eager to join their men in this strange exciting place, none with any idea of conditions in the port, all confident of finding a place in which to live. It was only human instinct; but as a result the city's hotels, boarding houses, tenements, apartments, and homes were jammed for six years. Many found themselves obliged to live in filthy rooms in the slums, and a tumorous growth of small shacks appeared and spread into the woods on the outskirts.

Unlike the first German war, when building supplies were comparatively plentiful and cheap until the final year, the new war created a dire shortage of lumber, an almost complete dearth of electrical and plumbing supplies, and a prohibitive price for what was available. Hence there was a scramble for existing accommodation, and the demand caused a sharp rise in rentals. Laws to curb the rapacity of landlords had no more effect in Halifax than in other crowded cities of the continent. The incoming swarm were ready and eager to pay bribes above the legitimate rental; the advertisement columns of Halifax newspapers were full of appeals and proffered "rewards" for the tenancy of rooms or apartments, and the Haligonian who did not own his own home found himself obliged to bribe in turn if he wished to keep a roof over his family.

Overcrowding had other unhappy results. The meager wartime supplies of civilian goods, especially clothing, bedding, and household utensils, were snapped up as soon as they appeared in the shops, for the throng of shoppers included not only the enlarged population but thousands of merchant seamen eagerly buying for their own folk in Britain and elsewhere. As the war went on the Halifax shops became so bare of necessities that every housewife found herself in the position of Old Mother Hubbard. As always in wartime there seemed to be no dearth of luxury goods. One could buy a fur coat, a diamond necklace, an exquisite watch; but only the lucky could find a kettle, a shirt, a stove, or a suit of child's underwear for months and years.

The food problem was severe always, for it was complicated by service requirements. When large troop convoys and their warship escorts were being provisioned at Halifax, not only warehouse stocks in the city but all food in transit east of Montreal was subject to service priority, and for days on end very little meat and few vegetables were to be had in the shops. Even fish, always a staple in Halifax, was hard to obtain, owing to the absence of so many fishermen with the forces. And the fuel supply, reduced by the poor production of the Nova Scotia mines and the scarcity of sea transport from the United States, had to fill service and merchant marine demands before civilian needs could be met.

Somehow, in a sufficient if sketchy fashion, the swollen population was fed, housed, and kept from freezing under conditions faced by no other city in North America—conditions in some ways like those of a beleaguered and refugee-crowded city in Europe. The resemblance was increased by the fact that for four of the six years the enemy was just outside the gates. Indeed the worst perils of war were within the gates from the first—the presence of the great magazine at Burnside and of the huge oil stores at Imperoyal, the endless handling of munitions at the docks, and the continual passage of ships laden with terrific explosives. The hideous memory of December 1917 hung over Halifax for six years.

One night in April 1942 the steamship *Trongate*, with a large quantity of explosives on board, caught fire as she lay at anchor off George's Island within a few hundred yards of South Terminal, the Nova Scotian Hotel, the main city electric and gas plants, and the crowded warren of small hotels, boarding houses, flats and shops which cluster about the railway station. The ship's crew and naval boarding parties made desperate attempts to put out the fire and, failing that, to get the ship towed out of the anchorage; but finally a Canadian warship had to sink the *Trongate* by gunfire where she lay. All this took place in the darkness of a spring night. The cannonade in the heart of the port aroused all Halifax and Dartmouth and there were many anxious hours before it was revealed that the ship and her deadly cargo were at the bottom of the harbor.

The arrival of damaged ships caused a constant leak of fuel oil into the harbor. The oil gathered under the wooden wharves and clung to the piling in masses of inflammable black slime, making a potential firetrap of the whole waterfront. Worst were the damaged tankers, one of which in August 1943 spread thousands of gallons of high-test aviation spirit over the surface of the harbor. A match, a hot coal, a cigarette flipped from any of the wharves, would have set the port aflame. All harbor traffic had to be stopped, while naval and civil police patrolled the waterfront and warned the crews of all ships. The danger did not pass for several days and nights; indeed it never passed entirely, for other tankers, and other ships with leaky oil bunkers, from time to time renewed the iridescent scum on the water until the war came to an end.

Apart from these dangers there was always the probability that the enemy would attempt to strike at the port by air, by sea, or by some secret means. Halifax set up a civilian emergency organization along the lines of London's famous ARP to prepare the people for such an event. Wardens, auxiliary police and fire services, first-aid squads, ambulance services, and emergency Red Cross stations came into existence and conducted frequent drills. A system of powerful electric sirens erected through the city uttered a characteristic warning wail at the throw of a switch. One difficulty was that the warning sirens, however loud and however numerous, could not penetrate homes and apartments in which the radio sets were pealing forth the words and music of stations outside the controlled area. This problem was solved by what became known as the "squawker," an apparatus contrived from an obsolete spark radio transmitter, which could break into any standard-wave broadcast with long and short blasts very offensive to the human ear.

For auxiliary fire-fighting purposes the government provided stirrup pumps of the sort which had proved so useful in London; these were distributed to certain houses at strategic points, which then displayed in a prominent window this notice: "An Emergency Stirrup Pump Is Kept

Here." Every citizen was commanded to provide himself with a bucket of sand, to deal with incendiary bombs; and each head of a family was urged to buy gas masks for his household. The masks were made available by the government and sold through city stores. Small sizes were not to be had until May 1943, when the following advertisement appeared triumphantly in Halifax newspapers:

> INFANTS' GAS MASKS AVAILABLE
>
> *Gas Masks for infants of 1-1/2 to 5 years of age have just arrived in the city and can be secured at the T. Eaton Company and Robert Simpson stores.*

In this case the Haligonians, surrounded by real dangers, were inclined to be indifferent to a hypothetical poison-gas attack, and only the most timid or cautious bought masks of any sort. And although the black-out was practiced frequently, and rigorously enforced when the sirens blew, the urgency of night work on the wharves, in the ship-repair plants, and at the Dockyard made a complete darkness undesirable except in the event of attack. During most of the war the night shifts on the waterfront worked under clusters of floodlights and the shipyards glowed in the intense violet flare of arc welders. Even the windows of naval headquarters blazed forth into the darkness; and the glare of the port could be seen at sea for miles. It was in its way a gesture of defiance which must have impressed the German submarine commanders hovering outside.

The enemy's failure to attack Halifax by air was due to his lack of suitable aircraft. The presence of powerful air defense and patrol squadrons at Eastern Passage, and of radar stations dotted along the Nova Scotia coast, made the success of such an attempt doubtful in any case. But the Germans' failure to mine the approaches of Halifax Harbor from the outset remains one of the mysteries of the war. Of course the Canadian Navy began a daily sweep of the approaches soon after war began, and one of the wartime features of the port was the parade of the coal-burning *Comox* and her grimy sisters heading out of the harbor into the dawn, and returning at nightfall after a long and fruitless day's work.

These ships were equipped for sweeping the orthodox moored contact mine. When the ingenious Germans introduced their magnetic mine in British waters, several former Norwegian whaling steamers were equipped with trailing electric cables to explode such mines and based at Halifax. Similarly when the Germans introduced the acoustic mine, special craft employing a device to detonate them harmlessly became part of the Halifax system. The minesweepers had the most monotonous job in the Navy; for the "war channel," reaching thirty miles to sea, had to be swept and explored with care every day for six years, and only once in that time did they get a "catch."

On the night of May 28, 1943, a German submarine mine vessel laid fifty-six mines of a new type (combining the features of contact and magnetic mines) in an arc across the approaches to Halifax Harbor. On the following afternoon two of the mines were seen afloat and the port was closed. At daylight on May 30, Commander R. M. Barkhouse went out with a minesweeping flotilla and by nightfall had a channel cleared through the field. The only casualty was a merchant ship which, contrary to instructions, ventured out of the channel, blew up, and sank. The mines were thoroughly examined by Lieutenant George Rundle, RCNR, and Petty Officer Simpson, who put off from a minesweeper in a small dory, and despite a rough sea fastened a line to one of them and towed it to the beach on McNab's Island, where Rundle coolly took it apart. Later on this skillful and courageous officer recovered two more and dismantled them. He was awarded the George Cross.

After this the Germans laid no more, depending as before on their torpedoes. They never attempted to sink the harbor lightships—these were too useful as seamarks for their operations—although often they were close enough to do it. Merchant ships were attacked near the harbor, the Canadian minesweeper *Clayoquot* was torpedoed and sunk five miles off the Sambro lightship on Christmas Eve, 1944, and a submarine sank the minesweeper *Esquimalt* and many of her crew within sight of it in April, 1945. This was the last stroke at the port, for within three weeks Germany collapsed and ordered her submarines to surrender.

From 1940 onward thousands of German prisoners arrived at Halifax from Britain and the Mediterranean, on their way to prison camps in northern Ontario. During the first three years they were insolent, firmly convinced of Germany's ultimate victory, and making every possible difficulty for their guards. A few managed to slip away from the Halifax docks or from the trains despite every precaution, but these were rounded up in a short time and sent on their way. After 1943 there was a change in their demeanor, although most of the officers, especially those of the S.S. Corps and the Luftwaffe, remained truculent to the end. The disheartening thing to most of them was the very ease of their transportation to Canada when, according to their newspapers, the German submarines had made the passage all but impossible.

A happier and much more welcome visitor was Winston Churchill, on his way back from the Washington Conference in 1943. He spent several hours moving about the city, strolled through the public gardens, and inspected the port from the top of Citadel Hill. The great man was in jovial mood (Italy had surrendered a few days before) and when he was recognized and cheered by groups of townsmen and servicemen he stopped and shook hands with many of them, made his famous V sign, playfully pinched a little boy, and told Mayor Lloyd, "Now, sir, we know your city is something more than a shed on a wharf." He sailed from Halifax in a battleship on September 14.

A year later he was back again, this time with a large staff and accompanied by Mrs. Churchill, entering the harbor aboard the *Queen Mary* on September 10 en route to the Quebec Conference. Hundreds of servicemen and citizens recognized the Prime Minister and his inevitable cigar. They gathered at a respectful distance about the train; and again "Winnie" rose to the occasion, asking the guards to stand aside, making a little speech from the platform of his car, and finally leading the crowd in a sing-song—"When the Lights Go On Again," "Tipperary," "O Canada" and "God Save the King." Once before this a British prime minister had made a speech in Halifax (Stanley Baldwin, with his memorable reference to "this old British city on which the flag was never lowered") but Churchill's informal chat from the train, and his "something more than a shed on a wharf," pleased the Haligonians more.

All sorts of ships and all sorts of visitors were arriving in Halifax in these days. On October 9, 1942, the eighty-ton motor schooner *St. Roch* arrived, manned by eight men of the Royal Canadian Mounted Police who had left Vancouver in June 1940 and traversed the Northwest Passage, wintering twice in the Arctic on the way and burying one of their crew in the northern wastes. In peacetime they would have commanded headlines in every newspaper; in the clamors of war, their achievement was barely noticed.

A few days later a very different sort of ship steamed into Halifax after a lone voyage across the Atlantic, a white hospital ship bearing the first Canadian wounded homeward—the men of Dieppe. It was the beginning of a long procession that did not end until 1946.

38.
1939–1945

The old story. Liquor rationing and theft. The women. The Ajax Club. The decline of naval shore discipline. The V-E Day riots.

THIS GREATEST OF ALL WARS AFFECTED THE LIFE OF Halifax much as earlier wars had done. There was the same excitement, the departure of young townsmen on service, the arrival of thousands of strangers in uniform, the inpouring of workers, wives and children, speculators, criminals, and prostitutes, the rigid martial authority, the flood of money, the congestion, the scarcities, the imminent danger of death *en masse*, the sermons, the sorrow, the reckless gaiety, and the same general result.

Notable were the sorrow and the gaiety. The young men and women of the city flocked into the forces; by 1945 the list of killed and wounded was very long and many a home was saddened. But mourning made only an undertone in a city largely given over to the navy and merchant marine whose men, facing terrific dangers and enduring great hardship for weeks on end, wanted pleasure when they reached port. For six years the theatres, restaurants, and dance floors were thronged with lively young wives and sweethearts and their servicemen, all rubbing elbows cheerfully with strumpets and kept women and the gayer dogs of every service in the long roll call of the Allies.

Apart from the personnel of the merchant ships, which in itself represented the whole world, the variety of men in the armed forces posted in or passing through the Halifax area was astonishing. This was demonstrated in a Victory Loan parade on June 9, 1941, when a representative column of several thousand marched through the streets. It included companies of the Regina Rifles, Canadian Grenadier Guards, Princess Louise Fusiliers, and the Governor General's Foot Guards, a motorized battery of Canadian artillery, bluejackets of the Royal Navy, the Canadian Navy, the Norwegian Navy, the Dutch Navy, and the navy of Free France, a company of Royal Marines in full dress uniform, and detachments of the Royal Air Force, the Canadian, Australian, and New Zealand air forces, the fleet Air Arm and the Veterans' Guard. As the war went on, most of the khaki and air force blue uniforms disappeared towards Europe and the dominant note in the streets became that of the sea.

In the delicate language of Archibald MacMechan, "When a sailor makes port after a voyage, two things he must have. One is a drink." Drink was a matter requiring some contrivance in Halifax during this war. The government liquor stores adopted a rigid rationing system under which the holder of a ration card or booklet could obtain not more than two quarts of gin or one quart of rum or whiskey per month, with the alternative of two dozen quarts of beer per month. The alcoholic content of the spirits was sharply reduced from that of peacetime; the qualities of the beer suffered also. If the bibulous Dyott had come back from the grave he undoubtedly would have counted this state of affairs among the worst horrors of modern war.

But he would have found that as love laughs at locksmiths so does thirst triumph over rationing and dilution. To oblige a soldier, or a seaman parched from the salt Atlantic, there were thousands of nondrinkers, service and civilian, willing to take out ration books in their own names, purchase the allotted amount, and pass it over. Enterprising bootleggers soon discovered that ration books could be purchased or "rented" from the owners, and so arose a brisk black market in liquor. One thing led to another. The profit to be made in this black market induced wholesale thefts at the wharves, where liquor shipments consigned to overseas canteens were passing constantly. Theft of liquor by stevedores led to theft of cocaine and similar drugs in transit to the medical services. Eventually the RCMP discovered an organized system of drug theft and disposal leading from the Halifax waterfront to Montreal and other inland cities.

So there were stimulants in plenty for the modern counterpart of Dyott, and it was not long before he found women to go with the wine and song—but not as Dyott found them. Since the old wars the face of prostitution in Halifax had undergone a vast change. It was especially noticeable after the captains and the queans departed in 1919, when the city was able to resume the shreds of its normal life and to sniff once more the starchy aroma left by the Age of Victoria. Most merchant seamen visiting the port in the 1920s and 1930s found the place extremely dull. In 1939 only a few furtive dives remained of the once-notorious quarter between Argyle Street and "the Hill," and in the purlieus of Water Street and the shabby ends of Barrington Street. The moral state of the city was attested by a low rate of venereal disease and other factors well known to the social student. Most of the surviving brothels had adapted their trade to the motor age and moved outside the city where there were no police to be troublesome. Roadhouses of this sort, masquerading in various disguise, had appeared on the Bay road and here and there on the Bedford highway as early as 1917; but they were always small and never numerous until after 1939 when the new war brought back the old evils with a rush.

Madames and harlots flocked to the city by rail and air, and set up their trade with small brothels, usually in a secluded house or bungalow in the outskirts. With them came the more adventurous sisterhood, drawn to Halifax by men they had met in camps or ports elsewhere, or merely seeking opportunity. Here they found it. For six years the port was a courtesan's paradise far surpassing the days of 1918. There had been nothing like it since 1815. But it was very different from the old naughty days. Gone were the squalid resorts, the tattered and drunken sluts of Prince Billy's day and the time of Waterloo. Vice was more dainty now—and more discreet. Doll Tearsheet of 1942 wore a fur coat and a smart dress, traveled in taxicabs, patronized the best shops and restaurants, let herself be seen at the best dances, exacted a high price for her favors, and bestowed them in snug flats and apartments or in secluded cottages well outside the city.

All this went on beneath the surface of the city's busy wartime life, but it was early seen and recognized and every effort was made to counteract it. The YMCA, the Salvation Army, the Knights of Columbus, the Canadian Legion, various church societies and other volunteer groups opened hostels for men and women of the services, and summer camps and seaside cottages were thrown open to their use. So were most homes in the city. But here occurred a difficulty not experienced by cities which in proportion to their populace had few servicemen to entertain. The Haligonian's hospitality was sharply pinched by his rations of tea, coffee, sugar, butter, and other things necessary to entertainment of the simplest kind. To the extent of his rations he did his best, and when they were exhausted he could offer little more than a comfortable chair at the fireside. To a young and active man this had a certain charm after the long strain of duty at sea, but the charm soon palled and then came the siren call of the city's other life.

As the war dragged its course across the years there was a noticeable and increasing ennui in the servicemen at Halifax, and with it a slow but steady decline in shore discipline. As before in the city's long story, the fact that four out of five men were well behaved was offset by the behavior of the fifth, especially when thousands were "broke" and bored and footloose in the streets. Once again theft, robbery with violence, malicious damage, and assault upon women by men in uniform became matters of daily and nightly occurrence. The service police patrols did their best, stolidly tramping the streets and picking up drunks and brawlers; but they could not be everywhere at once. In 1944 the navy added jeep patrols to cruise the city; but even these had their limitations. In fact the service police were fighting a problem as old as war itself, to which no one ever had found a satisfactory solution. The city police, hampered by a lack of recruits in the general manpower shortage, had their hands full with the swollen civil population and the swarm of merchant seamen of all nations.

As in former wars the general boredom found its expression in a disgust with the city, which reached its final vent in the "V-E" riots of 1945 but which had its beginning in one or two incidents of the earlier years. The first and most famous of these was the Ajax Club affair. The Ajax Club was founded chiefly through the efforts of Mrs. Janet McEuan, wife of a Canadian naval officer stationed at Halifax. The McEuans had seen British naval ratings wandering about the streets, unable to afford theatres and restaurants on their small pay, and Mrs. McEuan and a group of devoted helpers raised a large fund and established a club at the corner of Queen and Tobin streets. It was equipped with comfortable furniture and a small bar at which beer was dispensed under license from the Nova Scotia Liquor Commission. The club was amiably but strictly run, and it soon became the recognized home of British naval ratings ashore in Halifax.

To the city, so long a station of the Royal Navy, the Ajax Club struck a happy note, and there was general astonishment when early in 1942 its license was canceled on the petition of the Kirk Session of Port Massey, one of the most venerable churches in Halifax, which stood immediately opposite. The particular grounds for this petition were never fully revealed, but its general complaint was that the club had become a nuisance. There followed an acrimonious discussion in the letter columns of city newspapers. The supporters of the Ajax Club appealed for tolerance; but the Session, firm in its own reasons, remained adamant and the license was not restored. The Royal Navy men shrugged and went their way. The men of the Royal Canadian Navy were indignant, and most Haligonians sympathized with them; but naval resentment was aimed at the city as a whole and the feeling grew, fed by other incidents and by the exasperation of life in the port itself.

Crowded lodgings, exorbitant rents, overburdened laundries, scant supplies, all had a part in this ill feeling. So did the growing indifference of shopgirls, cafe waitresses, and others overworked in the incessant rush. Another cause of irritation was the scarcity of taxicabs, due partly to the absence of many peacetime cabbies in the services and the preoccupation of the rest with the more lucrative forms of hire. Here and there a cabby retained his honesty and manners, but the insolence and rapacity of the average Halifax taximan during the war became intolerable. The city set up a central call office and attempted to bring all the cabs under its direction; but this was defeated by cabbies who could always find excuses for failure to report and in various other ways (including the destruction of telephone call boxes) made the central office another bad wartime joke. Travel to and from the railway station depended largely on the whim of these arrogant profiteers, so that everyone arriving in the city received a bad impression from the start, and it was the last straw to those who left.

What the servicemen and others of the floating population overlooked was that all these conditions had been created by the war, in fact very largely by their own presence in the port, and that the native Haligonians suffered just as much as they. So the feeling grew, and at the war's end it came to a head.

About midmorning on May 7, 1945, the German Radio at Flensburg announced to the world the surrender of Germany's remaining forces on land and sea. There was no confirmation from Allied Headquarters until several hours had passed, and then the city officials and the heads of the armed forces at Halifax decided to hold an organized celebration of victory on the following day. In the meantime, however, thousands of servicemen and civilians had gathered in the downtown streets, wandering aimlessly up and down. The German surrender having been expected for some days, many of the city stores began to hang out flags and bunting carefully put away for this occasion. The liquor stores were closed as a precaution; but the crowds were cheerful and orderly and there was no sign of trouble until towards evening, when a crowd of naval personnel emerged from the Dockyard and with happy energy stormed a streetcar, cleared out the driver and passengers, and set it afire. They proceeded along Barrington Street gathering followers as they went, and upon reaching the downtown district smashed their way into two liquor stores and looted them.

The Halifax police force, always small, at this time numbered ninety men, including the staff at headquarters under City Hall. For duty in the downtown area there were available fifty or at most sixty constables. It had been recognized early in the war that the armed services must provide their own police if the city force was to perform its task among the enlarged civilian population, and by tacit consent each looked after its own. The possibility of a riot had been discussed and some preparation made, but the event broke so suddenly that the first damage was done before any plan could be put into effect. The liquor stores were well stocked, and the swift distribution of their contents satisfied the mob for the night. But the success of this adventure brought a change of mood. What had begun as a gorgeous lark, with no more criminal intent than a pack of boys stoning the schoolhouse windows on the first day of vacation, turned overnight to a fixed determination to "take the town apart."

On the sunny morning of May 8 there were in the port and its defenses about 24,500 servicemen, including 3000 army, 3500 air force, and 18,000 naval personnel. The city and the heads of the three services had arranged a mass meeting on the garrison sports ground behind Citadel Hill, with band music, songs and hymns, and addresses by officials and clergy. The police hoped that this would keep the crowd out of the downtown district. However, some of the naval personnel, with the taste of yesterday's loot in their mouths, had other plans; and they were encouraged and abetted by the city's own criminal element whose main habitat was in the lower streets.

The celebration began on the Garrison Grounds as scheduled, but very quickly word reached the crowd that a new riot had begun in the shopping district and the whole mass poured over the hill to watch or take part in the excitement. The Navy had managed to keep roughly half its personnel on duty at the Dockyard and in the various ships and barracks, but at noon on May 8 about ninety-five hundred were loose in the streets. Of these probably not more than a thousand took part in the actual rioting, but many others shared in the loot, and they were joined by about two thousand merchant seamen of all nationalities, an assortment of waterfront laborers and loafers, and a host of males and females of the criminal class. For the rest of the day and well into the evening the city was in a state of anarchy.

Sailors rushing along Barrington Street from the Dockyard again took the lead, smashing shop windows from North Street into the heart of the city. In the main shopping district on Barrington and Granville streets they tore the victory flags from the shops and used the poles to shiver the plate glass windows, leaping inside and tossing out jewelry, drugs, clothing, shoes—every sort of goods—to the mob. A city police car making its way through the crowd was seized, capsized and burned by the seamen. In fact the city police were only a drop in this seething bucket and their efforts were useless. The air force and army police, having comparatively few personnel to control, were able to keep most of their men out of mischief. The naval police, unwilling to intervene in a mob which contained so many civilians, accomplished nothing,

Before long the downtown area was a shambles of broken glass and littered goods. Another liquor store was stormed and looted, and so was Keith's Brewery on Lower Water Street which had a large stock of bottled beer. Bacchanalia followed. Two shops were set afire, and all along the downtown streets sailors, waterfront toughs, and women of all sorts from giddy young girls to wizened hags could be seen smashing bottlenecks on the curbs, drinking themselves senseless, and lolling among the strewn merchandise on the sidewalks and in the gutter. Others carried their loot to the upper parts of the city. Within the parks, on the Citadel slopes, drunken seamen and workmen capered and sang, sprawled with drunken or merely hilarious women, eased themselves, and made unabashed love in the full blaze of the afternoon sun. Alert photographers took pictures of the riot and the following carousal. Some of these appeared later in the city newspapers: some could not be published anywhere. The camera was too cold and too exact an instrument. It was a scene for Hogarth.

And while all this was going on, thousands of other servicemen and other townsfolk looked on amazed or turned their backs and strolled away to enjoy the peace and sunshine of Point Pleasant and the Northwest Arm. Most of the people in the residential West End knew nothing of the rioting until evening, and then could not believe it. Towards evening the senior naval officer, Rear-Admiral L.W. Murray, RCN, made his way through the streets in a car equipped with loudspeakers, urging his men to return to their ships and barracks. Eventually most of them did, getting rid of undrinkable loot by hurling it into doorways, alleys, and other places along the way (the railway tracks above the Dockyard were found littered next morning) or bestowing it upon a following of yelling urchins.

Rear-Admiral Murray was a keen and capable officer, respected throughout the Navy. He had directed the greater part of the war in the western Atlantic with skill and success, and it was unfortunate that the record of his command at Halifax should have been marred by this unsavory climax, which clearly was no fault of his. Admiral G.C. Jones, RCN, flew down from Ottawa to take personal charge of naval affairs at Halifax, and a strong force of troops came by rail from the camp at Debert. However, the troops found nothing to do. After Mayor Butler of Halifax proclaimed a curfew on the evening of May 8, all but the most tipsy naval personnel returned to their stations; the merchant seamen slipped back aboard their ships, and the civilian rioters to their homes. Naval, army, and air force police patrolled the streets in strength, while the city police gathered up drunken figures in the parks and from the gutters and arrested all persons caught with loot in their hands. The police cells under City Hall and the city prison at Rock Head soon were filled, and finally the Armouries had to be taken over as an emergency jail and courthouse.

Shocked by this spasm of anarchy, the law dealt sharply with convicted offenders, among whom several naval men received severe sentences. A persistent search recovered large quantities of stolen goods which were gathered, sorted, and if possible returned to their owners. A special commission (the Kellock Commission) appointed by the Dominion Government to investigate the riots placed the primary blame on naval personnel, and the owners of the damaged and looted premises received full compensation from the Canadian treasury.

This decision, and the probability that most of the merchant seamen had been in mufti, did not obscure the fact that many civilians had taken part. For Halifax that was the most disturbing feature of the whole affair. Not every city is afforded a chance to see all at once the evil face of its own criminal element, grinning and triumphant, in the broad light of day. One filthy harridan, staggering along Barrington Street at the height of the riot with her arms full of stolen finery, shrieked again and again, "Never had so much fun in my life!" There spoke the voice of Chaos, which lurks in every modern city waiting patiently for the sailors to break the windows.

39.
1945–1946

The magazine disaster. The refugees. RDX *and Mendelssohn. The troops come home.*

AFTER SIX YEARS OF WAR THE WARDEN OF THE Honor of the North had been sacked by an unruly mob of its own defenders and the dregs of its own population, and for complete irony all that remained was to blow it up with its own magazine. This occurred on July 18, 1945, when Halifax was slowly recovering from the riots.

Since V-E Day a procession of ships carrying veterans and war brides from Britain had been arriving at the Halifax docks. On June 21 the first complete unit to return from overseas, the 1st Canadian Parachute Battalion, very jaunty in its red berets, marched through the streets cheered by thousands of Haligonians who turned out in pouring rain to welcome it home. The enterprising RCAF had begun to fly home, and on June 9 several Lancaster bombers, part of the famous "Ghost" Squadron, touched down at the Eastern Passage field on their way from Britain.

Meanwhile the navy was busy calling in ships and men from the Atlantic reaches and preparing to switch its efforts to the Pacific. For two months Canadian naval craft of all sorts had passed up the harbor and put ashore their ammunition. By July 18 the Bedford Basin magazine held enough shells, bombs, mines, torpedoes, depth charges, and other powerful material (including a quantity of the new secret explosive RDX) to blow Halifax off the face of the earth. Much of this ammunition was stowed away in the carefully designed and segregated buildings, but of necessity a good deal had been stacked outdoors for lack of storage space, and these dumps extended close to the jetty on the Basin shore.

The summer of 1945 was very hot; on Wednesday July 18 the heat was stifling. At the end of a sweltering afternoon, as the city was sitting down to the evening meal, an ammunition barge suddenly blew up at the magazine jetty. The blast shook the whole metropolitan area and shattered windows at Rockingham, Fairview, and the North End. The report and the characteristic smoke cloud, a toadstool growing swiftly in the northern sky, were like those of December 1917 on a smaller scale, and to most Haligonians, running out of their houses and staring northward, the explosion seemed to come from the same point. There followed an uneasy silence. But the exposed dumps had caught fire and soon there began an incessant rumbling and concussion which went on for more than twenty-four hours.

As a spectacle it was magnificent. The sun went down in a fine red blaze that lit the whole of the west, and as the huge cloud of dust and burning explosives arose and diffused over Bedford Basin it produced a tint in the sky that Turner alone could have painted. It was a Turner sunset come to life. When the last daylight faded, the burning magazine produced its own display, a vast golden glow across the north, with crimson underlights, with sudden blue-white flashes as if a powerful battery of searchlights were being switched on and off, with fountains of rockets, and star shells, and flares.

At 9 P.M. naval headquarters broadcast a warning that all people living between North Street and Bedford Basin should evacuate their homes at once. Later the warning was extended to all living north of Quinpool Road—more than half the population of the city. Fortunately a disaster of this sort had been anticipated throughout the war, and the emergency organization, service and civilian, was still in existence. Army, navy, and air force sent lorries and drivers to assist in the evacuation, and civilian vehicles of every sort were put to use.

Some of the refugees went towards the south end of the city where the woods of Point Pleasant offered space and shelter; but most headed out of the peninsula altogether. And here arose a problem foreseen during the war. The Halifax isthmus is a perfect bottleneck. Only two roads lead out of it, and the main one runs along the Bedford Basin shore in full view of the magazine. The whole evacuation had to be made by the single road past the head of Northwest Arm. Some people turned off along the farther side of the Arm but most held on along the St. Margaret's Bay road, which soon became a solid mass of vehicles, ten miles long, crawling slowly towards the west.

Some of the cars and trucks carried mattresses and even a few chairs lashed to the top or the rear; and there were baskets of food, blankets, and luggage of all sorts crammed with family valuables. Along the roadside trudged a multitude on foot, many pushing perambulators, pulling handcarts, carrying babies, or leading little troops of wondering children. There was no panic. The faces were serious, the voices low. In the crowd were many soldiers wearing the stripes of long service, and now leading their families away from a scene such as they had often witnessed across the sea.

But thousands remained in the North End, refusing to abandon their homes. These threw open windows and doors to save them from air blast and went outside, sitting on pavements, in back yards and gardens, to watch the terrific fireworks. From time to time a major explosion sent a huge yellow flame towards the zenith and all threw themselves flat, counting the seconds aloud and waiting for the blast. The worst came in quick succession about four o'clock in the morning of the nineteenth, rocking the buildings, shattering more panes, tumbling crockery and plaster; but none had the single force of the 1917 explosion and the houses stood, shaken but intact.

In fact the design of the magazine prevented the whole thing from going up at once; but there was a particular store of RDX which could level the whole North End, and naval headquarters continued to warn the remaining population of a terrific blast yet to come. Still the stoics remained. The telephone, broadcasting, and powerhouse staffs stayed at their posts. Household radios, turned on full, blared through the open windows a succession of bulletins and warnings mingled with strains of music. This was the strangest part of a weird night for the enduring North Enders crouched or lying on the ground, watching a monstrous *aurora borealis* in the midst of summer and between the thump and rush of explosions listening to everything from jazz to Mendelssohn.

The morning sunshine of the nineteenth killed the glare in the northern sky, but there remained a mass of brown smoke writhing and dancing with the upward gush of burning explosives, and the continuous rumble and jar of the bedrock on which Halifax is built. The night had been warm and was followed by another hot day—a fortunate thing for the women and children lying in gardens and parks or in the woods about Northwest Arm. The long hours passed. Towards evening the radio stations broadcast an official report that the worst of the danger was past and that the people could return to their homes.

Behind this curt announcement was an epic of heroism and endurance on the part of the men who for twenty-four hours had been struggling to get the magazine fires under control. Chiefly the credit was due to naval volunteers who under the direction of the magazine staff dragged fire-fighting apparatus to the very edge of the inferno and remained there, throwing themselves to earth for the greater explosions and working tenaciously at the blaze in the intervals, in a rain of stones, broken brick, unexploded shells, and whizzing fragments. As if their dangers were not enough, the parched woods all about the magazine on the Burnside slope caught fire and burned for two days.

When the fires and the last small explosions had ceased, picked squads of naval officers and men began to work in the magazine area, removing to safety a great number of live shells, depth charges and other explosive objects which had been flung in all directions by the blasts. The curious Haligonians, staring across Bedford Basin, could see part of the Burnside slope scorched and torn, and a few charred pilings where the jetty had been. But they saw as well how many of the grim brick buildings had been saved, and knew how much Halifax had been spared. The recent resentment against the Navy vanished in admiration of the men whose devoted efforts had saved the city. Indeed it may be said that the old affection for the Navy, tested by nearly two centuries of contact, good and bad, came back literally with a bang. If the magazine disaster did nothing else it blew away in a night and a day what might have been years of bitterness between Halifax and the service to which it is bound by destiny.

The casualties were miraculously small. Only one man was killed by the first explosion in the vicinity of the barge and jetty. By good chance it happened after six o'clock, when nearly all of the magazine staff had withdrawn for the evening meal. During the rest of that violent night the long training of the people of Halifax and Dartmouth for just such an event served them well. There were few civilian casualties and no lives lost. The city itself received a bad shaking. Merchants who had just replaced the plate glass broken in the May riots found their shop fronts gaping once more. But this time there was no looting, no disorder of any sort.

As always with large explosions, the vagaries of the air blast were strange. In the quarters of the magazine staff many panes were left intact—yet the heavy ironstone masonry of All Saints Cathedral in the city's south end, five miles away, was rocked and severely cracked, and a lighthouse keeper seventy miles away along the coast reported a strange low rush of air about four o'clock in the morning of the nineteenth, "as if a cat had brushed against my legs."

The Dominion authorities investigated the widespread damage in the city and paid for the cost of repair. And henceforth surplus ammunition was stored in a new magazine in the remote woods of New Brunswick. Halifax breathed again. It had had a narrow escape.

On August 14 Japan surrendered, and on that evening and the following day the city and the forces celebrated the close of the war. As a precaution the streets were patrolled by strong groups of service police in steel helmets and armed with "billies," this time with clear instructions to strike at the first sign of disorder. There was none. In fact there was a different spirit in evidence. The more restless naval personnel had been sobered after the events of May by the experience of July.

On October 1 the city and province welcomed home their senior regiment overseas, the West Nova Scotia Regiment, in whose ranks many Haligonians had fought in Sicily, Italy, and Holland. The wearers of the sunrise badge disembarked from the *Ile de France* and marched six abreast through the streets amid a wild ringing of church bells and a chorus of ship and factory whistles, halting finally on the Garrison Grounds, where a great crowd of people covered the Citadel slopes. Here in the blaze of searchlights Premier Angus Macdonald in stirring words congratulated the regiment on its fighting record and presented its commander, Major H. M. Eisenhauer, with a Nova Scotia ensign, the last of a succession of such flags flown by the "West Novas" throughout their campaigns. It was five years and nine months since the regiment had sailed from Halifax with the 1st Division.

There were many more to be welcomed, in the process of winding up the war. In the returning stream from Europe came three more Nova Scotia regiments, the North Nova Scotia Highlanders, the Cape Breton Highlanders, and the Haligonians' own Princess Louise Fusiliers, all of whom received a tumultuous reception in the snowy January of 1946. The last Nova Scotia regiment to come home, the Pictou Highlanders, arrived in the transport *Mataroa* in April from duty in the West Indies.

One by one the army, navy and air force hostels, the merchant seamen's clubs, and the rest homes closed. The last of them, the Salvation Army hostel, ceased its work on May 9, 1946. By summer the streets of the city were filled once more with young men and women in civilian clothes.

40.
1946–1949

Postwar problems. A master plan. The changing times.

WITH THE COMING OF PEACE THE DEMAND FOR A roof or a room became frantic. Civilians who had swarmed to Halifax for the jobs and fat wages of wartime stayed in the city, hoping that somehow the jobs and wages would go on. Discharged service personnel with families, returning to their homes in other parts of Canada, were more than offset by Halifax veterans with wives and children returning from abroad. Many of these had to take shelter in warworn and shabby Chebucto Camp, in similar army huts along the Citadel side of Sackville Street, in the somewhat better though barren wooden barracks built for women personnel of the services at Gorsebrook, Willow Park, and behind All Saints Cathedral, and in various other structures of the kind.

All this brought up an older problem. Since the original town was sketched on a London drafting board in 1748 there had been no planning at all. Halifax had simply "growed" like Topsy in the tale, spreading out along tracks made by soldiers, dairymen, and suburban estate owners in colonial days. As a result the city's business heart was now encrusted with slums; industrial concerns had made a deep intrusion into what should have been a purely residential area about Willow Park; a beautiful residential site facing Bedford Basin was marred by the grim City Prison and the squalid shacks of Africville; and the pleasant slope to Northwest Arm was gashed by an ugly railway cutting along its whole length. All this in a city favored by nature with one of the finest situations in the world.

The blue fiords that make a magnificent haven for ships—the harbor proper, Bedford Basin, and Northwest Arm—almost enclose the city. In the midst of this vast anchorage the peninsula lies like a hobnailed boot, about five miles long and two miles wide. The isthmus forms the ankle. The boot is laced by the railway to South Terminal and the streets that cross it and run down to the Arm. Point Pleasant forms the toe, stepping towards the harbor entrance. The hobnails are the wharves of the main city waterfront, the naval dockyard lies at the instep, and the heel is shaped by the Narrows and the southerly curve of Bedford Basin. The ball of the living foot in this boot is the city's business and administrative district, standing on the original site laid off by Cornwallis' surveyors in 1749.

In 1763 for community cattle grazing the Crown authorities set off about 235 acres behind Citadel Hill, a strip running roughly from the present Cunard Street to South Street. It was then a long intervale of swamp and wild meadow, drained by a stream called Freshwater River, with a low wooded ridge on the west that ended in a knoll called Camp Hill. This rough pasture land was called the Commons and divided into two parts, north and south.

Part of the North Common remains intact, chiefly because imperial garrisons used it for field maneuvers for nearly one hundred and fifty years. Today it is the city's biggest and best playground. (The so-called "South Common" of modern times, a small triangle enclosed by Bell Road, Trollope Street, and Ahern Avenue, is a piece of the old North Common.)

The real South Common was cut in twain by Spring Garden Road in the early part of the nineteenth century, and most of it fell into private hands, to be covered with private roofs. Nevertheless patches of it remain green in an oddly assorted fashion in the Wanderers' Grounds, Camp Hill Cemetery, the Public Gardens, Victoria Park, and the grassy spaces in the hospital zone.

Not far from the southern fringe of this zone lay for many years the rolling lawns and park of Gorsebrook, a large and lovely estate owned by absentee heirs and descendants of Enos Collins. Although these heirs leased the old house and park to various tenants, and much of the open ground to the Gorsebrook Golf Club, they kept their possession intact for generations. Finally this ancient holding came on the market with the death of Carteret Fitzgerald Collins, at his home in Tunbridge Wells, England, in 1941. The Roman Catholic Archdiocese of Halifax bought a major part to form a new campus for St. Mary's University. (St. Mary's began as a downtown school for Roman Catholic boys in 1802, and was chartered as a degree-granting college in the west end of Halifax in 1841. It was confined to a small brick building on Windsor Street until 1951, when a new main structure of stone was built on the Gorsebrook campus. St. Mary's is the oldest English-speaking Roman Catholic university in Canada.)

In developing St. Mary's, the picturesque but rickety old Gorsebrook mansion was demolished in 1959. Additions to the university are in progress, but the playing fields and other parts of the campus will keep green much of the old estate. A short walk away lie the woods of Point Pleasant.

So, from the needs of colonial cowherds and of soldiers wanting ground for mimic war, of a graveyard, a football club, a horticultural society, a wealthy colonial estate owner with tenacious heirs, and garrison engineers who kept a forest to hide their forts, Halifax today has an irregular chain of breathing spaces running through its central and southern parts, plain from the air as a mottled green stripe between the old town and the new.

In contrast the North End, the home of many middle class and most laboring class Haligonians, has nothing of the sort. An unhappy compost of houses, small shops and factories, leaves nothing green to the sky except the grassy tip of old Fort Needham and a patch of the former Exhibition Grounds.

In the west end, soon after the Second World War, housebuilders covered the last open spaces on the slope leading down to Armdale. The temporary wooden barracks of Camp Chebucto, built over the city's old airport during the late war, were torn down in 1948 for the Westmount housing development. Across Chebucto Road the fields and market gardens of the Industrial School for Boys, established early in the century, were sold for the Armcrest housing development, and the school was spirited away to a new site far down the coast at Shelburne.

The Dutch Village Road, before the war a quiet semiwooded drive winding across the isthmus, had changed by 1949 to a bustling thoroughfare, with houses and industrial buildings along its sides and sprouting on adjoining lanes. The rock and scrub woods of the ridge beyond (known to colonial German settlers as the Westenwald and to their descendants as Geizer's Mountain) made building in that direction expensive.

The easier trend was around the tip of Northwest Arm towards St. Margaret's Bay or to the rustic villages of Spryfleld and Jollimore. By 1960 Spryfield had swollen to the size of a town, linked with Halifax at Armdale, and spreading over the rocky barrens to Jollimore and towards the harbor mouth. In the same way a scatter of small hamlets grew and merged their haphazard wooden architecture along the St. Margaret's Bay highway.

The main road exit from Halifax, enlarged and paved with concrete as far as Bedford during the late war, fostered a built-up area reaching around the Basin to Waverley, and the once virgin tree-shaded drive by the Waverley Lakes became pocked with houses and cottages all the way to northward-marching Dartmouth. Thus, although Halifax was confined by definition to the peninsula, soon after the war it had a metropolitan growth sprawling far into the hinterland.

In Halifax itself, mindful of the happy-go-lucky past, anxious for an orderly future, a Civic Planning Commission went to work under chairman Ira McNab in 1943, while the war was in full sound and fury. They made their report soon after the war's close. It was not only a guide to postwar development but a long term plan for remodeling the older parts of the city, to some people a futile and fantastic dream.

One step towards fulfillment of the dream came quickly. The Canadian Army, taking a clear view of their dwindling role at Halifax, handed over to the city many odds and ends of military property that had cluttered the central area ever since the eighteenth century. These pieces of land, a few yards here, several acres there, enabled the city to widen parts of Lower Water, Sackville, Queen, and Windsor streets. More important, the city now owned the sites of Cogswell Street Military Hospital, Glacis Barracks, Pavilion Barracks, the old garrison headquarters ("Bellevue") on Spring Garden Road, part of South Barracks and Royal Artillery Park, and the whole north shoulder of Citadel Hill. Duke Street could be extended over the hill to the Common, Gottingen Street could be joined to this extension, and Brunswick Street could be pushed through to Spring Garden Road. All this was done without delay; and the old brick hospital, the dingy red barracks, the shabby travesty of "Bellevue," were swept away in favor of commercial buildings, a useful addition to the tax roll.

A vital part of the new plan was a highway bridge across the harbor, the dream of generations. All former notions placed it at the Narrows, where the bygone railway bridges had collapsed one after the other. The McNab Report suggested a high-level bridge from the vicinity of the dockyard to north Dartmouth. Further, it sketched a bridge across Northwest Arm, wide improvement in the traffic bottlenecks at the isthmus, demolition of slums in the old part of the city (to be replaced by subsidized apartment blocks for people of low income), and broad thoroughfares to link the harborside with the western suburbs.

Citizens regarded these plans with mingled hope and doubt. Doubt came from the past, old memories of wartime booms and long depressions afterward. Even the optimists did not realize how utterly that ancient pattern had vanished. Like jinn out of the *Arabian Nights* two new and tremendous factors had emerged from the smoke of the late war.

One was a peaceful phenomenon, the people of nations all over the world flocking to their towns and cities. Whole populations were eager for the bustle and glitter and easy amenities of urban life. So the cities were bulging and bursting like volcanoes, pouring their contents over the countryside in a swiftly hardening pumice of houses, apartments, and (in North America) motor shopping centers. The cities pushed up towards the sky, too, with angular honeycombs of metal and glass in the architectural motif of mid-twentieth century—and the great paradox of the Atomic Age, in which these tall brittle structures were potential deathtraps of the most frightful kind.

The other postwar factor was the rise of Russia as a mighty industrial and military power, dwarfing every other in the world but that of the United States, and making no secret of its aim to subvert and destroy the "capitalist" societies of Europe and America. In 1949 the most important of these societies drew together in the North Atlantic Treaty Organization (NATO) for mutual support and defense. Canada was one, and the strategic position of Halifax made it vital to the whole alliance. Ships, squadrons, sometimes whole fleets of NATO warships, with accompanying aircraft and submarines, began to pass in and out of the port for joint practice of sea warfare.

Now, too, the Canadian Navy began to modernize and enlarge its fleet and its shore establishments, especially those at Halifax. (As one potent example, the Bedford magazine spread to several times its former size, with miles of asphalt roads linking the grim storehouses with each other and with the waterside.)

In truth, the Warden of the North had much more to guard now than the North Atlantic. In 1948 a Canadian naval force, including an aircraft carrier, sailed from Halifax to cruise in Hudson Strait and Hudson Bay. It was the beginning of a new and urgent interest in Canada's third ocean, and from this time Canadian and United States defense forces pushed ever farther northward among the Arctic islands. Within ten years the American submarine *Skate* was able to cruise beneath the ice, and surfaced at the Pole itself.

The new interest in far northern waters came to special notice in Canada in the late summer of 1954, when HMCS *Labrador*, a fleet icebreaker designed for Arctic service, sailed from Halifax to Vancouver through the almost legendary Northwest Passage. She was the biggest (and the first naval) ship ever to make the famous passage, and she did it in weeks where bygone explorers had taken years. (Returning to Halifax by way of the Panama Canal, she was also the first ship to circumnavigate the continent within a single season.) *Labrador* sat as deep in the water as the largest ocean liners. It was surprising to realize that, led by suitable icebreakers, ships like the great *Queen Mary* could make the Northwest Passage any summer.

41.
1949–1964

After the centuries. The newspapers. Naval changes. The old forts.

ON JUNE 21, 1949, HALIFAX CELEBRATED ITS TWO hundredth birthday. It was a cool day with gray skies after rain, but thousands stood in the streets to watch a parade of decorated floats and tableaux, soldiers, sailors, airmen, school cadet corps, clubs, societies—a procession more than three miles long, moving to the music of eighteen bands.

There were items here and there to remind John Halifax of his origin. One column of soldiers marched with the uniforms and muskets of British grenadiers, Mark 1749. A navy float showed a section of gun deck in a frigate of the olden time, with seamen trundling cannon in and out of the ports, and firing them with convincing bangs and smoke. A huge float from the Halifax Shipyards carried HMS *Sphinx*, with Governor Cornwallis in solemn chat with painted Indians on the deck.

The evening entertainment was a spectacular sham battle on the Citadel slope facing the Common, where a huge crowd gathered. Army engineers had built on the slope a mock-up "defended village," which was "bombed" by aircraft, "shelled" by artillery, and finally "stormed" by tanks and infantry, all using a great amount of fireworks and blank ammunition. It was all in the manner of the late war, in which many of the spectators themselves had fought so recently. But in the baleful light of the Atomic Age, with rocket missiles soon to reach any part of the earth (not to mention the moon and stars) it was quite another story. This little show in the twilight of a Halifax summer evening was as antique as the march of the red-coated grenadiers.

On New Year's Day, 1949, Halifax had a local shock to open its bicentennial year, as stunning in its way as anything produced by nuclear fission. For years the city and province had enjoyed two Halifax morning papers, the *Chronicle* and *Herald*, and the corresponding afternoon *Daily Star* and *Evening Mail*. They were sharp rivals in politics as well as trade, for the *Herald* and *Mail* trumpeted Tory opinions while the *Chronicle* and *Star* gave the clear Grit view. The lively competition of these papers made sure that no matter of public interest escaped the public eye, with sharp news reporting, pungent editorials, and frequently hilarious cartoons.

This feature of Halifax life, familiar as the bang of the noon gun on Citadel Hill, came to a sad end with the year 1948, for in its last days wealthy owner F. B. McCurdy sold the *Chronicle* and *Star* "up the hill" to the *Herald* and *Mail*. It was then discovered that the *Herald* and *Mail* themselves had lately passed into new ownership which had various financial and political interests in other parts of eastern Canada.

On New Year's morning, 1949, a hybrid appeared, the *Chronicle-Herald*, followed in the afternoon by another, the *Mail-Star*, both printed in the former *Herald* and *Mail* plant on Sackville Street. Except for the slight change of name they were to all appearance the old *Herald* and *Mail*, but with a new and tame neutrality in politics and other matters. The *Chronicle* and *Star* had been sunk without trace. Their old home across the street from Province House, where a long succession of editors and writers had looked forth for inspiration to the ripsnorting bronze figure of Joe Howe, became eventually part of the offices of a neighboring trust company.

Another change in city life, this with no regrets, was the end of the old yellow electric trams clattering along the streets on iron rails and (reputedly square) wheels. In March '49 they were replaced by trolley coaches swishing along on rubber tires.

And now in their bicentennial year the townsmen beheld something of much wider importance, the beginning of the end of Canada's seagoing merchant fleet. Since the late war, in which the Canadian merchant marine had grown to a great size, most of the crews had fallen into the grip of the Communist-tainted Canadian Seamen's Union, whose officials seemed to come chiefly from the United States. In the spring of 1949 these officials called one of their frequent strikes, tying up ships at home and in ports about the globe, and cabling dockers' unions abroad that Canadian ships were "hot" and must not be touched.

By that time, and by these methods, the Canadian merchant marine had become a dreary joke to shippers about the world. In the sharp competition of ocean trade it was doomed. As a last desperate measure the Canadian shipowners called in the rival Seamen's International Union, a branch of the American Federation of Labor. The SIU had the surface virtue of being violently opposed to communism in all its forms, including the CSU; but its leaders proved just as greedy and ruthless as those of the CSU, and with as little care for Canadian trade or for Canada itself.

On April 8, 1949, a special train drew alongside a Halifax dock where three of the (government-owned) Canadian National Steamships lay strikebound. On the train were 150 imported strikebreakers of the SIU, accompanied by about 100 railway police. Awaiting them at the dock were 250 members and bullyboy sympathizers rounded up by the CSU. Apart from the police, both sides were armed with baseball bats, brass knuckles, bottles, stones, and at least one sawed-off shotgun, all of which were used in the battle royal that followed. The SIU men won their way aboard the ships and eventually took them to sea. The reign of the CSU was broken, on salt water at least.

This bloody clash of five hundred men on the Halifax waterfront startled the city and indeed the whole country. Few Canadians had realized the plight of their once proud merchant fleet. Fewer saw now that the owners had "swapped a devil for a witch." In ten more years the Canadian merchant flag would all but vanish from the sea, while Halifax and other Canadian harbors bustled with foreign shipping.

At the same time as the heyday of the CSU, the Royal Canadian Navy was having labor trouble of its own, a series of incidents among ratings ashore and afloat, ranging from petty indiscipline to virtual mutiny. A committee of officers under Rear Admiral Mainguy was appointed to study the trouble and make suggestions for the cure. Beneath many things on the surface they noticed a strong dissatisfaction in the men because their Navy had little or nothing distinctively Canadian. In modeling itself upon the Royal Navy the tendency had been to shape an imitation that borrowed many sound qualities but also aped some less endearing habits, including in many cases a supercilious attitude of officers towards their men.

Canadians had a natural share in the proud history of the Royal Navy, for during the past two centuries many of them had served in it. One of Nelson's favorite captains, Benjamin Hallowell, was a Nova Scotian. When Nelson died in the cockpit of the *Victory*, a Nova Scotian middy, George Westphal, lay wounded at his side, with Nelson's coat tucked beneath his head. No less than seven lads from Nova Scotia, including young Westphal, became admirals in the Royal Navy.

So it was right and good to remember the great days of Britannia and to keep in touch with the modern British Navy. The huge and well-equipped navy of the United States rated even closer study and touch, for it was now the most powerful in the world. But study and emulation of what was good in other navies did not mean casting off a Canadian personality and outlook.

Canada had good sea traditions of her own in war and peace, not least the great days of the square-riggers, when her "wooden ships and iron men" were famous in every part of the globe. It was time for Canadian officers and men to think of such things and take pride in them. In 1948 a group of naval officers at Halifax, seeing the need, made a start with a Canadian sea museum, gathering a collection in a small building at the Dockyard. In 1952 it was moved to quarters in the Citadel, where it could be seen by the public as well. By 1962 more than two hundred thousand people were coming to see the Canadian Maritime Museum at Halifax every year. The Citadel quarters were then too cramped for what had become a magnificent collection, marking the story of transport (and warfare) on Canada's rivers and lakes, as well as her three seas. In the following year the city arranged to provide large and more suitable quarters at the harborside.

Meanwhile the "Canadianization" of the RCN was a quiet but steady process, working in various ways. Oddly enough, one was musical. Indeed the whole process began on a small but significant musical note at the Halifax dockyard in 1950. At that time the cornerstone of a large modern barrack block for naval ratings was laid with the full ritual of Ceremonial Divisions. Formerly at such ceremonies the Canadian naval bands had followed the practice of the Royal Navy, which was to play selections from *Iolanthe*, "Rule Britannia," and "In the Garb of Old Gaul."

On May 12, 1950, in the presence of the Lieutenant Governor of Nova Scotia, the General Officer of the Canadian Army Eastern Command, the Mayor of Halifax, and other guests, the naval ritual was carried out to the tunes of "O Canada," "The Maple Leaf For Ever," and a lively song of the French-Canadian voyageurs, "C'est l'aviron que nous mène en haut" (It's the oar that shoves us along).

These fresh musical notes carried far and created much fuss. In a public speech in England an aging Winston Churchill told his audience "with a bitter pang" that the Canadian Navy had abolished "Rule Britannia." Quizzed about it in the House at Ottawa, the Minister of Defense (Mr. Claxton) defended the substitution of "O Canada" as a change desirable to all Canadians. What nobody cared to say, out of respect for the gallant old gentleman in England, was that Britannia had not ruled the waves for quite some time, that if anyone ruled them now it seemed to be Columbia, and that in any case Canadians liked to call their own tune.

In August 1954, at a spot near Cornwall, Ontario, the builders of the long-argued St. Lawrence Seaway began to dig their great ditch, and in Halifax and St. John there was an almost audible scratching of chins. Obviously a waterway deep enough to pass ocean ships to the rich heart of the continent threatened to suck away a good deal of their sea traffic. The great question was, "Can this Seaway ever operate in winter?" At first the answer, in and outside the House at Ottawa, was, "No." Yet there was bound to be a powerful interest, especially at Montreal, in keeping the Seaway open through the year. In February 1959 a Danish steamer, helped by Canadian Government icebreakers, carried a cargo from Europe to Quebec, the first ocean ship ever to make the passage there in midwinter. This was a portent; but for the present the question had no answer. It was one thing to reach Quebec through the ice floes of the Gulf of St. Lawrence, quite another to melt or break the hard clutch of frost on canals and locks inland.

In April 1955 the new Angus L. Macdonald bridge, named in honor of Nova Scotia's beloved premier, opened its tollgates to an eager rush of motor traffic between Halifax and Dartmouth. The great steel suspension bridge, so high that the tallest ships and masts could pass underneath, added a new and imposing feature to the harbor scene.

That summer the city's first television station CBHT, operated by the Canadian Broadcasting Corporation, began to use a five-hundred-foot transmission tower on the old Westenwald beyond Dutch Village. Hitherto it had only a makeshift fifty-foot mast at its new building on Bell Road. Programs originating in Toronto, the heart of the Canadian television industry, came "canned" and were shown as much as a week later than in Ontario. This lag continued until a chain of tall microwave relay towers, linking the Maritime Provinces with Ontario and the West, was completed in February 1958.

In November 1955 contractors began work on a huge new Halifax airport in the forest at Kelly Lake, twenty miles from the downtown hotels. The city's first port for wheeled aircraft (Chebucto Field) had been too small, even for light planes, and after 1940 Air Canada and other passenger lines were permitted to use the runways built by the RCAF at Eastern Passage. After the Second World War the field at Eastern Passage became HMCS Shearwater, operated by the air arm of Canada's navy. All civilian use of it ceased on July 31, 1960, when the new international airport was opened at Kelly Lake.

The times were changing fast, and change had many faces. In 1956 the Canadian Army dismantled York Redoubt, the last fort guarding the entrance to Halifax harbor. Soon afterwards its garrison, the 49th Coast Artillery Battery, vanished not only from the redoubt but from the Army List.

The other outlying forts had been abandoned or left to the care of a lone watchman soon after 1945—Connaught Battery and Sandwich Battery on the west side of the harbor entrance; Fort McNab, Fort Hugonin, and Ives Point Battery on McNab's Island; and Hartland Point Battery (built 1942) at the mouth of Eastern Passage.

The inner (and much older) forts had crumbled into semiruin long ago—Point Pleasant Battery, Fort Cambridge, Fort Ogilvie, and Prince of Wales Tower, all in Point Pleasant Park, and Fort Charlotte on George's Island in the harbor.

The long reach of rocket missiles in the Atomic Age made all such defenses worthless. Halifax remained headquarters for the Army's Eastern Command, but nowadays the Command kept its strongest forces in the heart of New Brunswick at newly built Camp Gagetown, well removed not only from Halifax but from the whole vulnerable Nova Scotia peninsula. The regular soldiery at Halifax shrank to a khaki thread of engineer, signal, ordnance, and clerical personnel. The Halifax militia kept up routine practice with the weapons of ordinary warfare, but now their chief concern was the dire business of Civil Defense, the rescue and evacuation of survivors of the city population in case of a nuclear fission explosion.

With the closing of York Redoubt, the active defense of Halifax was left to the Navy and Air Force. It marked the end of an epoch long to be remembered in the story of Canada; for it was from their first rude forts on the shore of "Chebucto" that the British began the long march which carried them first to Louisburg and Quebec, and finally to the shore of the Pacific.

Lest any other nation dream of such a course, imperial soldiers and engineers had labored at Halifax for generations, siting batteries in the outlying wilderness, delving in the rock beneath for magazines and shelters, and from time to time replacing what was obsolete with the latest works and weapons. The isolation and secrecy of these defenses had been kept with care. No easy roads were allowed to approach them. The only ready access was by water, and then aboard one of the garrison's own harbor craft. As late as 1964 few Haligonians had ever set foot on George's Island, or inside York Redoubt or Fort McNab.

Wise heads in Halifax and Ottawa recognized the historic value in these old defenses and decided to repair and preserve them as public monuments. Working through the Parks Branch of the Department of Northern Affairs, the federal government began with the Citadel, a careful labor, going on for years. Even the ancient wooden clock tower, rotten to the foundation, was taken down piece by piece in 1960, and replaced two years later with an exact replica. As work advanced on the Citadel, historical museums of the Army, Navy, Air Force, and Merchant Marine were opened to the public in its barracks and casemates.

The general plan was to have the Citadel and the outlying forts and batteries ready for public inspection by 1967, Canada's centennial year. Most of the outer forts are framed by wild woods and crags, all have magnificent views of the harbor and the sea approaches, and together they provide Halifax with a new fringe of small parks and picnic grounds. Quite apart from the scene is the historic interest of works and weapons ranging in time from the young days of Napoleon to the last days of Adolf Hitler. In time to come they will draw visitors from many parts of the world, for these old Halifax defenses are a unique relic of the British Empire during its rise, through its greatest days, and its voluntary winding-up.

42.
A New Face For An Old

In the middle of the twentieth century Halifax found itself flourishing in its outskirts and decaying at the heart, like many other cities in the western world. The cause was, of course, the motor car. An expensive fad before 1914, a spreading luxury in the period between the wars, the motor car had become almost a substitute for human legs after 1945. In the cities, even in country towns, few people would walk the length of two blocks if they could ride. The poorest of the poor could buy for a few dollars a "jalopy" which, with a little tinkering, would carry them about the town and countryside, or for that matter across the continent.

The narrow and irregular streets of downtown Halifax, never meant for anything much larger or faster than a sedan chair at a jog trot, proved hopelessly inadequate for the motor age. The most ingenious rules and automatic signals could not cope with the traffic, except to keep it moving. Parking spaces were few, and rarely near the main shops. The inevitable result, common throughout North America, was the appearance of new and elaborate "shopping centers" in the suburbs, easy of access and with ample parking room. With so much of the populace on wheels these enterprises prospered and multiplied, while the old shopping districts in the heart of the cities withered like gourds on a choked vine.

At Halifax the future trend had been demonstrated in the early 1920s when a Canadian mail-order firm placed a branch plant and added a large department store in what was then the semirural village of Armdale. The department store seemed a wild venture, but a host of Halifax housewives quickly discovered that it was easy to reach by motor or tram. The store drew a swarm of shoppers that increased year by year. Yet such was the force of Halifax business habit, and of old property values on Barrington, Granville, and Hollis streets, that none of the downtown merchants considered this obvious omen. During a whole generation the single firm at Armdale enjoyed and profited from the growth of the motor age.

Not until that age came to its climax after the Second World War was anything further done, and then the new investments came, as before, from firms in central Canada. By 1954 various national chain grocery stores and other shops catering to the motor trade were spreading rapidly in the Armdale–Dutch Village area, drawing customers from the city itself, from the new metropolitan area outside the peninsula, and indeed from the whole provincial countryside. This shift of business reached a new mark in 1962, when another national enterprise opened a huge complex of shops, all under one roof, on Mumford Road, with nearby parking space for twenty-eight hundred cars.

As its customers drifted away, the old downtown shopping district changed from a stodgy gentility to a condition more and more like the nearby slums. The buildings were old and inconvenient. Except for government offices and a few banks and trust companies, nothing new had appeared between the Citadel and the harborside for at least thirty years, and most of the buildings dated back to the age of Victoria. Barrington, so long the main shopping street, had become notoriously down-at-heel for most of its length. City Hall was typical. In 1952 the police had moved from its dismal basement to new quarters in the former Market Building up the hill, otherwise nothing was changed. Built to serve a population of thirty thousand, City Hall was now dingy and cramped and obsolete.

What had become of the McNab Report of 1945? Some of its points had been made, notably the harbor bridge, but nothing had been done to abolish the slums on the harbor slope or to revive the drooping business district there. Since 1945 the problem of redevelopment had much wider aspects, so that new plans were necessary, and a new study had to be made. The basis was laid by Professor Gordon Stephenson of Dalhousie University in 1957, when his careful and frank report became the Bible of city committees devoted to future planning and redevelopment.

A firm of engineering consultants in 1960 estimated the population of the Halifax metropolitan area, including Dartmouth, at nearly two hundred thousand, and predicted from the present rate of growth that it would reach three hundred thousand by 1980. (Dartmouth took into incorporation several of its rapidly growing suburbs in 1962, with a total population of about fifty thousand.)

This raised a natural question. What were all these people living on? A study by Alasdair Sinclair of Dalhousie (*The Economic Base of the Halifax Metropolitan Area*, published 1961) showed that the city's income from manufacturing was relatively small. In fact the number of people so employed was only a fraction larger than that of 1921. The wholesale and retail trades, transportation, health services, shipbuilding and ship repair formed about 36 per cent of the economic base in 1951, and the national defense services accounted for 41 per cent. Since then the defense services had increased their proportion. For the years from 1956 to 1959, the average annual expenditures by the Department of National Defense in the Halifax area were about $95,000,000.

So the existence and growth of the Warden of the North had not changed their basis since 1749. The household eggs were still in one basket—the war basket. But now there was an important difference. All the past wars had been hot ones, each with a definite end. The new kind of war, the cold one, was a continual stalemate in which no nation dared to lay aside its weapons for a moment. In this condition Halifax was assured of a large and steady income which had no relation to the cycles of prosperity and depression in the manufacturing and trading world.

In 1960 the city authorities began to demolish the slums about Jacob and Buckingham streets, and within two years made almost a clean swath of the portion shown in the new plans as the "Central Redevelopment Area." Money for this came 75 per cent from the federal treasury, 12 1/2 per cent from the provincial treasury, and 12 1/2 per cent from the city itself.

Further plans for redevelopment include what is called "The Old North Suburb," running from the Citadel to North Street and down to the harborside along most of its length. In this area much is worth preservation, especially along Brunswick Street which (as the Stephenson Report observes) is, in an architectural sense, the most interesting in Halifax.

Among all the areas marked for redevelopment the most remarkable is Africville, whose 370 inhabitants are mostly of Negro blood. They occupy a squalid shack town without piped water or sewer facilities on the shore of Bedford Basin, where their predecessors "squatted" more than a century ago. It is, and has always been, a shifting population, and few of the present inhabitants have legal ownership of the land on which they live, which belongs mostly to the city and the Canadian National Railways. Here is a sad problem. The people of Africville want to stay where they are, and as a Negro community. They are indignant at any notion of removing them to new (subsidized) housing where they would mingle with whites of their own economic class. (Most of the other Negroes in Halifax have lived in integration with poor whites for generations, chiefly in the Old North Suburb.) The Stephenson Report says firmly: "Despite the wishes of many of the residents, it would seem desirable on social grounds to offer alternative housing in other locations within the city. The city is a comprehensive urban community, and it is not right that any segment of the community should continue to exist in isolation."

Another eyesore lies right in the center of things, the waterfront about the footing of Buckingham, Duke, and George streets, the city's oldest approach from the viewpoint of sailor and passenger. From early times, when this section was known simply as the Beach, it had been a hodgepodge of wooden wharves, warehouses, marine shops, brothels, and drinking dens. In more recent times the last two had given place to small offices and stores in the shipping trade, most of them using the same old buildings, largely of wood but sometimes of stone. By 1963 nearly all were shabby and decrepit.

Here the city plans to demolish a good deal and to create a new and trim appearance from the water as well as the land. The plan includes a "Civic Plaza" drawn about the old approach to the Dartmouth ferry. Here eventually will stand a new City Hall and a large and handsome building for the Law Courts.

Time and change have left little more than a memory of the Halifax which celebrated its first century in 1849. A tramp steamer anchors now where Cornwallis held his first council in the "Beaufort." The statue of a Boer War soldier stands where Cornwallis built his first small residency, a bare musket shot from the waterside. Suburban bungalows jostle each other where D'Anville's men perished of typhus by the Basin shore, where Prince Edward and his Julie played their game of hearts, where Father Bailly recited the Mass in secret to the faithful. A lighthouse flashes and a foghorn groans at Mauger's Beach, where naval mutineers and deserters once dangled from the gibbets. A hotel occupies the walls (of stone from conquered Louisburg) where Bulkeley played chess, dabbled with sketching and painting, entertained Wolfe and Cobbett, and outraged the naval officers. A dull concrete sidewalk runs where military beaux and town belles paraded the Mall on sunny afternoons. Students hurry about a campus where Judge Croke composed his naughty rhymes. Yachtsmen talk of tacks and sheets—and elegant cabin cruisers—on Melville Island where French and American prisoners once carved ship models from their own beef bones. Members of the legislature browse in the library where old Richard Uniacke tried his own son for manslaughter. Smart new Canadian warships and their NATO visitors moor at the dockyard which once knew only Britain's famous old wooden walls. Citizens bathe and splash in the Northwest Arm at Horseshoe Island, where long ago the Indians and their white friends held the feast of St. Aspinquid. Jesuit teachers walk with their pupils on the grounds where Enos Collins paced among the trees, scheming his way to the richest fortune in all of Canada in his time. A bijou repertory theatre, opened in 1963 (Neptune Theatre), stages live plays old and new where vaudeville and raucous girl-and-jingle shows played their last at the old Garrick.

Still, some things remain. Province House, whose walls once rang with Joe Howe's eloquence. Government House, where Johnnie Wentworth and his lady held their pompous little court. St. Paul's, where (as well as English) Indians and Hessian soldiers heard sermons in their own tongues. Admiralty House, where the incomparable Cochrane, captor of "El Gamo" and "Esmeralda" in the wars, inventor and stock exchange speculator in time of peace, once entertained six hundred guests. The Martello tower at Point Pleasant, where Howe fought his pistol duel with Haliburton one morning when the dew was on the grass. The old town cemetery where the pioneers were laid; the graveyard of old Fort Massey where generations of imperial soldiers buried their dead; of the old Dockyard Hospital where some of "Shannon's" men still sleep; of Fairview and Mount Olivet where the dead of the *Titanic* found rest in earth at last.

The Grand Parade, once a frame for scarlet-coated regiments, is now a place of rumination for old men on benches about the Cenotaph. The clock tower on the Citadel slope ticks off the hours as a reminder of the punctilious Duke of Kent. Above the little Dutch Church the steeple cock still turns to every breath from heaven. And the green cone of Citadel Hill stands over all like a volcano, extinct now but still the finest watch-post of the old fortress, a witness to the changing story and the unchanged duty of the Warden of the North.

New Chapters by Stephen Kimber

43.
1964–1977

Harbour Drive. Waterfront development. Scotia Square. The View from the hill. "Encounter on the Urban Environment." Africville. The Black United Front. The 4th Estate. *Annexation and regionalization. University expansion. Cultural renaissance.*

BY THE EARLY 1970S, HALIFAX WAS AT A CROSSROADS. Several of them, in fact. The central issue was the future of the city's historic downtown. On one side were the real estate developers, impatient to transform their consultants' visions of futuristic, fantastic expressways and heaven-headed high-rises into concrete urban renewal reality. On the other side was a ragtag collection of citizen activists and history buffs, equally adamant that the city's admittedly crumbling waterfront heritage buildings and priceless harbour views must not pay the price for progress.

The preservationists were led by Lou Collins, an affable, bearded, middle-aged schoolteacher, scout leader, and amateur historian. In 1964, while researching a book on downtown buildings, he discovered that the proposed Harbour Drive Expressway, which was to run through the downtown core, would wipe out a collection of dilapidated but historic waterfront buildings. Though his initial attempts to save these buildings were rebuffed, Collins persevered, eventually cajoling city council into appointing a landmarks commission, whose purpose was to preserve and protect the city's heritage, and which he chaired.

By 1970, the preservationists had been so successful in changing public opinion that the city had not only scrapped the Harbour Drive project—bequeathing just a strangely orphaned massive concrete from-nowhere-to-nowhere downtown interchange to posterity—but it had also issued a continent-wide call for proposals to bring a collection of seven abandoned waterfront warehouses back to commercial life.

The result was Historic Properties, a delightful harbourside complex that reinvented those dowdy warehouses as trendy boutiques, pubs, restaurants, and offices. Enos Collins's old stone warehouse, for example, once packed to the rafters with privateering loot, was reborn as—what else?— Privateers' Warehouse, a popular restaurant and pub.

The success of that restoration, in turn, spawned the establishment of the Waterfront Development Corporation (WDC), a Crown corporation whose mandate was to manage—in an accessible, tourist-friendly way—fifty-three acres of prime waterfront real estate on both sides of the harbour. The WDC became responsible for developing a walkable water's edge boardwalk that would eventually stretch from the Historic Properties to Pier 21, the old immigration shed and former prime entry point for generations of new Canadians, which itself would later become a museum.

The working waterfront, meanwhile, nudged southward to the edge of Point Pleasant Park with the opening of the Halifax International Container Terminal in 1970. "This historic event," noted the *Canadian Geographical Journal* in 1973, "must have brought back memories...of the days when fifty-odd percent of British North American shipping was Nova Scotia-owned." The article went on to boast, "Now Halifax is again to the fore with the largest container operation in Canada and the third or fourth in North America."

Although the new terminal's ability to accommodate the world's largest ships and Halifax's location at the edge of the Great Circle shipping route to Europe did make the port more attractive to international shippers, Halifax was already facing increasing competition from other, more aggressive, North American ports like New York, Montreal, and Quebec City, which had all entered into the container business before it.

In its article on the new terminal, the *Canadian Geographical Journal* noted hopefully, "virtually every registered stevedore in the Port of Halifax is reported to have had some work at the container terminal," but that good news couldn't mask the larger disappointment of the terminal's lackluster usage rate. "As of the winter of 1973, the container terminal is being used consistently and substantially," it said, "but well below planned capacity."

While those various changes made the downtown waterfront more publicly accessible, they did little to protect the iconic view of that same harbour from Citadel Hill. New and ever-taller office buildings had begun to pop up throughout the downtown like weeds: In 1965, Royal Bank announced plans for a thirteen-storey bank tower at the corner of George and Hollis Streets; the next year, Bank of Montreal one-upped its rival with a proposal to erect a seventeen-storey edifice on Hollis Street directly behind the Royal Bank building, thus enabling it to place its corporate sign strategically above that of Royal Bank for the enlightenment of anyone looking down from Citadel Hill.

Not everyone was amused with these developments. "The Citadel is Halifax," declared Brenda Large, one of the editors of *The 4th Estate*, a feisty new twice-monthly (later weekly) newspaper that served as an antidote to the establishment dailies, both of which were owned by the Dennis family and known simply as the "Dennis papers." "To hundreds of thousands of Canadians," Large continued, "[the Citadel] represents the spirit of the city. Strict views bylaws can be enacted which will still leave room for some high-rise buildings in the downtown. But high-rise buildings should never be allowed to overcome the dominance of the Citadel."

The debate over whether buildings should be allowed to overshadow the Citadel heated up in the late sixties after Halifax Developments Limited, a new corporate entity composed of some of the province's most successful business families—including the Sobeys, MacKeens, Jodreys, Connors, and Olands—broke ground on Scotia Square, a massive $29.5 million complex on the seventeen-acre site of a demolished slum neighbourhood on the northerwestern edge of downtown. The project, which boasted a shopping centre, two office towers, three apartment buildings, and a hotel, symbolized, for some, the new face of Halifax. *Maclean's* magazine raved about the project, gushing, "It generates an excitement about tomorrow that Canada east of Quebec hasn't felt since the death of sail a century ago."

But by the summer of 1969, with the first sixteen-storey office tower—complete with "computer-programmed elevators"—and high-rise apartment complex thrusting upward and blocking out part of the view of the harbour from Citadel Hill, some Haligonians began to have second thoughts.

The battle for Citadel Hill came to a head in late 1971, when another local developer, Ralph Medjuck, asked for permission to top his low-rise Citadel Inn motel on Brunswick Street with an eleven-storey addition.

City staff argued against the proposal, claiming, among other negatives, that it would interfere with the view north from Citadel Hill toward the Macdonald bridge.

The final decision about whether to allow the expansion landed in the lap of a freshly elected and already deeply divided city council, among whom was Robert Stapells, a thirty-year-old come-from-away entrepreneur whose pitch to voters was that the city needed "a slate of good hard-core businessmen who will take this city by the seat of its pants and try to put it back on the right path." Stapells's pro-high-rise views were counter-balanced by those of another councillor, David MacKeen, a thirtysomething black sheep son of a former Tory lieutenant-governor and nephew of industrialist J. C. MacKeen. MacKeen represented the city's poorest neighbourhood and had become a passionate advocate for its interests.

Ralph Medjuck was a bright young lawyer/developer who'd built his first six-storey office building on land where his father had operated a grocery and antique store for thirty years. He'd gone on to convince an earlier city council to waive its six-storey downtown height restrictions to allow him to build the twelve-storey office tower at the corner of Hollis and Sackville streets. This time he again won the day with the city's elected representatives, but the council's seven-to-three vote in favour of his Citadel Inn project came with a caveat: the council asked staff to study the issue of how to protect harbour views in future projects.

It took three more years of proposals, counter-proposals, counter-counter-proposals, and bitter wrangling—"I am so sick of this damn view from Citadel Hill I could scream," lamented alderwoman Margaret Stanbury at one point—but on January 31, 1974, city council unanimously approved a motion protecting ten different views from the Citadel, affecting three hundred acres of prime downtown real estate. "In the larger sense," author and activist Elizabeth Pacey would later note, "the decision represented a sweeping achievement in the pioneer field of environmental protection legislation."

The decision was one more sign of how much the Warden of the North had changed during the previous decade. But just one.

"In the final week of February 1970, twelve specialists—most of them men of international reputation—gathered in Halifax, Nova Scotia, to take part in an experiment utterly new to the Western Hemisphere," wrote Ken Hartnett, a Washington-based urban affairs reporter for the Associated Press. "Their assignment, although it was never explained to the twelve in precisely these terms, was to take a community of two hundred and fifty thousand persons and turn it upside down."

The summit, known as "Encounter on the Urban Environment," was the unlikely brainchild of the province's Voluntary Planning Board, a citizen's policy advisory forum set up by the Stanfield government and made up mostly of members of the local establishment. "I told [the board] exactly what was planned [for Encounter] and what the likely implications were," A. Russell Harrington, the president of Nova Scotia Light and Power Company and the chair of the planning board, explained later. "And they didn't believe me."

Over the course of the week, the carefully chosen specialists—six from Canada, five from the United States, and one an American working in England, whose day jobs ranged from economist to black community organizer to industrialist to labour leader to journalist—spent exhausting days and nights meeting with, listening to, and sometimes cajoling or arguing with, Haligonians from every stratum of society about what their city was and what it could be. The process allowed the traditionally powerless—indigenous blacks, the poor, students, women—to finally have a voice in regards to the way the city was being run, and forced the powerful to listen, and respond.

Why were there no black people working at Volvo, the Swedish car maker that had been lured with taxpayer dollars to set up shop in north-end Halifax cheek by jowl to a black neighbourhood? Why did Industrial Estates Limited, the province's business development agency, have such a lousy "batting average" when it came to attracting development to the provincial capital? Why were so few affordable housing units being built? Why was the city's daily newspaper failing to cover what was really happening in the city? Why was the school system so awful? Why had the police really raided that radical educational commune attended by the police chief's daughter? Why was the new container pier in a location everyone agreed was at the wrong end of town? Why had the city razed the poor but proud black community of Africville? And why had the new human rights commission, established in 1967, done nothing to support the residents of that community?

What made the process so powerful was that these questions—parochial, petty, sometimes profound—got asked and occasionally answered in the full glare of television cameras. Finlay MacDonald, the owner of CJCH-TV and one of the organizers of the Encounter process, broadcast the team's nightly town hall meetings live. With only two English-language television channels to watch, the sessions quickly became must-see events for Haligonians. No one knew what might happen next, or who might say words not otherwise permitted on television.

Although it is difficult to pinpoint specific changes that resulted from the Encounter sessions, there is no question that the process engaged a previously apathetic citizenry in the affairs of its city. Within months of the summit, thousands of blacks, trade unionists, and social activists staged a march on city hall to protest secret plans made by the council to hire an American city manager the groups claimed was an anti-union racist. They won; the candidate withdrew.

Race had become an increasingly volatile issue in Halifax, in part because of the civil rights movement elsewhere but also because of the fallout from the city's controversial decision to raze Africville. Although the motives for destroying the community were complex and often contradictory—some saw the land as a necessary link in the planned Harbour Drive Expressway or as prime industrial development land, while others honestly believed the residents would be better off in integrated, modern housing elsewhere—the reality was that few people, including black leaders, paid much attention to the wishes of the residents, who, almost to a person, wanted to stay where they were.

Regardless of how outsiders imagined Africville, its four hundred residents considered it home, a tight-knit community where everyone knew everyone, neighbour helped neighbour, and the adults looked after the children, their own as well as everyone else's. What they really wanted was for the city to provide them with long-denied services like sewers and water (which their leaders had been demanding unsuccessfully from city hall for decades), stop dumping facilities in their backyards that no one wanted (like the abbatoir, infectious diseases hospital, and city dump), and then just leave them alone.

It was not to be. In 1962, Halifax City Council approved a motion to remove the "blighted housing and dilapidated structures of the

Africville area." By 1969, the last resident was gone, the buildings had been bulldozed, and most of Africville's residents had been relocated to Uniacke Square, a soulless concrete public housing complex on Gottingen Street near Macdonald Bridge. Designed as a subsidized stepping stone on the road to home-owning middle-class suburbia for the former Africville residents, the area instead turned out to be a trap. By 2009, in fact, many of the residents of Uniacke Square were still descendants of those originally relocated from Africville.

The black leaders who had been intimately involved in the relocation process, negotiating for compensation with the city and serving on relocation committees, lost credibility and influence, especially among younger blacks. This younger contingent turned to a new champion, Burnley "Rocky" Jones—an articulate, forceful young radical who, along with his wife, Joan, had run a federally funded inner city youth project until the city fathers had successfully lobbied to have it closed. In the fall of 1968, Jones shook what was left of the city's racial complacency when he invited a number of members of the American Black Panther Party to visit Halifax. The Panthers' manifesto included a call for black people to take up arms against their "oppressors." Within months of the Panthers' visit, the federal government announced funding for a new black umbrella organization known as the Black United Front that it hoped would keep a lid on growing black power sympathies.

Although the BUF, as the organization became known, did help defuse tensions in the short term by co-opting community leaders to serve on its board, the fact that it depended on government funding for its survival meant it was never fully trusted by the broader community. It was also dogged by internal arguments over whether it favoured the interests of Halifax blacks over those in rural areas. The BUF, facing a deficit of more than one hundred thousand dollars, finally folded for good in 1996 under what the *Halifax Chronicle Herald* called "clouds of dissension and financial questions."

All of the social activism of the late sixties was faithfully recorded—not to mention aided and abetted—by *The 4th Estate*. Frank Fillmore, a horticulturalist and activist, and Nick, his twenty-six-year-old wire-service-journalist son, started the populist alternative paper in 1969 because of the failure of the staid and tepid Dennis newspapers—which they snidely dismissed in their own pages as "the Old Women of Argyle Street"—to provide quality reporting and analysis.

The paper established its editorial bona fides with an early campaign against the city's scourge of slum landlords. Thundered its opening salvo: "*The 4th Estate*, published in a city where the clear majority of civil servants and politicians don't seem to give a damn about cracking down on anyone except those who cannot defend themselves, is declaring war on those who profit from human misery." In each subsequent issue, the paper chronicled a dramatic case of people living under "barely believable conditions" in squalid housing, but didn't immediately identify the landlord responsible. Instead, the paper gave the landlord in question a week to make the necessary repairs; if the repairs weren't made, the landlord was warned that he could expect to see photos of his slum rental "alongside a photograph of his own home" in the pages of the paper. With its various scoops and crusades—not to forget a gossipy "Farmer Brown" column that gleefully skewered members of the local establishment—*The 4th Estate* soon became a must-read for anyone who wanted to know what was really happening in Halifax; by the end of its first year, the paper had more than eight thousand paying subscribers and had increased its publishing frequency to weekly.

One of the reasons for the paper's success was the public's unhappiness with the performance of the local dailies. In late 1970, a special national Senate committee studying the state of the country's mass media declared the Dennis newspapers guilty of "lazy, uncaring journalism" and concluded, "there is probably no large Canadian city that is so badly served by its newspapers [and] probably no news organization in the country that has managed to achieve such an intimate and uncritical relationship with the local power structure, or has grown so indifferent to the needs of its readers."

How intimate and uncritical? Well, according to a report in the December 20, 1969, issue of *Globe* magazine, "in the twelve years in which Robert Stanfield was premier, there wasn't one word of criticism of his administration in the Halifax papers. But it was that way even before Nova Scotia turned Conservative with Stanfield," added the magazine. "While Henry Hicks [a Liberal] was premier, he too was the apple of their eye."

The senators had received some help in reaching their unkind conclusions about the papers' lazy, uncaring journalism from *The 4th Estate*.

Its editors documented for the committee literally dozens of major local stories it had uncovered and that the *Herald* had then ignored or reported much later. To cite but one example, when the city's then-chief of police, Verdun Mitchell, used his service revolver to commit suicide in his police department offices one afternoon in the mid-1960s, the provincial newspaper of record did not deem the cause of his demise even worthy of note in its pages. Most Haligonians didn't know about it until years later when the newly launched *4th Estate* revealed the fact to its shocked readers.

Despite its damning conclusions, the Senate report's immediate impact was limited; the *Herald* itself dismissed it as the work of meddling outsiders, and readers looking for an alternative daily newspaper would have to wait another fourteen years until the launch of the feisty *Halifax Daily News* in 1984 to find one.

By then, Halifax would be a very different city. In more ways than one.

On January 1, 1969, the city annexed a swath of small outlying communities—Armdale, Jollimore, Purcells Cove, Spryfield, Kline Heights, Fairview, Rockingham, and Kearney Lake—west of the peninsula. The move instantly tripled the city's land mass to 13,500 acres and increased its population by 35,000 people, making Halifax not only the thirteenth-largest city in Canada but also the largest in Atlantic Canada, regaining a crown it had earlier lost to Saint John. The extension of city water and sewer services to the newly annexed areas allowed for the development of Clayton Park, a modern, upper-middle-class subdivision of family homes and apartment buildings located just beyond the peninsula. Unlike most homes in Halifax, which were made of wood, the new structures were primarily brick. That wasn't surprising considering that the prime developer of the project was Shaw Brick, the largest brick maker in Atlantic Canada.

A year and a half after the annexation, the Halifax-Dartmouth Bridge Commission opened a second harbour bridge, a four-lane span across the Narrows that created new residential and industrial development possibilities in Dartmouth, Bedford, and Sackville. Unlike the Macdonald bridge, which had been named in honour of a late, lamented, and legendary premier, bridge commission officials chose to name their new structure the A. Murray MacKay bridge to recognize the contributions of the chair of the commission itself, a man virtually unknown outside its boardroom.

For years after, many Haligonians refused to call it by its official name, preferring to refer to it simply as the "new bridge" instead.

To serve this growing metropolitan area, the city finally traded in its electric trolleys for diesel buses in 1970. While almost no one was unhappy to see the old trolleys replaced, service didn't improve much. In fact, it would be another eleven years before the Halifax and Dartmouth bus services were finally merged into one. Most commuters who had a choice still preferred to travel by car instead of bus.

Halifax's economic and social underpinnings were also shifting at this time. Although still vitally important, the navy was becoming a less dominant player in city life. The navy, which had been subsumed in the recently unified Canadian Armed Forces, seemed very much a junior player in this new military order. As a consequence, the local navy brass spent more time fighting turf wars in Ottawa than they did exerting their traditional influence over everyday life in the Warden of the North.

More significantly, other players, especially the universities, began to assume more important roles in community life. Dalhousie University, the province's largest post-secondary institution, went on a building spree in the late 1960s—between 1966 and 1971, the university officially opened the Weldon Law Building, the Sir Charles Tupper Medical Building, the Dalhousie Arts Centre, the Killam Memorial Library, the Student Union Building, and the Life Sciences Centre. Meanwhile, in 1966, Mount Saint Vincent, the small Roman Catholic women's college on the edge of Bedford Basin, reinvented itself as Mount Saint Vincent University and began admitting men the next year. And in 1970, Saint Mary's University, which had been run by the Jesuits for the past thirty years, officially became a secular, co-educational institution.

As Mount Saint Vincent and Saint Mary's became less religiously tied, the Roman Catholic, Anglican, and United churches got together in 1971 to found the Atlantic School of Theology to provide a degree-granting inter-denominational focus for religious education. That forced the Anglican-operated University of King's College to find a new role for itself too, which it did with the launch of the Foundation Year Programme—now an internationally recognized first-year "great books" program—in 1972 and the opening of a degree-granting School of Journalism in 1978.

In 1969, the Nova Scotia College of Art—founded in 1887 by Anna

Leonowens of *Anna and the King of Siam* fame—morphed into the degree-granting Nova Scotia College of Art and Design (NSCAD). The change was more than cosmetic. Under the direction of its charismatic new president, a thirty-two-year-old conceptual artist named Garry Neill Kennedy, the college quickly developed an international reputation as a centre for avant-garde artists to congregate and make and discuss art. In 1973, the magazine *Art in America* went so far as to call NSCAD "the best art school in North America."

In 1974, NSCAD helped bring the many threads of change in the city together when it relocated its campus from the edge of Dalhousie University to space in the new waterfront Historic Properties complex. The move was part of a concerted effort to make the city's downtown core livable—and lively—even after the army of nine-to-five office workers had left for the day.

The influx of NSCAD students became the catalyst in the development of a new and lively downtown scene that included not only bars and nightclubs but also art galleries and theatres. On July 1, 1963, Neptune Theatre, a new professional repertory company, launched its ambitious thirteen-play first season with a production of George Bernard Shaw's *Major Barbara*. The new theatre was housed in the dramatically and expensively renovated Garrick, a former vaudeville and burlesque house on Sackville Street that, as writer Harry Bruce put it, "nice mothers told their children [was] Off Limits." Though often financially precarious—the theatre, noted *Saturday Night* magazine in 1972, "experienced more fantastic ups and downs, and gorgeous triumphs and snatchings from the jaws of death than any theatrical production since *The Perils of Pauline*"—Neptune's umbrella also helped shelter a lively and eclectic collection of short-lived independent theatre companies.

Halifax's concentration of universities also created an intellectual hub that helped attract important new scientific and research-related institutions. The Bedford Institute of Oceanography, for example, which would become the largest ocean research facility in Canada, was launched on the shores of Bedford Basin in 1962. In 1969, Dalhousie University opened its new Life Sciences Centre, which allowed it to provide world-class facilities—including high-pressure labs that could stimulate deep-sea conditions as well as wet labs and aquatic tanks supplied by saltwater lines connected to the Northwest Arm—for researchers conducting sophisticated marine research. Then, in 1970, the Izaak Walton Killam Hospital for Children, a nationally recognized pediatric research centre as well as the region's only children's tertiary care hospital, opened its doors on University Avenue.

In turn, those new institutions helped make Halifax a logical regional centre for federal financial institutions and government departments, attracting an influx of well-educated, well-paid come-from-aways who refused to accept much of what the locals had long taken as the city's inevitable, inviolable social givens. Separate Catholic and Protestant schools, for example. Men-only taverns. The obvious lack of black faces in local business. The dearth of good restaurants. The inordinate role party politics played in determining whether you got a job or an appointment, or even an invitation to a weekend dinner party.

The ironic end result of all this social, political, and cultural upheaval was that the rest of the world began to see Halifax as "the next best place." In November 1979, *Chatelaine* described Halifax as "a beautiful city, a city fit for people to live in, big enough to compete successfully on just about any urban livability factory, small and personal enough for any individual to stay human." Added the *Star Weekly*: "Halifax need no longer borrow from the styles of others but is quite able, thank you, to create its own."

44.
1978–1995

The Buddhists arrive. Festivals city. Anatomy of "hip." Tall ships and tourism. The G7. Seeking a sewage solution. Africville again.

THE INCIDENT THAT MOST PROFOUNDLY CHANGED the face of Halifax during the last two decades of the twentieth century happened not in Halifax, but in Boulder, Colorado, physically almost an entire continent and psychically at least a world away from the venerable Warden of the North. It occurred in the summer of 1978, when Chögyam Trungpa Rinpoche—a Buddhist monk reputed to be the eleventh reincarnation of the supreme abbot of the Surmang Tibetan monasteries—unexpectedly and seemingly inexplicably announced to his several thousand mostly young, well-educated, middle-class American adherents (many of whom had already followed him to Boulder) that he had chosen Nova Scotia as the new world headquarters of his Tibetan Buddhist organization, Vajradhatu International.

The year before, the thirty-seven-year-old Trungpa—who had escaped Tibet when the Chinese invaded in 1959 and had eventually settled in America—had spent ten days quietly visiting, and falling in love with, the province. Whatever his reason for choosing Nova Scotia—and there is still speculation about why he selected such an outwardly unappealing and seemingly out-of-the-mainstream location—Trungpa's announcement touched off a wave of immigration that transformed Halifax culturally and commercially.

The transformation didn't happen immediately, or without controversy. Initially, many Haligonians greeted the roughly five hundred newcomers with skepticism, if not outright suspicion. Were they members of a religious cult? Were they here to convert—perhaps brainwash—the locals? It didn't help that memories of a 1978 mass suicide of nine hundred followers of Peoples Temple cult leader Jim Jones were still fresh when the first Buddhists arrived. Or that the *New York Times* reported in 1989 that Trungpa's chosen successor, Ösel Tendzin, was not only dying of AIDS but had also apparently knowingly infected others with the disease.

Over time, however, the locals came to accept these new arrivals, thanks in no small measure to the fact that most of them quietly integrated into life in the city, buying homes, raising kids, landing jobs, starting businesses, and making positive contributions to local life. Contributions? Halifax writer David Swick, in his 1996 book *Thunder and Ocean*, catalogued some of them: Buddhists, he wrote,

> *founded the Nova Scotia Sea School, the Great Ocean natural food market, the province's first mindfulness stress reduction clinic, and an internationally selling magazine. They have opened bookstores, cafés, bakeries, clothing stores, organic farms, a branch of peer lending, and the one and only Italian Market. The community boasts architects, lawyers, venture capitalists, photographers, economists, university professors, software designers, even a golf pro. Members have made movies, directed Symphony Nova Scotia and the Discovery Centre, won house design awards, received a Progress Women of Excellence Award and an honorary degree from St. Francis Xavier University. They have headed the Council of Nova Scotia Archives, the Nova Scotia Film and Video Producers' Association, NovaKnowledge, and the children's section of the Atlantic film Festival.*

And all of that within a few decades of landing in the city.

The arrival of the Buddhists coincided, perhaps not entirely coincidentally, with a cultural renaissance in Halifax that was spurred, in part, by the establishment of several annual festivals. In 1982, the Atlantic Film Festival premiered in Halifax. Its goal was to showcase not only new Canadian and international films but also—and more importantly—the work of the growing number of emerging local filmmakers. One year after the first festival, the Donovan brothers—Paul, a London Film School graduate, and Michael, a recently minted lawyer—launched their own film production company. They cheekily named their company Salter Street Films after the place where they'd once lived—in an apartment above a pornographic book store. Salter Street would go on to become an iconic name in the Canadian film and television industry, producing a number of successful feature films as well as the Oscar-winning documentary *Bowling for Columbine* and hit television series such as the long-running satiric *This Hour Has 22 Minutes.*

In 1986, the city was home to the first annual Halifax International Busker Festival, a ten-day summer celebration featuring what its promoters described as "gravity-defying acrobatics, mind-bending illusions, fiery feats of bravery, and many other amazing acts" by street performers from all over the world. In an earlier era, they might have all been arrested for loitering; now they made a decent living passing the hat among appreciative audiences at free shows along the waterfront.

In 1987, the mid-summer Atlantic Jazz Festival debuted. It would eventually become Atlantic Canada's largest music festival, featuring over 450 performers—local, national, and international—playing to more than 65,000 fans over nine days each summer. Then, in 1991, the East Coast Music Awards established itself as an important new annual showcase for local talent as well as a career catapult for many performers.

For the first time, local musicians of all styles—not just the fiddlers and other traditional music-makers—began attracting attention on the world stage. In the early nineties, both *Melody Maker*, an influential British pop music magazine, and *Billboard*, the American entertainment industry bible, heaped praise on Halifax and its exploding popular music scene. *Harper's Bazaar*, a New York fashion magazine, described Halifax as "the anatomy of a hip city."

Nothing encapsulated hip—or the new Halifax—as well as an event *Maclean's* magazine described in an article published in the spring of 1995. In a cavernous former waterfront warehouse, legendary New York beatnik poet Allen Ginsberg and infamous Nova Scotian fiddler Ashley MacIsaac performed together before a fashionable Halifax crowd in honour of Rangdröl Mukpo—the late Trungpa's son—who had just become the Halifax-based leader of his father's worldwide Buddhist community. "The conservative capital of Nova Scotia," *Maclean's* mused, "seems to have rediscovered a lost youth to go with its penetrating sense of history."

That sense of history, of course, was still very much in evidence. In 1979, Ian Fraser, a former-soldier-turned-impresario, staged the first Nova Scotia International Tattoo—a grand spectacle featuring traditional military pageantry, dancing, and music—to celebrate the Queen Mother's visit to Nova Scotia for the International Gathering of the Clans. The show was so popular with audiences that the organizers staged an encore performance, and the Tattoo very quickly became yet another annual extravaganza on the city's cultural calendar.

The Tattoo was staged in the Halifax Metro Centre, a new ten-thousand-seat arena on the edge of Citadel Hill. The centre—which was also home to the American Hockey League's Nova Scotia Voyageurs, the top farm team for the NHL's Montreal Canadiens (and later, the Halifax Mooseheads, an elite junior team initially owned by Moosehead Breweries)—gave the city its first large downtown venue capable of staging everything from rock concerts to trade shows to the two-thousand-performer Tattoo.

The 1978 opening of the Metro Centre also marked the end of the era of manufacturing in downtown Halifax. To make space for the centre, Moir's chocolate factory—home of the famous Pot of Gold brand—which had operated continuously on Argyle Street since Benjamin Moir opened his first bakery there in 1815, was demolished and the entire operation moved to the new Woodside Industrial Park on the edge of Dartmouth.

The 1984 opening, next door to the Metro Centre, of the World Trade and Convention Centre—which boasted "three floors of flexible and multi-purpose meeting and banquet space" featuring "more than a dozen rooms accommodating up to three thousand people for banquets and receptions...luxurious reception areas and comfortable conversation spaces," not to mention the proposed climate-controlled pedway that would link the new complex to all of the city's major downtown hotels and shopping areas—signalled the city's belated arrival as a player in the growing international convention and tourism business.

So too did the arrival that same year of the first Tall Ships festival, when a fleet of more than sixty sailing vessels from around the world filled Halifax Harbour as part of a North Atlantic sailing race. The sight of so many gloriously full-sailed ships—a powerful and poignant reminder of Nova Scotia's golden age of sail—attracted thousands of locals and visitors to the spiffed-up waterfront and helped spread the word that dowdy old Halifax welcomed tourists.

By 1995, the city was ready to take its real official bow on the world stage, hosting the twenty-first G7 economic summit, a gathering of the leaders of the most powerful industrialized countries in the world. Such meetings usually took place in political centres like London, Bonn, or Toronto, but Halifax proved an excellent host. While the business of the summit was being transacted in private—mostly inside a squat, green-glassed waterfront office building officially known as Summit Place but quickly dubbed the "Green Toad"—Halifax hosted a massive, continuous downtown street party for residents and visitors, including thousands of international government officials and members of the media. The city basked in the glow of the laudatory reviews that followed. "Even a few cynical journalists seemed, for a brief moment, to be touched by the hospitality," reported a Reuters correspondent, while a *Globe and Mail* reviewer summed up the summit-ending concert on Citadel Hill as having "the energy of a rock concert but the sentiment of a family gathering."

The city's tourism promoters couldn't have asked for more. Thanks to such favourable reviews, not to forget what had evolved into a summer-long, interconnected necklace of family-friendly events—from the Tattoo to the jazz, buskers, and film festivals, as well as the occasional stopover by the tall ships—tourism had become a major force behind the city's economy.

The burgeoning tourism industry made the worsening stench from Halifax Harbour all the more foul. In 1987, *Cities* magazine described what it called a "familiar" Halifax waterfront scene: "The sun shines, tourists stroll along the boardwalk taking pictures of the *Bluenose*. Some even sit on the rocks overlooking the harbour to enjoy the salt sea air. Then there's a faint rumbling, a muffled gurgling and the water in front of the hamburger shop boils with toilet paper, used condoms, and other detritus of personal life."

Halifax and Dartmouth residents had been dumping their effluent into the harbour ever since the cities were founded, but no one had paid much attention to the harm being done to the harbour until the 1960s, when the combination of an ever-growing—and polluting—population coupled with an awakening awareness of pollution's dangers to the environment made residents finally begin to take notice. In 1964, federal officials banned harvesting mussels and clams from the harbour because of public health concerns. In 1969, the Bedford Basin Pollution Committee, a citizens' group made up of engineers, scientists, students, and housewives, staged a set of well-attended public meetings to raise alarms about how pollution was affecting the basin. In 1973, the city fathers added a pollution control charge to water bills, supposedly to build a nest egg for a future sewage treatment plant (though those funds were soon diverted to pay for other projects the aldermen decided were more urgent).

By the 1980s, forty different sewage outfalls were pumping millions of gallons of untreated waste into the harbour every day and Tom MacMillan, the federal environment minister, was describing Halifax Harbour as "an open sewer" with a waste water management system so ancient it would have been "familiar to Caesar Augustus."

In 1987, the province proudly announced what it described as "Phase One of the Cleanup of Halifax Harbour"—a sixty-million-dollar project including two treatment plants that would clean up sixty percent of the city's untreated waste. Construction would begin, the government said, in the spring of 1988. It didn't happen. The problem was that the federal, provincial, and municipal governments couldn't agree on what was actually needed, let alone who would pay for it. In fact, the Halifax treatment plant wouldn't finally open for business for another twenty years.

Harbour pollution was not the only thorny issue whose final reckoning the city preferred to put off for as long as possible. On the eve of the arrival of the G7 leaders, Halifax officials had evicted two black squatters from the site of what had once been Africville. The squatters, former residents themselves, had camped out there that winter to protest what they saw as the city's continuing refusal to respond to the legitimate concerns of the community's former residents. While the eviction worked for the duration of the G7 summit, the squatters returned soon after the politicians left. They were still there in 2009.

Ironically, with the exception of a small chunk of land used as a footing for the bridge across the Narrows in 1970, the Africville lands had not been transformed into industrial land as many had expected, but had instead been set aside as parkland. Officials, perhaps not surprisingly, had chosen to call the park Seaview after the name of the community's razed black Baptist church rather than the more provocative alternative, Africville Park.

In the years since the expropriation of Africville, the former residents had become increasingly vocal about their loss. In 1983, they staged their first annual Africville reunion in Seaview Park, attracting former residents from across the continent for a weekend party. Irvine Carvery, a son of Africville who would later become president of the Africville Genealogy Society, petitioned city council to apologize for what it had done and allow the residents to return to their land. "My presentation," Carvery would explain later, "went to the basement or wherever those things go."

But Carvery refused to give up—or go away. By 1991, he had convinced the provincial government to rebuild Seaview United Baptist Church on the site of the former Africville settlement as a symbolic gesture of apology for the historic wrong that had been done to the community. But, like the province's grand plan to build a sewage treatment system, rebuilding the church—not to mention coming to terms with the former residents' demands for redress—remained little more than talk. In 2004, a United Nations report on racism and discrimination publicly criticized the Africville relocation and recommended Canada pay compensation to its former residents. The federal government ignored the report, but all three levels of government did begin to negotiate for a settlement of the dispute.

45.
1997–2009

Amalgamation. Hurricane Juan. And then white Juan. The great Harbour Solutions mess. HRM by Design. The future.

IN 1969, THE THEN-MAYOR OF HALIFAX, ALLEN O'BRIEN, mused to a reporter that amalgamating Halifax, Dartmouth, and the rest of Halifax County made practical sense. "If you look at the Halifax-Dartmouth area from the air, you would see only one city, which is united by the harbour that goes down the centre," he said. But O'Brien, a veteran municipal politician, was cautious about how long uniting the municipal units might take. "I think that it was unthinkable in the political sense five years ago, that five years from now it will be a very serious topic of discussion, and that ten years from now it may be realized," he explained.

As with others who have attempted to forecast Halifax's future, O'Brien wasn't nearly cautious enough. It wasn't until April 1, 1996—more than twenty years after the Graham Royal Commission on Education, Public Services, and Provincial-Municipal Relations, which had been set up to look into how to better deliver education and public services, had first formally proposed the idea—that Halifax, Dartmouth, Bedford, and the County of Halifax were finally pushed, kicking and screaming, into political matrimony by the Liberal provincial government, which had finally grown weary of all the debate and infighting.

The new entity—officially the Halifax Regional Municipality, unofficially HRM (sometimes pronounced "herm"), and generically still Halifax—was a sprawling, unwieldy 5,577-square-kilometre collection of 188 urban and rural communities. The city stretched 165 kilometres from the summer resort community of Hubbards in the west to the tiny fishing village of Ecum Secum in the east. To put its geographic size into perspective, the new HRM occupied an area slightly larger than Prince Edward Island and three times the size of London, England. To put that perspective into further perspective, compare London's population of seven million to the new HRM's total of just 330,000 people (which, however, still represented a full forty percent of Nova Scotia's total population).

No one, it seemed, was happy with the amalgamation. In Bedford, which had finally become its own town in 1980, the town staff staged a New Orleans-style funeral procession—complete with a jazz band, a town-flag-draped coffin, and two grim reapers—to mark its too-quick passing. In Halifax, Mayor Walter Fitzgerald—even though he was set to become the mayor of the newly amalgamated city—was in tears as he adjourned city council for the last time. "I love this town and I love each and every one of you," he declared.

In the outer rural reaches of the new city, there was puzzlement over why they'd been lumped in with downtown Halifax. In Ecum Secum, for example—where residents had no access to cell phone service or cable TV, the nearest banking machine was 130 kilometres away in Antigonish, and the biggest local issue was the presence of coyotes—people wondered what amalgamation would do for them. And what they would end up paying for. "What services do we need?" one resident asked a reporter. "The Mounties do the policing. Everybody has their own water and sewer system. And there's no street lights. We don't get any services here."

The ostensible reason for the amalgamation was that it would save money. A consultant's report had forecast that the new city could save over twenty million dollars a year by eliminating duplicate services and staff. Instead, most of those expected savings were instantly swallowed up by increased salaries for formerly lesser-paid rural municipal workers. The real cost of the amalgamation—from new stationery to new chairs for the expanded twenty-four-member council—was almost three times the initial estimates (from $9.8 million to $26 million).

The newly formed Halifax Regional Municipality experienced dramatic growth during the decade after the amalgamation, partly because of the impact of increasing urbanization, partly because of a booming economy goosed by increased offshore oil and gas revenues, and partly, in all likelihood, because of the synergies achieved by amalgamation. None of that made amalgamation any more popular, however.

The main issue remained the yawning gap between the interests of

HRM's urban and rural voters: from sewage to snow removal, from sidewalks to skyscrapers, the concerns in Ecum Secum were simply different than they were in downtown Halifax. In 2004, in fact, some Eastern Shore residents even briefly flirted with the idea of asking the province to carve their area off into a separate municipality of its own. Though that scheme never made it off the ground, Rodney MacDonald's foundering Progressive Conservative provincial government did promise during its 2009 election campaign that it would appoint an independent review of amalgamation if the party was re-elected. It wasn't. And the review idea died with it.

Thus, amalgamation become another one of those issues—like Nova Scotia's always unpredictable weather—that people liked to complain about but ultimately knew they couldn't change.

If Haligonians needed a reminder of just how unpredictable—and uncontrollable—their weather could be, they got it with a vengeance in the fall of 2003 and the winter of 2004.

At 12:10 AM on September 29, 2003, Hurricane Juan, a Category 2 storm packing sustained winds of 160 kilometres per hour with gusts estimated at up to 230 kilometres an hour, smashed fist-first into the heart of Halifax. Most residents had expected that the tropical storm, like dozens before it, would veer away from the province at the last moment or blow itself out before making landfall. It didn't.

The storm, the worst natural disaster in the city in more than a century, killed two people, including a paramedic, and resulted indirectly in the deaths of four others; cut off power for seven hundred thousand Nova Scotians, some of whom would not get their lights back for two weeks; forced evacuation of the Victoria General Hospital as well as dozens of high-rise apartment buildings; damaged close to one-third of all homes in HRM; created a two-metre-high storm surge with occasional twenty-metre-high waves that set new record high water levels for Halifax Harbour; flattened one hundred million trees, including seventy percent of the one hundred thousand trees in Point Pleasant Park; devastated the storied Halifax Public Gardens; and closed schools, universities, and many businesses for more than a week. By the time the cleanup was complete, Hurricane Juan was responsible for two hundred million dollars in damages, most of them in HRM where the storm had made landfall. Point

Pleasant Park didn't reopen to visitors until June 2004, and it will be at least a generation or two before the park's forests regenerate themselves.

In 2004, Environment Canada, "in consideration of the lost and damaged lives, the impact to economy, and the widespread destruction" Juan had caused, requested that the World Meteorological Organization, which is responsible for naming hurricanes, retire the name Juan from use. The WMO agreed.

Less than five months after Juan, Halifax got smacked by yet another "storm of the century," this time a devastating nor'easter with sustained winds of 60 to 80 kilometres per hour—and unofficially recorded gusts of up 147 kilometres an hour—that dumped a record 95.5 centimetres of snow on Halifax. Officials imposed a 10:00 nightly curfew to allow crews to clear snow from downtown streets, much of which was dumped into Halifax Harbour. Perhaps not surprisingly, locals dubbed the storm—which also shut down schools and businesses and knocked out power—"White Juan."

In 2009, yet another winter storm—a not untypically Nova Scotian mix of sloggy, slushy snow and rain—instantly transformed what had only recently seemed like one of the new HRM's major triumphs of political leadership, engineering know-how, economic wherewithal, and environmental good sense into an unmitigated disaster on every front.

In the early hours of January 14, 2009, the storm triggered a number of power outages across the city, including one inside Halifax's brand-new sewage treatment plant.

The plant, part of Harbour Solutions, the largest public works project in Halifax history, had only finally officially opened—amid much fanfare and congratulation—fifteen months before.

At the time, there seemed to be good reason to celebrate. Soon after the amalgamation in 1996, the new regional council had hosted the Harbour Solutions Symposium in order to kick-start a process that had seemed permanently stalled for more than a decade. It worked. By 1999, the council had not only agreed to fund two-thirds of the estimated $315-million "re-plumbing" project but had also invited bids for the construction of the plant from three different consortia. Two years later, the council had chosen one of the groups and began negotiating a deal. But then, two years after that, in 2003, it had dumped its private partner and announced it would build the project itself. Despite the skepticism of some, the new plant had officially opened in November 2007, just four years after the ceremonial groundbreaking.

The system initially appeared to be so successful at keeping raw sewage out of the harbour that, in August 2008, the mayor himself had ventured out for a brief, highly publicized swim at the long-closed-to-bathers Black Rock Beach in Point Pleasant Park. Two days later, however, after tests determined that E. coli bacteria levels were too high, officials had closed down the beach again.

Officials had claimed such "hiccups" were to be expected with any new and complicated facility like the sewage treatment plant, and insisted that everything was working as it should. Which it seemed to be—until early in the morning of January 14.

Immediately after the initial power failure at the plant, the system's backup electrical system did what it was supposed to do and kicked in. But then it failed too. After that, everything that could go wrong did go wrong. And quickly. The plant filled up with raw sewage, submerging and destroying the expensive equipment that was supposed to treat it.

While consultants prepared secret reports for councillors detailing what had gone so wrong and why; lawyers for the various parties argued behind closed doors over who was to blame and who should pay; and contractors desperately worked to get the plant up and running again, Halifax's sewage treatment system remained closed with no clear indication of when it would reopen. Until it did, Haligonians would continue to flush 150 million litres of untreated sewage into Halifax Harbour every day.

As Halifax approached the end of the first decade of the twenty-first century, it faced an all-too-familiar dilemma: how to steer a reasoned course between the push for progress and the pressure to preserve—put more generally, how to decide what kind of city it really wanted to be when it grew up.

In 2006, the city hired the Toronto-based Office for Urbanism as the lead consultant in a process that became known as HRM by Design, an attempt to re-envision Halifax twenty years into the future.

Some of the problems with the city were obvious. While suburban Halifax was experiencing dramatic growth, the regional centre—the eight thousand acres of Halifax and Dartmouth between the harbour and the circumferential highway—had actually seen its population shrink by thirty thousand over the previous fifty years. There were any number of reasons for this, the consultants suggested, including those much-debated seventies bylaws intended to protect the views from the Citadel. The bylaws had done what they were supposed to do, but they had also unintentionally made the development process in the downtown core long, needlessly complex, and expensive. The restrictions had also spawned the uninviting mess of what the *Halifax Daily News* called "massive concrete rectangles with sheer blank walls that cast cold, windy shadows on everything, and everyone" in those areas of the city not under the spell of the views bylaws.

"People didn't foresee the impact (the view planes) would actually have," explained Andy Fillmore, a young architect the city hired to help navigate the HRM by Design process. "They came from a motive to do a good thing for the city and to preserve its beauty," but the end result was a hodgepodge of new tall buildings clustered outside the construction-free view planes zones, creating a disconnected downtown core.

One result of all of this was that the city's centre was dying. While the overall population of HRM was nudging four hundred thousand, fewer and fewer of those people were choosing to live within the regional centre. The population density in the city's core had fallen to just fifteen hundred people per square kilometre—one-third of the density of Boston, almost one-twentieth of the density of Paris. The residents of the HRM preferred instead to commute each day from the suburbs to one of the more than 56 percent of HRM's 107,000 jobs based in the regional centre. As more residents fled to the suburbs, of course, the city had been forced to make massive investments in new infrastructure—roads, schools, and services—just to keep up with the growth. Between 1980 and 2004, in fact, HRM had spent eighty million dollars just to extend sewer and water services to new residential areas.

While this might have made some sort of sense in a late-twentieth-century world of gas-guzzling car commuters, sprawling suburbias, and monster shopping malls, that future was now past. Rising oil prices and global warming had changed the dynamics.

The new HRM by Design strategy envisioned a much more environmentally sustainable regional centre composed of pedestrian-friendly neighbourhoods, each with its own local schools and grocery stores; an easily navigable system of trails and green spaces to connect those neighbourhoods; and far more emphasis on public and alternative transportation. The goal was to convince twenty-one thousand more people to settle in the regional centre within twenty-five years, necessitating, among other things, the development of a minimum of fifteen thousand new housing units.

Ironically, the fact that Halifax was a late bloomer in the worldwide trend to suburbanization meant that it was now better positioned to turn the clock back to the future. In the absence of a lot of out-of-date infrastructure, explained Frank Palermo, a professor of planning at Dalhousie University, the city was ideally positioned to attract new, creative businesses. "From that point of view," he said, "it's possible that the best days are ahead for Halifax."

But are they really? As the city prepares to celebrate its 260th birthday, the only certainty is that, as has always been the case in the Warden of the North, history will be the judge.

Bibliography

Adams, James Truslow. *Album at American History*. In 3 vols. Scribner. New York, 1944.

Aspinall-Oglander, C. F. *The Admiral's Wife*. Longmans. London, 1941.

Bell, F. McKelvey. *The Halifax Disaster, 1917*. Royal Print & Lithograph. Halifax, 1918.

Brebner, John Bartlet. *The Neutral Yankees at Nova Scotia*. Columbia University Press. New York, 1937.

——. *New England's Outpost*. Columbia University Press. New York, 1927.

Brooks, Van Wyck. *The Flowering of New England*. Dutton. New York, 1936.

Bruce, Harry. *Happy Birthday, Dear Neptune*. Neptune Theatre. Halifax, 1973.

——. *An Illustrated History of Nova Scotia*. Nimbus. Halifax, 1997.

Chishohn, Joseph A. *Speeches and Public Letters of Joseph Howe*. Chronicle Pub. Halifax, 1909.

Collins, Louis W. *In Halifax Town*. Privately printed. Halifax, 1975.

Colquhoun, A. H. U. *The Fathers at Confederation*. Glasgow, Brook. Toronto, 1916.

Creighton, Helen. *Songs and Ballads from Nova Scotia*. Dent. Toronto, 1932.

Dennis, Clara. *Down in Nova Scotia*. Ryerson Press. Toronto, 1935.

——. *More about Nova Scotia*. Ryerson Press. Toronto, 1937.

Duguid, A. Fortesque. *Official History of the Canadian Forces in the Great War, 1914-1915*. Canadian Department of National Defence. Ottawa, 1925.

Forbes, Esther. *Paul Revere and the World He Lived In*. Houghton. Boston, 1942.

Fortesque, Sir John. *A History at the British Army*. In 13 vols. Macmillan. London.

Fulford, Roger. *The Royal Dukes*. Duckworth. London, 1933.

Grant, James. *British Battles on Land and Sea*. Cassell. London.

Grant, William Lawson. *The* Tribune *of Nova Scotia*. Glasgow, Brook. Toronto, 1915.

Greenwood, Alice D. *Horace Walpole's World*. G. Bell. London, 1913.

Haliburton, T. C. *A General Description of Nova Scotia*. C.H. Belcher. Halifax, 1825.

Hartnett, Ken O. *Encounter on Urban Environment: Historian's Report.* Voluntary Economic Planning. Halifax, 1971.

Harris, Reginald v. *History at King's Collegiate School.* "The Outlook" Press. Middleton, NS, 1938.

Kerr, W. B. *The Maritime Provinces and the American Revolution.* "Busy East" Press. Sackville, NS, 1941.

Kimber, Stephen. *Not Guilty: The Trial of Gerald Regan.* Stoddart. Toronto, 1999.

——. *More Than Just Folks.* Pottersfield. Halifax, 1996.

King, C. Cooper. *The British Army and Auxiliary Forces.* In 2 vols. Cassell. London, 1893.

Lescarbot, Marc. *Nova Francia.* Routledge. London, 1928.

Mackinlay, A. and W. *Halifax and Its Business.* G.A. White. Halifax, 1876.

MacMechan, Archibald. *The Book of Ultima Thule.* McClelland. Toronto, 1927.

——. *Old Province Tales.* McClelland. Toronto, 1924.

——. *The Winning of Popular Government.* Glasgow, Brook. Toronto, 1916.

McLennan, J. S. *Louisburg from Its Foundation to Its Fall.* Macmillan. London, 1918.

Mockler, Ferryman. *The Life of a Regimental Officer.* Blackwood. Edinburgh, 1913.

Murdoch, Beamish. *A History of Nova Scotia.* In 3 vols. James Baines. Halifax, 1865-67.

Nova Scotia, Bank of. *The Bank of Nova Scotia, 1832-1932.* Toronto, 1932.

O'Brien, Cornelius. *Memoirs of the Rt. Rev. Edmund Burke.* Thoburn. Ottawa, 1894.

Pacey, Elizabeth. *The Battle of Citadel Hill.* Lancelot Press. Hantsport, 1979.

Parkman, Francis. *A Half-Century of Conflict.* Musson. Toronto, 1892.

Patterson, George G. *Studies in Nova Scotian History.* Imperial Pub. Halifax, 1940.

Pope, Joseph. *The Day of Sir John Macdonald.* Glasgow, Brook. Toronto, 1915.

Rand, Silas. *Dictionary* of *the Language of the Micmac Indians.* Nova Scotia Printing Co. Halifax, 1888.

——. *Legends of the Micmacs.* Longmans. New York, 1894.

Sabine, Lorenzo. *The American Loyalists.* Little. Boston, 1847.

Simon, André L. *Bottlescrew Days.* Duckworth. London, 1926.

Skelton, Oscar D. *The Railway Builders.* Glasgow, Brook. Toronto, 1916.

Swick, David. *Thunder and Ocean: Shambala & Buddhism in Nova Scotia.* Pottersfield. Halifax, 1996.

Thacher, James. *American Medical Biography.* In 2 vols. 1828.

Vernon, C. W. *Bicentenary Sketches.* Chronicle Printing. Halifax, 1910.

Wallace, F. W. *Wooden Ships and Iron Men.* Hodder. London, 1924.

BROCHURES

Halifax Shipyards Ltd. *The Halship Saga*. Halifax, 1946.

Harvey, D. C. *Introduction to the History of Dalhausie University*. McCurdy. Halifax, 1938.

MacMechan, Archibald. *Halifax in Books*. Reprinted from *Acadiensis*, 1906.

Martin, John P. *A Pocket Guidebook of Historic Halifax*. McCurdy. Halifax, 1946.

Mosher, L. Weldon. *The Old Dutch Church*. McNab & Sons. Halifax, 1933.

Nova Scotia Light and Power Co., Ltd. *Now It Can Be Told*. Imperial Pub. Halifax, 1946.

Webster, John Clarence. *Abbé le Loutre*. Privately printed. Shediac, 1933.

——. *Wolfiana*. Privately printed. Shediac, 1927.

Weir, Gerald E. *Devastated Halifax* (1917).

PUBLISHED STUDIES AND PAPERS

In the following list the abbreviation NSARM *refers to publications of the Nova Scotia Archives and Records Management; the abbreviation* NSHS *refers to publications of the Nova Scotia Historical Society.*

Akins, T. B. *History of Halifax City*. NSHS Vol. 8.

——. *The First Council*. NSHS Vol. 2.

Allan, John. *Proposals for an Attack on Nova Scotia*. NSHS Vol. 2.

Allison, D. *Notes on a Return of the Townships of Nova Scotia*. NSHS Vol. 7.

Archibald, Adams G. *Life of Sir John Wentworth*. NSHS Vol. 20.

——. *Deportation of Negroes to Sierra Leone*. NSHS Vol. 7.

——. *Sir Alexander Croke*. NSHS Vol. 2.

Armstrong, Maurice W. *Backgrounds of Religious Liberty in Nova Scotia*. NSHS Vol. 27.

Bell, Winthrop. *A Hession Conscript in Halifax*. NSHS Vol. 27.

Brown, Andrew. *The Acadian French*. NSHS Vol. 2.

Brown, W. M. *Recollections of Old Halifax*. NSHS Vol. 13.

Bulmer, John T. *Trials for Treason, 1776-1777*. NSHS Vol. 1.

Comeau, J. W. *François Lambert Bourneuf*. NSHS Vol. 27.

Edwards, J. P. *The Militia of Nova Scotia, 1749-1867*. NSHS Vol. 17.

Flemming, H. A. *Halifax Currency*. NSHS Vol. 20.

Frame, Eliza. *Memoir of the Rev. James Murdoch*. NSHS Vol. 2.

Gottesman, R. S. *Arts and Crafts in New York, 1726-76*. New York Historical Society.

Harvey, D. C. *A Friendly Scot Looks at Nova Scotia in 1853*. NSHS Vol. 27.

Hattie, R. M. *Old Time Halifax Churches*. NSHS Vol. 26.

Hill, G. W. *History of St. Paul's Church*. NSHS Vols. 1, 2, and 3.

——. *Nomenclature of the Streets* of *Halifax*. NSHS Vol. 15.

Howe, Joseph. *Notes on Several Governors and Their Influence*. NSHS Vol. 17.

Johnson, George. *The* Trent *Affair*. NSHS Vol. 16.

Lynch, Peter. *Early Reminiscences of Halifax*. NSHS Vols. 16 and 17.

Macdonald, James S. *Lieutenant-Governor Michael Francklin*. NSHS Vol. 16.

——. *Life and Administration of Governor Charles Lawrence*. NSHS Vol. 12.

——. *Richard Bulkeley*. NSHS Vol. 12.

——. *Governor John Parr*. NSHS Vol. 14.

——. *The Honourable Edward Cornwallis*. NSHS Vol. 12.

Macdonald, S. D. *Ships of War Lost on the Coast of Nova Scotia*. NSHS Vol. 9.

Martell, James S. *Government House*. NSARM Vol. 1, No. 4.

——. *Immigration and Emigratian, Nova Scotia, 1815-38*. NSARM No. 6.

Mullane, George. *Old Inns and Coffee Houses of Halifax*. NSHS Vol. 22.

——. *Privateers of Nova Scotia*. NSHS Vol. 20.

——. *A Sketch of Lawrence O'Connor Doyle*. NSHS Vol. 17.

Murray, Walter C. *History of St. Matthew's Church*. NSHS Vol. 16.

Nichols, G. E. E. *Nova Scotia Privateers*. NSHS Vol. 13.

Partridge, Francis. *Early History of St. George's Church*. NSHS Vol. 6.

Payne, A. M. *Life of Sir Samuel Cunard*. NSHS Vol. 19.

Piers, Harry. *Old Peninsula Blockhouses at Halifax*. NSHS Vol. 22.

——. *Artists in Nova Scotia*. NSHS Vol. 18.

——. *Six Regiments Raised in Nova Scotia*. NSHS Vol. 21.

——. *Evolution of the Halifax Fortress, 1749-1928*. NSARM NO. 7.

Power, L. G. *Richard John Uniacke*. NSHS Vol. 9.

Regan, J. W. *Inceptian of the Associated Press*. NSHS Vol. 19.

Roche, Charles. *Dockyard Reminiscences*. NSHS Vol. 18.

Saunders, E. M. *Life and Times of the Rev. John Wiswell*. NSHS Vol. 13.

Smith, T. Watson. *The Slave in Canada*. NSHS Vol. 10.

Smith, William. *The Post Office in Nova Scotia, 1755-1867*. NSHS Vol. 19.

Stewart, J. J. *Early Journalism in Nova Scotia*. NSHS Vol. 6.

Story, D. A. *Halifax Naval Yard in the Early Sixties*. NSHS Vol. 22.

Story, Nora. *Church and State Party in Nova Scotia, 1749-1851*. NSHS Vol. 27.

Stubbing, C. H. *Dockyard Memoranda*. NSHS Vol. 13.

Thomas, John. *Diary of John Thomas.* NSHS Vol. 1.

Townshend, C. J. *Life of Alexander Stewart, C.B.* NSHS Vol. 15.

——. *Jonathan Belcher.* NSHS Vol. 18.

Wilson, Beckles. *Wolfe's Men and Nova Scotia.* NSHS Vol. 18.

Winslow, John. *Journal of Colonel John Winslow.* NSHS Vol. 3.

Index